THE PROPHET
JOSEPH

THE PROPHET JOSEPH

ESSAYS ON THE LIFE AND MISSION OF JOSEPH SMITH

EDITED BY LARRY C. PORTER AND SUSAN EASTON BLACK

Deseret Book Company
Salt Lake City, Utah

©1988 Deseret Book Company
All rights reserved
Printed in the United States of America

No part of this book may be reproduced in any
form or by any means without permission in writing
from the publisher, Deseret Book Company,
P.O. Box 30178, Salt Lake City, Utah 84130.
Deseret Book is a registered trademark of
Deseret Book Company.

First printing October 1988

Library of Congress Cataloging-in-Publication Data

The Prophet Joseph : essays on the life and mission of Joseph Smith /
    edited by Larry C. Porter and Susan Easton Black.
      p.   cm.
    Includes bibliographies and index.
    ISBN 0-87579-177-8 : $15.95 (est.)
    1. Smith, Joseph, 1805–1844. 2. Mormons—United States–
–Biography.   3. Church of Jesus Christ of Latter-day Saints–
–Presidents—Biography.   4. Mormon Church—Presidents—Biography.
I. Porter, Larry C. II. Black, Susan Easton.
BX8695.S6P76   1988
289.3′092′4—dc19
[B]   88-22638
                                            CIP

Contents

Preface

The miraculous beginnings of The Church of Jesus Christ of Latter-day Saints may surprise an inquirer who is not accustomed to having faith in a living God or listening to the words of a modern prophet. Yet these early beginnings are true. God did speak to the youthful Joseph Smith and while calling him by name said, *"This is My Beloved Son. Hear Him!"* (Joseph Smith–History 1:17.) Since Joseph's first vision of Deity, Joseph's name has been known "for good and evil." (Joseph Smith–History 1:33.) In this book we sincerely declare that we know Joseph's name for "good."

Joseph Smith was what he proclaimed himself to be — a prophet, seer, revelator, and translator for God. Joseph magnified these callings by testifying, prophesying, translating, and obeying the commandments of God. Unfortunately, most of his contemporaries rejected both Joseph and the word of the Lord. With this rejection came Joseph's continual foe — persecution. Ridicule, arrest warrants, and evil speaking were his common companions throughout his short life. Doctrines revealed by the Lord to Joseph Smith were distorted by apostates to disprove his claims of divine revelation and to arouse public sentiment against him.

Yet amid the persecution, suffering, and rejection by man, the Lord did not leave Joseph comfortless. While in

Liberty Jail, under the sentence of death, the Prophet was promised that he would be delivered and his friends would greet him again with "warm hearts and friendly hands." (D&C 121:9.) This prophecy was fulfilled.

Not until 27 June 1844 was Joseph's life taken. Assassins destroyed his body, but they could not destroy the "broad seal affixed to 'Mormonism' " which repeatedly affirms that Joseph, the religious martyr, sealed his testimony with his blood. (D&C 135:7.)

Volumes of literature have been written about the life, mission, persecution, and teachings of Joseph Smith. Some of these volumes lack detailed scholarship while expounding faith. Others declare their impeccable scholarship, yet deny faith. Most of the texts rewrite known facts as a historical narrative, while ignoring well-documented new discoveries concerning Joseph.

The unique characteristic of this book is that recognized Latter-day Saint scholars testify through their diligent study, expertise, and faith to the singularity of the divine calling of Joseph Smith as a prophet of God. These eminent authors have accurately documented through their meticulous research the life and mission of Joseph and proclaim in their writings their testimony. Through their writings, Joseph is clearly seen as the prophet of the Restoration. We humbly express to these scholars, who are our friends and colleagues, our gratitude for their contribution to this book. We also extend our appreciation to Don E. Norton and Jane Chapman of Brigham Young University for their assistance in the preliminary preparation of the manuscript of this book.

It is our hope that this book of essays on the life and mission of Joseph Smith will be rewarding reading for you. We hope that in your reading you will learn the details of his life and share our conviction that Joseph was what he professed to be—a prophet of God.

Chapter 1

Joseph Smith's
Family Background

Richard L. Bushman
H. Rodney Sharp Professor of History
University of Delaware

Because the Latter-day Saints love and honor Joseph Smith, we wish to create for him a family background in perfect harmony with his later life as a prophet. Not that his parents had to be wealthy or well-educated, for we know they certainly were not, but we believe they must have been devout people who taught their son faith in the Christian religion and surrounded him with their love. We are inclined to think they lived comfortably, though never opulently, with a large, happy family of brothers and sisters growing up together. We are not altogether in error when we imagine the Smith household this way. They did love and depend heavily on one another. Our mistake is to remove from the picture the stresses and strains the family felt. They labored under a burden of serious poverty during all the years when Joseph was growing up; accumulating the necessities and a few of the simplest amenities was a struggle that engaged the family nearly every day of their lives. As if this were not enough, there were deep disagreements over religion. All the Smiths were believers, but Lucy Smith and Joseph Smith, Sr., differed sharply over where and how to find God. When Joseph, Jr., was a young teenager, the mother and father split so badly that Lucy went off to church with some of the children, and Joseph, Sr., stayed home with the others. We err in trying to bury these real difficulties, because without them the Prophet's religious calling seems like an unbidden elevation, requiring little effort on his part, instead of one that emerged out of struggle and confusion. It may well be that the most important early preparation for his later call came from dealing with stresses within the family. It is certainly true that Joseph's organization of the Church played an important part in bringing the family together. It is equally clear that the achievement of unity within the family on religious questions meant a great deal to Joseph Smith.[1]

Both of Joseph's parents had been brought up in families who suffered from economic disruptions and religious perplexities. There was not a stable, conventional religious tradition in either family on which Lucy Mack Smith or Joseph Smith, Sr., could rely. Lucy's father, Solomon Mack, was indentured to a family in Lyme, Connecticut, when he was just four years old because his own father had lost his land and was unable to support his four children. Solomon complained later that the family of his master had no feeling for the needs of a little boy. "I was treated by my master as his property and not as his fellow mortal." The man gave young Solomon little education and no religious instruction. "His whole attention was taken up on the pursuits of the good things of this world; wealth was his supreme object. I am afraid gold was his God."[2] Late in life, at age seventy-five, Solomon went through a religious conversion and spent his declining years trying to persuade any who would hear of the folly of worldly pursuits, but until that time Solomon himself concentrated his efforts almost entirely on the acquisition of wealth, as he had seen his master do. He was engaged in many enterprises, from opening land in New York and New Hampshire, to running a coastal schooner off New England, manufacturing saltpeter for gunpowder, and serving on a privateer during the Revolution. At one time he was gone from his family for four years while they struggled on alone against a foreclosure on their farm. Solomon knew nothing of their loss until his return, probably because letters never passed between them.

Until his conversion, Solomon had little religion to offer his children. Lucy received instruction from her mother, the daughter of a deacon in the East Haddam, Connecticut, church near Lyme. Solomon gave his wife, Lydia Gates, full credit for teaching the children habits of "piety, gentleness, and reflection."[3] She was the one to call them together morning and evening to pray. The children showed signs of her gentle, pious touch. When Lucy's two elder sisters died, they called their families around them and reminded them to seek for eternity. Lucy's eldest brother Jason became a lay preacher at age twenty and taught the gospel in Nova Scotia. Lucy herself yearned to find God. In 1803 when sickness brought her to the edge of death, as she thought, she saw in despair "a dark and lonesome chasm, between myself and the Savior" and received comfort when she covenanted to "serve him according to the best of my abilities."[4] But she reached this reconciliation on her own, with little help from a minister or church. The religious people who visited her brought so little satisfaction that she refused to join one of their churches. She depended on Bible reading and meditation for her worship. Finally she found a minister who agreed to baptize her without requiring that she join his church; and that is where she stood for many years. Lucy inherited from her mother religious yearnings but no church. Her brother Jason at age sixteen considered himself a seeker, one who was looking for the true religion, and Lucy acted the part herself for most of her life. Perhaps in consequence of the incongruous combination of her father's lack of religion and her mother's piety, Lucy deeply wanted religion without knowing where to find it.

The ancestors of Joseph Smith, Sr., enjoyed prosperity and eminence in Topsfield, Massachusetts, for three generations, until the young manhood of his father, Asael. Asael's father, Samuel, was a highly respected person in the village, being frequently elected town selectman, town clerk, and representative to the Massachusetts legislature. When he died in 1785, the *Salem Gazette* said he "was esteemed a man of integrity and uprightness, . . . a sincere friend to the liberties of his country, and a strenuous advocate for the doctrines of Christianity."[5] Samuel died in a decade when the market for American farm products was in a deep slump, and the repayment of debts troubled thousands of Massachusetts farmers. As it turned out, Samuel's estate was actually insolvent. Asael's elder brother tried to pay the debts without success, and then Asael himself took over the family farm for another five years, until he also failed. Ultimately he was forced to sell the property and move. He rented land for a short period while he sent his two oldest sons north and west into Vermont to the newly opened town of Tunbridge. They cut trees through the summer of 1791 and built a tiny hut fourteen feet long and ten feet wide.

In the fall the entire family arrived and crowded into the little shelter to weather the winter. There the family fortunes began to mend. With the father and seven sons working together, land was cleared and prepared for farming. Jesse, the eldest, married a year after their arrival and received a fifty-acre plot from his father, enough land to make a living on. Supported by food from the cleared land, Asael opened additional farms and purchased more land. Joseph, Sr., received a farm when he married Lucy Mack in 1796, and Asael, Jr., received one in 1802.

Through cooperative effort and much hard work, the Smiths put together a complex of farms in southern Tunbridge and began to win the respect of their neighbors. After 1793 Asael was frequently elected to the office of selectman and occasionally elected as town meeting moderator. Jesse was chosen trustee of the school district in the southern portion of the town and in time rose to be selectman and town clerk. By 1800 the Smiths were well established in Tunbridge, enjoying a modest prosperity and the regard of their fellow townsmen.

Asael's economic stability, however, did not lead him

toward a religious position any more conventional than the Macks', whose lives were buffeted by Solomon's restless pursuit of wealth. Asael taught his children religion, as Solomon did not, reflecting Asael's own baptism and upbringing in the Topsfield Congregational Church, but his teachings were not the ordinary Calvinist doctrines of New England. Asael seems to have fallen under the influence of John Murray, who around the time of the Revolution began teaching what was called Universalism. Murray embraced the usual Calvinist teaching of salvation by grace alone and then carried it to an extreme which the Congregationalists considered heretical. Murray's central idea was that Christ's atonement was extensive and powerful enough to redeem all men, no matter the depth of their sin. All were saved; hence the name Universalism. In a letter to his offspring, Asael asked if they believed Christ came "to save mankind because they were sinners and could not save themselves or whether he [came] to save mankind because they had repented of their sins, so as to be forgiven on the score of their repentance." In Asael's opinion, "he came to save sinners merely because they were such" and not because of their repentance. Moreover, he saved not merely pious Christians but "the worst heathen in the darkest corner of the deserts of Arabia." The key point was that "sinners must be saved by the righteousness of Christ alone, without mixing any of their own righteousness with his."[6] Asael went so far as to help organize a Universalist society in Tunbridge that lasted for two years. Joseph, Sr., and Jesse were members before it dispersed and the Smith men returned to the Congregational meetinghouse. The end of the society did not mean Asael abandoned his Universalist beliefs. He held to those doctrines to the end of his life. Moreover, as a side effect of his Universalism, he seems always to have disliked the standard evangelical preaching. Lucy wrote late in life that Asael demanded that Joseph, Sr., stop going with Lucy to the Methodist church when she attended for a brief period around the time of her father's conversion. Whether this was an accurate memory or not, Joseph, Sr., in his mature years showed little tolerance for any of the churches, thinking their doctrines misplaced and the conduct of church people hypocritical. This deep-dyed mistrust he must have inherited in part from his father Asael. Like Lucy, Joseph, Sr., in consequence of his upbringing, moved along the margins of conventional Christianity, yearning, hoping, and uneasy.

Asael's religious heterodoxy did not divide his family as they were growing up. The tentative tone of his writings implies that he knew some of his children disagreed with him on Universalism. On the subject of family unity, he was much more direct and forceful, and all we know about his children suggests that they were exceptionally close-knit. In 1799, when each of his four married children was about to present him with a new grandchild, making eight in all, Asael wrote "a few words of advice" to his family. Amidst all that he said, including his doctrinal comments, the strongest injunction was stick together: "My last request and charge is that you will live together in an undivided bond of love. You are many of you, and if you join together as one man, you need not want anything. What counsel, what comfort, what money, what friends may you not help yourselves unto, if you will all as one contribute your aids.

"Wherefore my dear children, I pray, beseech, and adjure you by all the relations and dearness that hath ever been betwixt us and by the heart-rending pangs of a dying father, whose soul hath been ever bound in the bundle of life with yours, that you know one another. Visit as you may each other. Comfort, counsel, relieve, succor, help and admonish one another. And while your mother lives, meet her if possible once every year. When she is dead, pitch on some other place, if it may be, your elder brother's house; or if you cannot meet, send to and hear from each other yearly and oftener if you can. And when you have neither father nor mother left, be so many fathers and mothers to each other, so you shall understand the blessing mentioned in the 133 Psalm."[7]

Those sentiments were distilled from his own life ex-

6

periences. He had proven what a cooperative effort could accomplish by working with his sons to hack farms from the Vermont wilderness. The words of advice showed he acted from more than economic expediency. He loved his children, feeling his soul "ever bound in the bundle of life with yours." Those feelings welded them to one another. As the next generation of Smith children grew up, the clan repeated the Vermont venture in New York. Between 1809 and 1820 Asael and his wife Mary and at least seven of the eleven children moved from Tunbridge. Joseph, Sr., and Lucy were the exception in moving to Palmyra. Six of the seven who moved settled around their parents once again, this time in Stockholm and Potsdam in St. Lawrence County, where presumably they joined forces in opening farms for the next generation. Joseph, Sr., though removed from the main body of the clan, thought of them immediately when the Book of Mormon came from the press. He went at once to St. Lawrence County with the news. Jesse, the eldest, would hear nothing of it, but Asael and Mary and three other sons and all but two daughters believed what their brother Joseph told them. In 1836 the clan moved again, this time without Asael, who had died in 1830, to Kirtland. There with young Joseph, now the Prophet, there was a grand reunion in fulfillment of Asael's admonition that the children meet yearly and "live together in an undivided bond of love."

Lucy and Joseph, Sr., met through one of Lucy's brothers, Stephen Mack, then a merchant in Tunbridge and a friend of Asael Smith. The pair got off to a good start after their marriage in 1796. Asael gave his son a farm, and Stephen and his business partner, John Mudget, gave Lucy a thousand dollars, a munificent gift for the time. But they were not to enjoy prosperity for long. In 1802 they rented the farm and opened a store in Randolph, a neighboring town. Besides contracting for store goods brought up from Boston, they purchased ginseng root from surrounding farmers. Ginseng was a major cargo in the newly opened trade with China, and the Smiths stood to make a sizable profit by shipping their ginseng from New York. Unfortunately, the venture failed. Lucy reported later in her autobiography that a young man from the neighborhood who sailed with the ship and managed transactions in Canton swindled the family. He claimed there were no profits, when actually he came back with a chest of gold and absconded. That left the Smiths with heavy debts for their store goods and possibly for the ginseng purchased from the farmers. To meet their obligations, they had to sell their farm and dispense all of Lucy's thousand-dollar wedding gift. They were left with nothing.

From being established property holders, they abruptly descended to the ranks of tenant farmers. They first rented a farm from Solomon Mack, who had purchased a hundred-acre plot on the Sharon-Royalton line just south of the Smith holdings in Tunbridge. Joseph, Sr., taught school and farmed, so they were comfortable and basically prosperous when a baby boy whom they called Joseph was born on 23 December 1805. They remained on Solomon's property for only two years after that. Tenants rarely enjoyed stability on their property. If the owners did not devise other plans for the land, the tenants moved in hopes of working a better farm. After losing their property, the Smiths moved seven times in fourteen years.

They went from farm to farm in towns along the Connecticut River, crossing once from Vermont over into New Hampshire and then back again to Norwich. Finally they were ejected from this small orbit by a cataclysmic world event. The year 1816 is known in meteorological history as the year without a summer. In 1815 Tambora on Sumbawa erupted and blew fifteen cubic kilometers of volcanic ash and pulverized rock into the atmosphere. Climatologists generally credit the spread of this dust layer around the globe as the cause of erratic weather patterns across North America. On June 8 several inches of snow fell across the northern highlands of New York and New England, blighting the young crops just emerging from the soil. The entire summer was cold and dry, so decimating the fields that farmers had to import corn at extravagant prices. The Smiths, despairing of making any headway in their battle with poverty and tenantry, left in the fall along with thousands of other Vermonters, choosing for their destination Palmyra, New York.

Prospects brightened in Palmyra. It was a fast-growing little village, soon to be connected with Albany and Rochester via the Erie Canal, which passed just a few hundred feet north of the town's central crossroads. There was ample work helping established farmers, and the Smiths did a small business in various trade items. They sold simple refreshments from a small shop, and Lucy painted oil tablecloths. Mainly they benefited from the growth of their sons. A farm family's maximum earning power over the life cycle came in the years when the boys were old enough to do a man's work and still too young to marry. That was the time when the increased earning power enabled a family to purchase additional land or equipment. Alvin had reached that critical age by the time the Smiths arrived in Palmyra, and Hyrum and Joseph were not far behind. By 1818, after fifteen years of tenantry, the Smiths had contracted for a hundred-acre farm just two miles south of Palmyra over the boundary into Manchester township. They were to pay $100 a year on the mortgage, with the final payment due in 1825.

Ten people moved into the two-room log cabin they constructed on their new property. Besides the parents, there were six boys from two years to nineteen years, and two girls, ages six and fifteen. Although they added a bedroom wing soon after, they also added another daughter to complete the family. The close quarters did not prevent Lucy from remembering these years as a happy time in their "snug comfortable though humble habitation built and neatly furnished by our own industry."[8] The satisfaction did not last for long. In the first draft of her autobiographical sketches, Lucy recounted a tea party at which one of the women made a slightly disparaging reference to their log cabin. Though not intended to hurt, the comment stung, and Lucy lashed back in defense of her family's honor. She claimed they lived more happily in their cabin than others did in their grand houses. Nonetheless, Lucy's very next entry in the diary was the observation that they soon began work on a frame house.[9] Alvin took the lead in the construction. He was a sober, hard-working young man whose labors brought in the hundred dollars needed annually to make payments on the farm. With Hyrum and Joseph also able to take on outside jobs, the family's earning power seemed to justify the added costs of the house.

Alvin's death in 1823 dealt a severe blow to these plans. He fell ill in early November and died on November 19. Whatever his illness, Lucy thought that the prescription of calomel, a compound of mercury and chlorine, was the actual cause of death. On his deathbed Alvin charged Hyrum, the second oldest, to take responsibility for the house. He and Joseph did their best to raise the required funds, but the loss of Alvin handicapped their efforts. With the mortgage payment and payments to the carpenters hanging over their heads, in the fall of 1825 Joseph, Jr., and his father entered into an agreement with Josiah Stowell and others to dig for a supposed Spanish mine in Harmony, Pennsylvania. That enterprise came to nought, and in December the mortgage payment was due. Ordinarily the land agents tolerated missed payments: there was such a shortage of money in this largely barter economy that many people could not meet their due dates precisely on schedule. The agents were better off to be lenient, in hopes of getting the money eventually. They apparently had been lenient with the Smiths at least once, since Lucy reported they made "nearly all" of their first payment.[10] In 1825, however, according to Lucy, someone told the agent that the Smiths were tearing down fences and ripping up orchards, reducing the value of the property. The agent insisted they make full payment on the date due. Try as they would, the Smiths could not raise the money in the few days left to them, and the agent foreclosed. They lost not only the farm, but all the improvements in the form of house, outbuildings, fences, orchards, and cleared fields. A friendly party bought the land at once from the agent and allowed the Smiths to live there, but at the beginning of 1826 they were once again propertyless tenants, deprived of all they had worked so hard to acquire.

The ups and downs in their fortunes during the early years in Palmyra were no more disturbing to the Smiths than the turbulence in their religious lives. Although Lucy and Joseph, Sr., both stood along the edges of church life, their attitudes differed somewhat, and these differences came to a head in Palmyra. Lucy always hoped she could find a church or minister to suit her; Joseph, Sr., thought the churches were corrupt. When Lucy made her covenant with God in 1803, she talked with ministers and church people in hopes that one would speak the right words to her. She attended church again during the revivals of 1810 and 1811 when her father was converted. In Palmyra she again wanted to join a church. Joseph, Sr., would have none of it. He went for a few Sundays during the 1810 revivals and then refused further attendance. He was deeply skeptical of the authenticity of clergy and doctrine. He began having graphic dreams in 1811, reported to Lucy and recorded in detail, which showed how deeply he despaired of religion in the churches. In the first one, he saw a lifeless, barren field that he was told represented "the world which now lieth inanimate and dumb, in regard to the true religion or plan of salvation." When in the dream he tried to gain knowledge, "all manner of beasts, horned cattle, and roaring animals" sprang up, "tearing the earth, tossing their horns, and bellowing most terrifically." Lucy said that he concluded from the dream that the "class of religionists" knew no more of the kingdom of God than the unbelievers. And yet his dreams often contained a glimmer of hope. In one where he found himself sick and lame, a guide pointed him to a beautiful garden, filled with lovely flowers, where he found happiness and pleasure. In another a peddler told him, "There is but one thing which you lack, in order to secure your salvation."[11] In the dream, Joseph eagerly sprang to get paper for the peddler to write the answer, and inadvertently wakened himself and so never heard the message. He seemed always on the verge of truth and salvation, but they were just out of reach.

In 1820 these differences on religion divided the children as well as the parents in the family. It seems to have been about this time that Lucy made up her mind on a church. When revivals in the surrounding towns made religion and church membership a topic on everyone's mind, she decided to join the Western Presbyterian Church in Palmyra. For the first time she seemed resolved to attend regularly, and three of the children, Hyrum, Sophronia, and Samuel, went with her. Joseph, Sr., held back. Joseph, Jr., and presumably the other children were caught in the middle. In 1820 Joseph not only had to find a religion to meet his personal need for divine assurance, but he also had to choose between mother and father. He showed some partiality to the Methodists but was actually entirely undecided; moreover, he could not tell how he could possibly make a decision with conflicting direction from his parents and no clear answer in the scriptures. That was the time when he went to pray, carrying this heavy family and doctrinal burden. He wanted to know the truth about the churches in order to find salvation for himself and, on top of that, to resolve a deep family conflict. There were many parts to the answer he received to his prayer, but so far as the record shows, he told his mother only one part. When she asked about his condition following the First Vision, he replied somewhat abruptly, "Never mind, all is well—I am well enough off. . . . I have learned for myself that Presbyterianism is not true."(Joseph Smith–History 1:20.) The vision did not really resolve all the family tensions, but it gave Joseph an answer for the moment. He would side with his father.[12]

What was the religion of his father? On the one hand, it was a profound skepticism about the authenticity of the churches; on the other, it was a visionary yearning to find God and salvation. Joseph, Sr., had declared his independence of conventional religion without having lost the urge to make contact with the divine. In that position he was open to forms of religion that the educated Protestant clergy considered outlandish or heretical. Many of the Smith neighbors, along with countless others in early

America, believed in various forms of occult lore, such as astrology and treasure-seeking, which they thought could possibly both enrich them and invest them with super-natural power. The neighbors, after they had turned hostile to the Smiths, accused Joseph, Sr., of being one of the ringleaders of these money-digging ventures. Just how much he was involved is difficult to determine now amid the conflicting evidence, but it is probable that like many others of his time, Joseph, Sr., attempted to enlist the aid of supernatural powers in a quest for hidden treasures. The people who did such things were most often devout Christians who believed they needed the help of the God of heaven in their undertakings. They sensed no sharp division between religion and magic. We know from his dreams how strongly Joseph, Sr., wanted salvation; it is even possible that along with the hope for riches, treasure-seeking was part of his religious quest.[13]

Joseph, Jr., was a natural ally of his father in these ventures. In 1822 he came across an unusual stone while digging a well for a neighbor and identified it as a seer-stone. With it, because of his gifts, he was able to find lost objects. The gift and the stone naturally fit in with his father's treasure-seeking. His mother said that Josiah Stow-ell came to Joseph, Jr., for help in search for the Spanish mine "on account of having heard that he possessed certain keys, by which he could discern things invisible to the natural eye." The offer came in the summer of 1825 when the Smiths were recovering from Alvin's death and needed money for the last payment on their farm. Joseph, Jr., was obliged to help in the interests of saving the family's property. It is not entirely clear that he favored treasure-seeking. Lucy, in reporting the episode with Stowell, said that "Joseph endeavoured to divert him from his vain pursuit."[14] A few months after the money-digging episode with Stowell, a nephew of Josiah accused Joseph, Jr., of trying to swindle his uncle and pulled him into court. On that occasion Joseph said he "had been in the habit of looking through this stone to find lost property for three years, but of late had pretty much given it up on account of its injuring his health, especially his eyes—made them sore; that he did not solicit business of this kind, and had always rather declined having anything to do with this business." By 1826 Joseph may have been an unwilling participant in his father's treasure-seeking enterprises. At the same trial, Joseph, Sr., expressed his own hopes that something more than money would come from the quest. Considering his financial trials, Joseph, Sr., could not have been heedless of the hope for treasure, but he sought for something more. According to the hostile reporter at the trial, Joseph, Sr., "swore that both he and his son were mortified that this wonderful power which God had so miraculously given him should be used only in search of filthy lucre, or its equivalent in earthly treasures." "His constant prayer to his Heavenly Father was to manifest His will concerning this marvelous power. He trusted that the Son of Righteousness would some day illumine the heart of the boy and enable him to see His will concerning him."[15] Joseph, Sr., seemed to believe that through his son's gifts a connection with the heavens could be achieved that had not been attained through mere money-digging.

Since this trial took place in 1826, the hopes of Joseph, Sr., for his son may have been influenced by the angelic visions Joseph, Jr., had begun to receive in 1823. In those visions was the beginning of a true reconciliation of the father's frustrated quest for visionary truth and the mother's desire for a Christian church. On the one hand, the vision of Moroni told Joseph, Jr., of buried golden plates on which could be found the true religion. That part of the vision was consistent with the treasure-seeking of Joseph, Sr. The outlines of the story accorded with common lore about buried wealth. Moroni was the guardian of the golden plates, and treasure-seekers thought a spirit often protected buried boxes of money. Besides that, Moroni offered a connection with the heavens made independently, without going through minister and church, which were always obstacles to Joseph, Sr. On the other hand, the messenger told Joseph, Jr., that the plates contained "the fulness of the everlasting Gospel . . . as delivered by the Savior" to the keepers of the record. (Joseph Smith–History 1:34.) That was a Christian message that Lucy could appreciate. Probably never sympathetic to her husband's money-digging practices, she was a little apprehensive about the appearance of treasure-seeking when she wrote the story of the plates in her autobiography. When she began, she told her readers not to think "that we stopt our labor and went at trying to win the faculty of Abrae drawing Magic circles or sooth saying to the neglect of all kinds of business."[16] A book about the gospel was much more to her liking.

For his part, Joseph, Jr., had to purge the old money-digging impulses when he went for the plates. Moroni warned him that "Satan would try to tempt me (in consequence of the indigent circumstances of my father's family), to get the plates for the purpose of getting rich." There was one purpose alone for this quest for treasure: "to glorify God." (Joseph Smith–History 1:46.) Many of their old ideas had to be sloughed off or modified, but the golden plates at last provided a central meeting point in which all of the family could join. As Lucy put it, the golden plates gave them "something upon which we could stay our minds." She obviously took great happiness in telling how after the visit to the hill, Joseph told them what had happened, and they gathered to listen, "all seated in a circle, father, mother, sons and daughters," all "giving the most profound attention to a boy, eighteen years of age; who had never read the Bible through in his life." This son of hers, who had resisted her Presbyterianism and taken his own course, had provided at last a religious purpose that brought her family together. After decades of disagreement, during those evening discussions of the golden plates, "the sweetest union and happiness pervaded our house no jar nor discord disturbed our peace and tranquility reigned in our midst."[17]

All their troubles did not end at that point. This was 1823, and the loss of the farm still lay ahead. In 1824 another religious revival came to the region, and Lucy's search for a church was renewed, no more successfully than before.

Joseph, Sr., went on with his search for lost treasure, still hoping, as he said in the 1826 trial, that God would reveal the true mission of Joseph, Jr. Not until that mission unfolded further did the family achieve the religious unity and stability they had long sought.

Beginning in 1828 the revelations foreshadowed the organization of a new church; and after the translation of the Book of Mormon was complete, that organization took place in April 1830. On the evening after the organization occurred, Lucy Smith and Joseph Smith, Sr., were baptized. The Prophet was doubtless pleased with his mother's compliance, knowing that she had always wanted a church and now had found one she could wholly believe in. His father's baptism was much more of a triumph. This warm-hearted and spiritually sensitive man had fought with churches through his life, mistrusting ministers, doctrines, and people, all the while aching to find salvation. At last on 6 April 1830 he was baptized into the church his own son provided. Lucy said that as Joseph, Sr., came from the water, the Prophet Joseph's eyes filled with tears, and he grasped his father's hand. "Oh, My God! have I lived to see my own father baptized into the true church of Jesus Christ!" Joseph Knight, the Prophet's dear friend, was there for the occasion and remembered how after the baptism Joseph, Jr., "bast out with greaf and joy and seamed as tho the world Could not hold him. He went out into the Lot and appeared to want to git out of site of every Body and would sob and Crie and seamed to Be so full that he could not live."[18]

It must have been a moment of intense relief and reconciliation for the Prophet, to have his family united at last in a single faith and one church. To obtain and translate the plates, to overcome opposition from neighbors, to win the confidence of a few believers, and finally to organize a church had been a mighty labor for a young man. The stresses within his family, especially the division between the parents, had not made the task easier. The flood of tears on the day of the baptism revealed how deeply he felt the strain. But the yearning to bring mother and father together and to achieve peace and harmony in a divided family must have strengthened the will to go on. The problems in the family must have helped form the deep need to find the truth that was the wellspring of Joseph's religious life. Although flawed as all families are, the family of Lucy and Joseph Smith, Sr., gave their son a desire to know God and confidence that whether through scriptures, churches, or visionary quests, He could be found. Joseph's life was a fulfillment and resolution of their powerful and contradictory yearnings. We must not fault the Smiths for their shortcomings and disagreements, for it was their weaknesses, as well as their strengths, that suited them for the task of rearing a prophet.

Notes

1. The facts of Joseph Smith's family and early life can be found in Richard Lloyd Anderson, *Joseph Smith's New England Heritage: Influences of Grandfathers Solomon Mack and Asael Smith* (Salt Lake City, Utah: Deseret Book Co., 1971), and Richard L. Bushman, *Joseph Smith and the Beginnings of Mormonism* (Urbana and Chicago: University of Illinois Press, 1984).

2. Solomon Mack, *A Narrative of the Life of Solomon Mack* (Windsor, Vt.: The Author, [1811]), conveniently reprinted with excellent notation in Anderson, *Joseph Smith's New England Heritage*, pp. 35–36. Subsequent references are to this edition.

3. Lucy Mack Smith, *Biographical Sketches of Joseph Smith the Prophet* (1853; reprint, New York: Arno Press and the New York Times, 1969), p. 19.

4. Ibid., pp. 46–47.

5. *Salem* [Mass.] *Gazette,* 22 Nov. 1785, quoted in Anderson, *Joseph Smith's New England Heritage*, p. 91.

6. Asael Smith, "A Few Words of Advice" (holograph), Archives of The Church of Jesus Christ of Latter-day Saints, Salt Lake City, Utah. All references are to the best modern edition, in Anderson, *Joseph Smith's New England Heritage*; the quotations are on pp. 125–26.

7. Asael Smith, "A Few Words of Advice," pp. 127–28.

8. Lucy Mack Smith, Preliminary Manuscript of *Biographical Sketches of Joseph Smith*, Archives of The Church of Jesus Christ of Latter-day Saints, Salt Lake City, Utah, p. 38.

9. Ibid., p. 39.

10. Lucy Mack Smith, *Biographical Sketches*, p. 70.

11. Ibid., pp. 57, 74.

12. In the next revival, in 1824, Joseph, Sr., in his amiable way tried attending church a few times with Lucy; this time Joseph, Jr., was the one to hold back, warning his mother that she did not "know the wickedness of their hearts." Lucy Mack Smith, *Biographical Sketches,* p. 91.

13. The evidence for Smith family involvement in treasure-seeking is presented in a controversial book by D. Michael Quinn, *Early Mormonism and the Magic World View* (Salt Lake City, Utah: Signature Books, 1987), pp. 1–52. Quinn argues that magical practices were consistent with religious faith in Joseph Smith's time. The book has been criticized for exaggerating the degree of Smith family involvement in magic and for making speculative leaps without sufficient confirming evidence. For another view of the Smith family and magic, see Bushman, *Joseph Smith and the Beginnings of Mormonism,* pp. 69–76.

14. Lucy Mack Smith, *Biographical Sketches,* pp. 91–92.

15. The trial transcript appeared in an article written by Daniel Sylvester Tuttle in 1882 for the Schaff-Herzog Encyclopedia, and an account of the trial was written more informally by W. D. Purple and published in 1887. Both documents appear in Francis W. Kirkham, *A New Witness for Christ in America: The Book of Mormon,* 2 vols. (Independence, Mo.: Zion's Printing and Publishing Co., 1942, 1951); the quotations are from 2:360, 366.

16. Lucy Mack Smith, Preliminary Manuscript, p. 40.

17. Lucy Mack Smith, *Biographical Sketches,* p. 84, and Preliminary Manuscript, p. 43.

18. Lucy Mack Smith, *Biographical Sketches,* p. 151; Dean C. Jessee, "Joseph Knight's Recollection of Early Mormon History," *BYU Studies* 17 (Autumn 1976): 37.

Chapter 2

Lo, Here! Lo, There!
Early in the Spring of 1820

Milton V. Backman, Jr.
Professor of Church History and Doctrine
Brigham Young University

In the early nineteenth century, Joseph Smith, a young
man living in western New York, launched a serious quest
for religious truth. Because he was a farm boy from a poor
family, he did not attend school as frequently as other
children did. His formal education was minimal, being
limited to a study of the rudiments of reading, writing,
and arithmetic.[1] Meanwhile, he learned to derive dignity
and joy from his labors and developed qualities of strength,
endurance, self-reliance, and trust in God. While he was
unschooled in the traditions and philosophy of the world,
he possessed a pliable and inquisitive mind. He was a
rough stone that welcomed the polishing influence of God.

Joseph Smith's quest for truth initiated an extended
search. This search led to a humble prayer, and that prayer
resulted in one of the most remarkable visions in the history
of the world. This theophany near Palmyra, New York,
illuminated his understanding of many gospel principles
and initiated a call that eventually led to the restoration of
the fulness of the everlasting gospel.[2]

When Joseph was about twelve years old, he became

concerned about the welfare of his immortal soul. After recognizing that he was a sinner, he sought a faith that would provide him with a remission of sins. During his youthful years, he also pondered many things in his heart concerning the contentions, wickedness, and darkness that pervaded the minds of mankind. "I felt to mourn," he later reminisced, "for my sins and the sins of the world."[3] His quest for truth and redemption from sin led him to investigate the religious communities in the area where he lived. In modern terminology, Joseph Smith asked others, "What must I do to be saved?"

Joseph Smith's quest led to confusion and disappointment. Religious communities in western New York disagreed vehemently on a variety of doctrines that related to the general theme of salvation. A bitter war of words raged in that state during the early nineteenth century. Ministers and members, for example, unfolded to Joseph Smith conflicting views on the role of individuals in the salvation experience. Members of reformed churches (societies whose historical roots extended back to John Calvin), such as the Presbyterian church, the Congregational faith, and German and Dutch Reformed communities, and most Baptists in his neighborhood held that man played little or no role in his own conversion. Before the foundation of the world, Calvinists insisted, God decided, or determined, who would be saved. These Protestants would have admonished Joseph Smith to search his heart to see if God had elected him. On the other hand, Methodists, Episcopalians, Free Will Baptists, and Quakers insisted that man played a role in that experience: while God proffered the gift, man had the free will, or capacity, to accept or reject salvation. Seek and search, study and pray, they would have told Joseph Smith, and if you do not reject the gift and do not fall, you will be saved in God's heavenly kingdom. The subject of baptism was another major area of debate in Joseph Smith's world. Religious leaders disagreed on the relationship between faith and baptism, on the consequences or necessity of baptism, on candidates for this ordinance, on the mode of this ordinance, and on

qualifications or authority to perform this sacrament. Orthodox Lutherans and a few Baptists proclaimed at that
time that baptism was essential for salvation, that in order
to see God a person must be born of the water and of the
Spirit. Others, including Methodists, Episcopalians, Presbyterians, Congregationalists, and most Baptists, proclaimed that faith alone was necessary. Lutherans, Methodists, Presbyterians, and Congregationalists accepted
baptism of infants by sprinkling or pouring. Baptists disagreed with most Christians on that subject. Members of
this religious society proclaimed that only believers in
Christ were proper subjects and that immersion was the
only proper mode. Friends, or Quakers, rejected all physical sacraments or ordinances.

Who had the right to perform baptism was another
question that led to a contest of opinions in New York and
other parts of the young nation. Most Protestants embraced
the doctrine of priesthood of believers, a concept popularized by Martin Luther. According to this doctrine, all
believers in Christ were endowed by God with the authority to perform baptism and other sacraments. While
many embraced this view, religious leaders disagreed on
qualifications necessary to exercise the endowed priesthood. Some emphasized a call by a congregation. Others
insisted that one's internal call from God was the only
significant prerequisite. While advocates of the priesthood
of believers were arguing among themselves, Episcopalians, Methodists, and Roman Catholics insisted that authority was transmitted by the laying on of hands. This
authority, they declared, was passed from Christ to the
apostles, and from the apostles to bishops, and was held
by ministers of their respective faiths.

Doctrines relating to man's redemption were not the
only issues debated with intensity in the area where Joseph
Smith lived. Most Christians embraced creeds that defined
God as three persons of one divine essence. Others taught
that the Father and Son were distinct beings. Some believed
that only active church members should be permitted to
receive the Lord's Supper. Others taught that the Lord's

Supper should be viewed as a precursor and an encouragement to salvation. Some believed that the Lord's Supper was a memorial in which communicants partook of the emblems in remembrance of the body and blood of Christ. Others insisted that Christ was physically present during communion. Calvinists advocated that Christ was spiritually present. There were also major disputes in western New York concerning universal salvation, Christ's mission in paradise, the meaning of everlasting punishment in hell, the fate of those who failed to embrace Christ's gospel, and even the propriety of card playing and dancing.[4]

As Joseph Smith continued to explore many conflicting beliefs proclaimed by religious leaders, the young man asked himself, "What is to be done? Who of all these parties are right; or, are they all wrong together? If any one of them be right, which is it, and how shall I know it?" (Joseph Smith–History 1:10.) There was a time during his quest when he suspected that no society had retained the simple purity of the New Testament church. This conclusion he based on a comparison of biblical teachings and doctrines disclosed by religious leaders. Although as a consequence of intellectual analysis, he probably decided that not one of the churches he investigated was right, deep down in his heart he maintained a conviction that somewhere God's church existed.[5] Nevertheless, he reasoned that all churches could not be right, for they taught conflicting beliefs. "If God," he decided, "had a church it would not be split into factions." He would not teach "one society to worship one way, and administer in one set of ordinances" and teach another group principles and ordinances that were "diametrically opposed."[6]

Joseph Smith's interest in organized religion was intensified by the religious awakening that occurred in the area where he lived. "In the second year after our removal to Manchester," he explained, "there was in the place where we lived an unusual excitement on the subject of religion. It commenced with the Methodists, but soon became general among all the sects in that region of country.

Indeed, the *whole district of country seemed affected by it, and great multitudes united themselves to the different religious parties."* (Joseph Smith–History 1:5; italics added.)

An uncommon development in world history occurred in the young nation during the early nineteenth century. Religious liberty was advancing, becoming a legal reality. Following the transplanting to the thirteen colonies of all major religions of Western Europe and the rise of new faiths in the young nation, religious pluralism increased. In fact, there was greater religious diversity in the United States than in any other Christian land. Moreover, most Americans in the early Republic were not active members of a religious community. Many immigrants to this land gradually lost their identity with organized religion. Expanding into the frontier, most inhabitants lived on isolated farms and found it difficult to attend church with any degree of regularity. Following a long decrease in the ratio of church members to population, this decline reached its lowest level around 1800, when only about 7 percent of the citizens in the United States were active members of a church.[7] A combination of increased religious liberty, unusual religious pluralism, and a population that had lost its identity with organized religion created a unique environment. Seeds for a powerful revival had been planted.

One of the most extended, widespread, and consequential religious awakenings in history began in America about 1800 and reached a climax during the 1830s and 1840s. Amid a fruitful field, Methodist circuit riders, Baptist farm preachers, and itinerant Presbyterian ministers sought to carry their forms of Protestantism to others. During this Second Great Awakening, vast numbers confessed Christ, many claimed that they were saved, and the increase (in percentage) of church membership resulting from conversions was greater than at any other time in American history. Between 1800 and 1820, church membership increased from around 7 percent to 11 percent (also the ratio in the Manchester-Palmyra area in 1820), and during the next four decades it increased to about 23 percent.[8]

Joseph Smith's search for truth occurred during this powerful religious enlivenment. According to his account, the excitement that influenced him commenced with the Methodists and spread to others. Indeed, he emphasized, great multitudes joined churches in the whole region of country. In 1819 and 1820 the Methodist and Baptist faiths were the fastest growing religious communities in the United States, and there were in those years more reports of revivals in upstate and western New York than in any other state. Accounts of religious upsurges and increases in membership in New York appeared in periodicals and newspapers, including the *Palmyra Register*. Unusual meetings and revivals were also advertised by itinerant preachers and traveling businessmen. After learning the locations of prospective revivals, many people traveled to these neighborhoods in anticipation of witnessing an unusual growth of religiosity.[9]

Contemporaries of Joseph Smith affirmed his testimony regarding the spiritual awakening that occurred at the time of the First Vision. Brigham Young, who was living in Mendon, New York, about forty miles from the Smith farm in 1820, reminisced: "I very well recollect the reformation which took place in the country among the various denominations of Christians, the Baptists, Methodists, Presbyterians, and others — when Joseph was a boy . . . of fourteen. . . . And in the midst of these revivals among the religious bodies, the invitation, 'Come and join our church,' was often extended to Joseph."[10]

Daniel Wells, born in western New York in 1814, recalled religious conditions in that region of country during the era of Joseph Smith's quest for truth. "The days of my youth," he explained, "were days of religious excitement — the days of revivals, which so pervaded that section of country at that time — and I can well apprehend the effect these things must have had on the mind of Joseph. . . . I know how those revivals affected young minds in the neighbourhood in which I lived."[11]

While discussing the effect of this powerful religious awakening, Joseph Smith noted that it created bitter divisions among the people. Some cried, "Lo, here!" and others, "Lo, there!" Some contended for the Methodist faith, some for the Presbyterian, and some for the Baptist persuasion. As people "began to file off," Joseph observed, "some to one party and some to another, . . . the seemingly good feelings of both the priests and the converts" dissipated amid great confusion and bad feelings. (Joseph Smith–History 1:5–6.)

Members of Joseph's family were divided on the subject of religion. While living in New England, Joseph's father helped organize a Universalist church, but there were no formal organizations of that society in Manchester or Palmyra. The Prophet later recalled that after moving to western New York, part of his family, including his father, leaned toward Methodism; and his mother, Lucy, his brothers Hyrum and Samuel, and his sister Sophronia joined the Presbyterian church.[12]

Although Joseph Smith was deeply troubled by cries and tumults caused by religious divisions, he read the admonition of James, "If any of you lack wisdom, let him ask of God, that giveth to all men liberally, and upbraideth not; and it shall be given him." (James 1:5.) The fourteen-year-old boy was deeply moved by this counsel. "Never did any passage of scripture come with more power to the heart of man," he asserted, "than this did at this time to mine." Recognizing that he lacked wisdom, he reflected on this scripture again and again. Finally, he came to the conclusion that if he did not follow the admonition of James, he would "remain in darkness and confusion." (Joseph Smith–History 1:12–13.)

"On the morning of a beautiful, clear day" in the spring of 1820, the fourteen-year-old boy retired to a grove near his father's log farmhouse to petition his Heavenly Father. "It was the first time" in his life, he admitted, that he had attempted to pray vocally. After retiring to a predetermined sight, he looked around to see if anyone was near. Assuming that he was alone, he knelt in prayer. (Joseph Smith–History 1:14–15.) His early efforts were fruitless. His tongue seemed to be swollen in his mouth. After hearing a noise behind him that sounded like a person walking toward him, he sprang to his feet and looked around, but saw nothing.[13] Immediately thereafter, he was seized by a power that entirely overcame him. It had such astonishing influence over him that his tongue seemed bound. He could not speak. Thick darkness gathered around him, and for a time he seemed doomed to destruction. Exerting all his will, he called upon God to release him from the power of this enemy. At the very moment he was ready to sink into despair and abandon himself to "the power of some actual being from an unseen world," he saw descend over his head a pillar of light above the brightness of the sun. This fire-like brilliance gradually rested upon him. After being delivered from the power of the enemy, he experienced unspeakable joy. (Joseph Smith–History 1:16.)[14]

"When the light rested upon [him]," he saw standing above him two glorious Personages who exactly resembled each other in features and likeness. (Joseph Smith–History 1:17.)[15] "[Their] brightness and glory," he observed, defied all description. One of the Personages then spoke to Joseph, calling him by name, and said, pointing to the other — *"This is My Beloved Son. Hear Him!"* (Joseph Smith–History 1:17.) After being introduced by the Father, Jesus Christ instructed him: "Joseph, my son, thy sins are forgiven thee. Go thy way, walk in my statutes and keep my commandments. Behold, I am the Lord of glory. I was crucified for the world that all who believe on my name may have eternal life. Behold the world lieth in sin. . . . Behold . . . I come quickly as it is written of me in the cloud clothed in the glory of my Father."[16]

Since the object of his inquiry was to determine which church he should join, Joseph asked the Lord which of all the sects was right and which he should join. The answer was that he must join none of them, for they were all wrong. The Lord said in essence that all had turned aside from the gospel[17] — all religious denominations believed in incorrect doctrines[18] — "their creeds were an abomination in his sight." (Joseph Smith–History 1:19.)

The Lord also chastised professors of religion. The Personage said that their hearts were far from him, and they taught "for doctrines the commandments of men, having a form of godliness, but they deny the power thereof." (Joseph Smith–History 1:19.)

During this vision Joseph received additional instructions and perceived other truths. He was told a second time that he should not join any church (see Joseph Smith–History 1:20), and he was promised that the fulness of the gospel would at some future time be restored to him.[19] He also testified that he saw many angels during this first communication, or vision.[20] In an autobiography he added that for many days following this experience he rejoiced with great joy. The Lord was with him, he proclaimed.[21]

It is not possible to write a complete description of all that Joseph Smith learned during his remarkable theophany near Palmyra. In the most extended account of this experience, the Prophet concluded that he learned "many other things" which he could not write at that time. (Joseph Smith–History 1:20.) Some aspects of this experience perhaps were so sacred and profound that he could not explain in the language of mortals that which he learned and experienced. Or he might have been forbidden to reveal all that was disclosed at that time. (See D&C 76:115; 3 Nephi 26:16.)

A few days following this vision, Joseph Smith described his experience to a Methodist preacher who had been active in the awakening. The preacher responded with great contempt. Expressing the basic position of most Protestants, the minister said that "it was all of the devil, that there were no such things as visions or revelations in these days; that all such things had ceased with the apostles, and that there would never be any more of them." (Joseph Smith–History 1:21.) Joseph soon learned that relating his experience created prejudice against him and was the cause of bitter persecution and much sorrow. While describing his feelings regarding the opposition that occurred, the Prophet later bore a powerful testimony. "I felt much like Paul," he declared, "when he made his defense before King Agrippa, and related the account of the vision he had when he saw a light, and heard a voice; but still there were but few who believed him; some said he was dishonest, others said he was mad; and he was ridiculed and reviled. But all this did not destroy the reality of his vision. . . . So it was with me. I had actually seen a light, and in the midst of that light I saw two Personages, and they did in reality speak to me; and though I was hated and persecuted for saying that I had seen a vision, yet it was true. . . . I knew it, and I knew that God knew it, and I could not deny it." (Joseph Smith–History 1:24–25.)

Although Joseph Smith was cautious about what he related to others regarding this visitation of the Father and the Son, he gradually unfolded in his speaking and writing various aspects of this experience. By combining these declarations, one can gain a better understanding of the truths unfolded in 1820 and the significance of this remarkable event. Moreover, between his experience in the grove near Palmyra and his tragic death at Carthage, Joseph Smith's potential to learn and his knowledge and understanding of gospel truths increased. As explained by Orson Pratt, a close associate of Joseph, the Lord revealed as much to him in 1820 as Joseph had the capacity to receive.[22] Because Joseph Smith and others discussed this event in a setting of enriched knowledge, it is not possible to know exactly what Joseph Smith perceived as a fourteen-year-old boy. Nevertheless, the Prophet was specific on many basic truths that were unfolded in 1820, and all major concepts included in his writings were confirmed by contemporaries who bore witness of that which they learned from Joseph.[23]

When Joseph Smith walked from the Sacred Grove, he knew more about the Godhead than anyone then living on the earth. This knowledge was not based on his interpretation of the Bible nor on intense study but on that which he had seen and heard. "All his inquiries previously had been futile," Orson Pratt explained. "Now here was certainty . . . here were personages capable of instructing him. . . . One minute of instruction from personages clothed with the glory of God coming down from the eternal worlds is worth more than all the volumes that were ever written by uninspired men."[24]

The Prophet in various sermons later emphasized the importance of gaining a correct understanding of the Godhead. There are very few, he said in 1844, who understand correctly the character of God. The scriptures inform us that "this is life eternal, that they might know . . . God, and Jesus Christ, whom [he] hast sent." (John 17:3.) We cannot gain eternal life without such knowledge, he added. One of our first objectives should be to understand the character of the true God.[25] Included among the first principles unfolded to Joseph Smith in 1820 was that God lives; that he hears and answers prayers; that he intervenes in the affairs of his children; that our Father is a personal being with an actual body; that Jesus, his son, is a distinct Personage; and that our Father created man in his physical image.

Two major inaccuracies about the Godhead were exposed at the beginning of the vision. One related to the characteristics of the Godhead; the other pertained to the power of communicating God's will to others. Despite a growing belief in the early nineteenth century that the Father and the Son were separate and distinct spirits, every major creed of Christendom specified that God was a spirit (defined as immaterial) and was three persons of one divine essence or substance.[26] Since God was viewed as an immaterial being, essence did not imply that God created man in his physical image. By identifying the two Personages who appeared to him in 1820 as the Father and Son and by declaring that they resembled each other in features or likeness, Joseph Smith taught others the distinctiveness of these Personages and identified some of their physical attributes. The writings of Joseph and his contemporaries confirm this interpretation of truths unfolded in 1820.

The separate nature of the Father and the Son, for example, was disclosed in other latter-day visions and was the topic of discussion in the various sermons of Joseph Smith. In 1832, Joseph Smith and Sidney Rigdon saw Christ on the right hand of the Father. (See D&C 76:23.)[27] While speaking on the subject of the Godhead in 1843, Joseph Smith used as scriptural support of the separate nature of their bodies, Stephen's vision (see Acts 7:55), wherein he saw the Son of Man "standing on the right hand of God."[28] In other talks delivered during the 1840s, the Prophet insisted that the popular view of the Trinity (three beings in one essence) was wrong. "Any person that has seen the heavens opened," Joseph explained, "knows that there are three personages in the heavens who hold the Keys of Power."[29] In a sermon delivered on 16 June 1844, the Prophet emphasized that the concept of the separate nature of the Father and the Son was not a new doctrine. According to a record kept by Thomas Bullock, one of the Prophet's scribes, Joseph Smith on that occasion said that for "15 years" he had preached on the subject of the plurality of Gods. "I have always declared God to be a distinct personage and or separate and these 3 constitute 3 distinct personages and 3 Gods."[30]

Although available records do not provide us with specific information on what Joseph Smith learned in 1820 regarding the body of God, as Joseph reflected on his experience, he emphasized that our Father was a tangible being who created man in his own image. "God who sits in yonder heavens," he declared in 1844, "is a man like yourselves." Explaining the meaning of that statement, the Prophet said, *"If you were to see him today . . . you would see him like a man in form, like yourselves.* Adam was made in his image and talked with him."[31] In an article published in 1836, Truman Coe, Presbyterian minister of Kirtland, Ohio, affirmed that in the mid-1830s Latter-day Saints embraced an anthropomorphic concept of Deity. Mormons believe, he asserted, that "the true God is a material being, composed of body and parts, and that when the Creator formed Adam in his own image, he made him about the size and shape of God himself."[32]

After Joseph Smith learned in 1820 various characteristics of the Godhead, he learned about the mission of the Savior and the need to restore Christ's church. In addition to receiving instructions regarding the reality of the atoning sacrifice of Christ and the imminence of the Second Coming, he was told that the church of Christ was not upon the earth. Others, he was told, taught incorrect beliefs and denied the power of God. When Orson Pratt explained the meaning of this latter phrase, he emphasized that after early Christians strayed from the ancient faith, they "lost the gifts and power of the Holy Ghost." They lost, he added, the "spirit of revelation and prophecy" and other gifts enjoyed by the ancient Church. Subsequently, they denied God's power to communicate and reveal his will to others directly or through the administration of angels.[33] While interpreting this same basic message, Brigham Young said that Joseph Smith was informed that the "Christian churches were all wrong because" they did not have the "priesthood and have strayed from the holy commandments of the Lord precisely as the children of Israel did."[34]

Before Joseph Smith learned characteristics and attributes of the Godhead and the status of religious communities, he felt the penetrating power of Satan. Although he recognized that such influence was real, he was taught that the power of God is stronger than that wielded by Satan.

Joseph Smith's prophetic call was briefly mentioned by the statement that the fulness of the gospel would be restored to him. Orson Pratt amplified the nature of this call. Recalling that which was related to him by Joseph, Elder Pratt declared that Joseph not only learned in 1820 that gospel truths would be unfolded to him, but he would be an "instrument in the hands of God of laying the foundations of the kingdom of God."[35]

Throughout the history of the Restored Church, Latter-day Saints have borne witness that the visitation of the Father and the Son in 1820 to Joseph Smith was the beginning of a series of visions and revelations that led to the reestablishment of the church and kingdom of God among men. The Prophet's account of the First Vision is the only surviving record (from the days of Adam to our time) of both the Father and the Son appearing and speaking to man. Once the Father introduced the Son, he always communicated to his latter-day prophets through other channels. In addition to emphasizing this principle of authority, Elder James E. Faust, a modern apostle, expressed another popular belief of Latter-day Saints: "There has been no event more glorious, more controversial, nor more important in the story of Joseph Smith than this vision. It is possibly the most singular event to occur on the earth since the Resurrection."[36] And another twentieth-century leader, President Spencer W. Kimball, added his testimony to the reality and significance of this sacred experience.

"Nothing short of this total vision to Joseph, could have served the purpose to clear away mists of the centuries. Merely an impression, a hidden voice, a dream could [not] have dispelled the old vagaries and misconceptions.

"The God of all these worlds and the Son of God, the Redeemer, our Savior, in person attended this boy. He saw the living God. He saw the living Christ.

"Of all the great events of the century, none compared with the first vision of Joseph Smith."[37]

Notes

1. Joseph Smith, "History of the Life of Joseph Smith," 1832, Archives of The Church of Jesus Christ of Latter-day Saints, Salt Lake City, Utah; hereafter cited as 1832 History.

2. On four different occasions, Joseph Smith wrote or dictated to scribes accounts of his First Vision that have been preserved. There is a different emphasis in each of the accounts. They were prepared at different times, for different audiences, and for different purposes. Each of them emphasizes a different aspect of his experience. These accounts have been published in Milton V. Backman, Jr., *Joseph Smith's First Vision* (Salt Lake City, Utah: Bookcraft, 1980), and Dean C. Jessee, *The Personal Writings of Joseph Smith* (Salt Lake City, Utah: Deseret Book Co., 1984), pp. 4–6, 75–76, 199–200, 213. A harmony of the writings of the Prophet on this vision appears in Milton V. Backman, Jr., *Eyewitness Accounts of the Restoration* (Salt Lake City, Utah: Deseret Book Co., 1986). For a discussion of the contents and background of each of the four accounts, see also Milton V. Backman, Jr., "Joseph Smith's Recitals of the First Vision," *Ensign* 15 (Jan. 1985): 8–17.

3. 1832 History.

4. For a more detailed discussion of the theological confrontations that occurred in the area where Joseph Smith lived at the time of the First Vision, see Backman, *Joseph Smith's First Vision*, pp. 92–105.

5. 1832 History; Joseph Smith–History 1:18; hereafter cited as 1838 History.

6. Joseph Smith, "Church History," *Times and Seasons* 3 (1 Mar. 1842): 706–7; hereafter cited as 1842 History.

7. Milton V. Backman, Jr., *American Religions and the Rise of Mormonism* (Salt Lake City, Utah: Deseret Book Co., 1965), pp. 277, 283, 301, 309; Backman, *Joseph Smith's First Vision*, pp. 76–78.

8. Backman, *Joseph Smith's First Vision*, pp. 68, 76, 78.

9. One contemporary of Joseph Smith, David Marks, traveled in 1821 to Brutus and Camillus, twenty to thirty miles from his father's house, to attend meetings because he learned that there was a great revival in that area. Marks referred to an area which included towns thirty miles from his home as the "vicinity of Junius." When Joseph Smith discussed the increased number of church members in his 1838 History, he not only described conditions in Palmyra village but aptly described an awakening that led to increased church membership in a much larger geographical area, or in the "whole region of country." Marilla Marks, ed., *Memoirs of the Life of David Marks* (Dover, N.H., 1846), pp. 17, 32.
For a more detailed discussion of the awakening of 1819–20, see Backman, *Joseph Smith's First Vision*, pp. 80–89.

10. Brigham Young, in *Journal of Discourses*, 26 vols. (Liverpool: Latter-day Saints' Book Depot, 1855–86), 12:67.

11. Daniel Wells, in *Journal of Discourses*, 12:71–72.

12. 1838 History; Backman, *Joseph Smith's First Vision*, pp. 67–69, 76; Joseph Smith–History 1:7; Richard Lloyd Anderson, *Joseph Smith's New England Heritage* (Salt Lake City, Utah: Deseret Book Co., 1971), pp. 105–6.

13. Diary of Joseph Smith, 9 Nov. 1835, Archives of The Church of Jesus Christ of Latter-day Saints, Salt Lake City, Utah; hereafter cited as 1835 History.

14. Ibid.

15. 1842 History.

16. 1832 History. Spelling and punctuation has been standardized.

17. Ibid.

18. 1842 History.

19. 1842 History.

20. 1835 History.

21. 1832 History.

22. Orson Pratt, in *Journal of Discourses*, 12:355.

23. For a more complete discussion of that which was related by Joseph Smith to his contemporaries regarding the First Vision, see Milton V. Backman, Jr., "Confirming Witnesses of the First Vision," *Ensign* 16 (Jan. 1986): 32–37.

24. Orson Pratt, in *Journal of Discourses*, 12:354.

25. Andrew F. Ehat and Lyndon W. Cook, eds., *The Words of Joseph Smith* (Provo, Utah: Religious Studies Center, Brigham Young University, 1980), pp. 344, 348–49, 356.

Most of the quotations from Joseph Smith's talks are based on sermons delivered during the 1840s. It is difficult to know concepts he taught earlier, because contemporaries, with very few exceptions, did not record his earlier sermons.

In this chapter I have sought to limit the discussion to principles that were probably unfolded in 1820: I do not examine a fourteen-year-old boy's perception of all these views. As Joseph received additional light and knowledge, his understanding of what had been disclosed in 1820 must have been enlarged.

26. See Backman, *American Religions and the Rise of Mormonism,* pp. 207–13, for a discussion of the increased numbers of people who believed in the separate nature of the Father and the Son, at the time of the First Vision.

27. Milton V. Backman, Jr., *The Heavens Resound: A History of the Latter-day Saints in Ohio, 1830–1838* (Salt Lake City, Utah: Deseret Book Co., 1983), pp. 86, 267, 288.

28. Ibid., p. 212. In an article published in the *Millennial Star,* Orson Pratt used the same basic argument used by Joseph Smith to teach the separate nature of the Father and the Son. He taught in essence that Joseph Smith saw "both the Father and Son" during the First Vision and Joseph Smith and Sidney Rigdon saw these same Personages in 1832. *Millennial Star* 15 (Sept. 1849): 281–84; 15 (Oct. 1849): 309–12.

29. Ehat and Cook, *Words of Joseph Smith,* p. 214. This statement should be considered in light of what Joseph Smith later learned about the Holy Ghost. We do not know what he learned in 1820 about this member of the Godhead. Nevertheless, the thrust of this sermon was that members of the Godhead were separate and distinct beings (with different bodies) and that anyone who had seen members of the Godhead would know this truth. Possibly some of the truths he did not discuss in his accounts of the First Vision pertained to characteristics of the Holy Ghost. While discussing that which Joseph Smith learned in 1820, Joseph Fielding Smith wrote that "it was further revealed to him that the Holy Ghost is a personage of Spirit, distinct and separate from the personalities of the Father and Son." *Improvement Era* 23 (Apr. 1920): 496.

There is no way to know when Joseph Smith initially learned the doctrine he enunciated in a sermon delivered on 2 April 1843 that "The Father has a body of flesh and bones as tangible as man's; the Son also; but the Holy Ghost . . . is a personage of Spirit." Doctrine and Covenants 130:22.

30. Ehat and Cook, *Words of Joseph Smith,* p. 378. The spelling in this quotation has been revised to coincide with current English usage. Some of the words were abbreviated in Bullock's notes.

31. Ibid., pp. 344, 349, 357, 380, 382.

32. Truman Coe, "Mormonism," [Hudson,] *Ohio Observer,* 11 Aug. 1836; reprinted in *Cincinnati Journal and Western Luminary,* 25 Aug. 1836.

33. Orson Pratt, in *Journal of Discourses,* 12:354–55; 14:141.

34. Brigham Young, in *Journal of Discourses,* 12:67.

35. Orson Pratt, in *Journal of Discourses,* 7:220–21.

36. James E. Faust, in Conference Report, Apr. 1984, p. 91.

37. Spencer W. Kimball, *The Teachings of Spencer W. Kimball,* ed. Edward L. Kimball (Salt Lake City, Utah: Bookcraft, 1982), pp. 428, 430.

Chapter 3

Joseph, a Family Man

LaMar C. Berrett
Professor of Church History and Doctrine
Brigham Young University

"The home is the basis of a righteous life and no other instrumentality can take its place nor fulfil its essential functions," said the First Presidency when David O. McKay was President of the Church.[1] President McKay later added, "No other success can compensate for failure in the home."[2]

It is readily apparent to one who reads about Joseph Smith that he had an extremely busy life. How, then, could he spend enough time with his family to be considered a successful family patriarch? With the pressures of being a prophet of God, mayor of the city of Nauvoo, businessman, missionary, editor of newspapers, temple builder, writer, student of languages, military leader, political candidate, and city planner, was it possible that he could also be a successful patriarch? The Prophet Joseph's own writings in the form of letters, diaries, and written histories attest that he was devoted to his family and they to him, and that he did take the time necessary to be a successful member of his father's family and patriarch in his own home. Joseph learned early in life about his role as a child and his relationship to his parents and brothers and sisters; and this understanding carried through his own marriage in his responsibility to his wife and children.

Joseph, a Child

When the Father and Son appeared to Joseph in a grove of trees in the spring of 1820, Joseph knew that God the Father was in charge. The Father introduced his Son and said, "This is My Beloved Son. Hear Him!" (Joseph Smith–History 1:17.) With this pronouncement, the Father taught Joseph that there was order in the organization of the kingdom of God on earth. Jesus was responsible under the direction of his Father. It was also the Father who established the most basic social structure of mankind, the patriarchal family. (See Moses 2:27.) Originally the patriarchal family was the sole form of government on the earth. In a God-ordained patriarchal family organization, the father was to be the head of the family. The patriarch was to direct, guide, counsel, rebuke, and bless his family. His assignment as patriarch was a divine arrangement of family government, and "there is no other authority paramount."[3]

A proper relationship existed between a father and his son when Joseph Smith told his father about the visit of the angel Moroni. His believing father, the first person to have faith in Joseph's experience with Moroni, replied that Joseph's experience with Moroni "was of God, and told me to go and do as commanded by the messenger." (Joseph Smith–History 1:50.) Joseph's father showed respect and trust to his son concerning an experience that would cause most fathers to question, criticize, or disregard. Joseph showed proper respect to his father, who in turn expressed continual esteem for the integrity of his son.

When Joseph and his brother William had a physical confrontation, Joseph called on his father to be the patriarchal judge and arbitrator. Through the father's prayers and inspired counsel, a reconciliation was made between the divided brothers. Joseph wrote of this occasion:

"Brothers William and Hyrum, and Uncle John Smith, came to my house, and we went into a room by ourselves, in company with father and Elder Martin Harris. Father Smith then opened our interview by prayer, after which he expressed himself on the occasion in a very feeling and pathetic manner, even with all the sympathy of a father, whose feelings were deeply wounded on account of the difficulty that was existing in the family; and while he addressed us, the Spirit of God rested down upon us in mighty power, and our hearts were melted. Brother William made a humble confession and asked my forgiveness for the abuse he had offered me. And wherein I had been out of the way, I asked his forgiveness. And the spirit of confession and forgiveness was mutual among us all, and we covenanted with each other, in the sight of God, and the holy angels, and the brethren, to strive thence-forward to build each other up in righteousness in all things, and not listen to evil reports concerning each other; but, like brothers indeed, go to each other, with our grievances, in the spirit of meekness, and be reconciled, and thereby promote our happiness, and the happiness of the family, and, in short, the happiness and well-being of all. My wife and mother and my scribe were then called in, and we repeated the covenant to them that we had entered into; and while gratitude swelled our bosoms, tears flowed from our eyes. I was then requested to close our interview, which I did, with prayer; and it was truly a jubilee and time of rejoicing."[4]

When Joseph's father acted in his divinely appointed role under the inspiration of the Holy Ghost, the difficulties were resolved. Joseph could have said to himself, "I am the prophet, and am therefore more qualified than my father to settle the difficulty," but he did not. He was a submissive son to a patriarchal father who had the responsibility and right to seek the Lord's help in solving the family differences.

Joseph's parents taught their children to have faith in God. They had family prayers, with the father doing most of the praying; and the children were taught in a "family home evening" atmosphere. After Joseph's first experience with Moroni, mother Lucy said: "We continued to get the children together every evening for the purpose of listening" while Joseph described the dress and mode of living of the ancient inhabitants of the American continent. Lucy said the family were "all seated in a circle, father, mother, sons and daughters, and giving the most profound attention to a boy, eighteen years of age."[5] Not only the parents were teachers but the children were also. Learning was a "two-way street." The parents respected their children's right to contribute to the welfare of the whole family.

Lucy and Joseph Smith, Sr., provided an atmosphere of love and harmony in their home that won the deep respect of Joseph. Joseph dearly loved his parents and sought their parental counsel. On an occasion when his father was ill, Joseph said, "I waited on him all this day with my heart raised to God in the name of Jesus Christ, that He would restore him to health, that I might be blessed with his company and advice, *esteeming it one of the greatest earthly blessings to be blessed with the society of parents, whose mature years and experience render them capable of administering the most wholesome advice.*" (Italics added.)[6] Only a son matured in love and respect could pen such a sublime statement about his parents. The fact that he wrote it bears witness of the relationship that existed between son and parents. Regardless of spoken praise or love, however, the real test comes in the doing, for actions speak louder than words. How did Joseph show by his works that a loving and caring relationship existed between him and his parents? Consider the following entries in the Prophet's writings:

"Went to visit my father, found him very low, administered some mild herbs, agreeably to the commandment."[7] "At home. Waited on my father."[8] For several days Joseph nursed his father back to health and did his father's chores: "Labored in father's orchard, gathering apples."[9]

Joseph had the same kind of respect for his mother, Lucy. He said in his journal: "Mother came to my house to live."[10] "At home all day. My mother was sick with inflammation of the lungs, and I nursed her with my own hands."[11] "I stayed at home all day to take care of my mother, who was still sick."[12] "Rode out with mother and others for her health."[13]

39

Many more journal entries show that Joseph had a loving respect for his parents; and though he was an extremely busy man, he still had time to render proper esteem for his parents. Joseph had learned well his role as a child to a parent.

Joseph, a Brother

The love and respect Joseph had for his brothers and sisters was expressed in both words and deeds. They supported him with their faith, prayers, and works as he organized and conducted the affairs of the kingdom of God on earth. Joseph had seven brothers (two of whom died in infancy) and three sisters. His oldest brother, Alvin, was a strong believer in the Book of Mormon even before the Prophet Joseph received the golden plates. Lucy said that Alvin manifested greater anxiety and zeal over the Book of Mormon record than any of the rest of the family, "in consequence of which we could not bear to hear anything said upon the subject. Whenever Joseph spoke of the Record, it would immediately bring Alvin to our minds."[14] Because the Church was not organized before Alvin's death in 1823, he had not been baptized. For thirteen years this matter worried Joseph. In Kirtland the Prophet received a revelation that Alvin would be in the celestial degree of glory, because "all who have died without a knowledge of this gospel, who would have received it if they had been permitted to tarry, shall be heirs of the celestial kingdom of God." (D&C 137:7.) This revelation must have brought great comfort to Joseph, because of his deep love for his brother. Joseph said of Alvin, "He was the oldest and the noblest of my father's family. In him there was no guile. He lived without spot from the time he was a child."[15]

Hyrum was nearly six years older than his brother Joseph, but even twins could not have had a stronger love for each other. Joseph said of Hyrum, "What a faithful heart you have got! O how many are the sorrows we have shared together."[16] It was Hyrum who sat beside six- or seven-year-old Joseph day and night for a long time holding the infected part of Joseph's leg and pressing it between his hands to help Joseph endure the excruciating pain. Doctors finally cut out the infected bone, and Joseph was eventually cured of this painful ailment. Mother Lucy felt that Hyrum was "remarkable for his tenderness and sympathy" and desire to be of service to his mother and brother.[17] Of Hyrum, Joseph said: "And I could pray in my heart that all my brethren were like unto my beloved brother Hyrum, who possesses the mildness of a lamb, and the integrity of a Job, and in short, the meekness and humility of Christ; and I love him with that love that is stronger than death, for I never had occasion to rebuke him, nor he me, which he declared when he left me today."[18] Hyrum shared in the joys and trials of Joseph and stood by him in life and in death—always bearing witness that his brother was the prophet of God.

Samuel Harrison, just younger than Joseph, was always faithful to the building up of the Church established through his brother. He was one of the witnesses of the golden plates of the Book of Mormon, a member of the high council in Kirtland, and a faithful member of the Church. He died in Nauvoo a month after his brothers Joseph and Hyrum were martyred.

Of all the brothers, William seems to have been the most independent and stubborn. Apparently it was rather difficult for him be in harmony with the Prophet all the time, and on at least one occasion the disagreement came to physical contact. But in spite of William's negative feelings, Joseph loved him. "Brother William is as the fierce lion, . . . and in the pride of his heart he will neglect the more weighty matters until his soul is bowed down in sorrow; and then he shall return and call on the name of his God, and shall find forgiveness, and shall wax valiant, therefore, he shall be saved unto the uttermost, . . . notwithstanding his rebellious heart."[19] With a Christlike love, Joseph could accept William as a brother.

Don Carlos, Joseph's "little brother," was very active in the Church and was ordained the first president of the high priests quorum; he was a professional printer and helped establish the *Times and Seasons* newspaper in Nauvoo; he served with his brother Joseph in the Nauvoo Legion as a brigadier general. Joseph's love for him was manifested when he named his seventh child Don Carlos. "Don Carlos Smith . . . was a noble boy; I never knew any fault in him," said Joseph. "He was a lovely, a good-natured, a kind-hearted and a virtuous and a faithful, upright child; and where his soul goes, let mine go also."[20]

Entries in Joseph's journal indicate that he spent time with his brothers: "Rode out to the prairie with my brothers, William and Samuel."[21] "My brother William arrived from New Jersey . . . I spent some time with him in the evening."[22]

Although Joseph wrote less about his sisters—Sophronia, Catherine, and Lucy—he undoubtedly loved them as he loved his brothers. Joseph not only treated his brothers and sisters with love and respect but also wrote down his feelings, and thus he left a clear example of how siblings should treat one another.

Joseph, a Husband

Joseph's marriage to Emma Hale in 1827 was the beginning of an affectionate relationship that was to last for seventeen earthly years. Emma had religious training in her youth, and she along with Joseph had desires to serve the Lord. In a revelation, Emma was told that she was an "elect lady," later interpreted by the Prophet to refer to her election to be the first president of the Relief Society in Nauvoo. The Lord told her to comfort her husband, to go with him at the time of his going (which was often), to be a scribe for him, to make a selection of hymns, and to murmur not because of things she had not seen; her soul was to delight in her husband and the glory which should come upon him. (See D&C 25:1–14.)

Emma supported her husband through trials, arrests, ridicule, attacks, imprisonments, threats, and anxiety. It was not easy for Emma to have nine pregnancies, nor was it easy to be uprooted from her home time after time. But her love and support helped calm troubled waters.

An occasional disagreement was settled through discussion, prayer, and repentance. While finishing the translation of the Book of Mormon with the help of Emma, Joseph was unable to continue the work because of a minor problem between him and Emma. Going into the Whitmer orchard where he could be alone, Joseph spent an hour in supplication with the Lord. When he returned to the house, he asked Emma's forgiveness. He was then in the proper spiritual position to continue the translation, and at the same time he had renewed the love between him and his wife.

Did Joseph have time in his busy and turbulent life to spend quality time with Emma? The record tells us that he took time to be with his wife, whether he had it or not. Journal entries are replete with evidence of this: "Continued translating and revising, and reading letters in the evening, Sister Emma being present in the office."[23] "In the afternoon rode to Brother John Benbow's, on horseback, accompanied by Emma and others."[24] "Walked to the store with Emma."[25] "Rode to the big mound on the LaHarpe road, accompanied by Emma."[26] "Spent the forenoon chiefly in conversation with Emma on various subjects, and in reading my history with her — both felt in good spirits and very cheerful."[27] When Emma was ill, Joseph took personal care of her. Perhaps he could have hired nurse Jane Johnson to take care of Emma. Or perhaps his mother could have taken care of her; but Joseph's journal entries indicate that he played the role of nurse himself, and this at a time when he was, as usual, extremely busy. Joseph's writings further attest to his love and care for Emma: "Emma began to be sick with fever; consequently I kept in the house with her all day."[28] "Emma is no better. I was with her all day."[29] "Emma was a little better. I was with her all day."[30] The entries go on and on. He spent much time with Emma when she was ill, caring for his wife tenderly and lovingly. Mercy Thompson said, "I saw him [Joseph] by the bed-side of Emma, his wife, in sickness, exhibiting all the solicitude and sympathy possible for the tenderest of hearts and the most affectionate of natures to feel."[31]

Joseph's journal tells of riding horses often with Emma. He also tells of going in a sleigh with her. He records how well Emma fed him: "I took dinner in the north room, and was remarking to Brother Phelps what a kind, provident wife I had,—that when I wanted a little bread and milk, she would load the table with so many good things, it would destroy my appetite."[32]

Joseph's love and compassion for Emma is clearly displayed in his private letters to her. He addresses them "My dear and beloved companion, of my bosom, in tribulation, and affliction," or simply "Affectionate Wife" or "Dear and Affectionate Wife." The contents of his letters reflect a warmth toward Emma that continued over the years.

When Joseph was secluded on an island in the middle of the Mississippi River to escape the attempted arrests by the Missourians, he had time to contemplate and write about his true friends. He recorded names and blessings of those he felt were his choice friends and called the book of blessings *The Law of the Lord*. Joseph's feelings toward Emma are carefully preserved in this book, and we are not left in doubt about his feelings toward the sweetheart of his youth.

"With what unspeakable delight, and what transports of joy swelled my bosom, when I took by the hand, on that night, my beloved Emma—she that was my wife, even the wife of my youth, and the choice of my heart. Many were the reverberations of my mind when I contemplated for a moment the many scenes we had been called to pass through, the fatigues and the toils, the sorrows and sufferings, and the joys and consolations, from time to time, which had strewed our paths and crowned our board. Oh what a commingling of thought filled my mind for the moment, again she is here, even in the seventh trouble—undaunted, firm, and unwavering—unchangeable, affectionate Emma!"[33]

As a helpmate to her husband, Emma was successful. She sustained him through all of his trials and shared with him in his joys. The love that brought stability and happiness to their lives is clearly taught through the personal writings of Joseph the Prophet. The time he spent with Emma and their family shows that he truly was a devoted husband.

Joseph, a Father

Certainly Joseph and Emma were family oriented. Joseph came from a family of eleven, and he, Emma, and their children were also a family of eleven. In addition to the nine children born to Emma, however, two more children were adopted; thus their family actually numbered thirteen:

1. Alvin was born and died 15 June 1828, at Harmony.
2. Louisa, a twin, was born and died 30 April 1831, at Kirtland.
3. Thaddeus, a twin, was born and died 30 April 1831, at Kirtland.
4. Joseph III was born 6 November 1832, at Kirtland. He died 1914.
5. Frederick Granger Williams was born 20 June 1836, at Kirtland. He died 1862.
6. Alexander Hale was born 2 June 1838, at Far West. He died 1909.
7. Don Carlos was born 13 June 1840, at Nauvoo. He died 1841.
8. A boy was born and died 26 December 1842, at Nauvoo.
9. David Hyrum was born 17 November 1844, at Nauvoo. He died 1904.
10. Joseph Smith Murdock, adopted twin, was born 30 April 1831, at Kirtland. He died 1832.
11. Julia Murdock, adopted twin, was born 30 April 1831, at Kirtland. She died 1880.

One cannot be a family man without a family, and Joseph and Emma believed that a large family was a special blessing to them. Bathsheba W. Smith wrote that while she was in Nauvoo playing with her baby boy, Joseph Smith said to her that children were the "honor, glory, and royal diadem of women."[34]

Again the personal writings of Joseph tell us that he

himself took the time out of his busy schedule so that his family could enjoy his company and influence. The Prophet said, "Spent the day at home in the enjoyment of the society of my family, around the social fireside."[35] "At home all day. Took solid comfort with my family."[36] "In the evening, several of the Twelve and others called to visit me. My family sang hymns, and Elder John Taylor prayed and gave an address."[37] "I was engaged in reading, meditation, &c., mostly with my family."[38] "I rode out to my farm with my children, and did not return until after dark."[39]

Joseph took time not only to work with his children but also to play with them. "At four in the afternoon, I went out with my little Frederick, to exercise myself by sliding on the ice."[40] "In the morning I took my children [on] a pleasure ride in the carriage."[41] "One, p.m., called and gave licence for a circus performance, which I attended with my family until five, p.m."[42] "This morning, I, with my family and a large company of brethren and sisters, started for Quincy, on a pleasure voyage on the steamboat *Maid of Iowa*, had a fine band of music in attendance."[43]

Other observers also wrote about Joseph's time spent with his children. Joseph Taylor wrote that "Sister Emma Smith said that he [Joseph] and his son Joseph had just gone up the river near Nauvoo to shoot ducks."[44] Joseph's tender feelings toward his children are reflected in another journal entry: "At home at nine o'clock, a.m., reading a magazine to my children."[45]

To the world, Joseph Smith is known because of such things as his extraordinary nature and charisma, his tremendous accomplishments, his leadership as a prophet of God, and his martyrdom. The true greatness of the Prophet Joseph must also include the qualities and characteristics that made him a successful husband and father. Those things done behind closed doors and unknown to the masses must be considered if one is to get a true picture of Joseph Smith, the man of God.

Joseph Smith grew up in a family that was taught to love freedom, work, the Lord, and spiritual unity. They united their work efforts to earn money to purchase a farm in Manchester, New York. They worked on the farm and made maple syrup together; worked to build a new home for Joseph and Lucy to enjoy; and walked or rode horses together as they went to nearby churches for worship. As a family they moved one thousand miles to faraway Missouri. They cared for and loved each other and were successful in showing outwardly their positive feelings of "family togetherness."

An essential part of the restored gospel was to turn the hearts of fathers to children and the hearts of children to fathers, as Malachi had foretold and for which Elijah restored keys. (See Malachi 4:5–6; D&C 110:13–16.)

The Prophet Joseph understood well his exemplary role in a family unit. A busy life did not excuse him from a divine appointment, because he understood that the home is the basis of a righteous life and that it was the Lord's will for him to be an exemplary child, brother, husband, and father.

Notes

1. First Presidency, David O. McKay, quoted by Harold B. Lee, "The Correlation Program," *Improvement Era* 66 (June 1963): 502.

2. David O. McKay, "Blessed Are They That Do His Commandments," *Improvement Era* 67 (June 1964): 445.

3. Joseph F. Smith, *Gospel Doctrine* (Salt Lake City, Utah: Deseret Book Co., 1939), p. 287.

4. Joseph Smith, *History of The Church of Jesus Christ of Latter-day Saints,* 7 vols., 2d ed. rev., ed. B. H. Roberts (Salt Lake City, Utah: The Church of Jesus Christ of Latter-day Saints, 1932–51), 2:353–54.

5. Lucy Mack Smith, *History of Joseph Smith* (Salt Lake City, Utah: Bookcraft, 1956), pp. 82–83.

6. Smith, *History of the Church,* 2:289.

7. Smith, *History of the Church,* 2:288.

8. Smith, *History of the Church,* 2:289.

9. Smith, *History of the Church,* 2:290.

10. Smith, *History of the Church,* 5:271.

11. Smith, *History of the Church,* 5:290.

12. Smith, *History of the Church,* 5:298.

13. Smith, *History of the Church,* 6:65.

14. Lucy Mack Smith, *History of Joseph Smith,* p. 89.

15. Smith, *History of the Church,* 5:126–27.

16. Smith, *History of the Church,* 5:107–8.

17. Lucy Mack Smith, *History of Joseph Smith,* p. 55.

18. Smith, *History of the Church,* 2:338.

19. Smith, *History of the Church,* 1:467.

20. Smith, *History of the Church,* 5:127.

21. Smith, *History of the Church,* 5:371.

22. Smith, *History of the Church,* 6:342.

23. Smith, *History of the Church,* 4:548.

24. Smith, *History of the Church,* 5:21.

25. Smith, *History of the Church,* 5:21.

26. Smith, *History of the Church,* 5:25.

27. Smith, *History of the Church,* 5:92.

28. Smith, *History of the Church,* 5:166.

29. Smith, *History of the Church,* 5:166.

30. Smith, *History of the Church,* 5:167.

31. "Recollections of the Prophet Joseph Smith," *Juvenile Instructor* 27 (1 July 1892): 399.

32. Smith, *History of the Church,* 6:165.

33. Smith, *History of the Church,* 5:107.

34. "Recollections of the Prophet Joseph Smith," *Juvenile Instructor* 27 (1 June 1892): 344.

35. Smith, *History of the Church,* 2:405.

36. Smith, *History of the Church,* 2:344.

37. Smith, *History of the Church,* 6:79–80.

38. Smith, *History of the Church,* 4:601.

39. Smith, *History of the Church,* 5:182.

40. Smith, *History of the Church,* 5:265.

41. Smith, *History of the Church,* 5:369.

42. Smith, *History of the Church,* 6:2–3.

43. Smith, *History of the Church,* 5:418.

44. "Recollections of the Prophet Joseph Smith," *Juvenile Instructor* 27 (1 Apr. 1892): 202.

45. Smith, *History of the Church,* 6:133.

Chapter 4

"Upon You My Fellow Servants": Restoration of the Priesthood

William G. Hartley

Research Historian, Joseph Fielding Smith Institute for Church History, Brigham Young University

If asked when and how the priesthood was restored, most Church members would answer, "In 1829, John the Baptist and Peter, James, and John gave Joseph Smith and Oliver Cowdery the Aaronic and the Melchizedek priesthoods." Such a simple answer, however, is but a part of the story, the beginning segment of Joseph Smith's receiving authority and implementing it. For priesthood to be restored, it must not only be bestowed but also implemented—put into effect.[1]

Priesthood, which encompasses powers, keys, ordinances, offices, duties, organizations, and attitudes, did not come to Joseph Smith in full bloom. Like a tree, priesthood restoration unfolded from seed to shoot, to trunk, to branches, to leaves, to blossoms. Moroni promised priesthood would be restored. From that announcement (the seed) until 1843, when Joseph first exercised the highest temple sealing powers (the blossom), priesthood progressively unfolded.

Joseph Smith did not record all he experienced or was

taught about priesthood, so our picture of priesthood restoration is incomplete. In 1835 he lamented that gaps in his and others' records meant that "we cannot bear record to the Church and to the world, of the great and glorious manifestations which have been made to us with that degree of power and authority we otherwise could."[2] Unlike the details he recorded about John the Baptist's visit, Joseph mentioned visits from Peter, James, and John, Adam, Elijah, Elias, Moses, and other messengers but gave few details of what they said or how they gave him keys and authority. Joseph received a revelation about the Seventy which he did not put into writing.[3]

Preliminaries to Priesthood

In 1823, when Joseph Smith was seventeen, Moroni planted the priesthood seed in Joseph's heart by instructing him not only about plates but also about priesthood. Quoting Malachi, Moroni four times said the Lord would reveal "the Priesthood, by the hand of Elijah the prophet." (D&C 2:1.) Moroni said nothing of John the Baptist or Peter, James, and John, only that Elijah would reveal priesthood to someone, someday.

While Joseph Smith was translating the plates, priesthood seed found roots. Joseph encountered many Nephite references to priesthood, which made him ponder what priesthood was. The Book of Mormon was his first primer on priesthood and how it functioned in ancient times. He learned that even the people of Limhi, who desired baptism, could not receive it, because "there was none in the land that had authority from God." Lacking authority, "they did not . . . form themselves into a church." (Mosiah 21:33–34.) Alma, their contemporary who was hiding in the wilderness, however, received "authority from the Almighty God" by which he began baptizing. (Mosiah 18:13.)

Joseph Smith no doubt paid keen attention to the Nephite account of church operations at Zarahemla. Alma, Joseph learned, was a "high priest" and "founder of their church," and "none received authority to preach or to teach except it were by him from God." (Mosiah 23:16–17.) In time, Alma established churches throughout the land of Zarahemla and ordained priests and teachers "over every church." (Mosiah 25:19.) A priest preached "according as it was delivered to him by the mouth of Alma." (Mosiah 25:21.)

Among the Nephites there was a priestly "order of God" or "holy order of God." Alma the Younger "ordained priests and elders, by laying on his hands according to the order of God, to preside and watch over the church." (Alma 6:1.) Alma referred to "the order after which I am called" (Alma 5:49) and explained in detail the "high priesthood being after the order of his Son," which made men "high priests forever" (Alma 13:7, 9). Melchizedek, Alma taught, was "a high priest after this same order." (Alma 13:14.) Alma and his co-workers "preached after the holy order of God by which they were called." (Alma 43:2.) Further, Joseph Smith learned that Ammon was a "high priest" in Jershon (see Alma 30:19–20) and that Helaman and "high priests" guided the church (Alma 46:38).

If the young translator grew curious about the high priest's office and consulted his Bible, he would have found one reference to Jesus Christ being a high priest after the order of Melchizedek (see Hebrews 5:10) and one reference in the Psalms to "the order of Melchizedek" (Psalm 110:4). But such references produce questions, not answers. What does "the order of Melchizedek" refer to? Why would Jesus be a high priest in that order? What connection did Jesus' being a high priest after the order of Melchizedek have with the Book of Mormon's "order of the Son of God"? In Genesis, Joseph found that Melchizedek was a contemporary of Abraham, a king of Salem, and a "priest of the most high God" who blessed Abraham and received tithes from him. Genesis is silent about any order of priests that Melchizedek headed. (See Genesis 14:18–20.)

While translating, Joseph Smith learned that Nephi, son of Helaman, taught that "there were many before the days of Abraham who were called by the order of God; yea, even after the order of his Son." (Helaman 8:18.) This same Nephi, much like Moses, who parted the sea, possessed power from God to smite the earth, split a temple, level a mountain, and have God smite people. (See Helaman 10:6–10.) This Nephi received from God "power, that whatsoever ye shall seal on earth shall be sealed in heaven; and whatsoever ye shall loose on earth shall be loosed in heaven." (Helaman 10:7.) Probably the translator recognized that this power Nephi received was the same binding and loosening power that Jesus gave his apostle Peter. (See Matthew 16:18–19.)

By the time Joseph Smith finished translating the plates, they had taught him that baptisms must be performed only by proper authority, God must give that authority, there exists "an order" of priesthood, and the churches had high priests, priests, and teachers. He knew that before Abraham's time there existed "an order of God," that Moses and other prophets received great power over the elements, and that Nephite prophets had power to seal on earth, an act which heaven would honor.

From Jesus' ministry in the Americas, Joseph Smith learned that Jesus chose twelve disciples to lead his church, gave men power to baptize (see 3 Nephi 11:21), to ordain others, to administer the sacrament (see 3 Nephi 18:5), to bestow the Holy Ghost (see 3 Nephi 18:37), to form churches (see 4 Nephi 1:1), and to choose replacements for the Twelve (see 4 Nephi 1:14). Joseph found that Jesus' twelve disciples had authority to bestow the Holy Ghost and to ordain priests and teachers, and that elders and priests could administer the sacrament. (See Moroni 2–6.)

It needs to be stressed that Joseph Smith, during the priesthood restoration process, firmly believed in the Book of Mormon and revered its teachings about priesthood. He did not treat them casually or lightly.

Restoration of the Aaronic Priesthood

When Joseph Smith told others what the translations said, believers asked what they should do. He inquired of the Lord, who said that believers who were "called to the work" should thrust in their sickles and study. (D&C 4:3.)[4]

At first the believers needed no particular priesthood authority to preach repentance and to convert people to gospel principles explained in the forthcoming Book of Mormon.

While translating material relating to baptism—probably in 3 Nephi—Joseph Smith and Oliver Cowdery needed and sought divine advice. "Our souls were drawn out in mighty prayer," Oliver said, "to know how we might obtain the blessings of baptism and of the Holy Spirit, according to the order of God" (the Book of Mormon phrase) "and we diligently sought for the right of the fathers and the authority of the holy priesthood, and the power to administer in the same." The two "repaired to the woods" and there "called upon the name of the Lord."[5]

Joseph said they went into the woods "to pray and inquire of the Lord respecting baptism for the remission of sins, that we found mentioned in the translation of the plates."[6] According to Oliver, they "called upon him in a fervent manner," after which they heard "the voice of the Redeemer," which "spake peace to us."[7] Joseph's version says that while they were praying and calling on the Lord, "a messenger from heaven descended in a cloud of light."[8] Oliver's description said "the veil was parted." He said "our eyes beheld—our ears heard." The angel came as in the "blaze of day, above the glitter of the May sunbeam" then shining.[9]

Joseph and Oliver's experience of seeing, hearing, feeling, and being physically touched by a celestial being overwhelmed their senses and emotionally shook them to the core. They heard the angel's voice, "I am thy fellow-servant." This soft answer dispelled their fears. Said Oliver: "We listened, we gazed, we admired! 'Twas the voice of the angel from glory—'twas a message from the Most High, and as we heard we rejoiced." While hearing the voice, Oliver said, the messenger's "love enkindled upon our souls" and wrapped them "in a vision of the Almighty!" He added: "Where was room for doubt? Nowhere; uncertainty had fled."[10]

Continuing, Oliver struggled to verbalize what they

53

had experienced: "The angel of God came down clothed with glory and delivered the anxiously looked for message, and the keys of the Gospel of repentance. What joy! what wonder! what amazement!"[11]

Oliver, in the earliest recorded account of the Aaronic Priesthood restoration, written in 1833, said that Joseph "was ordained by the angel John unto the lesser or Aaronic priesthood, in company with myself . . . , after which we repaired to the water, even to the Susquehannah River and were baptized, he first ministering unto me and after—I to him."[12]

The men bowed themselves down, filled with surprise and wonder. According to Oliver they "received under his hand the Holy Priesthood" and heard these words: "Upon you my fellow servants, in the name of Messiah, I confer this Priesthood and this authority, which remain upon earth, that the sons of Levi may yet offer an offering unto the Lord in righteousness!"[13]

Surprisingly, Joseph's early accounts do not contain the terms *Aaronic* or *lesser priesthood*.[14] Not until about ten years later, when he wrote what is now section 13 of the Doctrine and Covenants,[15] did Joseph make clear that John the Baptist bestowed the Aaronic Priesthood : "Upon you my fellow servants, in the name of Messiah I confer the Priesthood of Aaron, which holds the keys of the ministering of angels, and of the gospel of repentance, and of baptism by immersion for the remission of sins; and this shall never be taken again from the earth, until the sons of Levi do offer again an offering unto the Lord in righteousness."

Oliver wrote of "the majestic beauty and glory that surrounded us." He said that each sentence John uttered carried with it "joy, peace, and wisdom" and was delivered "by the power of the Holy Ghost. You will believe me when I say, that earth, nor men, with the eloquence of time, cannot begin to clothe language in as interesting and sublime a manner as this holy personage." Oliver felt this encounter with an angel was "past description" and an "expression of the Savior's goodness."[16]

54

The angel instructed Joseph and Oliver to baptize each other — Joseph baptized Oliver first, then Oliver baptized Joseph. Then Joseph reordained Oliver, and Oliver, Joseph. "Immediately on our coming up out of the water after we had been baptized, we experienced great and glorious blessings from our Heavenly Father. No sooner had I baptized Oliver Cowdery, than the Holy Ghost fell upon him, and he stood up and prophesied many things which should shortly come to pass. And again, so soon as I had been baptized by him, I also had the spirit of prophecy, when standing up, I prophesied concerning the rise of this Church, and this generation of the children of men. We were filled with the Holy Ghost, and rejoiced in the God of our salvation."[17]

Possessing power and authority to baptize, Joseph and Oliver baptized several people. By the time three months had passed, Samuel and Hyrum Smith and David, John, and Peter Whitmer, Jr., had been baptized. What would be part of the main trunk of the priesthood tree was now in place.

Restoration of Melchizedek Priesthood

Joseph and Oliver became anxious to receive authority to bestow the Holy Ghost, as promised them by John the Baptist. "We had for some time made this matter a subject of humble prayer," Joseph said, and while staying at the home of Peter Whitmer, Sr., they "engaged in solemn and fervent prayer" to obtain that blessing. In response, "the word of the Lord came unto us in the chamber, commanding us that I should ordain Oliver Cowdery to be an Elder in the Church," that Oliver should ordain Joseph to the same office, and that then they should ordain others. But, they were told, they should defer the ordination.[18] Apparently, shortly after this revelation, Peter, James, and John visited them and restored the Melchizedek Priesthood. But the exact date of their visit "has always been a puzzle in Mormon history," because early records fail to mention the event.[19] A positive circumstantial case can be made that Peter, James, and John must have appeared in late May or early June 1829—soon after the visit of John the Baptist.[20]

In Doctrine and Covenants 27:12 the Lord discusses "Peter, and James, and John, whom I have sent unto you, by whom I have ordained you and confirmed you to be apostles, and especial witnesses of my name, and bear the keys of your ministry."[21] This verse, which was added after 1833 to the record of the revelation, indicates that Joseph and Oliver received authority to be apostolic special witnesses—the term *Melchizedek Priesthood* is absent.

Oliver Cowdery, late in 1833, said that after the visit of John the Baptist, "we received the high and holy priesthood" but gave no details.[22] Joseph, writing in 1842, rejoiced that he heard "the voice of Peter, James, and John in the wilderness" near the Susquehanna River, "declaring themselves as possessing the keys of the kingdom, and of the dispensation of the fulness of times!" (D&C 128:20.)

Through hindsight and better knowledge of the Melchizedek Priesthood obtained after 1835, Joseph and Oliver's later writings linked Peter, James, and John with bestowing upon them the Melchizedek Priesthood. Joseph Smith's 1838 history indicates that the visit of John the Baptist had been directed by Peter, James, and John, "who held the keys of the Priesthood of Melchizedek, which Priesthood, he said, would in due time be conferred on us."[23] Joseph, in July 1839, asked: "How have we come at the Priesthood in the last days?" and then answered: "It came down, down, in regular succession. Peter, James, and John had it given to them and they gave it to others."[24] Oliver Cowdery in 1849 told a few Saints that "Peter, James, and John, holding the keys of the Melchizedek Priesthood," ordained men to that priesthood.[25]

Joseph and Oliver's ordinations made each of them "an apostle of Jesus Christ" and "an elder." (D&C 20:2–3.) Joseph Smith, as apostle and first elder, now was caretaker for a priesthood whose main trunk already supported small branches. Brigham Young later explained that Joseph Smith had first to be an apostle in order to organize and

build the kingdom of God. "The keys of the eternal Priesthood, which is after the order of the Son of God, are
comprehended by being an Apostle. All the Priesthood,
all the keys, all the gifts, all the endowments and everything preparatory to entering into the presence of the
Father and the Son, are in, composed of . . . [are] incorporated within the circumference of, the Apostleship."[26]

Organizing a Church

Joseph and Oliver knew during 1829 that they would
organize a church. Revelations that year told of "the rising
up and the coming forth of my church" (D&C 5:14) and
"the foundation of my church" (D&C 18:4). In 1829
Cowdery drafted a version of what became in 1830 the
first manual for church government—now Doctrine and
Covenants, section 20. Called "Articles of the Church of
Christ," it was a revelation to Oliver, who is "called with
the same calling as Paul," to "baptize those who repent."
The revelation explained the method of baptism, the words
to use when ordaining priests and teachers, and the sacrament prayer. The document was signed, "Behold I am
Oliver I am an Apostle of Jesus Christ."[27]

During 1829, Joseph and Oliver baptized and ordained
others to the priesthood. David Whitmer, in old age, said
that by August 1829, six elders had been ordained, the
other four being himself, Samuel and Hyrum Smith, and
Peter Whitmer. David said that "we preached, baptized,
and confirmed members into the Church of Christ" during
the next eight months. He added, "We were an humble
happy people."[28]

Preaching, converting, baptizing, ordaining, holding
meetings of believers—these activities show that an infor-
mal church was in operation in 1829. Then, Whitmer said,
in part because "the world had been telling us that we
were not a regularly organized church, and had no right
to officiate in the ordinance of marriage, hold church property, etc.," a more formal, legal entity needed to be
formed.[29] Sometime early in the spring of 1830, Joseph

Smith told his friend Joseph Knight, Sr., that "there must be a church formed."[30] Joseph received a revelation giving the exact date for this formal organizing to occur.[31]

On April 6 more than fifty people met at the Whitmer house in Fayette to formally create the Church of Christ.[32] By vote, Joseph Smith was sustained as First Elder and Oliver as Second Elder, and they ordained each other as such. Joseph and Oliver blessed bread and wine and administered the sacrament, then they laid hands on various members and bestowed the Holy Ghost. Joseph and Oliver ordained a few men to the priesthood. Father Joseph Knight reported that "Joseph gave them instructions how to Bild up the Church."[33]

This meeting followed the blueprint given to Joseph Smith in Father Whitmer's chamber in June 1829, which outlined that at a future meeting of the baptized, the group must vote to sustain Joseph and Oliver to be ordained as First and Second Elders in the Church of Jesus Christ, vote to sustain Joseph and Oliver as their spiritual teachers, partake of the sacrament, allow Joseph and Oliver to ordain each other and then ordain others, and then confer the gift of the Holy Ghost upon those baptized. (See D&C 18.)

At the meeting, a revelation was received which said Joseph should be called and recognized by the Church as "a seer, a translator, a prophet, an apostle of Jesus Christ, an elder." (D&C 21:1.)

A revelation that month said that prior baptisms in other churches were not valid and that "although a man should be baptized an hundred times it availeth him nothing." (D&C 22:2.)[34]

At the first conference of the Church, on 9 June 1830, the members received and canonized the church government manual Oliver had penned by revelation the previous year, "The Articles and Covenants" (D&C 20).[35] It was read at succeeding conferences and carried about by elders on missionary journeys and preaching assignments to be read to the believers.[36]

Regarding priesthood, the Articles stipulated that Joseph Smith was called of God and "ordained an apostle of Jesus Christ, to be the first elder of this church." (D&C 20:2.) Oliver was second elder, and "an apostle is an elder" authorized to baptize, administer the sacrament, bestow the Holy Ghost, teach, expound, and conduct meetings under the guidance of the Holy Ghost. (See D&C 20:38–45.) Taking the revelation literally, Joseph and Oliver tried to perform their duties, and they did baptize, administer the sacrament, bestow the Holy Ghost, teach, and conduct meetings. They not only received authority but used it diligently.

The Articles gave specific duties to each of four priesthood offices—main branches—of elder, priest, teacher, and deacon. Taken together, the four offices had responsibility to perform ordinances, conduct meetings, and visit members to see that all did their duty. (See D&C 20:38–59.) Various churches, or branches, would be guided and coordinated at quarterly conferences of the elders. (See D&C 20:62–65.)[37]

This revelation on church organization built upon the Book of Mormon pattern, with the addition of deacons. The offices had a graded order from least (deacon) to highest (elder), with the First and Second Elders as the top officers, all unpaid.[38]

During the conference, new officers were ordained: Samuel H. Smith, an elder, by Oliver Cowdery; Joseph Smith, Sr., Hyrum Smith, and Martin Harris as priests; and Hiram Page and Christian Whitmer as teachers. The conference gave licenses to the seven elders present and to three priests and two teachers to preach and teach.

By 1830 the priesthood tree had a sturdy trunk with several branches. Authority had been restored, that is, bestowed and shared. Joseph and early members called it "authority," but not Melchizedek or Aaronic Priesthood or even priesthood.[39] Priesthood bearers proselyted, baptized, confirmed, administered the sacrament, ordained, and conducted meetings as "they [were] directed and guided by the Holy Spirit," and managed the church. (D&C 46:2.) By February 1831, elders were blessing the sick through the laying on of hands. (See D&C 42:43–48.)[40]

Nevertheless, priesthood restoration was not complete. Still lacking were several branches, leaves, and blossoms: offices, understanding of greater and lesser priesthoods, the sealing keys, the priesthood temple ordinances, and the discovery of how priesthood offices should intermesh into a workable whole.

Higher and Lesser Priesthoods

During the next five years, Church relocations and growth and new revelations caused the single priesthood trunk to fork into clearly defined Aaronic and Melchizedek main branches, each properly budded. Many converts, like Solomon Humphrey, "got baptized and ordained an elder" and preached.[41] Increasing numbers of priesthood officers required that men be grouped into quorums, their duties clearly differentiated by office, and units governed and coordinated.

Quarterly elders conferences supervised ordaining and preaching assignments. In December 1831 the Lord said converts were to "be ordained and sent forth to preach"— all men (and selected older boys)[42] were to receive ordination to an office. (D&C 36:5.) But in February 1831, the Lord instructed that no one was to preach or build up the Church "except he be ordained by some one who has authority, and it is known to the church that he has authority and has been regularly ordained by the heads of the church." (D&C 42:11.) Two years later, Joseph Smith taught that "there has been too much haste" in ordaining men to the priesthood, and some had not "magnified their calling at all."[43]

A new office, a vital new limb of the priesthood tree, appeared on 4 February 1831, when Joseph Smith received a revelation calling Edward Partridge to be "ordained a bishop unto the church," an office not foreshadowed in the available Nephite records. (D&C 41:9.) Two months earlier the office was anticipated, however, when the Lord asked that men be appointed by the voice of the Church "to look to the poor and the needy" and to "govern the affairs of the property of this church." (D&C 38:35–36.)

The bishop was to be assisted by elders as his counselors. (See D&C 42:72.)[44] By year's end, Newel K. Whitney became the second bishop. He served Ohio Saints, and Partridge served those in Missouri.

Both bishops received the duty "to keep the Lord's storehouse," manage consecrated properties, receive funds, keep elders' accounts, pay church expenses, and care for the poor. (See D&C 72:8–19.) Bishops were not considered Aaronic Priesthood officers until later. For a few months "bishops and elders," by revelation, governed local affairs.[45] An August 1831 revelation said that elders in Missouri should be governed by conferences and that the bishop should direct the conference. (See D&C 58:58–61.)

By late 1831 the first deacons were ordained.[46]

In 1831 Joseph introduced another new office—a shoot that quickly became a branch of the trunk—high priest. No identifiable revelation announced or explained it, although high priests in the Book of Mormon led the church before Christ's visit to the Americas. On 3 June 1831, Joseph Smith directed that more than twenty men, including himself, be ordained to the "high priesthood."[47] Not until 1835 was this called "Melchizedek Priesthood"; rather, contemporaries used its Book of Mormon name, the "high priesthood of the holy order of God." (Alma 13:6.)

This new calling produced a priesthood trunk divided into "higher" and "lesser" branches. Only high priests received this higher priesthood; elders, priests, teachers, and deacons held the lower priesthood.[48] Because the high priests were the highest officers in the Church, the high priests' president was the presiding officer in the Church. Joseph Smith, who had led the Church as its First Elder, now led because he was the President of the High Priesthood. Within a year, he called counselors to assist him—the first First Presidency, in current terms.[49] As usual, Joseph took his duties seriously and labored diligently to preside over the expanding priesthood.

On 16 February 1832, as part of the vision of the three degrees of glory, Joseph and Sidney were shown that among those who would receive God's fullest rewards in the hereafter were "priests of the Most High, after the order of Melchizedek" — the earliest reference in revelations to a Melchizedek Priesthood. (D&C 76:57.)

During September 1832, Joseph received a major revelation concerning priesthood. (See D&C 84.) It told of the temple to be reared at Kirtland — implying a priesthood tie to temples yet to come. The revelation traced the "Holy Priesthood" (D&C 84:6) back from Moses through Noah to Adam, told of a priesthood placed upon Aaron and his seed, and said the "Holy Priesthood" was the "greater priesthood" (D&C 84:25–26). Anciently, God had removed the Holy Priesthood from Israel, but "the lesser priesthood continued." (D&C 84:26.) This lesser priesthood held keys of the preparatory gospel of repentance and baptism and "the law of carnal commandments" that passed down from Aaron to John the Baptist. (D&C 84:27.)

The priesthood revelation explained that the "offices of elder and bishop are necessary appendages belonging unto the high priesthood" and that the "offices of teacher and deacon are necessary appendages belonging to the lesser priesthood." (D&C 84:29–30.) Holders of both priesthoods one day would offer sacrifices in a temple to be built. The Lord covenanted with those who received both priesthoods and magnified their callings that they would receive "all that my Father hath." (D&C 84:38.) In the revelation, the Lord compared the priesthood to the human body, which needs head and feet and "every member" so that "the system may be kept perfect." (D&C 84:110.) He instructed high priests to "take with [them] those who are ordained unto the lesser priesthood" as assistants. (D&C 84:107.) "Let every man stand in his own office, and labor in his own calling." (D&C 84:109.) The high priests, elders, and priests "should travel" as proselyters. (D&C 84:110.) Deacons and teachers should be standing ministers locally.

High priest councils governed church operations in Missouri and Ohio until 1834, when stakes were created.[50] The creation of the first stake high council — "the standing council" at Kirtland — occurred on 17 February 1834. (D&C

102:1, 3.) The First Presidency served as council presidency, much like a stake presidency today.[51] Missouri received a twelve-man "council of high priests"[52] and a presidency of Zion (the Second Presidency) on 3 July 1834. By early 1835, high councils were considered stake entities. (See D&C 107:36.)

More main branches sprang forth on the priesthood tree. Joseph Smith bestowed the first patriarchal blessing on 18 December 1833 upon his father and mother, two brothers, and Oliver Cowdery. Then Joseph's father was ordained to the Patriarchal Priesthood and given the keys of blessings.[53]

Then, commanded by God and shown in vision and by the Holy Spirit what to do, Joseph conducted a special priesthood conference on 14 February 1835, where the Three Witnesses selected Twelve Apostles.[54] Two weeks later Joseph explained the calling of the Twelve: "They are the Twelve Apostles, who are called to the office of traveling high council, who are to preside over all the churches of the Saints among the Gentiles, where there is no presidency established, and they are to travel and preach among the Gentiles, until the Lord shall command them to go to the Jews. They are to hold the keys of this ministry to unlock the door of the kingdom of heaven into all nations and to preach the Gospel to every creature. This is the power, authority and virtue of their Apostleship."[55]

Two weeks later a quorum of Seventy was called into being, perhaps bearing some relationship to the seventy elders Moses called or to seventy missionaries the Savior ordained.[56] "The Seventies," Joseph Smith taught, "are to constitute traveling quorums, to go into all the earth, whithersoever the Twelve Apostles shall call them." He and his counselors ordained the number who were present.[57] By December 1836 two more quorums of seventy had been formed. Questions arose concerning which priesthood office had the higher authority, high priests or seventies? Joseph instructed that high priests could not be ordained as seventies, but the controversy lasted for decades.[58]

A month after the Apostles and the Seventy were called, Joseph Smith received another key priesthood revelation which, like a manual of instructions, clearly explained Melchizedek and Aaronic priesthood offices, duties, and interrelationships. (See D&C 107.) It provided the first details about structuring Aaronic Priesthood work.

"There are, in the church, two priesthoods," the revelation begins. The first is Melchizedek and "all other authorities or offices in the church are appendages to this priesthood. . . . The office of an elder comes under the priesthood of Melchizedek." (D&C 107:1, 5, 7.) High priests administer in spiritual things and can officiate in the office of elder, priest, teacher, or deacon. The Aaronic priesthood is a lesser priesthood that has power in administering "in outward ordinances." (D&C 107:20.) A high priest can serve as bishop.

The revelation taught that the Church's three Presiding High Priests are the "quorum of the Presidency" of the Church. The Twelve Apostles are a traveling high council directed by the Church Presidency. The Seventy are to travel into the world to preach. Stake high councils govern within their stake. The Twelve have a duty to ordain patriarchs (evangelical ministers[59]) and "to ordain and set in order all the other officers of the church." (D&C 107:58.) Groups of ninety-six elders, forty-eight priests, twenty-four teachers, and twelve deacons are each to have their own presidencies, and the priests' president is a bishop. Literal descendants of Aaron can be bishops and serve without counselors. "The bishopric is the presidency" of the Aaronic Priesthood. (D&C 107:15.) The Seventy have a seven-man presidency. The high priests have a Presiding High Priest, who "is to preside over the whole church, and to be like unto Moses." (D&C 107:91.) Church court systems are outlined. The revelation concludes with a call for all officers to learn and do their own duties.

In the fall of 1835 the Church published the first edition of the Doctrine and Covenants. Unlike the Book of Commandments of 1833, this collection featured the priesthood revelations first. It opened with the Articles and Covenants (D&C 20), the newly received priesthood revelation (D&C 107), and the 1832 priesthood revelation (D&C 84).

Elijah and Sealing Authority

Even though all the priesthood offices had been revealed and their duties and organizations explained, the priesthood restoration process still lacked the promised visit of Elijah and the connection to temples. Moroni had promised Joseph Smith that Elijah would come to reveal "the priesthood." (D&C 2:1.) Sidney Rigdon had been told by revelation that his labors had been preparing the way for Elijah, "which should come." (D&C 35:4.) The Prophet pushed the completion of the Kirtland Temple because the Lord in 1833 had commanded him that "you should build a house, in the which house I design to endow those whom I have chosen with power from on high." (D&C 95:8.)[60]

Designed according to revelation, the temple's lower auditorium had elevated pulpits on the east end for Melchizedek Priesthood presidencies and on the west for Aaronic Priesthood presidencies.[61] For the first time in this dispensation, priesthood and temple were firmly intertwined. On 27 March 1836 Joseph Smith dedicated the temple; and during subsequent days the priesthood quorums and their leaders received the ordinance of washing of feet, anointings, and the beginnings of temple endowments.

On 3 April 1836 the Prophet and Sidney Rigdon bowed in solemn prayer in the temple and beheld several remarkable visions about which they recorded neither details nor emotional reactions. (See D&C 110.) The Lord appeared and accepted the temple. Moses appeared and committed the keys of the gathering of Israel. Elias committed to them keys of the dispensation of the gospel of Abraham. Then came the visit promised by Malachi and reiterated by Moroni in 1823. Elijah "stood before us," Joseph said, and bestowed the keys for turning hearts of fathers to children and children to fathers — the sealing powers. (D&C 110:13–15.)

But Joseph, now possessing great priesthood keys and powers, did not implement the higher priesthood ordinances made possible by the sealing powers until the Nauvoo Temple was under construction. Early in 1841 the Lord instructed his prophet that when the Nauvoo Temple was built, He would show Joseph "all things" pertaining to "the priesthood thereof." (D&C 124:42.) Rooms should be prepared in the temple for all the grades and offices of the priesthood. Joseph Smith started using the sealing powers on behalf of deceased people in 1842 by authorizing baptisms for the dead. Even as workmen built the temple, the Lord promised that "I am about to restore many things to the earth, pertaining to the priesthood." (D&C 127:8.)

In 1842, after giving the Twelve responsibility for leadership at home as well as abroad, Joseph Smith introduced them and other leaders to the full temple endowment by personally "instructing them in the principles and order of the Priesthood, attending to washings, anointings, endowments and the communication of keys pertaining to the Aaronic Priesthood, and so on to the highest order of the Melchisedek Priesthood."[62]

During his final five years, Joseph Smith, after serious meditations in Liberty Jail, did more teaching than ever before. As prophet-teacher, he taught in depth about the priesthood. By letter from Liberty Jail, he explained crucial priesthood principles of success and failure. (See D&C 121:34–46.) Men might receive the priesthood, he said, but lose it by caring too much about worldly matters, seeking honor and power, covering their sins, and exercising authority through compulsion or unrighteous dominion. Priesthood bearers lacked power or influence unless they practiced persuasion, long-suffering, gentleness, meekness, and genuine love. Men must learn "this one lesson," he emphasized, that the priesthood must connect with the powers of heaven "and that the powers of heaven cannot be controlled nor handled only upon the principles of righteousness." (D&C 121:35–36.) Unrighteousness causes the Spirit to withdraw, which in turn causes the priesthood power to withdraw.

In Nauvoo, Joseph Smith preached several vital discourses to explain priesthood. In September 1842 he told of various beings from Adam forward who had declared their dispensations to him and given him keys and "the power of the priesthood." (D&C 128:20–21.) In mid-1843 he taught that a man receives the fulness of the priesthood by keeping the commandments and obeying all the ordinances of the temple.[63]

In October 1843 the prophet-teacher explained that there are three "grand orders" of priesthood, Melchizedek, Patriarchal, and Levitical. Regarding the Patriarchal order he said: "Go to and finish the temple, and God will fill it with power, and you will then receive more knowledge, concerning this priesthood."[64]

A year before his death, Joseph Smith recorded the capstone revelation of the priesthood restoration sequence. On 12 July 1843 he dictated the celestial marriage revelation, wherein the Lord said he would "give unto thee the law of my Holy Priesthood, as was ordained by me and my Father before the world was." (D&C 132:28.) He conferred upon Joseph "the keys of the power of this priesthood" so that whatsoever Joseph sealed or loosed on earth would be sealed or loosed in heaven and be eternally valid, including marriages. (D&C 132:46–48, 59.) Joseph taught the Twelve that only one man on the earth at a time — the President of the Church — could hold the keys of the sealing power, and sealings had to be performed by him or "by his dictation."[65]

Three months before his death, Joseph delivered his last priesthood sermon, and emphasized the importance of Elijah and the sealing authority. In it he asked: "What is this office and work of Elijah? It is one of the greatest and most important subjects that God has revealed." He taught that "the spirit, power, and calling of Elijah is, that ye have power to hold the key of the revelations, ordinances, oracles, powers and endowments of the fulness of the Melchizedek Priesthood," and have power to turn hearts of children on earth to deceased fathers. It is by the Spirit of Elijah, he said, "that we redeem our Dead" and "connect ourselves with our fathers which are in heaven, and seal up our dead to come forth in the first resurrection." By the power of Elijah we "seal those who dwell on earth to those who dwell in heaven." He added that "the power of Elijah is sufficient to make our calling and election sure."[66]

The Prophet introduced complete temple endowments to selected confidants, who became part of what was called the Holy Order. Men received endowments first, but, as charter members of the Nauvoo Female Relief Society were told by Bishop Whitney, in Joseph's presence, "without the female all things cannot be restor'd to the earth—it takes all to restore the Priesthood."[67] The final step of priesthood restoration came during 1843, when Emma Smith became the first woman to obtain temple endowments, and she and Joseph received the highest temple rites.[68] On September 28 the Prophet introduced the "fullness of priesthood ordinances" to a few dozen trusted believers. This group, or Holy Order, was kept small, he explained, to restrict the knowledge of the ordinances until the temple was completed and members could receive them in a properly dedicated edifice.[69]

With the granting of temple endowments, sealings of spouses for eternity, and granting the fulness of the priesthood, Elijah's part of the priesthood restoration work was fully implemented. The priesthood tree stood complete with trunk, branches, and leaves and was bearing good fruit. Twenty years after Moroni's first visit, through the Prophet Joseph Smith, "the fullness of priesthood" was operational on earth and available to tried, tested, and worthy Latter-day Saints. Joseph had faithfully restored and nurtured the mighty priesthood tree to mature size, shape, beauty, and usefulness.

Joseph Smith was both priesthood restorer and priesthood bearer. He received and honored the Aaronic Priesthood. He received and honored the Melchizedek Priesthood. Like all other priesthood holders, he received powers and duties and had to learn how to exercise and magnify them. His history is peppered with incidents when, as priesthood bearer, he taught, visited and cared for members, administered the sacrament, presided, anointed and blessed the sick, dedicated sites, bestowed and radiated the Holy Ghost, gave blessings, ordained, blessed children, and baptized.

For Joseph, priesthood was restored not only to the Church but to him as well. He received, honored, exercised, and cherished the power and authority God had granted him, and he felt great joy when others did the same — all of whom traced their priesthood lineage back to and through him.

Notes

1. Basic priesthood history is outlined in John A. Widtsoe, *Priesthood and Church Government*, rev. ed. (Salt Lake City, Utah: Deseret Book Co., 1965); Joseph B. Keeler, *The Lesser Priesthood and Notes on Church Government* (Salt Lake City, Utah: Deseret News, 1904); D. Michael Quinn, "The Evolution of the Presiding Quorums of the LDS Church," *Journal of Mormon History* 1 (1974): 21–38; and Lee A. Palmer, *Aaronic Priesthood through the Centuries* (Salt Lake City, Utah: Deseret Book Co., 1964).

2. Joseph Smith, *History of The Church of Jesus Christ of Latter-day Saints*, 7 vols., 2d ed. rev., ed. B. H. Roberts (Salt Lake City, Utah: The Church of Jesus Christ of Latter-day Saints, 1932–51), 2:198–99.

3. Ibid., 2:202.

4. References in Doctrine and Covenants 5 to Martin Harris's waiting to be ordained were added a few years later.

5. Joseph Smith, Sr., Patriarchal Blessing Book 1, 18 Dec. 1833, pp. 8–9.

6. Smith, *History of the Church*, 1:39.

7. Smith, *History of the Church*, 1:43n.

8. Smith, *History of the Church*, 1:39.

9. Smith, *History of the Church*, 1:43n.

10. Ibid.

11. Ibid.

12. Ibid.

13. Smith, *History of the Church*, 1:43n.

14. Doctrine and Covenants 27:8 notes John's bestowing the Aaronic Priesthood on Joseph and Oliver, but the reference was added to the revelation years later. See Robert John Woodford, "The Historical Development of the Doctrine and Covenants," 3 vols., Ph.D. dissertation, Brigham Young University, 1974, 1:394.

15. Doctrine and Covenants 13 was written by Joseph Smith for his history about ten years after the appearance of John the Baptist. Section 13 was first printed in the Doctrine and Covenants in 1876. Woodford, "Historical Development," 1:233.

16. *Messenger and Advocate* 1 (Oct. 1834): 16.

17. Smith, *History of the Church,* 1:42.

18. Smith, *History of the Church,* 1:60–61.

19. Richard L. Bushman, *Joseph Smith and the Beginnings of Mormonism* (Chicago and Urbana: University of Illinois Press, 1984), p. 240, n. 55.

20. Larry C. Porter, "Dating the Melchizedek Priesthood," *Ensign* 9 (June 1979): 5–10. Others see evidence pointing to a later restoration date: see Bushman, pp. 162–63, 240–41; and Lyndon Cook, "Joseph Smith and the High Priesthood," address to *Sunstone* Symposium, 26–29 Aug. 1987.

21. Woodford, "Historical Development," 1:394. See Book of Commandments (1833), section 28; 1835 Doctrine and Covenants, section 50.

22. Joseph Smith, Sr., Patriarchal Blessing Book 1, 18 Dec. 1833, pp. 8–9.

23. Smith, *History of the Church,* 1:40.

24. Smith, *History of the Church,* 3:387.

25. Smith, *History of the Church,* 1:42n.

26. In *Journal of Discourses,* 26 vols. (Liverpool: Latter-day Saints' Book Depot, 1855–86), 1:134–35.

27. Woodford, "Historical Development," 1:293.

28. David Whitmer, *An Address to All Believers in Christ* (Richmond, Mo.: Author, 1887; reprint, Concord, Calif.: Pacific Publishing Co., 1959), p. 32.

29. Ibid., p. 33.

30. Hartley, *"They Are My Friends": A History of the Joseph Knight Family, 1825–1850* (Provo, Utah: Grandin Book Co., 1986), pp. 207, 208.

31. Smith, *History of the Church,* 1:64–65.

32. Joseph Smith in writing to John Wentworth on 1 March 1842 said that the Church was first organized "in the town of Manchester." See Dean C. Jessee, *The Personal Writings of Joseph Smith* (Salt Lake City, Utah: Deseret Book Co., 1984), p. 216.

33. Ibid., pp. 143–48.

34. Bushman, *Joseph Smith and the Beginnings of Mormonism,* p. 153.

35. Donald Q. Cannon and Lyndon W. Cook, eds., *The Far West Record: Minutes of The Church of Jesus Christ of Latter-day Saints, 1830–1844* (Salt Lake City, Utah: Deseret Book Co., 1983), p. 1.

36. Woodford, "Historical Development," 1:292–93.

37. Doctrine and Covenants 20:66–67, which mentions bishops, high councilors, and high priests, was not part of the original revelation.

38. Bushman, *Joseph Smith and the Beginnings of Mormonism,* pp. 147–48.

39. Cook, *Sunstone* address; Bushman, *Joseph Smith and the Beginnings of Mormonism*, p. 240.

40. In July 1830 Joseph was told he had power to heal the sick (D&C 24:13), and in December he and Sidney Rigdon were told that those who asked in faith could "heal the sick" and disabled (D&C 35:9).

41. Larry C. Porter, "A Study of the Origins of the Church . . . in the States of New York and Pennsylvania, 1816–1831," Ph.D. dissertation, Brigham Young University, 1971, p. 265.

42. Robert L. Marrott, "History and Functions of the Aaronic Priesthood and the Offices of Priest, Teacher, and Deacon . . . 1829 to 1844," Master's thesis, Brigham Young University, 1970.

43. Joseph Smith, *Teachings of the Prophet Joseph Smith*, sel. Joseph Fielding Smith (Salt Lake City, Utah: Deseret Book Co., 1976), p. 42.

44. The reference in Doctrine and Covenants 42:71 to high priests assisting the bishop was added later. It is not in the 1833 Book of Commandments version (44:54), p. 95.

45. See Book of Commandments 44:56; 49:23; 51:6. The latter reads "bishop and elders" but was later changed in Doctrine and Covenants 48:6 to read "presidency and the bishop."

46. The first deacons of record were Titus Billings, Serenes Burnett, and John Burk, who attended a 25 October 1831 conference. Cannon and Cook, *Far West Record*, p. 19; Smith, *History of the Church*, 1:219.

Revelations in January and February 1831 list elders, priests, and teachers but not deacons, indicating that no deacons were then functioning. Doctrine and Covenants 38:40; 42:12, 70.

47. Cannon and Cook, *Far West Record*, p. 7. Joseph Smith in retrospect said that "the authority of the Melchizedek Priesthood was manifested and conferred for the first time upon several of the Elders." Smith, *History of the Church*, 1:175–76.

48. For a good analysis of high priesthood versus Melchizedek Priesthood problems, see Lyndon W. Cook, *The Revelations of the Prophet Joseph Smith* (Provo, Utah: Seventies Mission Bookstore, 1981), pp. 136–37, n. 6.

49. Quinn, "The Evolution of the Presiding Quorums of the LDS Church," p. 25.

50. James B. Allen and Glen M. Leonard, *The Story of the Latter-day Saints* (Salt Lake City, Utah: Deseret Book Co., 1976), pp. 78–79.

51. Smith, *History of the Church*, 2:29.

52. Cannon and Cook, *Far West Record*, p. 70.

53. Quinn, "The Evolution of the Presiding Quorums of the LDS Church," p. 26; Smith, *Teachings of the Prophet Joseph Smith*, p. 39; *History of the Church*, 3:381.

54. Smith, *History of the Church*, 2:182–200.

55. Kirtland Council Minute Book, 27 Feb. 1835, p. 88, quoted in Quinn, "The Evolution of the Presiding Quorums of the LDS Church," pp. 27–28.

56. Numbers 11:16, 17, 24, 25; Luke 10.

57. Smith, *History of the Church,* 2:202.

58. James N. Baumgarten, "The Role and Function of the Seventies in LDS Church History," Master's thesis, Brigham Young University, 1960.

59. "An Evangelist is a Patriarch, even the oldest man of the blood of Joseph or of the seed of Abraham. Wherever the Church of Christ is established in the earth, there should be a Patriarch for the benefit of the posterity of the Saints, as it was with Jacob in giving his patriarchal blessing unto his sons, etc." Smith, *History of the Church,* 3:381.

60. See also Doctrine and Covenants 38:32.

61. On the east were seats for the Melchizedek Presiding Council (First Presidency), Presiding Melchizedek High Priesthood (the Twelve, or the Kirtland High Council), the Melchizedek High Priesthood (high priests quorum), and the Presiding Elder Melchizedek (elders quorum) and on similar west pulpits for the Bishop Presiding Aaronic (Bishop), Presiding Aaronic Priest (Priests), Presiding Teacher Aaronic (Teachers) and Presiding Deacon Aaronic (Deacons). See Milton V. Backman, Jr., *The Heavens Resound* (Salt Lake City, Utah: Deseret Book Co., 1983), p. 160.

62. Smith, *History of the Church,* 5:2.

63. Smith, *Teachings of the Prophet Joseph Smith,* p. 308.

64. Ibid., p. 323; see also note 59, above.

65. Quorum of the Twelve Apostles to William Smith, 10 Aug. 1845, Brigham Young Papers, Archives of The Church of Jesus Christ of Latter-day Saints, Salt Lake City, Utah.

66. Smith, *Teachings of the Prophet Joseph Smith,* pp. 337–38.

67. Carol Cornwall Madsen, "Mormon Women and the Temple: Toward a New Understanding," in Maureen Ursenbach Beecher and Lavina Fielding Anderson, eds., *Sisters in Spirit: Mormon Women in Historical and Cultural Perspective* (Urbana and Chicago: University of Illinois Press, 1987), p. 85.

68. It appears that Joseph Smith and Emma were sealed in eternal marriage on 28 May 1843. (By then, at least, the Prophet was sealing eternal marriages.) Andrew F. Ehat, "Joseph Smith's Introduction of Temple Ordinances and the 1844 Mormon Succession Question," Master's thesis, Brigham Young University, 1982, pp. 61–63, 263–65.

69. Madsen, "Mormon Women and the Temple," p. 85.

Chapter 5

"The Field Is White Already to Harvest": Earliest Missionary Labors and the Book of Mormon

Larry C. Porter
Director of Church History Area, Religious Studies Center
Brigham Young University

The exact point in this dispensation at which active proselyting began with the object of restoring a formal religious society, the Church of Jesus Christ, is difficult to determine. From the time of his First Vision and the visits of Moroni, Joseph Smith, Jr., had been given assurance that "the true doctrine—the fulness of the gospel, should, at some future time, be made known unto [him]" and that "God had a work for [him] to do." (Joseph Smith–History 1:33.)[1] Between 1820 and 1827, he had conversed with his family, friends, and acquaintances concerning the visitations he had received from heavenly beings. His discussions of these matters with Martin Harris, Josiah Stowell, Emma Hale, Joseph Knight, Sr., Newel Knight, and others certainly had a telling effect on them and laid the groundwork for their conversions when the Church was organized.

In 1828, Joseph Smith, with Martin Harris acting as scribe, began the translation of the Book of Mormon plates.

Although disastrous in its immediate effects, even Martin's loss of the 116-page manuscript entailed some redemptive aspects for some of the Harris family. By covenant, Martin was to show the document only to his parents, Nathan and Rhoda Harris; his brother Preserved; his wife, Lucy; and his wife's sister, Mrs. Mary (Polly) Harris Cobb.[2] Martin disobeyed his solemn pledge. In Lucy Mack Smith's words, "Passing by his oath, he showed it to any good friend that happened to call on him, . . . to any one whom he regarded prudent enough to keep the secret."[3] Nevertheless, Martin's participation in the translation of the first manuscript and his personal testimony in the publication of the second were deciding factors in his own later baptism and that of his brothers Emer and Preserved, his sister Naomi, and others within the extended Harris family.

The final translation of the Book of Mormon and its publication in book form in 1829–30 were the stimulus to formal organization by converts to the restored gospel. The Book of Mormon was not only a doctrinal measure against which inquirers could examine their personal beliefs, but it was also a test of existing Christian dogma. We tend nowadays somehow to link the first missionary efforts solely with the published Book of Mormon and the organization of the Church: many see this as the starting point for active proselyting. Too little recognition has been given to the amazingly intense missionary thrust that preceded these events. Using extracts from the unpublished Book of Mormon manuscript, missionaries had done productive proselyting in the year before the organization of the Church, April 1829 to April 1830. When David Whitmer was asked about how many people were present for the organizational meeting at the Peter Whitmer, Sr., farmhouse in Fayette, New York, on 6 April 1830, he specified that "2 rooms were filled with members — about 20 from Colesville, 15 from Manchester Church and about 20 from around about Father Whitmers. About 50 members & the 6 Elders were present."[4] Though few in number, these people represented a rapidly growing interest in the teachings of the Book of Mormon.

Indeed, while the official organization of the Church occurred on 6 April 1830, to meet "the laws of our country, by the will and commandments of God" (D&C 20:1), it was not the beginning point for proselyting. Let us examine further certain events that took place in the spring of 1829, a year prior.

Soon after arriving at Joseph Smith's Harmony, Pennsylvania, homestead on 5 April 1829, Oliver Cowdery wrote a letter to his friend David Whitmer in Seneca County, New York, alerting him that Joseph did have the records as claimed and that it was the "will of heaven" that Oliver should serve as scribe in the translation process. In a second letter, Oliver shared a "few lines of what they had translated." David said, "I showed these letters to my parents, and brothers and sisters."[5] Thus very early in the translation of the Book of Mormon, a small extract from its pages was transmitted to the Whitmer household. This is but one early example of efforts of a handful of faithful adherents sharing the contents of the Book of Mormon with other persons the year before the Church was officially organized.

As the work of translation progressed, Joseph and Oliver sought answers to their questions regarding the teaching of baptism for the remission of sins, mentioned in the record. The Lord directed John the Baptist to visit them, to instruct them concerning baptism, and also to confer upon them the keys of the priesthood of Aaron. This event happened on 15 May 1829. At first Joseph and Oliver kept the circumstances of their baptism and priesthood ordination secret, because of a very real spirit of persecution in that neighborhood. The two had already been threatened by a local mob.

Nevertheless, despite intimidations, they felt that opposition should not thwart the spread of their urgent message. Now vested with the authority of the Aaronic Priesthood, they began to "reason out of the scriptures" with friends and acquaintances. Among the first to hear them was Samuel H. Smith, brother of the Prophet. Joseph and Oliver taught him out of the Bible and "also showed him that part of the work which [they] had translated, and labored to persuade him concerning the Gospel of Jesus Christ, which was now about to be revealed in its fulness."⁶ After fervent prayer, Samuel expressed faith in their message and authority and was baptized by Oliver on 25 May 1829. He returned home to Manchester "greatly glorifying and praising God, being filled with the Holy Spirit."⁷

Immediately after Samuel's baptism, Hyrum Smith came to Harmony to inquire about the Book of Mormon and ask what the Lord would have him do. Through the Prophet, Hyrum received a revelation admonishing him to "Wait a little longer, until you shall have my word, my rock, my church, and my gospel, that you may know of a surety my doctrine." (D&C 11:16.) The time and conditions being appropriate, both Hyrum and his wife, Jerusha, were baptized in Seneca Lake in June 1829.⁸

Lucy Mack Smith said it was during this period that "evil-designing people were seeking to take away [Joseph's] life, in order to prevent the work of God from going forth to the world."⁹ Experiencing such increased hostility toward their labors, the Prophet urged Oliver to ask David Whitmer to provide a place of refuge where they could complete the translation. The Whitmers were willing. David moved the translators to his parents' home in Fayette Township, Seneca County, New York. David affirmed that "the translation at my father's occupied about one month, that is from June 1, to July 1, 1829."¹⁰

Commenting on Joseph and Oliver's dedication to complete the translation, David reported: "It was a laborious work for the weather was very warm, and the days were long and they worked from morning till night. But being both young and strong, they were soon able to complete the work."¹¹ While laboring on the translation they were besieged by a host of people who wanted to hear about the plates and the doctrines they contained. Joseph detailed this situation when he stated:

"We found the people of Seneca county in general friendly, and disposed to enquire into the truth of these strange matters which now began to be noised abroad.

Many opened their houses to us, in order that we might have an opportunity of meeting with our friends for the purpose of instruction and explanation. We met with many from time to time who were willing to hear us, and who desired to find out the truth as it is in Christ Jesus, and apparently willing to obey the Gospel, when once fairly convinced and satisfied in their own minds. . . . From this time forth many became believers, and some were baptized whilst we continued to instruct and persuade as many as applied for information."[12]

Those engaged in proselyting received some direction by letter from Joseph and Oliver. On 14 June 1829, Oliver wrote to Hyrum, "These few lines I write unto you feeling anxious for your steadfastness in the great cause which you have been called to advocate and also feeling it a duty to write to you at every opportunity." Then he told Hyrum to "stir up the minds of our friends against the time we come unto you that they may be willing to take upon them the name of Christ for that is the name by which they shall be called at the last day."[13] These brethren clearly had a "cause to advocate" and were actively teaching the doctrines of the Book of Mormon and the Bible. They called upon the people to believe and take upon themselves the name of Christ. Many accepted the teachings and applied for baptism. Estimates of those baptized between 15 May 1829 and 6 April 1830 run from thirty to seventy-six persons.[14]

Those touched by the gospel message characteristically used every means at their disposal to share with family and friends the newly found precepts. Joseph Smith, Sr., wrote to his father, Asael Smith, at Stockholm, St. Lawrence County, New York, as early as 1828 to inform him "of some of the visions the youthful Prophet had received."[15] Asael was also apprised that Joseph, Jr., "had discovered, by the revelations of the Almighty, some gold plates, and that these gold plates contained a record of great worth."[16] This letter was followed by one from the Prophet, who himself bore witness of the fallen state of the Christian world.[17] Hyrum Smith similarly wrote to his grandfather about these matters, and Asael in turn shared these letters with his sons and daughters who lived near him.

Mentioning the miraculous accounts stirred a terse response from Asael's son Jesse Smith, uncle of the Prophet, on 17 June 1829. Supposedly writing on behalf of his father, Jesse unloaded his own pent-up emotions on his nephew Hyrum Smith in a scathing denunciation of the Book of Mormon. Especially interesting is a chance line in which he rails, "Your good, pious & methodistical uncle Asahel [Asahel, Jr., the son of Asahel, Sr.] induced his father to give credit to your tale of nonsense, your abominable wickedness."[18] While news of the Book of Mormon met a mixed reception in that household, it is obvious not everyone there shared Jesse's irateness toward it. Recognizing that the door was not closed to further proselyting, in August 1830 Joseph Smith, Sr., and Don Carlos Smith personally delivered a copy of the Book of Mormon to the aged patriarch, Asael Smith, and other family members in St. Lawrence County. All of Joseph Smith, Sr.'s, living brothers and sisters eventually believed their message except Jesse, Mary, and Susan.[19]

The month of June 1829 was filled with activities pertinent to the Restoration. The main work of translation was complete, and the copyright application filed with R. R. Lansing, clerk of the Northern District; the Three Witnesses were shown the plates by Moroni in Fayette; the Eight Witnesses "handled with their hands" and "hefted" the gold plates at Manchester; and many individuals were taught from the scriptures as they inquired after these "strange matters." After much difficulty, arrangements were finally made for Egbert B. Grandin to publish the Book of Mormon. John H. Gilbert, principal compositor for Grandin, told James Cobb that "as quick as Mr. Grandin got his type and got things all ready to commence the work, Hyrum Smith brought to the office 24 pages of manuscript on foolscap paper, closely written and legible, but not a punctuation mark from beginning to end. This was about the middle of August 1829."[20]

David Whitmer remembered a very exacting period of proselyting throughout the entire time the Book of Mormon was being printed and bound at Palmyra, New York. He later wrote, "In August, 1829, we began to preach the gospel of Christ. . . . We preached . . . from August 1829, until April 6th, 1830, being eight months in which time we had proceeded rightly."[21] The Prophet Joseph confirmed David's observations when he himself declared, "Whilst the Book of Mormon was in the hands of the printer, we still continued to bear testimony and give information, as far as we had opportunity."[22] In addition to the original manuscript and the printer's copy of the Book of Mormon, which was a copy of the original made by Oliver Cowdery, some handwritten excerpts from the record were used by those teaching the doctrines of the still unpublished volume. Recalling the contribution of one of his brothers, David Whitmer said, "The Book of Mormon was still in the hands of the printer, but my brother, Christian Whitmer, had copied from the manuscript the teachings and the doctrine of Christ, being the things which we were commanded to preach."[23] The effectiveness of the preaching is evident in David's description: "The heavens were opened to some, and all signs which Christ promised should follow the believers were with us abundantly. We were an humble happy people, and loved each other as brethren should love."[24]

As soon as the first pages of the Book of Mormon were "struck off" the Grandin press in the fall of 1829, still another phase of the missionary effort commenced. Not waiting for the printing and binding to be completed, many drew proof sheets and used them extensively in proselyting. The experience of Thomas B. Marsh, a resident of Charleston [or Charlestown, now part of the city of Boston], Massachusetts, who stayed briefly with a family in Lyonstown [Lyons], New York, is typical. The lady of the house asked whether he had heard of the "Golden Book" found by a youth named Joseph Smith. Marsh said he knew nothing of it but was eager to learn more. The lady then informed him that Martin Harris in Palmyra could tell him of it. Thomas related the following circumstances:

"I returned back westward and found Martin Harris at the printing office, in Palmyra, where the first sixteen pages of the Book of Mormon had just been struck off, the proof sheet of which I obtained from the printer and took with me. As soon as Martin Harris found out my intentions he took me to the house of Joseph Smith, sen., where Joseph Smith, jun., resided who could give me any information I might wish. Here I found Oliver Cowdery, who gave me all the information concerning the book I desired. After staying there two days I started for Charleston, Mass., highly pleased with the information I had obtained concerning the new found book."[25]

Thomas's wife, Elizabeth, was shown the sixteen-page proof sheet of the Book of Mormon; she believed it to be the work of God, but others did not so approve. Having received a letter from Thomas Marsh dated 25 October 1829, Oliver Cowdery corresponded with the Prophet at Harmony, Pennsylvania, reporting that Thomas had "talked considerable to some respecting our work with freedom but [to] others [he] could not because they have no ears."[26] It seems that as early as the fall of 1829, Thomas B. Marsh (later senior member of the first Quorum of the Twelve Apostles) was personally engaged in spreading the news of the Book of Mormon in the Charleston-Boston area of Massachusetts. Thomas was later baptized in Cayuga Lake, Seneca County, New York, on 3 September 1830.

The use of proof sheets from the Grandin press was not an isolated incident. Before the binding of the Book of Mormon sheets into a book, a man by the name of Solomon Chamberlain, a cooper (barrel maker) from Lyons, New York, was on his way to Upper Canada. By his own account, he was traveling westward via the waterway in the fall of 1829 on the Erie Canal when he was constrained by the Spirit to get off the boat at the village of Palmyra. Walking three miles south of the community, he lodged at a farmhouse for the night. In the morning the occupants of the house asked him if he had ever heard of the "Gold Bible." The mere mention of such a volume stirred him to the core. Solomon said, "There was a power like electricity went from the top of my head to the end of my toes." In 1816 an angelic visitor had informed him that "there would be a book come forth, like unto the Bible and the people would be guided by it, as well as the Bible." Solomon, having maintained a constant vigil, anticipating the appearance of just such a work, could not neglect the investigation of so "electrifying" a source. The same angelic informant had also instructed him that the gospel of Christ had been taken from the earth and the true Church would soon be restored in its fulness.

On inquiry from his host of the evening, Solomon learned he was just one half mile from the Smith home and the location of the "Gold Bible." Mr. Chamberlain anxiously made his way "across lots" to the Smith home, where he met Joseph Smith, Sr., Hyrum Smith, Christian Whitmer and others. Unfortunately, the Prophet was away at the time in Harmony, Pennsylvania. Solomon, on explaining to those present the nature of his mounting interest, was instructed for two days directly from the manuscript of the Book of Mormon. He quickly recognized this as the very work he had been searching for.

Hyrum Smith and others accompanied Solomon to the E. B. Grandin Printing Office, where he was given sixty-four printed pages of the volume then in progress (four sixteen-page proof sheets). He observed: "I took them with their leave and pursued my journey to Canada, and I preached all that I knew concerning Mormonism, to all both high and low, rich and poor, and thus you see this was the first that ever printed Mormonism was preached to this generation [in that particular section of country]." He continued, "I did not see any one in traveling for 800 miles, that had ever heard of the Gold Bible (so called) I exhorted all people to prepare for the great work of God that was now about to come forth, and it would never be brought down nor confounded."[27] Unordained, but nevertheless sent with the blessings of Oliver and Hyrum, Solomon preached the Book of Mormon and the principles of the restored gospel to whoever would listen on his trek through an unspecified section of Upper Canada. Upon his return from Canada, Solomon went into Massachusetts and preached the restored gospel in that state.

Not long after the publication of the Book of Mormon, Solomon Chamberlain visited a large gathering of the Reformed Methodist Church in Manlius, New York. Of his experience with that sect he recorded: "I accordingly went to one of their conferences, where I met about 40 of their preachers and labored with them for two days to convince them of the truth of the Book of Mormon, and they utterly rejected me, and the Book of Mormon. One of their greatest preachers so called, by the name of Buckly, (if I mistake not) abused me very bad, and ordered me off from their premises. . . . At this conference was Brigham and his brother Phineahas [sic] Young, they did not oppose me but used me well."[28]

Solomon also took the scripture into a Baptist gathering and reported some success: "I stopped at a free will Baptist Church, and preached to a large congregation, and they received the work, but there was no one to baptize them, the Church was not yet organized, but was soon after, April 6th, 1830."[29]

Oliver Cowdery gave loose sheets of the Book of Mormon to his brother Warren A. Cowdery as they came from the press. Warren then showed them to others in the town of Freedom, Cattaraugus County, New York. William Hyde, an early proselyte, verified this matter, saying: "In the year 1830 or 31, we began to hear something concerning the Book of Mormon, and the setting up of the Kingdom of God on earth in the last days. The little information that we gained upon this subject, until the Elders came preaching, was through Warren A. Cowdery, whose farm joined with ours. Warren A. obtained from his brother Oliver, at an early date, some of the proof sheets to the book of Mormon some of which we had the privilege of perusing, and we did not peruse any faster than we believed."[30]

William, his father and mother, and other family members were baptized at Freedom in 1834.

Apparently the Prophet Joseph Smith also used proof sheets of the Book of Mormon to spread the work in Harmony. Pomeroy Tucker recorded such an instance, remarking, "The first and second books of 'Nephi,' and some other portions of the forthcoming revelation were printed in sheets;—and armed with a copy of these, Smith commenced other preparations for a mission to Pennsylvania, where he had some relatives residing."[31] The existence of such sheets would have also confirmed the actuality of the forthcoming volume. In his correspondence to Oliver Cowdery from the Susquehanna, 22 October 1829, Joseph explained that the reality of the book's printing was creating quite a stir locally: "There begins to be a great call for our books in this country. The minds of the people are very much excited when they find that there is a copyright obtained and that there is really a book about to be produced."[32]

This same letter also informs us that the pending publication generated no small interest in the household of Josiah Stowell, who lived immediately south of South Bainbridge, Chenango County, New York. Josiah, always a benefactor of the Prophet, was again making plans to lend his assistance. Joseph told Oliver, "Mr. Stowell has a prospect of getting five or six hundred dollars. He does not know [for] certain that he can get it but he is going to try and if he can get the money he wants to pay it in immediately for books."[33] Years later, while reminiscing on these early scenes, Josiah Stowell spoke of Joseph Smith, declaring to John S. Fullmer, I "know him to be a Seer & a Prophet and Believe the Book of Mormon to be true."[34]

While the Book of Mormon was being printed, there was an attempt to publish some of its pages in advance of the regular volume. Under the pseudonym of Obadiah Dogberry, Jun., Esquire Abner Cole, a former justice of the peace, held sway from his "Bower" on Winter Green Hill (Winter Green Hill is the name of the drumblin immediately north of the village of Palmyra, visible en route to the Martin Harris farm). In his publication *The Reflector,* Esquire Cole ran a series of articles on the "Gold Bible" and even reproduced actual segments from the Book of Mormon. His running commentary on the progress of the work picked up in the very first number of *The Reflector,* 2 September 1829, with the wry comment, "The Gold Bible, by Joseph Smith Junior, author and proprietor, is now in press and will shortly appear. Priestcraft is short lived!"

It is almost ironic that Cole was using the very same press, evenings and Sundays, that was used by the Prophet to publish the Book of Mormon on weekdays. It was no idle boast when Obadiah Dogberry (Abner Cole) announced to his readership: "As much curiosity has been excited in this section of the country on the subject, and as the work itself will not be ready for delivery for some months to come, — at the solicitation of many of our readers we have concluded to commence publishing extracts from it on or before the commencement of the second series."[35]

Cole availed himself of certain pages from the Book of Mormon, probably discarded, or otherwise acquired sheets that were conveniently available at the press where Grandin published the *Wayne Sentinel.* In his 2 January 1830 number he printed a portion of the text of "The First Book of Nephi. His reign and Ministry, Chapter I," running for the first thirteen paragraphs in the original edition of the Book of Mormon. A second extract from First Nephi, Chapter I, was printed on 13 January, and was soon followed on 22 January by copy from the Book of Alma, Chapter XX. Abner Cole's use of the text was cut short, however, when the Prophet himself confronted him one Sunday evening in the Palmyra printing office. Joseph had been summoned by his own father, who had gone all the way to Harmony to warn him of Cole's actions. The Prophet's threat of a lawsuit for violation of the copyright law stopped further borrowings.[36] Esquire Cole's articles did serve to heighten local awareness of the Book of Mormon and the activities of those who had espoused the work.

The Book of Mormon was printed on a "Smith" Press, single pull; old fashioned "Balls" were used. Small printing offices generally did not have composition rollers.[37] E. B. Grandin had a self-contained unit under one roof in "Exchange Row," which he rented from his brother, Phillip Grandin. The printing was done on the third story and west end, while the binding operation was accomplished by Luther Howard on the second story. The lower story, or ground level, housed the bookstore.[38]

The *Wayne Sentinel* of 19 March 1830 alerted prospective readers, "We are requested to announce that the 'BOOK OF MORMON' will be ready for sale in the course of next week." On 26 March 1830, the volumes were made available to the patrons of the store. Pomeroy Tucker recalled that "the book . . . fell dead before the public. . . . It found no buyers, or but very few."[39] Lucy Mack Smith has given us a plausible explanation for the poor reception: "The inhabitants of the surrounding country perceived that the work still progressed. . . . They resolved, as before, never to purchase one of our books, when they should be printed."[40] Nevertheless, Joseph, Martin, Oliver, and others made extended efforts to promote the sale of the work. Albert Chandler recorded: "Martin Harris . . . gave up his entire time to advertising the Bible to his neighbors and the public generally in the vicinity of Palmyra. He would call public meetings and address them himself."[41] While out soliciting with a "Bunch of morman [sic] Books," Martin encountered the Prophet Joseph and Joseph Knight just arriving from the Susquehanna. After a moment of greeting, Martin dejectedly observed, "The Books will not sell for no Body wants them." The Prophet tried to console his friend with a ready response, "I think they will sell well."[42] Eager to promote the work of the Lord and in the process to save himself, if possible, from having to liquidate some of his property to pay for the publication of the Book of Mormon, Martin used every avenue available to him to sell the volume. He obviously talked to numbers of people about the content of the publication.

At this same time, March-April 1830, Joseph Knight said that he remained in the Palmyra-Manchester area for "a few Days waiting for some Books to Be Bound." While there he was witness to the organization of the Church in Fayette on 6 April. He then observed that "after he [the Prophet] had set things in order and got a number of mormon Books we Returned home,"[43] to Colesville. These copies of the Book of Mormon were used judiciously among the people of that region. The Colesville converts brought into the fold in succeeding months were later organized into the first branch of the restored Church, under the presidency of Hyrum Smith.

Oliver Cowdery was certainly no less committed to the dissemination of the new volume. Esquire Abner Cole, editor of *The Reflector*, confirmed that in the spring of 1830 Oliver journeyed to the East, with multiple copies of the Book of Mormon, on a proselyting mission: "The apostle to the NEPHITES (Cowdery) has started for the EAST, on board a boat, with a load of 'gold bibles,' under a command, (as he says) to declare the truth (according to Jo Smith,) 'in all the principal cities in the Union.' "[44] Just how far Oliver traveled along the route of the Erie Canal is not known, but the fact that he went demonstrates that the gospel was carried in yet another direction from that which our histories have generally reported.

The Prophet Joseph Smith commented on the reception of the Book of Mormon by the public in April-May 1830 and confirmed the simple philosophy of proselyting that he and the other missionaries adopted as they sought to expound the newly restored faith. "The Book of Mormon, ('The stick of Joseph in the hands of Ephraim') had now been published for some time, and as the ancient prophet had predicted of it: 'It was accounted as a strange thing.' No small stir was created by its appearance; great opposition and much persecution followed the believers of its authenticity; but it had now come to pass that truth had sprung out of the earth; and righteousness had looked down from heaven—so we feared not our opponents, knowing that we had both truth and righteousness on our side; that we had both the Father and the Son, because we had the doctrines of Christ, and abided in them; and therefore we contined to preach, and to give information to all who were willing to hear."[45]

Active proselyting did not begin with the organization of the Church. The principal parties involved in the translation and publication of the Book of Mormon were already actively engaged in promulgating the ancient record and many of the precepts of the restored gospel before 6 April 1830. In anticipation of that event, these early servants considered "the field [to be] white already to harvest." (D&C 4:4.) During most of 1829 and in the early part of 1830, the gospel was preached to a great many people over a wide geographic area. Just eleven days following the first public sale of the Book of Mormon on 26 March 1830, the Church of Jesus Christ was officially organized at the Peter Whitmer, Sr., home. For the Prophet Joseph Smith and others in attendance, that great milestone marked the opening of the pleasing prospect of their becoming members of the Church and kingdom of God on earth, with all its attendant blessings—not the least of which was a new volume of holy writ, the Book of Mormon—Another Testament of Jesus Christ.

Notes

1. Orson Pratt, *An Interesting Account of Several Remarkable Visions* (Edinburgh: Ballantyne and Hughes, 1840), p. 5; Joseph Smith, *History of The Church of Jesus Christ of Latter-day Saints,* 7 vols., 2d ed. rev., ed. B. H. Roberts (Salt Lake City, Utah: The Church of Jesus Christ of Latter-day Saints, 1932–51), 1:11.

2. Smith, *History of the Church,* 1:21. Polly Harris Cobb was the widow of Freeman Cobb, who was drowned in a shipwreck on Lake Ontario on 19 December 1821. See Madge Harris Tuckett and Belle Harris Wilson, *The Martin Harris Story* (Provo, Utah: Press Publishing Ltd., 1983), p. 177. Polly was a first cousin to Martin Harris.

3. Lucy Smith, *Biographical Sketches of Joseph Smith the Prophet, and His Progenitors for Many Generations* (Liverpool: S. W. Richards, 1853), p. 123.

4. Journal of Edward Stevenson, 2 Jan. 1887, p. 129, Archives of The Church of Jesus Christ of Latter-day Saints, Salt Lake City, Utah.

5. David Whitmer interview with a reporter of the *Kansas City Journal,* 5 June 1881; emphasis added.

6. Smith, *History of the Church,* 1:44.

7. Ibid.

8. Ibid., 1:51; Statement of Hyrum Smith, 16 Feb. 1839, Archives of The Church of Jesus Christ of Latter-day Saints, Salt Lake City, Utah.

9. Lucy Smith, *Biographical Sketches*, p. 135.

10. *Kansas City Daily Journal,* 5 June 1881.

11. Interview of James H. Hart with David Whitmer, *Deseret Evening News,* 25 Mar. 1884, p. 2.

12. Smith, *History of the Church,* 1:51.

13. Letter of Oliver Cowdery to Hyrum Smith, Fayette, New York, 14 June 1829, Joseph Smith Collection, Archives of The Church of Jesus Christ of Latter-day Saints, Salt Lake City, Utah.

14. Smith, *History of the Church,* 1:76–77n.

15. Ibid., 1:285n.

16. *Journal of Discourses,* 26 vols. (Liverpool: Latter-day Saints' Book Depot, 1855–86), 5:102–3.

17. Ibid., 5:103.

18. Letter of Jesse Smith to Hyrum Smith, Stockholm, New York, 17 June 1829, Joseph Smith Collection, Archives of The Church of Jesus Christ of Latter-day Saints, Salt Lake City, Utah.

19. Smith, *History of the Church,* 4:190; Richard Lloyd Anderson, *Joseph Smith's New England Heritage* (Salt Lake City, Utah: Deseret Book Co., 1971), pp. 111, 211–12.

20. Letter of John H. Gilbert to James T. Cobb, Palmyra, Wayne County, New York, 10 Feb. 1879, New York Public Library, New York City, New York.

21. David Whitmer, *An Address to All Believers in Christ* (Richmond: David Whitmer, 1887), p. 32.

22. Smith, *History of the Church,* 1:74–75.

23. Whitmer, *An Address to All Believers in Christ,* p. 32.

24. Ibid., p. 33.

25. "History of Thos. Baldwin Marsh," *Deseret News,* 24 Mar. 1858.

26. Letter of Oliver Cowdery to Joseph Smith, Jr., Manchester, New York, 6 Nov. 1829, Joseph Smith Collection, Archives of The Church of Jesus Christ of Latter-day Saints, Salt Lake City, Utah.

27. Solomon Chamberlain, "A Short Sketch of the Life of Solomon Chamberlain," 11 July 1858, Archives of The Church of Jesus Christ of Latter-day Saints, Salt Lake City, Utah; Dean C. Jessee, ed. "The John Taylor Nauvoo Journal, January 1845–September 1845," *BYU Studies* 23 (Summer 1983): 45–46.

28. Ibid.

29. Ibid.

30. Journal of William Hyde, Archives of The Church of Jesus Christ of Latter-day Saints, Salt Lake City, Utah, p. 46.

31. Pomeroy Tucker, *Origin, Rise, and Progress of Mormonism* (New York: D. Appleton and Co., 1867), p. 56.

32. Letter of Joseph Smith, Jr., to Oliver Cowdery, Harmony, Pennsylvania, 22 Oct. 1829, Joseph Smith Collection, Archives of The Church of Jesus Christ of Latter-day Saints, Salt Lake City, Utah.

33. Ibid.

34. Letter of Josiah Stowell, Jr., to John S. Fullmer, Chemung County, New York, 17 Feb. 1843, Archives of The Church of Jesus Christ of Latter-day Saints, Salt Lake City, Utah. Josiah Stowell, Sr., dictated this statement to his son, who included it as an addendum in his letter to Fullmer.

35. *The Reflector* [Palmyra], 9 Dec. 1829.

36. Lucy Smith, *Biographical Sketches*, pp. 148–50.

37. "Memorandum, made by John H. Gilbert, Esq., Sept. 8th 1892," p. 3, located in Kings' Daughters' Library, Palmyra, New York.

38. Ibid.

39. Pomeroy Tucker, *Origin, Rise, and Progress of Mormonism*, p. 60.

40. Lucy Smith, *Biographical Sketches*, p. 150.

41. William Alexander Linn, *The Story of the Mormons* (New York: Macmillan, 1902), p. 48.

42. Dean C. Jessee, "Joseph Knight's Recollection of Early Mormon History," *BYU Studies* 17 (Autumn 1976) : 36–37.

43. Ibid., p. 37.

44. *The Reflector,* 1 June 1830.

45. *Times and Seasons* 4 (Dec. 1842): 22.

Chapter 6

The Prophet Joseph Smith in "the Ohio": The Schoolmaster

Keith W. Perkins

Chairman of the Department of Church History and Doctrine
Brigham Young University

Kirtland, Ohio, was the schooling period for Joseph Smith as New York had been the foundation for him. Probably no period of training and schooling of the Prophet Joseph Smith was more intense than that which occurred in Ohio. It was here that the Lord schooled the Prophet in the basic doctrines of the Restoration. Here he received more revelation than at any other time in his life. Revelations on the priesthood came in Ohio, and here the organization of the Melchizedek and Aaronic Priesthood quorums had their beginning. Here the first temple was constructed, and here Joseph Smith received those keys that fulfill the threefold mission of the Church: missionary work, family history and temple work, and the perfecting of the Saints. Because of the keys restored in the Kirtland Temple, we now perform ordinances for the living and the dead in many temples throughout the world. Kirtland saw the beginning of temple ordinances: a partial endowment. Some of the greatest spiritual outpourings of the Spirit occurred while the Prophet resided in Ohio. In New York the Prophet had received the First Vision and many visits from Moroni, but in Ohio he was privileged to see the Father and the Son on at least four occasions and to enjoy many visits from the Savior. The welfare program also had its beginning in Kirtland.

In Ohio, Joseph Smith produced under the inspiration of the Lord a number of important additions to our scriptural library. A special conference in Hiram, Ohio, voted to publish the revelations given to the Prophet. The attempt to accomplish this in Jackson County, Missouri, was thwarted by a mob, which destroyed the press and most of the copies of the Book of Commandments. So the revelations came to light for the first time in complete form in the Doctrine and Covenants, which was published in Kirtland. Michael Chandler sold to Joseph Smith in Kirtland the papyri from which the book of Abraham was translated. This translation was begun in Kirtland. Much of the Joseph Smith Translation of the Bible was also completed in Ohio. A major edition of the Book of Mormon, the second, was published. Emma Smith compiled and the Church published the first hymnal of the Church, and the first Church choir was begun.

The Prophet greatly expanded missionary work while he resided here. With renewed energy missionaries again took the gospel outside the United States into Canada, some of the missions being personally undertaken by the Prophet during his most active missionary period. The missionary work became truly worldwide when Joseph Smith called Heber C. Kimball, Orson Hyde, and others to serve missions to the British Isles.

To prepare missionaries for this widely expanded missionary effort, the Lord instructed the Prophet to begin the School of the Prophets. The school was held during several winter months, beginning in the winter of 1832–33. Great outpourings of the Spirit attended this first school. Students studied languages and other secular subjects. It was the beginning of our current missionary training centers throughout the world.

Patriarchal blessings were first given under the hands of patriarchs who had been ordained by Joseph Smith. To fulfill the great desire of Church members for these blessings, patriarchal blessing meetings were held in various locations in Kirtland.

The Word of Wisdom was received here and implemented among the leaders of the Church. Few things about the Church are better known in the world today than the principles of the Word of Wisdom.

The Book of Mormon continued to be used as the most effective missionary of the Church.

Many visitors met with the Prophet in Ohio. Some were touched by the Spirit and were converted. Others were impressed and left their testimonies of his power and influence. Some departed only to ridicule and criticize one whom they did not comprehend.

The great work for the dead had its genesis in Ohio. The keys for that work were restored by Elijah in the Kirtland Temple. By revelation Joseph Smith learned that all who die without the gospel who would have received it with all their hearts are heirs of the celestial kingdom. Although he did not fully understand the marvelous ramifications of this precept at this stage of his life, he rejoiced because it included his beloved brother Alvin. He also learned that all children who die before the age of accountability are saved in the celestial kingdom. This doctrine would be expounded more fully in Nauvoo.

There was probably no greater training of future leaders of the Church than that which came during this Ohio period. The Saints began to understand and comprehend a little better the life and mission of the Prophet Joseph Smith. The School of the Prophets really began this process. Its success was greatly enhanced when many future leaders marched at the call of the Prophet from Ohio and Michigan to redeem the Saints in Missouri in Zion's Camp. What invaluable training these men received during this time of close, around-the-clock contact with the Prophet. The marchers saw his seership firsthand.

A closer scrutiny of the events of the Ohio period reveals the great importance of the schooling experienced by the Prophet in that state. While still in New York, Joseph Smith began the translation of the Bible, "which the Lord had appointed." (D&C 76:15.) Hardly had he begun the task than the Lord directed him to change his residence: "Behold, I say unto you that it is not expedient in me that ye should translate any more until ye shall go to the Ohio, and this because of the enemy and for your sakes." (D&C 37:1.) He clarified this in a later revelation. (See D&C 38:31–32.) The Lord herein gave the Prophet four specific reasons for his going to Ohio: (1) a place to escape the power of the enemy (Satan and his co-workers), (2) the first gathering place for the Saints in this dispensation, (3) revelation of the law, (4) an endowment with power from on high. Within a few weeks after arriving in Kirtland, the Prophet saw all these promises fulfilled, except the last. He was to wait five years to receive that portion of the Lord's promise.

It was a cold winter day when Joseph Smith, his wife, Emma, Sidney Rigdon, and Edward Partridge arrived by sleigh in front of the Newel K. Whitney Store. Whitney was a frontier merchant who had one of the largest retail stores in the Western Reserve. Alighting from the sleigh, the athletic figure of Joseph Smith bounded into the store and extended his hand to the owner. He exclaimed, "Newel K. Whitney! Thou art the man!" Seeing Newel so confused at being known by a stranger, Joseph assured and amazed Newel with his reply: "I am Joseph, the Prophet. . . . You've prayed me here; now what do you want of me?"[1]

Thinking back to a particularly ardent prayer that he and his wife, Elizabeth, had uttered in their home some time before, Newel was now witness to the literal fulfillment of a promised answer. How he must have been amazed at the seership of the prophet of God then standing before him. How did Joseph know? How could he possibly know what Newel and his beloved Elizabeth had prayed for that night? How many times before had Joseph Smith astonished others, like David Whitmer, with his seeric vision,[2] and how many times would he astound others in the future with the same prophetic seership? A grandson of Newel K. Whitney later related in general conference his feelings about this event:

"By what power did this remarkable man, Joseph Smith, recognize one whom he had never before seen in the flesh? Why did not Newel K. Whitney recognize him? It was because Joseph Smith was a seer, a choice seer; he had actually seen Newel K. Whitney upon his knees, hundreds of miles away, praying for his coming to Kirtland. Marvelous—but true!"[3]

Sometime previous to Joseph's arrival and the coming to Kirtland of the missionaries to the Lamanites, the Whitneys had been inquiring of the Lord how they might receive the Holy Ghost. Elizabeth explained the vision which then opened to their view:

"It was midnight—as my husband and I, in our house at Kirtland were praying to the father to be shown the way, the spirit rested upon us and a *cloud* overshadowed the house. It was as though we were out of doors. The house passed away from our vision. We were not conscious of anything but the presence of the spirit and the cloud that was over us. We were wrapped in the cloud. A solemn awe pervaded us. We saw the cloud and we felt the spirit of the Lord. Then we heard a voice out of the cloud saying, 'Prepare to receive the word of the Lord, for it is coming.' At first we marveled greatly; but from that moment we knew that the word of the Lord was coming to Kirtland."[4]

Six months pregnant with her second child, Emma was glad to be able to rest after a long and tiresome journey. The few weeks spent in the Whitney home must have been a comfort to her, and she must also have been pleased with the announcement that in fulfillment of the Lord's injunction (see D&C 41:7), the newly baptized Saints were to construct a home for the Prophet and his Emma on the Isaac Morley farm just one mile northeast of the Whitney home and store.

Their experience at the Isaac Morley farm brought both much joy and much sadness to the Prophet and his wife. The joy came when Emma gave birth to twins, who, they hoped, would replace the loss of their first son, Alvin; but this was quickly followed by the sadness that came when the twins died a short time after birth. The sadness was partially compensated in the news of the opportunity to adopt twins of John and Julia Murdock, born the day after. Whereas Joseph and Emma lost their twins, John lost his wife in the twins' birth. It was with some reluctance but also with a sense of gratification that John Murdock consented to the request of the Prophet to let him and Emma adopt the twins and provide for them a home. They were named Joseph and Julia, after the Prophet and after their biological mother. Now Joseph and Emma's longing for children was partially satisfied. We know how much the Prophet loved children, because of the many hours he spent playing with them.

The Saints in Kirtland had been plagued with false spirits that brought confusion among them, but now the Prophet was in their midst, and the Lord would soon show them legitimate spiritual experiences.[5] The occasion was a conference held in June 1831 at the Isaac Morley farm. The meeting began with another attempt by Satan and his host to confuse the Saints with an imitation of genuine spiritual experiences. "The man of sin was revealed," the Prophet Joseph Smith recorded.[6] Several of the elders were attacked by Satan, who had to be rebuked by the Prophet Joseph Smith. Levi Hancock's reaction to this terrifying experience must have been typical: "I was so scared I would not stir without [Joseph's] liberty."[7] That Satan will be present before or after significant spiritual experiences, attempting to disrupt the work, is a principle which the Saints have had to learn. Satan, knowing the great things about to happen, tried to stop his servants and deceive them. For it was on this sacred occasion that the first high priests in this dispensation were ordained in a small log schoolhouse on the Isaac Morley farm.

Then the Spirit of the Lord descended upon the Prophet Joseph Smith in an unusual manner, and he arose in great majesty and power and prophesied that John the Revelator was at that time working with the ten tribes of Israel, preparing them for their return from their long dispersion. He reminded the Saints of the parable of the mustard seed. He likened the present kingdom of God to a grain of mustard seed that was putting forth its branches, and he said that angels would come like birds to its branches. With foreboding he said some of the Saints would have to die for their testimony of the work, sealing their testimony of Jesus Christ with their blood. Did he know even at this early date that he and his brother Hyrum would be two of those? Finally the Prophet concluded his great prophecy with this testimony: "I now see God, and Jesus Christ at his right hand, let them kill me, I should not feel death as I am now."[8]

Not only the Prophet Joseph Smith saw the Father and Son on that occasion, but also Lyman Wight, thus fulfilling the divine law of witnesses: "In the mouth of two or three witnesses shall every word be established." (D&C 6:28.) Five of the sixty-two men present were ordained high priests by the Prophet Joseph Smith, and eighteen by Lyman Wight.

It was also while the Prophet was living on the Morley farm that another spiritual experience of particular note occurred. Mary Elizabeth Rollins Lightner had gone to the Prophet's home for a visit with all the Smiths. Joseph was not there initially, but he soon walked in with Martin Harris. Seeing the group gathered, the Prophet announced that there were enough persons to hold a meeting. When he arose to speak, his countenance changed, and he stood silent. His face glowed with internal light. He looked as though a search light was inside his face. Mary was astounded: "I never saw anything like it. . . . I could not take my eyes off him." It was while he was enveloped with the power of God that he asked those present if they knew who had been in their midst that night. Several responded questioningly, "An angel?" Martin Harris, however, arose and said, "I know, it was our Lord and Saviour, Jesus Christ," to which the Prophet responded: " 'Martin, God revealed that to you. Brothers and Sisters, the Saviour has been in your midst. I want you to remember it. He cast a veil over your eyes, for you could not endure to look upon Him.' " Mary was almost as deeply touched by the prayer that he uttered. "I have never heard anything like it since. I felt he was talking to the Lord and the power rested upon us all."[9]

The power that rested upon Joseph Smith in his prophetic calling manifested itself in many other ways in Kirtland. The power to heal, as taught by James (see James 5:14–15), was also frequently exercised by the Prophet in Ohio. One of the earliest evidences of the gift of healing led to the conversion of the John Johnson family, as well as of a Methodist minister, Ezra Booth. John and Elsa Johnson had come from Hiram, Ohio, with Ezra Booth to meet this man of God they had heard so much about since his arrival in Kirtland. In their first interview, the Prophet asked Elsa Johnson if she believed that God could heal her arm, using him as an instrument. Her reply was yes. Joseph remarked simply that he would visit her the next day. The next day he went to the home of Bishop Newel K. Whitney, where the Johnsons were staying. During a conversation concerning the supernatural gifts conferred in the days of the apostles, someone said, "Here is Mrs. Johnson with a lame arm; has God given any power to man on earth to cure her?" In a few moments the conversation had turned to another subject, when quietly Joseph Smith got up from his chair and walked to Elsa Johnson. Taking her by the hand, he said, "in the most solemn and impressive manner: 'Woman, in the name of the Lord Jesus Christ I command thee to be whole.' " Immediately he left the house. "The company were awe-stricken at the infinite presumption of the man, and the calm assurance with which he spoke." Ezra Booth then asked Elsa if her arm was healed. "She immediately stretched out her arm straight, remarking at the same time, 'it's as well as the other.' "[10]

This experience helped convince John and Elsa Johnson that Joseph was what he claimed to be, a prophet of God. So impressed were they that they invited him and Sidney Rigdon to move to Hiram, Ohio, and live with them. This invitation appealed to the Prophet, for persecution was beginning to mount, and he was finding it difficult to continue his important work on the translation of the Bible. Once more Joseph gathered his family and his meager belongings and made the thirty-mile move to Hiram, Ohio.

Here he and Sidney could work more intensely on their translation. A few months earlier the Lord had instructed the Prophet to divert his attention from his translation of the Old Testament and move immediately to the translation of the New. There were important reasons for this change: "Wherefore I give unto you that ye may now translate it, that ye may be prepared for the things to come. For verily I say unto you, that great things await you." (D&C 45:61–62.) Little did they realize what great things awaited them in the translation of the New Testament. With the quietude and lessened responsibility of temporal affairs he enjoyed at the Johnson farm, Joseph Smith was moving rapidly through the New Testament when the work was briefly interrupted by the apostasy of Ezra Booth. Miracles do not necessarily convert unless those touched by the witnessing of a miracle build their testimony on the sure foundation of the scriptures. Having left the Church, Ezra began to publish the first anti-Mormon literature against the Church by an apostate. Because of the negative effect of his vitriolic letters, published in the *Ohio Star,* the Lord directed Joseph Smith and Sidney Rigdon to suspend their translation for "a season." Their mission was to counter the falsehoods of Booth by proclaiming the gospel "unto the world in the regions round about." (D&C 71:1–2.) They were to call upon Ezra Booth and their other enemies to engage in public and in private debate. As they would do this, "their shame [that of the enemies of the Church] shall be made manifest." (D&C 71:7.) The Lord further promised them that "no weapon that is formed against you shall prosper; and if any man lift his voice against you he shall be confounded in mine own due time." (D&C 71:9–10.) So successful were they in this mission that finally Ezra Booth refused to debate with them in public, and the anti-Mormon articles ceased to be published in the newspapers.

With this temporary obstacle out of the way, the Prophet was told to intensify the translation of the Bible until it was finished. (See D&C 73:3–4.) With the continuation of the work on the Bible, they were now ready to receive the "great things" (D&C 45:62) the Lord had promised.

Joseph and Sidney had now arrived at John, chapter 5, in the New Testament. As they worked on verse 29, they marveled at the new information the Lord revealed to them about this verse. They meditated upon what they had learned. "The Lord touched the eyes of [their] understandings and they were opened, and the glory of the Lord shone round about." (D&C 76:19.) Then unfolded one of the great visions of all time. Truly this was a "transcript from the records of the eternal world."[11] Herein were revealed the eternal possibilities for God's children. In this vision once again the Prophet saw the Father and the Son, and as in the case of every appearance of these glorious Beings in Ohio, someone else was present and also saw them. This time it was Sidney Rigdon. In this vision they received of the Lord's fulness. So moved were they by this experience that they left this powerful testimony: "And now, after the many testimonies which have been given of him, this is the testimony, last of all, which we give of him: That he lives! For we saw him, even on the right hand of God." (D&C 76:22–23.)

Philo Dibble, who was present on this glorious occasion, recorded what took place. Although the twelve or so other people in the room at the time did not see the same visions, they "saw the glory and felt the power" present on that occasion. Periodically during this experience, which lasted an hour or so, Joseph would say, "What do I see?" and then relate what he had seen and was looking at. Sidney would then remark, "I see the same." Then Sidney would ask the same question, describing what he was seeing; Joseph would reply in the same manner as Sidney, "I see the same." Philo said in review of this glorious experience:

"This manner of conversation was repeated at short

intervals to the end of the vision, and during the whole time not a word was spoken by another person. Not a sound nor motion made by anyone but Joseph and Sidney, and it seemed to me that they never moved a joint or limb during the time I was there, which I think was over an hour, and to the end of the vision, Joseph sat firmly and calmly all the time in the midst of a magnificent glory, but Sidney sat limp and pale, apparently as limber as a rag, observing which Joseph remarked, smilingly, 'Sidney is not used to it as I am.' "[12]

This vision was further expanded and clarified in another vision received in the Kirtland Temple before its dedication. On the evening of 21 January 1836, the First Presidency met in the west room of the attic of the temple for the purpose of administering the ordinance of anointing. After Joseph received a blessing under the hands of the rest of the First Presidency, the heavens were opened, and once again Joseph Smith saw the Father and the Son, as well as past prophets, his parents, and his brother Alvin, all in the celestial kingdom. From this vision he learned that "all who have died without a knowledge of this gospel, who would have received it if they had been permitted to tarry, shall be heirs of the celestial kingdom of God." (D&C 137:7.) He further learned, "All children who die before they arrive at the years of accountability are saved in the celestial kingdom of heaven." (D&C 137:10.) This knowledge was a precursor of the greater knowledge he would receive in Nauvoo: the reason those who die without a knowledge of the gospel can be heirs to the celestial kingdom is the principle of vicarious work for the dead. (See D&C 124; 128.)

The John Johnson home in Hiram was also the setting of a series of important conferences. During one session the decision was made to publish for the first time the revelations given to the Prophet Joseph Smith. When some discussion arose during one of the conferences about the language of the revelations, the Lord issued the following challenge to those who questioned them: "Seek ye out of the Book of Commandments, even the least that is among them, and appoint him that is the most wise among you; or, if there be any among you that shall make one like unto it, then ye are justified in saying that ye do not know that they are true." (D&C 67:6–7.) If they failed to duplicate a revelation, they would be under condemnation if they did not bear record of the truthfulness of the revelations given to the Prophet Joseph Smith. William E. McLellin accepted the challenge and failed. As a result, those present bore the following testimony of the truthfulness of the revelations to be published in the Book of Commandments, and later in the Doctrine and Covenants:

"The testimony of the witnesses to the book of the Lord's commandments, which He gave to His Church through Joseph Smith, Jun., who was appointed by the voice of the Church for this purpose; we therefore feel willing to bear testimony to all the world of mankind, to every creature upon the face of all the earth and upon the islands of the sea, that the Lord has borne record to our souls, through the Holy Ghost, shed forth upon us, that these commandments were given by inspiration of God, and are profitable for all men, and are verily true. We give this testimony unto the world, the Lord being our helper; and it is through the grace of God, the Father, and His Son, Jesus Christ that we are permitted to have this privilege of bearing this testimony unto the world, that the children of men may be profited thereby."[13] This testimony, like the one found in the Book of Mormon, stands as a witness to the world that this book is true and is the word of the Lord.

The peace and the great inspiration of the Lord that came to the Prophet Joseph in Hiram, Ohio, was soon ended. Apostates and citizens from Hiram, antagonized by the revelations and inspiration given to the Prophet, violently attacked Joseph Smith and Sidney Rigdon. Encouragement came from several sources, not the least of which was a woman, Mrs. Gresham Judson, who used her influence with some men from Mantua, Ohio, to accomplish this unprovoked attack on the Lord's anointed.[14]

The Smiths had settled for the night. Joseph was sleeping in a downstairs bedroom of the Johnson home. The twins, Joseph and Julia, had been sick with measles. Emma had lost considerable sleep taking care of them, and so out of consideration for his wife, Joseph told her to go to bed. He would watch young Joseph, the sicker of the two. Finally the Prophet had lain down on the trundle with his little son and fallen asleep. He was rudely awakened by being dragged out of the room and into the cold winter night. Threatening to kill him, the mobsters tried to poison him; then they covered his body with tar and feathers. If that were not enough, a madman mutilated Joseph by jumping on him and scratching his flesh with his nails— "like a mad cat," he cried out, "That's the way the Holy Ghost falls on folks!"[15]

Recovering somewhat, Joseph stumbled toward the house. In the dim light the tar looked like blood. Emma, thinking the worst, fainted. She later said that when the men dragged him out of the house, she was in terror. She spent the evening in prayer, because she never expected to see him alive again.[16] Joseph's friends spent the rest of the night removing the tar by scraping his body and cleaning it with lard. Joseph's commitment to his calling was greater than the ferocity of the mob. The result of this attack only served to highlight the determination and persistence of the Prophet Joseph Smith. Even though badly weakened by the attack, with a scarred body and without any sleep, true to his commitment, he preached the following day, the Sabbath, to a congregation of Saints, as well as to some of the mobsters. He baptized three people at the conclusion of his discourse.[17]

The Ohio period was one of intense missionary work by the Prophet Joseph Smith. During the major conference of the Church held in June 1831, the Lord gave a revelation calling a number of missionaries to Missouri, including the Prophet Joseph Smith and his companion, Sidney Rigdon. (See D&C 52:3.)

On 19 June 1831, the Prophet Joseph Smith, in company with seven others, departed from Kirtland for Missouri to fulfill an earlier command of the Lord. How eagerly they

looked forward to this mission, since they had been told
that if they were faithful, the Lord would reveal the location
of the City of Zion, where the New Jerusalem would be
built. The Prophet recorded something of this in his missionary journal:

"We went by wagon, canal boats, and stages to Cincinnati, where I had an interview with the Rev. Walter
Scott, one of the founders of the Campbellites, or Newlight
church. Before the close of our interview, he manifested
one of the bitterest spirits against the doctrine of the New
Testament (that 'these signs shall follow them that believe,'
as recorded in Mark the 16th chapter,) that I ever witnessed
among men. We left Cincinnati in a steamer, and landed
at Louisville, Kentucky, where we were detained three
days in waiting for a steamer to convey us to St. Louis. At
St. Louis, myself, Brothers Harris, Phelps, Partridge and
Coe, went by land on foot to Independence, Jackson
county, Missouri, where we arrived about the middle of
July, and the rest of the company came by water a few
days later.

"Notwithstanding the corruptions and abominations
of the times, and the evil spirit manifested towards us on
account of our belief in the Book of Mormon, at many
places and among various persons, yet the Lord continued
His watchful care and loving kindness to us day by day;
and we made it a rule wherever there was an opportunity,
to read a chapter in the Bible, and pray; and these seasons
of worship gave us great consolation."[18]

On the first Sabbath they held a meeting where the
Prophet said there were present "specimens of all the families of the earth; Shem, Ham and Japheth."[19] The climax
of the meeting was the baptism of two individuals. In
addition to their missionary work, they laid a log for a
house in Kaw Township, which would be the beginning
of the foundation of Zion in Missouri. They also dedicated
the land of Zion for the gathering of the Saints, and the
Prophet dedicated a site in Independence for a temple.

On 9 August 1831, while returning to Ohio on the
Missouri River, Joseph and his party had a dramatic en-

counter with the "destroyer" riding upon the water. Concerned, the Prophet prayed for an understanding of the event and received the revelation recorded in Doctrine and Covenants 61. Following this direction from the Lord, they continued by land and arrived in Kirtland on 27 August. The Prophet summarized this missionary journey in these words: "Many things transpired upon this journey to strengthen our faith, and which displayed the goodness of God in such a marvelous manner, that we could not help beholding the exertions of Satan to blind the eyes of the people, so as to hide the true light that lights every man that comes into the world."[20]

The Lord called Joseph on his next mission in March 1832. (See D&C 78:9–10.) Joseph was appointed, with Sidney Rigdon and Newel K. Whitney, to "sit in council with the saints which are in Zion." (D&C 78:9.) Differences had arisen between the Saints in Zion, Jackson County, Missouri, and Kirtland. The Lord warned that because of these difficulties, "Satan seeketh to turn their hearts away from the truth, that they become blinded and understand not the things which are prepared for them." (D&C 78:10.) The Prophet left Kirtland and was joined by his two counselors, Sidney Rigdon and Jesse Gause, and by Bishop Newel K. Whitney and Peter Whitmer, Jr. This was not an easy journey, as the Prophet later recounted: "Traveling from this country to Zion amidst a crooked and perverse generation leaving our families in affliction amidst . . . death [and] upon the mercy of mobs."[21] Joseph had just lost his son, Joseph Murdock Smith, who had died as a result of exposure after the Prophet had been tarred and feathered in Hiram, Ohio. Sidney had left his family sick with the measles. As if this were not enough, the mobs continued to threaten their families, and so they had to leave Hiram, Emma and Julia going to Kirtland and Sidney's family moving to Chardon. But the mobs, still not willing to leave them alone, followed them all the way to Cincinnati.[22]

This mission to Missouri succeeded in bringing about a reconciliation, at least temporarily, between the Saints in Missouri and the Saints in Ohio. The Lord, pleased with this reconciliation, gave a revelation to the Prophet: "Verily, verily, I say unto you, my servants, that inasmuch as you have forgiven one another your trespasses, even so I, the Lord, forgive you." (D&C 82:1.) In addition, the Lord commanded the two bishops in Zion and Kirtland, as well as other leaders, "to be bound together by a bond and covenant, . . . to manage the affairs of the poor, and all things pertaining to the bishopric both in the land of Zion and in the land of Kirtland." (D&C 82:11–12.) The two centers of the united order in Zion and Kirtland operated out of two stores, the Gilbert Whitney & Company store in Missouri and the Newel K. Whitney & Company store in Kirtland.[23]

Having completed a successful mission, they began their journey home. As this mission had begun with difficulty, so it ended. Between Vincennes and New Albany, Indiana, the coach in which they were riding experienced a runaway in which Newel's leg was badly broken. Sidney continued on to Kirtland, while the compassionate and loving Prophet stayed with his friend. In the busy life of Joseph Smith this brief layover extended to a month. Joseph's compassion and concern show in the letter he wrote from Greenville, Indiana, to his beloved Emma:

"My situation is a very unpleasant one although I will endeavor to be contented, the Lord assisting me. I have visited a grove which is just back of the town almost every day where I can be secluded from the eyes of any mortal and there give vent to all the feelings of my heart in meditation and prayer. I have called to mind all the past moments of my life and am left to mourn and shed tears of sorrow for my folly in suffering the adversary of my soul to have so much power over me as he has had in times past, but God is merciful and has forgiven my sins and I rejoice that he sendeth forth the Comforter unto as many as believe and humbleth themselves before him. I was grieved to hear that Hyrum had lost his little child. I think we can in some degree sympathize with him, but we all must be reconciled to our lots and say the will of the Lord be done. . . .

105

"I will try to be contented with my lot knowing that God is my friend in him I shall find comfort. I have given my life into his hands I am prepared to go at his call. I desire to be with Christ. I count not my life dear to me only to do his will."[24]

Joseph Smith tells in his history even more about his care and concern for Bishop Whitney, as well as a major problem that beset him: "I tarried with Brother Whitney and administered to him till he was able to be moved. While at this place I frequently walked out in the woods, where I saw several fresh graves; and one day when I rose from the dinner table, I walked directly to the door and commenced vomiting most profusely. I raised large quantities of blood and poisonous matter, and so great were the muscular contortions of my system, that my jaw in a few moments was dislocated. This I succeeded in replacing with my own hands, and made my way to Brother Whitney (who was on the bed), as speedily as possible; he laid his hands on me and administered to me in the name of the Lord, and I was healed in an instant, although the effect of the poison was so powerful, as to cause much of the hair to become loosen from my head. Thanks be to my Heavenly Father for His interference in my behalf at this critical moment, in the name of Jesus Christ. Amen."[25]

After this long ordeal he and Bishop Whitney returned home, to the joy and satisfaction of themselves, family, and friends. Nevertheless, the Prophet hadn't been home very long when he received a disturbing letter. After this long, laborious journey, beset with many difficulties and problems, he learned that there were still some serious problems with the Saints in Missouri. He wrote a letter to William W. Phelps, expressing these concerns and relating something of their return trip and their difficulty in Indiana. He then told of their prayers in behalf of the Saints in Missouri. Once more his great love and compassion for people was demonstrated. But he also loved them so much that he rebuked and chastened them when needed:

"After our detention on the road I often times wandered alone in the lonely places seeking consolation of him who is alone able to console me, while my beloved Brother Whitney (who is without guile) poured out his soul with much weeping upon his pillow for you or for Zion. While I in the lonely places communed with him who is altogether lovely, witnessed your case and viewed the conspiracy with much grief and learned the displeasure of heaven and viewed the frowns of the heavenly hosts upon Zion and upon all the earth. . . . I have ever been filled with the greatest anxiety for them, and have taken the greatest interest for their welfare. I am a lover of the cause of Christ and of virtue, chastity and an upright steady course of conduct and a holy walk. . . . I appeal to your consciences, and if appealing to your consciences, by all the ties which bind man to man, which are stronger than death, will not open your eyes & let you see the state and standing which you are in and bring you to repentance, I then appeal to a higher court even the court of heaven the tribunal of the great God and there I and my Brethren (I mean Brothers Sidney and Newel) will meet you to be weighed in the balance and there the innocent shall not suffer and the guilty go unpunished for the Lord God Almighty will do right. I bear you record that myself Bro. Sidney and Newel as far as any thing that I know have ever maintained the purest desires for your welfare and do still. Our object in going to Zion was altogether to keep the commandment of the most high."[26]

The Prophet was home only a few months when once more he was called on a mission. This time it was a financial mission to acquire goods and commodities for the recently organized united order. The Whitney and Gilbert stores in Kirtland and Missouri were to be the nucleus of the order. During the organizational meeting in Missouri, Bishop Whitney was directed to negotiate a $15,000 loan to assure the stability of the order. Again the Lord had issued a missionary call through a revelation to the Prophet Joseph Smith:

"And the bishop, Newel K. Whitney, also should travel round about and among all the churches, searching after

the poor to administer to their wants by humbling the rich
and the proud.

"He should also employ an agent to take charge and
to do his secular business as he shall direct.

"Nevertheless, let the bishop go unto the city of New
York, also to the city of Albany, and also to the city of
Boston, and warn the people of those cities with the sound
of the gospel, with a loud voice, of the desolation and utter
abolishment which await them if they do reject these
things.

"For if they do reject these things the hour of their
judgment is nigh, and their house shall be left unto them
desolate.

"Let him trust in me and he shall not be confounded;
and a hair of his head shall not fall to the ground unnoticed." (D&C 84:112–16.)

This mission would have been especially difficult for
Joseph, because Emma was expecting any day. To fill these
assignments, Joseph Smith and Newel K. Whitney headed
east in October 1832. Summarizing their travels, Bishop
Whitney later wrote: "My leg was not perfectly well, but
I proceeded with Joseph . . . to N. York, Providence and
Boston, and through New England. We visited Bishop
[Benjamin T.] Onderdonk of the Episcopal Church of the
United States while at New York, and returned back to
Kirtland. This journey was taken to fulfill the revelation."[27]
While they were in New York City purchasing goods for
the united order, Joseph and Newel lodged at the Pearl
Street House on Manhattan Island. Pearl Street, located
near the southern end of the island, was the location of
the merchants of dry goods warehouses. The Prophet's
poignant letter to Emma shows his loving concern for his
wife as well as his commitment to the Lord. It also gives
us some good insight into his great love for people — friends
or strangers. Finally, it shows his great commitment to
preaching the gospel:

"This day I have been walking through the most splendid part of the city of New York. The buildings are truly
great and wonderful to the astonishing of every beholder

and the language of my heart is like this. Can the great God of all the earth, maker of all things magnificent and splendid, be displeased with man for all these great inventions sought out by them. My answer is no it can not be, seeing these works are calculated to make men comfortable wise and happy, therefore not for the works can the Lord be displeased only against man is the anger of the Lord kindled. Because they give him not the glory, therefore their iniquities shall be visited upon their heads and their works shall be burned up with unquenchable fire. The inequity of the people is printed in every countenance and nothing but the dress of the people makes them look fair and beautiful. . . . After beholding all that I had any desire to behold I returned to my room to meditate and calm my mind and behold the thoughts of home of Emma and Julia rushes upon my mind like a flood and I could wish for a moment to be with them. My breast is filled with all the feelings and tenderness of a parent and a husband and could I be with you I would tell you many things. Yet when I reflect upon this great city like Ninevah not discerning their right hand from their left, yea more than two hundred thousand souls, my bowels [are] filled with compassion towards them and I am determined to lift up my voice in this city and leave the event with God who holdeth all things in his hands and will not suffer an hair of our heads unnoticed to fall to the ground. . . .

"I hope you will excuse me for writing this letter so soon after writing for I feel as if I wanted to say something to you to comfort you in your peculiar trial and present affliction. I hope God will give you strength that you may not faint. I pray God to soften the hearts of those around you to be kind to you and take the burden off your shoulders as much as possible and not afflict you. I feel for you for I know your state and that others do not, but you must comfort yourself knowing that God is your friend in heaven and that you have one true and living friend on earth. . . .

"While Brother Whitney [is] selecting goods I have nothing to [do] but to sit in my room and pray for him that he may have strength to endure his labors . . . I prefer reading and praying and holding communion with the Holy Spirit and writing to you. [While] walking the streets and beholding the distraction [of] man I have had some conversation with [a] few which gave satisfaction and one very beautiful young gentleman from Jersey whose countenance was very solemn. He came and sat by my side and began to converse with me about the cholera and I learned he had been seized with it and came very near dying with it. He said the Lord had spared him for some wise purpose. I took advantage of this and opened a long discourse with him. He received my teaching apparently with much pleasure and became very strongly attached to me. We talked till late at night and concluded to omit conversation till the next day, but having some business to do he was detained until the boat was ready to go. . . . He came to me and bid me farewell and we parted with much reluctance. Brother Whitney is received with great kindness by all his old acquaintances. He is faithful in prayer and fervent in spirit and we take great comfort together."[28]

Hurrying home to make it back in time for the birth of the new baby, the Prophet was disappointed in arriving "immediately after" the birth of his son, Joseph Smith III. Knowing Emma's difficulty in giving birth and knowing that they had already lost three children, Joseph must have been greatly disappointed, and Emma also, that he should arrive after the birth and not before. But to their great joy, this child survived. Just two days later the Prophet met for the first time two men who would have as great an effect upon the Church, as well as upon him personally, as any pair of converts: Brigham Young and Heber C. Kimball.

Upon his return to Kirtland, Joseph Smith organized the School of the Prophets in the Newel K. Whitney Store. In this school the visions of the Prophet continued. Of this Zebedee Coltrin, a member of the school, said:

"I saw a person passing through the room as plainly as I see you now. Joseph asked us if we knew who it was and answered himself, 'That is Jesus our Elder Brother, the Son of God!' " After the vision closed, Joseph then told those present to resume their former position of prayer. "Again I saw passing through the same room, a personage whose glory and brightness was so great, that I can liken it to nothing but the burning bush that Moses saw, and its power was so great that had it continued much longer I believe it would have consumed us." After this personage had disappeared from the room, Joseph announced that the men had seen the father of the Lord Jesus Christ. Zebedee Coltrin concluded his testimony by saying, "I saw him."[29]

There were also sad days for the Prophet. His brother William and others rebelled against him. Daniel Tyler, describing Joseph Smith's sorrow over their rebellion, reports that he saw tears streaming from Joseph's eyes. Joseph knelt down, but instead of facing the congregation as he prayed, he turned his back. Daniel Tyler felt it was to hide his sorrow. He said, "Never until then had I heard a man address his Maker as though He was present listening as a kind father would listen to the sorrows of a dutiful child."[30]

Certainly some of the greatest events that schooled the Prophet Joseph Smith in the ways of the Lord were the spiritual events surrounding the building, dedication, and ordinances associated with the Kirtland Temple. Those events connected with the temple, in which he was tutored by heavenly beings concerning mankind's destiny and possibilities, made a lasting impression on his life. The climax came with events following the dedication of the Temple. (See D&C 110.) The Savior of the world appeared to Joseph Smith and Oliver Cowdery, accepting the workmanship of their hands as His house: "For behold, I have accepted this house, and my name shall be here; and I will manifest myself to my people in mercy in this house." Hundreds of Saints present at this historic event testified of this same truth. "I will appear unto my servants, and speak unto them with mine own voice, if my people will keep my commandments, and do not pollute this holy house." (D&C 110:7–8.)

Following the visit of Jesus Christ to the temple, three other heavenly messengers came: Moses, Elias, and Elijah. Each came to Joseph and Oliver to restore keys to men on earth. The keys restored at that time were probably the keys to the threefold mission of the Church: missionary work, family history and temple work, and the perfecting of the Saints. Moses restored the keys to missionary work when he gave to the Prophet the keys of the gathering of Israel. (See D&C 110:11.) The mysterious prophet Elias restored the dispensation of the gospel of Abraham. The few reports of Elias indicate that that dispensation applied to the family—the eternal family unit.[31] I also believe that Elias restored keys for the perfecting of the Saints. Where is the best and really the only effective place to perfect the Saints? In the family!

Finally, Elijah came on 3 April 1836 and restored the keys to family history and temple work. Those keys, promised by Moroni on his first visit to Joseph Smith in September 1823 (see D&C 2:1) and again in July 1830 (see D&C 27:9), were now bestowed to Joseph Smith and Oliver Cowdery (see D&C 110:13–16). Because these keys were restored, in Kirtland, Ohio, temples now dot the earth.

I have rehearsed some of the salient events that schooled the Prophet Joseph Smith in Kirtland, Ohio. So effective was this schooling period that conditional promises of the Lord to the Prophet in the first three years of his administration were now made unconditional. Earlier in his ministry the Prophet had been told: "And I have given unto [Joseph Smith] the keys of the mystery of those things which have been sealed, even things which were from the foundation of the world, and the things which shall come from this time until the time of my coming, if he abide in me, and if not, another will I plant in his stead." (D&C 35:18; see also D&C 27:8; 64:5.)

But after two brief years of schooling the Prophet in Kirtland, the Lord removed this conditional promise to Joseph Smith and made it unconditional: "Verily I say unto you, the keys of this kingdom shall never be taken from you, while thou art in the world, neither in the world to come; nevertheless, through you shall the oracles be given to another, yea, even unto the church." (D&C 90:3–4.)

The Lord confirmed, clarified, and reiterated this promise even more strongly in Nauvoo just a year before the Prophet's death, as He had done to many of the prophets before (see Mosiah 26:20; 3 Nephi 28:3): "For I am the Lord thy God, and will be with thee even unto the end of the world, and through all eternity; for verily I seal upon you your exaltation, and prepare a throne for you in the kingdom of my Father, with Abraham your father." (D&C 132:49.)

Notes

1. Orson F. Whitney, "Newel K. Whitney," *Contributor*, vol. 6, no. 4 (Jan. 1885), p. 125.

2. *Millennial Star* 40: 772.

3. Orson F. Whitney, in Conference Report, Apr. 1912, p. 50.

4. Elizabeth Ann Whitney, in Edward W. Tullidge, *Women of Mormondom* (New York, 1877), pp. 41–42.

5. Parley P. Pratt, *Autobiography of Parley Parker Pratt*, edited by his son Parley P. Pratt (Salt Lake City: Deseret Book Co., 1950), p. 61.

6. Joseph Smith, *History of The Church of Jesus Christ of Latter-day Saints*, 7 vols., 2d ed. rev., ed. B. H. Roberts (Salt Lake City, Utah. The Church of Jesus Christ of Latter-day Saints, 1932–51), 1:175.

7. Journal of Levi Hancock, n.p., n.d., p. 33; see also Typescript, Harold B. Lee Library, Brigham Young University, Provo, Utah.

8. Ibid.

9. "Diary of Mary Elizabeth Rollins Lightner," pp. 4–5; see also Typescript, Brigham Young University, Provo, Utah.

10. Oliver B. Huntington, *Young Woman's Journal*, vol. 2, no. 5 (Feb. 1891), pp. 225–26. See also Amos Sutton Hayden, *Early History of the Disciples in the Western Reserve* (Cincinnati, Ohio: Chase and Hall, 1876), pp. 250–51; Smith, *History of the Church*, 1:215–16.

11. Smith, *History of the Church*, 1:252.

12. Philo Dibble, *Juvenile Instructor*, vol. 27, no. 10 (15 May 1892), pp. 303–4.

13. Smith, *History of the Church*, 1:226.

14. Gertrude Van Rensselaer Wickham, ed., *Pioneer Women of the Western Reserve* (1896), 3:415.

15. Smith, *History of the Church*, 1:263.

16. Buddy Youngreen, *Reflections of Emma, Joseph Smith's Wife* (Orem, Utah: Grandin Book Co., 1982), p. 93.

17. Smith, *History of the Church,* 1:261–65.

18. Smith, *History of the Church,* 1:188–89.

19. Smith, *History of the Church,* 1:190–91.

20. Smith, *History of the Church,* 1:206.

21. Dean C. Jessee, *The Personal Writings of Joseph Smith* (Salt Lake City, Utah: Deseret Book Co., 1984), p. 245; spelling and punctuation have been modernized.

22. Smith, *History of the Church,* 1:266.

23. Smith, *History of the Church,* 1:270.

24. Jessee, *Personal Writings of Joseph Smith,* pp. 238–39; spelling and punctuation have been modernized.

25. Smith, *History of the Church,* 1:271.

26. Jessee, *Personal Writings of Joseph Smith,* pp. 245–46; spelling and punctuation have been modernized.

27. Jessee, *Personal Writings of Joseph Smith,* p. 252.

28. Jessee, *Personal Writings of Joseph Smith,* pp. 252–54; spelling and punctuation have been modernized.

29. High Priests Records of Spanish Fork, 5 Feb. 1878, Archives of The Church of Jesus Christ of Latter-day Saints, Salt Lake City, Utah; Salt Lake School of the Prophets, 3 Oct. 1883, Archives of The Church of Jesus Christ of Latter-day Saints, p. 60.

30. Daniel Tyler, *Juvenile Instructor,* vol. 27, no. 4 (15 Feb. 1892), pp. 127–28.

31. Bruce R. McConkie, *The Millennial Messiah* (Salt Lake City, Utah, Deseret Book Co., 1982), pp. 119, 268; Theodore M. Burton, *God's Greatest Gift* (Salt Lake City, Utah: Deseret Book Co., 1976), p. 201.

Chapter 7

Joseph Smith, Builder of Ideal Communities

Leonard J. Arrington
Lemuel Redd Professor of Western History, Emeritus
Brigham Young University

Joseph Smith is known to most Latter-day Saints as a great religious leader, preacher, and revelator. But he was also a man of affairs — political leader, community organizer, entrepreneur, and planner. This was a necessary part of his stewardship as a prophet.

As early as September 1830, six months after the organization of the Church, a revelation was announced, stating, "Verily I say unto you that all things unto me are spiritual, and not at any time have I given unto you a law which was temporal . . . ; for my commandments are spiritual." (D&C 29:34–35.) As the nucleus of the kingdom of God, the Church must see to the gathering of God's people, organize them, and assist them in building a community worthy of God's blessings. The Prophet must exercise leadership in these affairs; he must concern himself with the daily activities and welfare of his people, both individually and collectively. The temporal side of life was inextricably connected with spiritual goals. Religion, as an editor who knew Joseph wrote, was not only "a matter of sentiment, good for Sunday contemplation and intended for the sanctuary and the soul," but it also had to do with "dollars and cents, with trade and barter, with the body and the daily doings of ordinary life."[1]

When the Prophet announced in December 1830 that the Lord had commanded the Saints to "assemble together at the Ohio" (D&C 37:3), he began his first activity as a community builder. He was called upon to procure lands, assist the New York (and other) members of the Church to migrate to Ohio, and help them get started making their living. Through his efforts a community of more than twelve hundred Saints was soon established at Kirtland and other locations on the Western Reserve.

A series of revelations gave counsel for the government of the Saints. They were to be united, to live in harmony, and to strive to work together to build the Lord's kingdom. Some of those in Ohio who had joined the Church had been followers of Alexander Campbell, a prominent Disciples of Christ preacher, who had established a communal society at Kirtland called "The Family." This was an attempt to duplicate the common sharing of the early Christians, as described in the Acts of the Apostles: "All that believed were together, and had all things common; And sold their possessions and goods, and parted them to all men, as every man had need." (Acts 2:44–45.)

When Joseph Smith arrived in Kirtland, he announced, on 9 February 1831, that "The Family" should abandon the common-stock principle in favor of what he called "the more perfect law of the Lord." The revelation, now recorded in Doctrine and Covenants 42, outlined what was referred to as "the Lord's law," or the law of consecration and stewardship. On the basic principle that the earth and everything on it belong to the Lord, Church members were asked to "consecrate," or deed, their property to the Presiding Bishop of the Church, Edward Partridge. The bishop would then grant an "inheritance," or stewardship, to each family out of the properties so received, the amount depending on the "just" wants and needs of the family as determined jointly by the bishop and the prospective steward. The stewardship might be a farm, building lot, store, workshop, mill, or simply an appointment to serve the community as a teacher, physician, or musician. Family heads were asked to consecrate, or donate, annually their surplus production to the bishop's storehouse. This surplus would be distributed to the poorer and the younger members of the Church who had no property to consecrate or who had too little to procure an adequate "inheritance." The surplus would also be used to provide funds for the purchase of lands and for such Church projects as printing, building a temple, and supporting schools. Should anyone leave the group, he or she might keep his or her inheritance but not the surplus donated to the Church. There was to be freedom of enterprise, freedom in the management of properties, and freedom to buy and sell; but at the same time, the interests of the group were protected and the growth of the Church was facilitated. Above all, the plan would provide the poor Saints migrating from New York with sufficient property to care for the needs of their families. Basic equality would be retained by the provision that members would periodically donate their surplus, for, as the revelation stated: "It is not given that one man should possess that which is above another, wherefore the world lieth in sin." (D&C 49:20.)

Among the earliest migrants to northeastern Ohio were the Saints from Colesville, New York. They had sold their land and improvements to help finance their trip and to assist those who had no means. Sixty-four of them moved as a group, and the Prophet settled them sixteen miles northeast of Kirtland on the thousand-acre farm of Leman Copley, who had consecrated some of his land to the cause. As instructed, each of the newcomers consecrated his or her property to the bishop and received back a stewardship. After two months of labor on the farm, however, Copley apostatized and sued for the return of his property. The courts, which were oriented in favor of individual property rights, supported Copley's demands, and the Colesville settlers had to give up their land and their newly constructed homes.

As the Church continued to grow and immigration increased, the Prophet received a revelation announcing a new gathering place in Jackson County, in western Missouri. (See D&C 84:3.) This gathering place was to be "Zion," the "New Jerusalem." Families in Ohio were encouraged to go to Missouri and other converts were as well. In particular, the Prophet instructed the Colesville Saints to go there. They moved, once more as a group, to Jackson County, traveling in twenty-four wagons. As one of the party wrote, "People all along the road stared at us as they would at a circus or a caravan. . . . We most truly were a band of pilgrims, started out to seek a better country. . . . We were told [by teamsters] we were the most peaceable and quiet emigrants they had ever carried west; 'no profanity, no bad language, no gambling, and no drinking.' "2

Arriving in Jackson County on 25 July 1831, the Colesville Saints and several dozen other families from the Kirtland area received a leased, landed inheritance from Bishop Partridge and worked cooperatively to build houses and fences and to sow grain. Visiting Jackson County in 1832, the Prophet was so impressed with the spirit of unity and self-abnegation that he called the Colesville Branch together "and sealed them up to Eternal Life."3

The Prophet was particularly pleased with how these Saints consistently demonstrated a self-reliance and resourcefulness for which the Saints in later years were particularly noted. Warned that some freeloaders might take advantage of the consecrations of others, the Prophet directed the Jackson County bishop to caution those intending to migrate to Zion that they should pay their debts, husband their property and savings carefully, and secure pure varieties of seeds and improved breeds of cattle, sheep, and hogs to bring with them: "For the disciples to suppose that they can come to this land without ought to eat, or to drink, or to wear, or any thing to purchase these necessaries with, is a vain thought. For them to suppose that the Lord will open the windows of heaven, and rain down angel's food for them by the way, when their whole journey lies through a fertile country, stored with the blessings of life from his own hand for them to subsist upon, is also vain. . . .

"And notwithstanding the fulness of the earth is for the saints, they can never expect it unless they use the means put into their hands to obtain the same in the manner provided by our Lord. When you flee to Zion, we enjoin the word, prepare all things, that you may be ready to labor for a living, for the Lord has promised to take the curse off the land of Zion . . . , and the willing and the obedient, will eat the good of the same: not the idle."[4]

The results of this frontier communitarianism are difficult to assess. Official communications mention that the disciples were "in good health and spirits" and "doing well." They also mention that the burden of migrating, of puchasing land, of establishing the printing office and store, and, above all, of transforming a "wilderness and desert" into a "garden of the Lord" was greater than most had anticipated.[5] By and large, those who participated and left recollections wrote of their experience with pronounced nostalgia: "There was a spirit of peace and union, and love and good will manifested in this little Church in the wilderness, the memory of which will be ever dear to my heart. . . . Peace and plenty had crowned their labors, and the wilderness became a fruitful field, and the solitary place began to bud and blossom as the rose. . . . In short, there has seldom, if ever, been a happier people upon the earth than the Church of the Saints now were."[6]

In Kirtland, where, despite the removal of several hundred Saints to Jackson County, there were more than a thousand residents by 1835, Joseph Smith established a planning, coordinating, and funding body to help him be more effective in gathering the Saints and developing the city. Inspired by an 1832 revelation, the Prophet and six others formed the United Firm, or United Order, with one branch to operate in Kirtland, the other in Jackson County. (See D&C 78; 82.) This group, organized as a partnership, held property and conducted general Church business, supported the migration to Kirtland and to Jackson

County, purchased land for the settlement of the Saints, operated as an agency to buy supplies for general stores, and supervised the printing of Church periodicals, books, and pamphlets. This group was split into two firms in 1834, one to function in Ohio and the other in Missouri. Eventually there were nine persons in the partnership. By purchasing large tracts of land, one or more square miles at a time, they were able to avoid competitive bidding on smaller tracts and thus provide land more economically. Eventually they bought about 250 square miles of land in Missouri, including one whole county and parts of others.

Once gathered, the Saints were to devote themselves assiduously to the task of building up Zion: "Thou shalt not be idle; for he that is idle shall not eat the bread nor wear the garments of the laborer." Plainness in living and financial self-sufficiency were to characterize this New Jerusalem: "let all thy garments be plain, and their beauty the beauty of the work of thine own hands." (D&C 42:40.) Thus, an industrious, frugal, independent society was to be established under the direction of the priesthood. In contrast with many contemporary communitarian societies, each family was to live separately, possessed of its own stewardship, and communal living was eschewed.

In administering the law in Missouri, the revelation specified that each person was to have as much as was sufficient for himself and family; that every man should receive "equal according to his family, according to his circumstances and his wants and needs." (D&C 51:3; Book of Commandments 51:6.) What were a family's wants and needs? Who was to determine them? In June 1833 the Prophet explained the procedure to be followed:

"Every man must be his own judge how much he should receive and how much he should suffer to remain in the hands of the Bishop. I speak of those who consecrate more than they need for the support of themselves and their families.

"The matter of consecration must be done by the mutual consent of both parties; for to give the Bishop power to say how much every man shall have, and he be obliged to comply with the Bishop's judgment, is giving to the Bishop more power than a king has; and upon the other hand, to let every man say how much he needs, and the Bishop be obliged to comply with his judgment, is to throw Zion into confusion, and make a slave of the Bishop. The fact is, there must be a balance or equilibrium of power, between the Bishop and the people, and thus harmony and good will may be preserved among you.

"Therefore, those persons consecrating property to the Bishop in Zion, and then receiving an inheritance back, must reasonably show to the Bishop that they need as much as they claim. But in case the two parties cannot come to a mutual agreement, the Bishop is to have nothing to do about receiving such consecrations; and the case must be laid before a council of twelve High Priests, the Bishop not being one of the council, but he is to lay the case before them."[7] These instructions came too late to be applied in the Jackson County settlement.

The Prophet took very seriously the planning for Kirtland and Jackson County. These were to be communities of *Saints*; they were erecting a city that would be a light unto the world, a place to which the Savior would delight to come, an ideal city. Other cities in the United States (for example, Philadelphia in 1683 and Washington, D.C., in 1791) had been laid out according to a definite plan; didn't Kirtland and the new City of Zion in Missouri deserve one as well? On 23 June 1833, the Prophet sent to the brethren in Jackson County a sketch for a proposed Plat of the City of Zion. It was not in the form of a revelation, although it may have been inspired in part by the descriptions of the New Jerusalem in Revelation 21 and Ezekiel 48. The original Plat, with the Prophet's handwriting, is in the Church Archives, and may be summarized as follows: [8]

All the people were to live in the city, which would be one mile square. The city was laid out on a grid pattern oriented to the cardinal points of the compass, with straight streets crossing at right angles. The streets were to be eight rods wide. Each block was to be ten acres, except that the blocks in the center were fifteen acres in size. These larger blocks were reserved for temples, schools, bishops' store-houses, and other public buildings. Each residential block was divided into twenty lots of one-half acre each. The houses were to be set back uniformly twenty-five feet from the street so as to allow room for an ample lawn and front yard. Gardens and orchards would be in the rear. All houses would be constructed of brick and stone. The lots were alternated so that no house would be exactly opposite another, and there was to be only one house per lot. Barns and stables were to be located outside the city, and the area around the city was to be used for farming.

The city was to hold from fifteen to twenty thousand persons. (In counting up the lots on the Plat and apportioning families, one can see that the original Plat would actually serve only about ten thousand persons.) As the Church grows, the Prophet wrote, a new city would be gathered and designed the same way, "and," wrote the Prophet, "so fill up the world in these last days; and let every man live in the city, for this is the city of Zion."[9] The outstanding feature of the plan was the location of the Saints in a village rather than on scattered farms, as was typical of most American settlements. In a letter accompanying the City of Zion plan, the Prophet mentioned the advantages:

"The farmer and his family, therefore, will enjoy all the advantages of schools, public lectures and other meetings. His home will no longer be isolated, and his family denied the benefits of society, which has been, and always will be, the great educator of the human race; but they will enjoy the same privileges of society, and can surround their homes with the same intellectual life, the same social refinement as will be found in the home of the merchant or banker or professional man."[10]

Particularly important in bringing the Saints together, he indicated, was the importance of education: "The glory of God is intelligence." (D&C 93:36.) The Saints must gather together so they can be educated about religious and secular matters: "The advantages of [gathering together in villages] are numerous. . . . As intelligence is the great object of our holy religion, it is of all things important, that we should place ourselves in the best situation possible to obtain it. . . . Intelligence is the result of education, and education can only be obtained by living in compact society; so compact, that schools of all kinds can be supported."[11]

The Plat was obviously intended only as a general guide, with the stipulated arrangements to be modified according to the circumstances and geography of each settlement. Kirtland, which was surveyed shortly after the Plat was prepared, followed the plan rather closely. Kirtland blocks were square, with twenty lots per block, alternate blocks having their lots oriented so as to protect privacy. With these arrangements the residents did, indeed, enjoy a rich social and cultural life. Moreover, the economy prospered. The consecrations of the faithful made possible a substantial missionary effort, the acquisition of needed machinery and equipment, and the construction of the Kirtland Temple. The Prophet's gratification with the faithfulness of the Saints is suggested in his response to a questioning immigrant. Despite rumors to the contrary, he wrote, the Saints did not practice "common stock business," but in fact, "every man enjoys his own property." Each person, he wrote, is free to "consecrate liberally or illiberally to the support of the poor and needy, or the building up of Zion."[12]

Even though stewardships over specific pieces of property had been assigned to certain individuals (members of the United Firm), every member of the Church, in fact, was a steward "over earthly blessings," responsible to the Lord for his or her stewardship. The Prophet said it was within the stewardship of all members to "be anxiously engaged in a good cause, and do many things of their own free will, and bring to pass much righteousness," for "the power [of the Spirit of God] is in them." (D&C 58:27–28.)

As for consecrations, Joseph gave the following explanation: "Now for a man to consecrate his property . . . to the Lord, is nothing more nor less than to feed the hungry, clothe the naked, visit the widow and fatherless, the sick and afflicted, and do all he can to administer to their relief in their afflictions, and for him and his house to serve the Lord. In order to do this, he and all his house must be virtuous, and must shun the very appearance of evil."[13]

Before the Plat of the City of Zion could be implemented in Jackson County, however, and before the Prophet and his associates could perfect the administration of the law of consecration and stewardships there, an angry mob, led by a militant Protestant minister, damaged the bishop's storehouse and destroyed the printing establishment, tarred and feathered the bishop, and finally, in November 1833, drove the twelve hundred or more Saints from their homes and farms with whippings and plunder. Many houses were burned, livestock killed, and furniture and other domestic property seized and carted away. The Saints moved north to Clay and Ray counties, where they formed small settlements on the Missouri bottoms. But before permanent arrangements could be put in place, they were forced to go still farther north to what became Caldwell County. The mutual sharing of provisions and teams and the camaraderie of the Saints in their persecution and poverty astonished observers and set a pattern of behavior that has characterized Latter-day Saints to this day.

By 1836 Kirtland had a population of about two thousand. There were three hundred houses and nine mercantile firms, all but two owned by Latter-day Saints. There was a blacksmithy, sawmill, gristmill, two carding mills, and a fulling and clothing factory, all owned by non-Mormons. Latter-day Saints operated a brickyard, printing office, hashery, tannery, shoe shop, forge, pottery, and steam sawmill. This was a reasonably well-supplied community for its size.[14]

Recent studies have demonstrated that under the development program administered by the Prophet the Kirtland economy was viable; land prices rose, not because of speculation but because of the increase in population; and in his borrowing programs the Prophet provided his creditors with valuable and substantial assets. In January 1837,

Oliver Cowdery, editor of the *Messenger and Advocate*, wrote:

"Our streets are continually thronged with teams loaded with wood, materials for building the ensuing season, provisions for the market, people to trade, or parties of pleasure to view our stately and magnificent temple. Although our population is by no means as dense as in many villages, yet the number of new buildings erected the last season, those who in contemplation and under contract to be built next season, together with our every day occurrences, are evincive of more united exertion, more industry and more enterprise than we ever witnessed in so sparse a population."[15]

Wilford Woodruff, who had been away for many months on a proselyting mission, wrote in his diary the magical change Joseph had wrought on the Kirtland economy: "Now I behold a cheerfulness beaming upon every countenance that indicates Prosperity and the noise of the ax and the hammer and the sight of their walls and dwellings newly erected and their Bank and market and especially house of God speaks in language loud as thunder that the saints will have a City in prosperity in spite of all the fals Prophets . . . because God is with them."[16]

The best evidence of Kirtland's viability and comparability with Ohio in general was its rapidly rising population and land values. The number of families rose from 128 in 1830 to 181 in 1834, 246 in 1836, and 304 in 1837. In 1837 the town was larger than Akron, Canton, and Youngstown, and not much smaller than Cleveland, Columbus, and Dayton.[17]

On the expectation that Kirtland would continue to grow in population and the land values rise at the customary growth rate, the Prophet and his associates in the United Firm had continued to make development loans, for which they were able to pledge substantial assets. But their cash flow failed to meet expectations. With the money shortage precipitated by the Panic of 1837, their creditors demanded payment. Under other circumstances the Prophet would have insisted on cash payments from those owing him for land, groceries, and other favors. But his role as religious leader worked against him. Brigham Young recalled the difficulties the Prophet encountered as a storekeeper in Kirtland:

"Joseph [Smith] goes to New York and buys 20,000 dollar's worth of goods, comes into Kirtland and commences to trade. In comes one of the brethren, 'Brother Joseph, let me have a frock pattern for my wife.' What if Joseph says, 'No, I cannot without the money.' The consequence would be, 'He is no Prophet,' says James. Pretty soon Thomas walks in. 'Brother Joseph, will you trust me for a pair of boots?' 'No, I cannot let them go without the money.' 'Well,' says Thomas, 'Brother Joseph is no Prophet; I have found *that* out, and I am glad of it.' After a while, in comes Bill and sister Susan. Says Bill, 'Brother Joseph, I want a shawl, I have not got the money, but I wish you to trust me a week or a fortnight.' Well, brother Joseph thinks the others have gone and apostatized, and he don't know but these goods will make the whole Church do the same, so he lets Bill have a shawl. Bill walks off with it and meets a brother. 'Well,' says he, 'what do you think of brother Joseph?' 'O he is a first-rate man, and I fully believe he is a Prophet. See here, he has trusted me this shawl.' Richard says, 'I think I will go down and see if he won't trust me some. . . . ' 'Well,' says Joseph, 'these goods . . . are of less value than the people . . . ,' and so it goes. Joseph was a first-rate fellow with them all the time, provided he never would ask them to pay him. In this way it is easy . . . to trade away a first-rate store of goods, and be in debt for them."[18]

The Prophet's cash flow deficiencies could have been alleviated had there existed in Kirtland a means to transform land assets into liquid cash. Upon the advice of trusted advisers, Church leaders decided to establish a bank, to be called the Kirtland Safety Society Bank. If successful, the bank would provide a local currency, a safe depository, a source of commercial and consumer credit, the opportunity to borrow using existing assets as security, and a potentially profitable business for their backers because of the ability to "create" money by issuing notes.[19] In short, it would transfer landed wealth into a more liquid form. Kirtland could surely support a modest bank, and the bank could play an important role in the development of the community.

But the bank failed; the timing was bad. Dominated by antibank forces, the state legislature refused to grant a charter to any bank. After having ordered plates for the currency they planned to circulate, the officers were induced by optimistic business interests and bad legal counsel to convert the proposed bank into an antibank, something that seemed to be both legal and practical. But the lack of a corporate charter was lethal. It meant bad publicity; it raised doubts in the minds of those who might otherwise have accepted the notes. Then occurred the national economic collapse known as the Panic of 1837. Like other banks in Ohio affected by the Panic, the Kirtland antibank suspended payments. The Prophet made courageous attempts to save it, further draining his own resources. On 8 June 1837 Joseph publicly removed himself from the bank's operations, and in August warned his followers against the ill-advised and perhaps fraudulent effort of Warren Parrish to revive the ill-fated bank.[20] The Prophet, burdened with suits, eventually had to leave Kirtland. In doing so, he not only fled his creditors but also had to leave behind his beloved temple and the thousand or more Saints who had accepted so willingly the doctrines of the Restoration. Five hundred of the Saints migrated in one large group, "Kirtland Camp," to Missouri under an arrangement of mutual sharing of wagons, teams, and provisions that assured all of them, even the most destitute, of means to make the journey.

The ten thousand Saints in northern Missouri, fifty miles north of Independence, welcomed the Prophet, who arrived at Far West in March 1838. Once again, the Prophet laid plans for a new mile-square headquarters city, laid cornerstones for a proposed temple, and supervised the planning of agricultural, commercial, and industrial enterprises. Within one year of the first settlement of Far

127

West, wrote Parley Pratt, "there were from one hundred to one hundred and fifty dwelling houses erected in that place, six dry good stores in operation, one grocery and several mechanic shops. There were in the county, nearly or quite three hundred farms opened and several thousand acres under cultivation also, four saw and five grist mills doing good business."[21]

Remembering the obligation of the Saints with respect to the law of consecration and stewardship, the Prophet announced on 8 July 1838 a clarified form of the law. The new revelation (D&C 119) required the consecration of surplus property at the time the convert joined the community of Saints, just as the 1831 revelation had specified. But whereas in 1831 the new convert consecrated all his property and received a stewardship, he would now consecrate only the surplus and keep the remainder. And whereas the 1831 revelation required all surplus income be placed in the storehouse for distribution to the poor and needy and for use on Church projects of various kinds (purchasing lands, building temples, printing scriptures, etc.), the new law required that a tenth be paid on the annual increase. This was regarded as a more precise definition of the surplus income to be consecrated. In any case, there would be a transfer of annual savings to the Church for community use. At the same time, the Twelve Apostles assumed some central Church administrative duties, and the United Firm ceased to operate. The Saints apparently accepted the new revelation. Less than three weeks after the revelation was announced the Prophet mentioned that he and other officials met at Far West "to dispose of the public properties of the Church in the hands of the Bishop, many of the brethren having consecrated their surplus property according to the revelations."[22]

Some of the Saints took a further step to consolidate their property by forming voluntary cooperative enterprises called united firms. Groups of farmers organized the Western Agricultural Company, the Eastern Agricultural Company, and the Southern Agricultural Company.[23] There were also plans to organize three other corporations, uniting mechanics, shopkeepers, and laborers. John Corrill explained: "Every man was [urged] to put in all his property by leasing it to the firm for a term of years; overseers or managers were to be chosen from time to time, by the members of the firm, to manage the concerns of the same, and the rest were to labor under their direction. . . . Many joined these firms, while many others were much dissatisfied with them, which caused considerable feeling and excitement in the Church. [Joseph] Smith said every man must act his own feelings, whether to join or not."[24]

Once more, however, the original settlers did not welcome the influx of Saints, and certain Church members reacted against some of the Prophet's policies. Ministers and apostates organized mobs to oppose the Saints and attempt to drive them out. Finally, Governor Lilburn W. Boggs, fearful of civil war, ordered the Saints to leave the state or be exterminated. Homes of the Saints were burned, livestock was killed, and seventeen Church members were massacred at Haun's Mill. Joseph and some of his closest associates were imprisoned, and under the direction of Brigham Young, the senior apostle, the Saints abandoned Missouri and migrated to Quincy, Illinois. The Saints left behind their cooperative hopes and more than $300,000 worth of property.

As in previous migrations, with Joseph's obvious approval, the Twelve induced the Saints to pool their material resources in order to remove all the Saints from Missouri to Illinois. On 29 January 1839, all the propertied heads of families signed what was called the Missouri Covenant:

"We, whose names are hereunder written, do for ourselves individually hereby covenant to stand by and assist one another, to the utmost of our abilities, in removing from this state in compliance with the authority of the state; and we do hereby acknowledge ourselves firmly bound to the extent of all our available property, to be disposed of by a committee who shall be appointed for the purpose of providing means for the removing from this state of the poor and destitute who shall be considered worthy, till there shall not be one left who desires to remove from the state: with this proviso, that no individual shall be deprived of the right of the disposal of his own property for the above purpose, or of having the control of it, or so much of it as shall be necessary for the removing of his own family, and to be entitled to the over-plus, after the work is effected."[25]

The relocation went on for several months, the means of those of substance becoming a common fund for the benefit of all, until the twelve thousand members of the Church had left Missouri and found refuge in Illinois. The widespread suffering occasioned by this exodus was greatly reduced by the orderly manner in which it was conducted.

When Joseph was given his liberty in April 1839 he established a new gathering place. Through a fortunate set of circumstances, he acquired considerable land in Commerce, Illinois, and recommended that the Saints gather there. Within a year, most of the Saints who had left Ohio and Missouri began to build a new city, which Joseph named Nauvoo.

Joseph and his colleagues laid out a city one mile square, on the gridiron pattern, with blocks and lots the same size as in Far West. Nauvoo had narrower streets, fifty feet wide. Many fine residences were erected, and officials prepared for a stream of immigrants from Great Britain and from the eastern and southern United States. A university was chartered by the state legislature, a municipal militia was organized, schoolhouses were built, and artisans began working on the construction of a temple.

In establishing the basic framework for their economy, the Prophet's priorities were clear. The gospel must be taken to the world, and the thousands of converts must be gathered to the new Zion. All energies must now be directed toward proselyting, immigration, and settlement. The Lord, who had commanded them to move forward with the expansion of the kingdom, had also commanded modifications in the law first announced in 1831. In Nauvoo, every member was made steward over his own properties.[26]

With respect to consecrations, the Prophet declared: "The law of consecration [as originally applied in Jackson County] could not be kept here, and that it was the will of the Lord that we should desist from trying to keep it; and if persisted in, it would produce a perfect defeat of its object, and that he assumed the whole responsibility of not keeping it until proposed by himself."[27]

There was a further clarification of the requirement to consecrate surplus income upon joining the Church. Announced in December 1841, this process specified that every person should consecrate a tithe, or ten percent, of his wealth upon joining the group and then consecrate ten percent of his annual increase. Those who were without property should donate their labor, one day in ten. Also in 1841 the Corporation of the Trustee-in-Trust of the Church was organized to hold and deal in properties, both real and personal, on behalf of the Church. Joseph Smith was sustained as Trustee-in-Trust. All donations to the Church, for whatever purpose (for building the temple, printing scriptures, supporting the Presidency, etc.) were regarded as consecrations. Those who made honest consecrations were regarded as having obeyed the injunctions in the law of consecration and were assured that they might "realize the fullness of the blessings of the celestial kingdom."[28]

Freedom of enterprise was encouraged. In Nauvoo, the Prophet, as mayor of the city, spoke "for the repeal of the ordinance of the city licensing merchants, hawkers, taverns, and ordinaries, desiring that this might be a free people, and enjoy equal rights and privileges."[29] The ordinances were repealed. Further reflecting this policy of economic freedom, the Prophet urged the city council to refrain from enacting any ordinances except those that "would promote peace and good order." Let the people improve the city, he said. Encourage capitalists to come in to build mills, factories, and machinery. He prophesied that "if the council would be liberal in their proceedings, they would become rich, and spoke against the principle of pay for every little service rendered."[30]

At the same time, the Prophet argued for various kinds of civic improvements — roads, schools, and a public market. The latter was important, he said, "so that the poor should not be oppressed, and that the mechanic should not oppress the farmer."[31] Rather than sales from open wagons, a farmer's market in a paved or sheltered area could be rented out in sections for short terms so that produce or other goods could be sold by individuals. The Prophet also approved the establishment of a cooperative store, calculated to "give employment to our own mechanics, by supplying the raw material, and manufacturing all sorts of domestic goods, and furnishing the necessaries and comforts of life on the lowest possible terms."[32]

The Prophet was well aware of the best policy to pursue in building a great city. The following remarks in a sermon delivered on the temple grounds in 1843 are typical:

"I will now speak a little on the economy of this city. I think there are too many merchants among you. I would like to see more wool and raw materials instead of manufactured goods, and the money be brought here to pay the poor for manufacturing goods. Set our women to work. . . . Instead of going abroad to buy goods, lay your money out in [this] country, and buy grain, cattle, flax, wool, and work it up yourselves. . . . We cannot build up a city on merchandise. . . . The temporal economy of this people should be to establish and encourage manufactures, and not to take usury for their money. I do not want to bind the poor here to starve. . . .

"Some say it is better to give to the poor than build the Temple. The building of the Temple has sustained the poor who were driven from Missouri, and kept them from starving. . . .

"Oh, all ye rich men of the Latter-day Saints from abroad, I would invite you to bring up some of your money . . . and give it to the Temple. We want iron, steel, spades, and quarrying and mechanical tools.

"It would be a good plan to get up a forge to manufacture iron, and bring in raw materials of every variety, and erect manufacturing establishments of all kinds, and surround the rapids with mills and machinery."[33]

In order to achieve these goals the Prophet established a joint-stock corporation called the Nauvoo Agricultural and Mechanical Association, which raised money through the sale of stock "to promote agriculture and husbandry in all its branches, and for the manufacture of flour, lumber, and such other useful articles as are necessary for the ordinary purposes of life."[34]

Joseph was always more concerned with the people and their needs than with "system." People were more important than profits; people's welfare was more important than regulations. In a private letter written shortly after Christmas 1841 to Edward Hunter, a wealthy landowner who was about to migrate from Pennsylvania, the Prophet confessed that he had spent the previous day behind the counter in his store, "dealing out goods as steady as any clerk you ever saw," to provide goods for his people who, because of the tardy arrival of sugar, molasses, raisins, and other condiments, had been obliged to go without their usual Christmas and New Year's dinner. "I love to wait upon the Saints," he wrote, "and be a servant to all, hoping that I may be exalted in the due time of the Lord."[35]

The steady flow of goods from the shelves and bins of his store, however, did not indicate that the enterprise was prospering; in fact it was approaching insolvency. Joseph was more interested in supplying the people with much needed goods than with the financial integrity of the business.[36] A visitor to Nauvoo said that he had "readily learned" the magic by which the Prophet had built up the city. "They believe in him," he wrote, "and in his honesty."[37]

In 1843 the Prophet turned his attention to harnessing the river, which swept around the Nauvoo peninsula, falling enough to provide an adequate head of water to drive machinery. On 22 November 1843, Joseph recorded in his journal that he had walked down to the river "to look at the stream, rocks, etc." He suggested that they petition Congress for "a grant to make a canal over the falls, or a dam to turn the water to the city, so that we might erect mills and other machinery." The city council passed a facilitating ordinance, and plans were developed. But politics and persecution preoccupied the Prophet, and he was assassinated in June 1844; so nothing more was done in his lifetime.[38]

The industries that were planned for Nauvoo were large and extensive, but the Saints lacked capital, large-scale power sources, and machinery. Nevertheless, their progress was phenomenal. By the time of the Prophet's death there were, in Nauvoo, two steam sawmills, one equipped with a gristmill. There were several brickyards, a match factory, leather manufactory, tan yard, rope and cord maker, and lime kiln. As Robert Flanders found, there was a glove and strawbonnet shop, a brewery, a bakery and confectionery, a pottery, a tool factory, a carpenter's and joiner's shop, a water gristmill, a blacksmithy, and a cast-iron foundry. There was also a jeweler, gilder, and watchmaker; comb factory; spinning-wheel maker, cabinetmaker, printing office and book bindery, "and several tailors, weavers, cobblers, cordwainers, and wagoners."[39]

The city had an appealing look. The lots and streets were laid out "in nice order." As one English immigrant wrote, "We have many good brick houses, and others are frame, wood and log houses. . . . A great many are quite smart large brick houses, which would look well in any city. . . . Brick houses, stone, and others are building as fast as they can."[40]

But the days of Nauvoo were numbered. Joseph was arrested, mobs continued to threaten the city and outlying settlements, and a mob of men with blackened faces, mostly members of the state militia, broke into the jail in Carthage, Illinois, and killed the Prophet and his brother Hyrum. The anti-Mormon raids continued, and with pitifully inadequate protection from the state militia, the Saints left Nauvoo in the late winter and spring of 1846.

The "City of Joseph," as it had been renamed after the death of the Prophet, now lay deserted.

Joseph had proved to be an innovative, imaginative, compassionate, and aggressive leader. He had implemented a variety of economic and social programs designed to carry out the Lord's commandments. The Saints, highly committed to "the Lord's law," consecrated their time, talent, and material resources to realizing the goals embodied in these revelations. The Prophet's instructions, different for each phase of the Church's experience, always contributed to the building of the kingdom of God on earth. This spirit of consecration and stewardship created and energized a cooperative commonwealth of peoples that blossomed phoenix-like in the Great Basin, and indeed is alive and growing throughout the world today.[41] After Joseph's death, his associates declared that he had done more for the salvation of men in this world, save Jesus only, "than any other man that ever lived in it." (D&C 135:3.)

Notes

1. Cited in Leonard J. Arrington, *Great Basin Kingdom: An Economic History of the Latter-day Saints, 1830–1900* (Cambridge, Mass.: Harvard University Press, 1958), p. 6.

2. Emily M. Austin, *Mormonism; or, Life among the Mormons* (Madison, Wis.: 1882), pp. 63–64.

3. Cited in William G. Hartley, *"They Are My Friends": A History of the Joseph Knight Family, 1825–1850* (Provo, Utah: Grandin Book Co., 1986), p. 86.

4. "The Elders Stationed in Zion to the Churches Abroad . . . ," *The Evening and the Morning Star* 2 (July 1833): 110–11.

5. See *The Evening and the Morning Star* 1 (July 1832): [13].

6. Parley P. Pratt, *Autobiography of Parley Parker Pratt*, edited by his son Parley P. Pratt, 6th ed. (Salt Lake City, Utah: Deseret Book Co., 1966), pp. 72, 93.

7. Joseph Smith, *History of The Church of Jesus Christ of Latter-day Saints*, 7 vols., 2d ed. rev., ed. B. H. Roberts (Salt Lake City, Utah: The Church of Jesus Christ of Latter-day Saints, 1932–51), 1:364–65.

8. See especially Richard H. Jackson, "The Mormon Village: Genesis and Antecedents of the City of Zion Plan," *BYU Studies* 17 (Winter 1977): 223–40.

9. Smith, *History of the Church,* 1:358.

10. "Zion, the City Plat," in B. H. Roberts, ed., *A Comprehensive History of The Church of Jesus Christ of Latter-day Saints,* 6 vols. (Salt Lake City, Utah: The Church of Jesus Christ of Latter-day Saints, 1930), 1:311–12.

11. Letter to the Saints from the First Presidency, *Elders Journal* [Far West, Missouri], Aug. 1838, p. 53.

12. Smith, *History of the Church,* 2:295–96.

13. Smith, *History of the Church,* 3:231.

14. Marvin S. Hill, C. Keith Rooker, and Larry T. Wimmer, "The Kirtland Economy Revisited," *BYU Studies* 17 (Summer 1977): 403.

15. "Our Village," in *Messenger and Advocate* [Kirtland] 3 (Jan. 1837): 444.

16. Dean C. Jessee, "The Kirtland Diary of Wilford Woodruff, 25 November 1836," *BYU Studies* 12 (Summer 1972): 371. Ampersand changed to *and.*

17. Hill, et al., "The Kirtland Economy Revisited," p. 405.

18. *Journal of Discourses,* 26 vols. (Liverpool: Latter-day Saints' Book Depot, 1855–1886), 1:215; 3:121. Also Edwin F. Parry, *Stories about Joseph Smith the Prophet* (Salt Lake City, Utah: Deseret News Press, 1934), pp. 126–28, where there is an account of the Prophet's giving away boots from his store when he saw that some of his men had bruised feet.

19. Hill, et al., "The Kirtland Economy Revisited," p. 433.

20. Ibid., p. 449.

21. "A History of the Persecution of the Church . . . ," *Times and Seasons* [Nauvoo, Illinois], 1 (Mar. 1840): 66.

22. Smith, *History of the Church,* 3:47.

23. Smith, *History of the Church,* 3:63–64.

24. John Corrill, *A Brief History of the Church of Christ of Latter-day Saints* (St. Louis, 1839), p. 46, as cited in Leonard J. Arrington, Feramorz Y. Fox, and Dean L. May, *Building the City of God: Community and Cooperation among the Mormons* (Salt Lake City, Utah: Deseret Book Co., 1976), p. 36.

25. Smith, *History of the Church,* 3:251.

26. Smith, *History of the Church,* 6:37–38.

27. Smith, *History of the Church,* 4:93.

28. Smith, *History of the Church,* 6:265.

29. Smith, *History of the Church,* 5:8.

30. Smith, *History of the Church,* 5:270.

31. Smith, *History of the Church,* 5:271.

32. Smith, *History of the Church,* 6:263.

33. Smith, *History of the Church,* 6:58–59.

34. Robert Bruce Flanders, *Nauvoo: Kingdom on the Mississippi* (Urbana: University of Illinois Press, 1965), pp. 148–50.

35. Smith, *History of the Church,* 4:492.

36. Flanders, *Nauvoo*, p. 162.

37. Smith, *History of the Church,* 4:381.

38. Flanders, *Nauvoo*, pp. 150–53.

39. Ibid., pp. 153–54.

40. Letter of James Needham, Nauvoo, 7 July 1843, to Thomas Ward, Church Place, England, in *Millennial Star* 4 (Oct. 1843): 87–88.

41. In addition to the sources cited, the following have been especially helpful: Kent W. Huff, *Joseph Smith's United Order: Instrument of the Gathering and Forerunner of the Corporation of the President* (Privately distributed, 1987); Mario S. DePillis, "The Development of Mormon Communitarianism, 1826–1846" (Ph.D. diss., Yale University, 1960); Lyndon W. Cook, *Joseph Smith and the Law of Consecration* (Provo, Utah: Grandin Book Co., 1985); Milton V. Backman, Jr., *The Heavens Resound: A History of the Latter-day Saints in Ohio, 1830–1838* (Salt Lake City, Utah: Deseret Book Co., 1983); Leland H. Gentry, "A History of the Latter-day Saints in Northern Missouri from 1838 to 1839" (Ph.D. dissertation, Brigham Young University, 1965); and Max H. Parkin, "A History of the Latter-day Saints in Clay County, Missouri, from 1833 to 1837" (Ph.D. dissertation, Brigham Young University, 1976).

Chapter 8

Joseph Smith and the Beginning of Mormon Record Keeping

Dean C. Jessee
Research Historian, Joseph Fielding Smith Institute
for Church History, Brigham Young University

Responding to an inquiry by Hubert H. Bancroft in 1880 on how the Mormons came to have an Historian's and Recorder's office when other people "generally are so careless of recording their proceedings," Franklin D. Richards wrote that "at the organization of this Church the Lord commanded Joseph, the Prophet, to keep a record of his doings in the great and important work that he was commencing to perform. It thus became a duty imperative."[1] This 1830 revelation referred to by Franklin Richards not only initiated record keeping among the Latter-day Saints but also placed Joseph Smith at the center of that enterprise. (See D&C 21:1.) It was the inspiration of his mind and the effect of his influence that laid the groundwork for the vigorous record keeping that has characterized the Latter-day Saints. Although some of his contemporaries played a more visible role in preserving Church records and writing its history, Joseph Smith was the dominant personality in establishing that work.

Record keeping as currently conceived in the Church is a complex process that embodies several related and highly specialized functions. These include procedures for creating records; their periodic and orderly collection and channeling into the archives; skills for identifying, describing, organizing, arranging, filing, and preserving the materials collected; facilities for housing the records; personnel to administer the whole process; and others to assimilate, chronicle, and interpret the material for the understanding and benefit of Church members and other interested persons.

When Joseph Smith read the revelation that initiated record keeping to the small group assembled in the Whitmer home at Fayette, New York, in April 1830, the principles of record keeping and writing history — well defined in our time — did not exist. Dewey's classification system for arranging printed works on a shelf and Shellenberg's exposition of archival theory were far in the future. Furthermore, history as a profession had not yet been born but rather was a branch of literature in a world where it was not uncommon to borrow other writers' thoughts, a world where primary sources could be altered at will, a world where history was a form of promotional literature with a deep sense of mission.[2]

If the first words given to the newly established Church in 1830 bluntly announced the need for records, further instruction and years of diligent work were required to create essential documents and develop methods for handling and housing them. In his effort to "move forward the cause of Zion," Joseph Smith saw the keeping of records as essential for perpetuating the divinely instituted work he had been called to perform, for understanding the ideas and ideals upon which it rested; he saw the records and their use as the thread that would bind one generation of Saints to the next.

In considering the role Joseph Smith played in the establishment of record keeping among the Latter-day Saints, it should be noted to begin with that there was little in his New England background to motivate such activity or to foster necessary skills. He no doubt learned of the need for records from his youthful study of the Bible and his work on the Book of Mormon. Several statements in the Book of Mormon deal with the importance of records: "I have received a commandment of the Lord that I should make these plates, for the special purpose that there should be an account engraven of the ministry of my people." (1 Nephi 9:3.) "We labor diligently to engraven these words upon plates, hoping that our beloved brethren and our children will receive them with thankful hearts, and look upon them that they may learn with joy and not with sorrow, neither with contempt, concerning their first parents. For, for this intent have we written these things, that they may know that we knew of Christ." (Jacob 4:3–4.) "It has hitherto been wisdom in God that these things should be preserved; for behold, they have enlarged the memory of this people, yea, and convinced many of the error of their ways, and brought them to the knowledge of their God unto the salvation of their souls." (Alma 37:8.) "I do make a record of the things which I have seen with mine own eyes. And I know the record which I make to be a just and a true record." (3 Nephi 5:17–18.) "I command you that ye shall write these sayings after I am gone." (3 Nephi 16:4.) "Their names were taken, that they might be remembered and nourished by the good word of God, to keep them in the right way." (Moroni 6:4.) Whatever Joseph Smith's understanding of record keeping may have been before 6 April 1830, his motivation to keep records came at that time; his influence established lasting precedents.

While specific details governing the creation and management of records were not given, early revelations designated the first records that were kept. The Articles and Covenants, later known as Doctrine and Covenants, section 20, stipulated that "each priest or teacher, who is ordained by a priest, is to take a certificate from him at the time, which when presented to an elder, he is to give him a license, which shall authorize him to perform the duty of his calling."[3]

Minutes of the elders conference held 9 June 1830 list ten men who received their licenses that day, and later meetings indicate the continuation of the practice.[4] Licenses were issued to those holding the priesthood and missionaries as a tangible evidence of authority and association with the Church. The issuance or retraction of a person's license designated his standing in the Church. Following an October 1835 altercation with his brother Joseph, William Smith returned his license as a symbol of resignation from his quorum; and in November when one member who had withdrawn from the Church made application to return, he was given a "severe chastisement" and his license was restored to him. At a conference in Massachusetts in 1835, one elder had his license taken from him because of gambling, and another, in consequence of a longstanding disagreement with his wife. A third elder was excommunicated, and upon refusing to give up his license, his excommunication was ordered to be published in the *Messenger and Advocate*.[5]

By 1836 it became necessary to evaluate the licensing procedure in the Church. At a meeting of the priesthood bearers, presided over by Joseph Smith, on 24 February, a committee consisting of Oliver Cowdery, Orson Hyde, and Sylvester Smith was appointed "to draft and make regulations concerning licenses," and Thomas Burdick was appointed to officiate as recorder of licenses and receive pay for his services.[6] A week later, Joseph Smith again presided when the assembled priesthood bearers heard Oliver Cowdery read the resolutions respecting licenses formulated by the committee.

Because records of several conferences[7] held by elders of the Church and because ordinations of members "in many cases" had been imperfectly kept since the organization of the Church, six resolutions governing licenses were adopted at this February 1836 meeting:

1. Henceforth, all licenses were to be recorded by a clerk in a book kept at Kirtland, each license endorsed on the back by the clerk, and the precise reference given to its notation in the general record.

2. Two people were appointed to sign licenses, one as chairman and the other as clerk of the conference, and to deliver the same to the recording clerk.

3. All conferences were to follow these rules.

4. All members of the Church were to forward their licenses, accompanied by a certificate signed by the chairman and clerk of the conference or branch where the person resided, to the conference clerk, who would then issue a new license. Licenses signed, recorded, and endorsed were to be considered valid in any country where clergy were entitled to special privileges.

5. The recording clerk must publish quarterly a list of those for whom he had recorded licenses during the previous quarter.

6. The elders were directed to appoint a chairman and clerk of conference to act in the absence of the regular chairman and clerk.[8]

The implementation of these resolutions is evident in the records that followed. For example, in accordance with the first and second resolutions, the elder's license issued to Joseph Smith was signed by Sidney Rigdon as Chairman, and Oliver Cowdery, Clerk; and one issued to Charles C. Rich was signed by Joseph Smith, Chairman, and Frederick G. Williams, Clerk. A notation by Thomas Burdick, Recording Clerk, on the reverse side of the Joseph Smith license issued at Kirtland, Ohio, 21 March 1836, indicates that the document was recorded the same day "in the License Records, Book A. Page 1," and the Charles Rich license was recorded on 18 April in Book A, page 85. In addition, records of the Nauvoo high priests quorum contain a list of quorum members who had received their licenses and the dates of their ordinations.[9]

In compliance with resolution number five, a list of "ministers of the gospel" whose licenses had been recorded during the previous quarter was published by Thomas Burdick in the *Messenger and Advocate* beginning in June 1836 and continuing for five successive quarters. The June listing was evidently an attempt to include all who had previously received their licenses in the Church.

The list counted 244 elders, 11 priests, 3 teachers, and 5 deacons, and included Joseph Smith and his counselors in the First Presidency, Oliver Cowdery, and members of the Council of the Twelve. The succeeding quarterly listings were not as extensive—the largest being 52 elders in the September 1836 issue of the paper.[10] Almost from the beginning, clerks were appointed in the branches to record licenses and keep other local records. In August 1835 instructions were given that "the clerk of every church should keep a record of all marriages solemnized in his branch."[11]

In addition to licenses, the Articles and Covenants of the Church also designated the creation of membership records, consisting of a letter or certificate that would identify the bearer as a member of the Church in good standing. According to instructions, the certificate was to be presented to the presiding officer of the branch with which the bearer desired to affiliate.[12] "It shall be the duty of the several churches, composing this church of Christ, to send one or more of their teachers to attend the several conferences, held by the elders of this church, with a list of the names of the several members, uniting themselves to the church since the last conference, or send by the hand of some priest, so that there can be kept a regular list of all the names of the members of the whole church, in a book kept by one of the elders; Whomsoever the other elders shall appoint from time to time: And also, if any have been expelled from the church, so that their names may be blotted out of the general church record of names. Any member removing from the church where he resides, if going to a church where he is not known, may take a letter certifying that he is a regular member and in good standing; Which certificate may be signed by any elder or priest, if the member receiving the letter is personally acquainted with the elder or priest, or it may be signed by the teachers or deacons of the church."[13]

As conferences met, representatives from the conference branches reported the membership in their jurisdiction. For example, at the Freedom, New York, conference already referred to, it was reported that of the twelve branches that made up the conference, the Freedom branch consisted of 65 members; Rushford, 28; Burns, 30; Holland, 15; and Aurora, 4; but the numbers of the remaining six branches could not be ascertained.[14]

These records show that by 1835, procedures for numbering all the members of the Church were being established, but they were not always followed nor did all records survive. Hence, a comprehensive and accurate enumeration of "all the names of the members of the whole Church" from the beginning was not possible. Responding in 1843 to an editor who was compiling information for a volume containing a history of religious denominations in the United States, Joseph Smith noted, "There are no correct data by which the exact number of members comprising this . . . Church . . . can be known."[15]

In addition to licenses and certificates of membership, early Church records also included minutes of meetings. Those who met at the 6 April 1830 organization meeting of the Church at Fayette, New York, evidently did not keep a memorandum, or official report, of what transpired that day. In response to the revelation Joseph Smith received there commanding the keeping of records, however, minutes of meetings became a regular institution, beginning with Oliver Cowdery's report of the elders conference at Fayette on 9 June 1830. Cowdery recorded the proceedings and was "appointed to keep the Church record and Conference minutes until the next conference." At the second conference of the elders, also held at the Whitmer home in Fayette, New York, David Whitmer was "appointed to keep the Church records." When the elders met in Kirtland on 9 April 1831, John Whitmer was given the record-keeping responsibility previously assigned to Cowdery and David Whitmer.[16]

Joseph Smith emphasized the value of keeping complete and accurate minutes, when he addressed the newly organized Quorum of the Twelve in 1835: he began, "I have something to lay before this council . . . which they will find to be of great importance," then told them that if he had in his possession every important decision regarding doctrine and duties since the beginning of the Church, that record would be of "incalculable worth to the saints"; however, he lamented, "we have neglected to keep records of such things, thinking that perhaps they would never benefit us afterwards." And because such records were not kept, "we cannot bear record to the Church and to the world, of the great and glorious manifestations which have been made to us with that degree of power and authority which we otherwise could." He then outlined a course the Twelve could pursue that would benefit them. If every time they assembled, in addition to appointing someone to preside, they would call one or more to keep a record of their proceedings, their important decisions would ever after "remain upon record as law." He told them that during their meetings their deliberations might not seem important, but later they would find them of "infinite worth." He warned them that if they were to discuss important matters and make decisions and fail to record them, "by and by you will be driven to straits from which you will not be able to extricate yourselves, not being in a sufficient situation to bring your faith to bear with sufficient perfection or power to obtain the desired information." By neglecting to keep a record, "the spirit may withdraw and God may be angry, and . . . knowledge of infinite importance . . . is lost"; and the cause would be "slothfulness or neglect to appoint a man to occupy a few moments in writing." The Prophet then prophesied that if the Twelve failed to keep adequate records, "the time will come when . . . you will fall by the hands of unrighteous men." He concluded by promising them that if they would be careful to keep a record of their proceedings, "it will be one of the most important and interesting records ever seen." In conformity with the instruction received that day, the Twelve appointed William McLellin and Orson Hyde as their clerks, and the proceedings of the meeting were recorded.[17]

The format of early meetings in the Church was to choose a moderator or chairman to preside and a clerk to record the proceedings. Records containing minutes of early Church quorums and other organizations that survive include those of the Kirtland, Missouri, and Illinois high councils, the Quorum of the Twelve, the Kirtland elders quorum, the seventies, and the Nauvoo Relief Society.

Another type of record produced under Joseph Smith's direction in the early 1830s contained copies of patriarchal blessings. The first blessing book includes an account of the meeting held 18 December 1833 in which Joseph Smith's father was ordained a patriarch under the hands of the Church presidency. Preceding the ordination, the Prophet, "by vision and the spirit of prophecy," blessed his father's family, and his counselors in the presidency. Oliver Cowdery, who recorded the proceedings of the meeting, prefaced his report with his own personal statement as a witness of Joseph Smith's authority. Cowdery's description is the earliest substantial account of the Aaronic Priesthood restoration in Church annals.[18]

The blessing record also contains a report of a meeting and feast held at the home of Joseph Smith, Jr., on 9 December 1834, at which his father, the patriarch, reflected upon his own life and family, blessed them, and bore record of his son Joseph's prophetic calling and personal character.[19]

The systematic copying of blessings in the patriarchal record book was started in September 1835. According to the first recorder, Oliver Cowdery, "many blessings" were given before that, but a book for recording them was not obtained until that date. The recording procedure was to give the recipient a copy of his or her blessing at the time it was given, with the expectation that it would be returned to the patriarch to be recorded.[20]

Besides these records, another point of Joseph Smith's influence in record keeping in the early years of Mormonism was the writing of a Church history. Oliver Cowdery evidently produced the first historical narrative, but in March 1831 the Prophet asked John Whitmer to continue the history, because Cowdery had been given another responsibility. Whitmer told the Prophet he would "rather not do it" but added, "the will of the Lord be done, and if he desires it, I desire that he would manifest it through Joseph the Seer." Whereupon Joseph received a revelation stating that "John Whitmer should write and keep a regular history, and assist you my servant Joseph, in transcribing all things which shall be given you." The revelation charged Whitmer "to keep the Church record and history continually," because Oliver Cowdery had been "appointed to another office." Addressing Whitmer's feelings of inadequacy, the revelation declared, "it shall be given him, inasmuch as he is faithful, by the Comforter, to write these things."[21]

At "a special meeting of the Elders of the Church" at Kirtland, Ohio, on 9 April 1831, Whitmer's calling was confirmed, and he was "appointed to keep the Church record & History." After explaining that Oliver Cowdery had "written the commencement of the church history, commencing at the time of the finding of the plates, up to June 12th, 1831," Whitmer started his own chronicle with the words, "I shall proceed to continue this record."[22]

Later in the year 1831 John Whitmer was called by revelation to travel to Missouri with Oliver Cowdery to carry revelations intended for publication there. The revelation also directed him to "continue in writing and making a history of all the important things which he shall observe and know, concerning my church. . . . Let my servant John Whitmer travel many times from place to place, and from church to church, that he may the more easily obtain knowledge: preaching and expounding, writing, copying, selecting and obtaining all things which shall be for the good of the church, and for the rising generations."[23]

In the following summer Joseph Smith wrote to the Saints in Missouri and requested John Whitmer to number "the disciples that have arrived in Zion," determine how many had received their inheritances, and give "the standing of each branch of the church." Whitmer was further admonished "to remember the commandment to him to keep a history of the church . . . and be sure to show himself approved" in his calling.[24] In November, the Prophet again expressed his concern for Church records to the Missouri Saints: "It is the duty of the Lord's clerk whom he has appointed to keep a history and a general church record of all things that transpire in Zion and of all those who consecrate properties and receive inheritances legally from the bishop and also their manner of life and the faith and works and also of all the apostates who apostatize after receiving their inheritances."[25]

Whatever the historical records of the Church may have contained by 1832, they evidently did not adequately reflect Joseph Smith's own experience—so fundamental to Church history. Sometime in the summer of 1832 the Prophet became directly involved in the writing of Church history when he began alternately writing and dictating a work he designated "A History of the life of Joseph Smith Jr. an account of his marvelous experience and of all the mighty acts which he doeth in the name of Jesus Christ the son of the living God of whom he beareth record, and also an account of the rise of the church of Christ in the eve of time." Although this manuscript was discontinued after six pages, it contained the earliest account of the Prophet's First Vision, the only one written with his own hand.[26]

Two years later, another start was made on a Church history, a work that underwent three changes of format and involved Joseph Smith but was written entirely by Oliver Cowdery, Frederick G. Williams, Warren Parrish, and Warren Cowdery before it too was discontinued.[27] Finally, in 1838 the Prophet began the work that was eventually published under his name as the multivolume, documentary history of the Church.[28] According to George A. Smith, the plan of compiling was commenced by the Prophet: "extracting items of necessary information in regard to general and particular movements, from the Times & Seasons, Mill. Star, Wasp, Neighbor, and other publications, extracts from City Councils, Municipal Courts, and Mayor's Dockets and Legion Records, which were all kept under his direction; also the movements of the Church as found in Conference Minutes, High Council records, and the records of the several quorums, together with letters and copies preserved on file; also noted remarkable occurrences throughout the world, and compiled them under date of transaction, according to the above plan which he while in prison just previous to his murder requested Elder Willard Richards to continue."[29]

The records produced personally by Joseph Smith and other records created under his influence are the basic sources for understanding his life and the foundation years of Mormonism. His influence remained after his death, as institutional records he conceived continued to be written. Manuscript histories, such as the voluminous Brigham Young and John Taylor histories, and the Journal History of the Church, perpetuated the format he created.

Even in the later years of his life, as harrassment from his enemies and administrative responsibilities increased, Joseph Smith continued his active commitment to history. Writing from Liberty Jail in 1839, he urged "all the saints" to gather up knowledge of "all the facts, and sufferings and abuses put upon them . . . and also all the property and amount of damages . . . and also the names of all persons that have had a hand in their oppressions . . . and to take statements and affidavits; and also to gather up the libelous publications that are afloat; and all that are in the magazines, and the encyclopedias, and all the libelous histories that are published, and are writing, and by whom."[30]

Among the first official acts of the Church after the Saints had arrived in Illinois in 1839 was the conference, chaired by the Prophet, in which a committee was appointed to gather historical data. Consisting of Almon Babbitt, Erastus Snow, and Robert B. Thompson, the committee was directed to "obtain all the libelous reports and publications which have been circulated against our Church, as well as other historical matter connected with said Church, which they can possibly obtain."[31]

In March 1843, the Prophet told Willard Richards that the one thing he failed in as a historian was noticing current events, such as the weather, etc.[32] Two months later, the

Prophet told W. W. Phelps of a dream he had experienced that "the history must go ahead before anything [else]."[33] And later that year, when noise from a school hindered the writing of the history, Joseph told the schoolmaster he would have to find another place, "as the history must continue and not be disturbed."[34] To a gathering of the Saints in Nauvoo a month before he was killed, the Prophet rejoiced that during the past three years his "acts and proceedings" had been recorded by "efficient clerks in constant employ" who had accompanied him everywhere "and carefully kept my history, and they have written down what I have done, where I have been, and what I have said."[35]

When vicarious work for the dead was begun in Nauvoo, Joseph Smith wrote the Saints that a recorder should be present, an "eyewitness," and "let him hear with his ears, that he may testify of a truth. . . . And . . . let all the records be had in order, that they may be put in the archives of my holy temple."[36] Continuing his instruction a week later, the Prophet wrote that there should be "a recorder appointed in each ward of the city, who is well qualified for taking accurate minutes; and let him be very particular and precise in taking the whole proceedings, certifying in his record that he saw with his eyes, and heard with his ears, giving the date, and names, and so forth, and the history of the whole transaction." And in addition to the local clerks, "let there be a general recorder, to whom these other records can be handed. . . . Then the general church recorder can enter the record on the general church book."[37] The Nauvoo Temple records and those of temples that followed reflect the accuracy and precision advocated in this instruction; and in addition to preserving a record of the transactions contained therein, these provide a significant source of family history data.

Joseph Smith not only encouraged the production of institutional records but he was also a strong advocate of personal records. Oliver B. Huntington introduced his lengthy diary with the statement that the "one object that induces me to write" was the "requirement, oft repeated by the Prophet Joseph Smith that every man should keep a daily journal."³⁸ Wilford Woodruff attributed his "enthusiasm" as a diarist and keeper of records to instructions Joseph Smith had given the Twelve. He regarded it not only a privilege, but a duty, to keep an accurate account of his proceedings: "It is to this intent that I shall endeavor henceforth to keep a journal of my travels that when required of may give an account of my stewardship."³⁹ The Prophet himself began his own diary on 27 November 1832 for the purpose of making "a minute account of all things that come under my observation." His diary became the basis for the textual narrative of a large part of the History of the Church during his lifetime.

Speaking at a bishops' meeting in Salt Lake City in 1857, Wilford Woodruff emphasized "the importance of every Elder in Israel keeping a Journal, or history of things as they transpire" and referred to Joseph Smith's early regrets "for not writing or caus[ing] to be written the dealings of God with this people." Woodruff "strongly urged on the Bishops to keep an account of how they spend their time, which would form an important History in Generations to come."⁴⁰

Once records are created, an important aspect of record keeping is the channeling of the records into a depository for preservation and safekeeping. Perhaps the earliest effort to collect and preserve documents of importance to the Church was undertaken in 1832 when Joseph Smith and his newly appointed clerk, Frederick G. Williams, began gathering correspondence, revelations, and other writings of importance and copying them into blank books. This was the beginning of three such volumes created during the Prophet's lifetime. The first item copied into the letter book was a letter of Joseph Smith to W. W. Phelps, dated 27 November 1832.⁴¹ The arrangement of subsequent materials indicates that after copying the 27 November letter, six earlier items were evidently located and copied before a chronological sequence resumed. Joseph Smith's personal involvement in the copy work is seen from his handwriting on six of the first thirteen pages and on later documents in the book. In addition to the handwriting of the Prophet, the writing of others close to him in the record-keeping work also appears in the volumes, including the writing of Orson Hyde, Oliver Cowdery, John Whitmer, James Mulholland, and Howard Coray. Much of the correspondence and other documentary source material pertaining to the Church between 1832 and 1843, later used in the Prophet's History, are contained in these books.

Another volume, kept concurrently with the first letter book, contained copies of revelations; and like the letter book, it reveals a personal involvement of the Prophet in the copy work. This volume, titled "Kirtland Revelations," contains the earliest known manuscript copy of some of the revelations given to the Church before 1835.

The process of gathering and preserving early records was not always a smooth one. According to Joseph Smith's History, one of the factors that complicated record keeping during his lifetime was the "treachery" of some who had assisted in that work. When John Whitmer left the Church in 1838, he kept the history he had been designated by revelation to write seven years previous. From Far West, Caldwell County, Missouri in 1844, Whitmer wrote William Phelps, who was assisting with the Joseph Smith History, and offered to sell the earlier history "at a fair price." Whitmer told Phelps that the Saints had land in Missouri "which is going to distruction," and the timber "prety much destroyed." His proposition was, "If you will come here in the spring I will sell to you the history for property &c. provided we can agree as to price." And he added, "I think there will be but little difficulty in that."[42]

No doubt chagrined at the prospects of a former Church historian bargaining to return an official history, Willard Richards, the Church recorder and historian at the time, responded: "We have already compiled about 800 pages of church history (Large Demi, closely written one page probably contains about 4 times the amount of matter of 1 which you wrote) which covers all the ground of which you took notes, therefore anything which you have in the

shape of church history would be of little or no consequence to the church at large."[43]

Although a small work by comparison with the Joseph
Smith History referred to by Richards, the Whitmer History
nevertheless contained valuable information about the
early Church. Not until 1893 was a copy of the record finally
obtained. On 5 September of that year, during a history-
gathering assignment in the Midwest, Andrew Jenson visited George Schweich and David J. Whitmer, son of the
Book of Mormon witness David Whitmer, at Richmond,
Missouri, and was shown the John Whitmer History. Convinced that the manuscript was indeed the history written
by the former historian, Jenson was reluctantly allowed to
take "the old book with faded writing" to his hotel room,
where he spent an entire night copying it. "I was very
pleased . . . to obtain a copy of this old Whitmer record; . . . it is well known that he, when he apostatized,
refused to give up this record to the Church authorities;
and now, when found, we discovered that it contained
only a little of historical value. Yet John Whitmer recorded
events which are not recorded elsewhere."[44]

Another important volume that was nearly lost through
devious means was the first book of patriarchal blessings,
containing those given by Joseph Smith and his father.
Shortly after Joseph Smith, Sr., arrived at Far West, Missouri, from Kirtland, Ohio, with the book in 1838, Cyrus
Smalling, a dissenter from the Church, stole the record.
Approximately two years later, it was purchased from
Smalling by the Church agent at Kirtland, Oliver Granger.
But when Granger suddenly died in August 1841, the volume fell into the hands of his son, Gilbert, who claimed
it as his own property. The Prophet tried to obtain the
book from the young Granger during the settlement of his
father's estate in March 1842 but failed. Gilbert Granger
later sent it to Nauvoo to the care of his sister's husband,
Hiram Kimball, authorizing him to sell it to the Church.
When Joseph Smith learned Kimball had the record, he
recovered the book with a search warrant on 7 February
1843. But the wanderings of the record were not over. The

binding being worn and damaged and two-thirds of the book blank, it was taken apart and rebound.[45]

In 1845 William Smith, the patriarch, borrowed his father's patriarchal record and left Nauvoo without returning it. Five years later, William was living with Isaac Sheen in Covington, Kentucky, when a disagreement developed between them, and William left Covington without taking the record with him. Sheen kept the book and later gave it to his brother-in-law, Almon W. Babbitt, with instructions to sell it to the Church for three thousand dollars if possible but not to take less than five hundred dollars for it. After Babbitt was killed by Indians while crossing the plains in 1854, one of the administrators of his estate, Benjamin F. Johnson, took possession of the patriarchal record, knowing it belonged to the Church. Finally, on 31 January 1859 Johnson delivered the book into the hands of George A. Smith, the Church historian.[46]

The acquisition of records and the writing of history presupposes facilities for housing them. During the early years of the Church the writing of history and filing of records took place in a variety of locations, including the Prophet's home, the homes of those who assisted him, rooms in the Kirtland printing office and temple, his "smoke house," an upper room in his brick store, and a room in the Nauvoo temple. But even under the best conditions, heat, humidity, and frequent moves took their toll upon the records.[47]

There is little evidence of how Church records were transported and cared for during the early migrations of the Saints. When the Prophet suddenly left Kirtland by night in December 1837 to save himself from mob violence, followed by his family and the faithful population of the town, it is not known how the Church records were carried to Missouri, nor who transported them from Missouri to Illinois during the removal of the Saints in 1838–39. Family members or close friends, appointed to that responsibility, probably cared for the records, as they did when the Saints left Nauvoo for the Great Basin. The Prophet's History indicates that important records "were destroyed or lost" at the time of the driving of the people from Far West, Missouri.[48] And the early records bear physical evidence of hard times. George A. Smith, who later used the early sources for compiling the Prophet's History, wrote that "many records are nearly obliterated by time, damp, and dirt, others lost; some half worked into mouse nests, and many important events were never written except in the hearts of those who were concerned." He noted that his progress on the history was slowed because many of the Prophet's papers had been "badly kept, and seriously damaged during our migratory movements."[49]

Beginning with Oliver Cowdery, eight men were appointed to the office of general Church recorder or historian during Joseph Smith's lifetime, and at least two dozen others served the Prophet in a clerical capacity. Of these, some died, others left the Church, and the remainder were more or less competent and faithful in helping to further the historical responsibility given to Joseph Smith in 1830. John Whitmer, George Robinson, Warren Parrish, and John Corrill left the Church, taking important records or resources with them. Robert B. Thompson, at age thirty, and James Mulholland, at age thirty-five, both men of talent and productivity at a crucial time in the writing of the Prophet's History, died suddenly within two years of each other. Add to this the mobbing, the imprisonment, the harrassment, the heavy burden of administration, and the migrations of the Church from New York to Illinois, and one can understand the gaps, the periods of silence, and the lack of continuity that exist in the historical records of early decades of the Church.

The influence of Joseph Smith upon record keeping and writing of history among the Latter-day Saints is clearly seen in records produced during his lifetime and in the vigorous historical work that continued in the Church after his death. In his effort to accomplish the work he was called to do, and at the same time "disabuse the public mind" of falsehoods that militated to destroy his reputation, Joseph Smith's attention to history was a paramount feature of his life after 1830. For him, record keeping had three purposes: first, to perpetuate the heritage of the kingdom through the creation, preservation, transmission, and use of its historical resources; second, to strengthen the effectiveness of the Church's administrative structure by recording the decisions and actions of each branch of the organization; and third, to provide an avenue for each participant in the kingdom to give an account of his stewardship. As the work Joseph Smith helped establish increases in size and influence, his role in perpetuating the knowledge of that work becomes increasingly important.

Notes

1. Franklin D. Richards, "Bibliography," July 1880. Unless otherwise indicated, manuscript sources are in the Archives of The Church of Jesus Christ of Latter-day Saints, Salt Lake City, Utah.

2. Reference is made to T. R. Schellenberg, *The Management of Archives* (New York, 1965), and his *Modern Archives: Principles and Techniques* (Chicago, 1956). On historical writing in America, see Elmer Barnes, *A History of Historical Writing* (New York, 1963), and James Loewenberg, *American History in American Thought* (New York, 1973). Treatments of LDS historiography are in David J. Whittaker, "Historians and the Mormon Experience: A Sesquicentennial Perspective," in *The Eighth Annual Sidney B. Sperry Symposium* (Provo, Utah, 1980), pp. 293–327, and Howard C. Searle, "Early Mormon Historiography: Writing the History of the Mormons, 1830–1858," Ph.D. dissertation, UCLA, 1979.

3. Book of Commandments 24:44; Doctrine and Covenants 20:64. A pathbreaking study of licenses is Donald Q. Cannon, "Licensing in the Early Church," *BYU Studies* 22 (Winter 1982): 96–105.

4. Donald Q. Cannon and Lyndon W. Cook, *Far West Record: Minutes of The Church of Jesus Christ of Latter-day Saints, 1830–1844* (Salt Lake City, Utah: Deseret Book Co., 1983), p. 1.

5. Diary of Joseph Smith, 31 Oct. 1835; 22 Nov. 1835; Joseph Smith, *History of The Church of Jesus Christ of Latter-day Saints*, 7 vols., 2d ed. rev., ed. B. H. Roberts (Salt Lake City, Utah: The Church of Jesus Christ of Latter-day Saints, 1932–51), 2:241.

6. Diary of Joseph Smith, 24 Feb. 1836; published in Dean C. Jessee, *The Personal Writings of Joseph Smith* (Salt Lake City, Utah: Deseret Book Co., 1984), p. 163. See also Diary of Oliver Cowdery under same date; published in Leonard J. Arrington, "Oliver Cowdery's Kirtland, Ohio, Sketch Book," *BYU Studies* 12 (Summer 1972): 424–25.

7. Before the organization of wards and stakes, early Church units consisted of branches and conferences. Periodically, a conference was held in a central location to which surrounding branches would send represen-

tatives. For example, the conference at Freedom, New York, in 1835 extending from Lodi on the west to Avon on the east, and from the Pennsylvania border on the south to Lake Ontario to the north, consisted of twelve branches: Freedom, Rushford, Portage, Grove, Burns, Genesee, Avon, Java, Holland, Aurora, Greenwood, and Niagara. And the Black River Conference embraced "all the northern part" of the state of New York. Smith, *History of the Church,* 2:224–25.

8. Kirtland Council Minutes, 3 Mar. 1836; the proceedings were published in *Latter Day Saints' Messenger and Advocate* 2:266–68; see also Jessee, *Personal Writings of Joseph Smith,* pp. 662–63.

Oliver Cowdery wrote, "I confess the hand of God in this matter, in giving me his Holy Spirit, to indite this valuable article, as by it the elders will enjoy their privileges as citizens, and the churches be freed from imposition." (Diary, 3 Mar. 1836.)

9. The Charles Rich License is located at the Daughters of Utah Pioneers Museum, Salt Lake City, Utah.

James Sloan, who served as the general Church clerk from 1841 to 1843, wrote that his business was "to keep a Record of the Names of the Members, give Licenses to the Elders Ordained to Preach," and also to record the baptisms for the dead. James Sloan to Andrew T. McReynolds, 27 Mar. 1842, published in "Mormon Nauvoo in 1842," *Journal of the Illinois State Historical Society* 46 [1953], pp. 313–14.

10. *Messenger and Advocate* 2:335–36, 383; 3:432, 472, 528. In the May *Advocate* the high priests quorum presidency published the form of a certificate to be given members of that quorum called to preside over churches and settle difficulties in the Church. *Messenger and Advocate* 3:511, 575.

11. Smith, *History of the Church,* 2:247.

12. See Cannon, "Licensing in the Early Church."

13. Book of Commandments 24:61–65; Doctrine and Covenants 20:81–84.

14. Smith, *History of the Church,* 2:224.

15. I. Daniel Rupp, *An Original History of the Religious Denominations at Present Existing in the United States* (Philadelphia, 1844), p. 409.

16. Cannon and Cook, *Far West Record,* pp. 1–3, 5.

17. "A Record of the Transactions of the Twelve Apostles of the Church of Christ," pp. 1–3. Ms. The report contains Joseph Smith's instructions, and much of the record book is in the hand of Orson Hyde.

18. Patriarchal Blessing Book 1, pp. 8–9. Ms. "He [Joseph Smith] was ordained by the angel John unto the lesser or Aaronic priesthood, in company with myself, in the town of Harmony, Susquehannah County, Pennsylvania, on Fryday, the 15th day of May, 1829, after which we repaired to the water, even to the Susquehannah River, and were baptised, he first ministering unto me and after - I to him. But before baptism, our souls were drawn out in mighty prayer - to know how we might obtain the blessings of baptism and of the Holy Spirit, according to the order of God, and we diligently saught for the right of the fathers and the authority of the holy priesthood, and the power to administer in the same. . . . Therefore, we

repaired to the woods, even as our father Joseph said we should, that is to the bush, and called upon the name of the Lord, and he answered us out of the heavens, and while we were in the heavenly vision the angel came down and bestowed upon us this priesthood; and then, as I have said, we repaired to the water and were baptized. After this we received the high and holy priestood but an account of this will be given elsewhere, or in another place."

19. "The Lord thy God has called thee by name out of the heavens: thou hast heard his voice from on high from time to time, even in thy youth. The hand of the angel of his presence has been extended toward thee by which thou hast been lifted up and sustained. . . . Thou hast been called, even in thy youth to the great work of the Lord: to do a work in this generation which no other man would do as thyself, in all things according to the will of the Lord. A marvelous work and a wonder has the Lord wrought by thy hand." Father Smith also focused on his son's early years: "From thy childhood thou hast meditated much upon the great things of [God's] law. Thou hast suffered much in thy youth; and the poverty and afflictions of thy father's family have been a grief to thy soul. Thou hast desired to see them delivered from bondage, for thou hast lov'd them with a perfect love. . . . Thou hast been an obedient son: the commands of thy father and the reproofs of thy mother, thou hast respected and obeyed." Patriarchal Blessing Book 1, p. 3. Ms.

20. Ibid., p. 16.

21. F. Mark McKiernan and Roger D. Launius, eds., *An Early Latter Day Saint History: The Book of John Whitmer* (Independence, Mo., 1980), p. 56; Book of Commandments 50; Doctrine and Covenants 47.

22. Cannon and Cook, *Far West Record,* p. 5; McKiernan and Launius, *An Early Latter Day Saint History,* pp. 25, 56.

The location of the Cowdery history, which was rumored to have "contained the record of the restoration of the Melchisedek Priesthood," was the object of a search in Missouri by Andrew Jenson in 1893. Evidently George Schweich, David Whitmer's brother-in-law, had communicated to the LDS Church historian, Franklin D. Richards, that the Cowdery history was in Missouri. When Andrew Jenson quizzed him, Schweich "did not think there was anything" in the Whitmer papers "bearing on this point, although he admitted that there was a whole box full of old documents which had not been examined since David Whitmer died." Jenson added, "If Mr. Schweich admits to you that they are in possession of the Oliver Cowdery record he denies it to me." Andrew Jenson to Franklin Richards, 14 Sept. 1893.

Schweich "conveyed the idea" to Jenson that Oliver Cowdery's papers were in possession of his heirs in Southwest City, Missouri. A letter by Maria Johnson, Oliver Cowdery's daughter, to David Whitmer in 1887 indicates that a chest containing a "great many letters and papers" belonging to Cowdery had become so "old and worn out" that "we burned them all up." Maria Johnson to David Whitmer, 14 Jan. 1887. Ms. RLDS Archives.

On the basis of the absence of a Cowdery manuscript, Richard L. Anderson has argued that references to Cowdery's history refer to his writing of early church documents and not to a narrative history. Richard L.

Anderson, "The Alvin Smith Story: Fact & Fiction," *Ensign,* Aug. 1987, pp. 65–67.

23. Doctrine and Covenants (1835 edition), section 28; see also current edition, 69:3, 7–8.

24. Joseph Smith to William W. Phelps, 31 July 1832; published in Jessee, *Personal Writings of Joseph Smith,* pp. 249–50.

25. Joseph Smith to William W. Phelps, 27 Nov. 1832; Jessee, *Personal Writings of Joseph Smith,* pp. 259–60.

26. Joseph Smith Letter Book 1, pp. 1–6. Ms. Jessee, *Personal Writings of Joseph Smith,* pp. 4–8.

27. Joseph Smith, "History of the Church," A-1. Ms.

28. Ibid. The 1834 history composes the first part of a large leather-bound book which was turned over and became the front cover for the 1838 History.

See also Dean C. Jessee, "The Writing of Joseph Smith's History," *BYU Studies* 11 (Summer 1971): 439–73, and "The Reliability of Joseph Smith's History," *Journal of Mormon History* 3 (1976): 23–46.

29. George A. Smith to Wilford Woodruff, 21 Apr. 1856. Ms.

30. Joseph Smith and others to the Church at Quincy, Illinois, 20 Mar. 1839. See also Doctrine and Covenants 123:1–5. The original text of the letter is published in Jessee, *Personal Writings of Joseph Smith,* pp. 389–407.

31. "Minutes of a General Conference held by the Church of the Latter Day Saints, at the Presbyterian Camp Ground New Quincy, Adams County, Illinois, on Saturday the 4th of May 1839." Ms. in hand of James Mulholland. Published in Smith, *History of the Church,* 3:344–45.

32. Diary of Joseph Smith, 4 Mar. 1843; Smith, *History of the Church,* 5:298.

33. Diary of Joseph Smith, 19 May 1843; Smith, *History of the Church,* 5:394.

34. Diary of Joseph Smith, 7 Nov. 1843; Smith, *History of the Church,* 6:66.

35. Joseph Smith address, 26 May 1844, in Andrew F. Ehat and Lyndon W. Cook, eds., *The Words of Joseph Smith* (Provo, Utah: Religious Studies Center, Brigham Young University, 1980), p. 374; Smith, *History of the Church,* 4:409.

36. Joseph Smith to the Saints in Nauvoo, 1 Sept. 1842; published as Doctrine and Covenants 127.

37. Joseph Smith to the Church, 6 Sept. 1842; published as Doctrine and Covenants 128.

38. Oliver B. Huntington, Autobiography and Journal, p. 25; Type-script, Brigham Young University, Provo, Utah.

39. Diary of Wilford Woodruff, 20 Jan. 1872, and the introduction to the first volume of his diaries.

40. Minutes of Presiding Bishop's Meetings with Bishops, 17 Mar. 1857. Ms.

41. According to his diary, on 5 December 1832 Joseph Smith was "copying letters."

42. John Whitmer to William W. Phelps, 8 Jan. 1844. Ms.

43. Willard Richards to John Whitmer, 23 Feb. 1844.

44. Andrew Jenson, *Autobiography of Andrew Jenson* (Salt Lake City, Utah, 1938), pp. 208–9.

45. The wanderings of the patriarchal blessing book are recorded in a statement signed by George A. Smith and Wilford Woodruff inside the front cover of the book; the statement is also entered in Journal History of the Church, 11 February 1859.

The blank two-thirds of the blessing book was subsequently rebound and used as Volume B-1 of Joseph Smith's history of the Church beginning in August 1843 when Volume A-1 of the manuscript of the history was filled.

On the dating of the first writing in Volume B-1, see Diary of Willard Richards, 24 August 1843. References to efforts of Joseph Smith to obtain the blessing book are in Smith, *History of the Church,* 4:542–43; 5:265.

46. Statement of George A. Smith and Wilford Woodruff.

47. On 29 October 1835, when Warren Parrish began writing for Joseph Smith, the Prophet noted that after meeting with the high council in Kirtland that day, he "returned to our writing room" and then went to Frederick Williams' place, obtained his journal or history, "returned home, and my scribe commenced writing in my journal a history of my life." Diary of Joseph Smith. Ms.

In December 1842, the Prophet "called on William W. Phelps to get the historical documents," and afterward "commenced reading and revising history." Smith, *History of the Church,* 5:198.

48. Smith, *History of the Church,* 3:323.

49. George A. Smith to John L. Smith, 28 Feb. 1855; George A. Smith to C. C. Waller, 31 July 1855. Mss.

Chapter 9

Hiram, Ohio: Tribulation

Susan Easton Black
Associate Professor of Church History and Doctrine
Brigham Young University

Twenty-five-year-old Joseph Smith was well accustomed to verbal threats and abuse. He wrote, "They were persecuting me, reviling me, and speaking all manner of evil against me falsely." (Joseph Smith–History 1:25.) But it was not until 1832, in Hiram, Ohio, that the abuse escalated from verbal to physical brutality.

Hiram mobs introduced to Joseph a new depth of hostile fury, anger, and rage. Joseph's hope of Hiram's becoming a continuing refuge for pondering the scriptures and translating the Bible ended abruptly when a violent mob sought to do him bodily harm or even take his life on 24 March 1832.

It is ironic that this barbaric scene occurred in an avowed Christian farming community.[1] Yet one night the inhabitants of this town formed a vicious mob bent on savagery. This seeming contradiction between upright and vicious prevailed in the town because Hiram shared with other societies the English tradition of "appropriate" mob rule. Although not legal, the practice of tarring and feathering was considered a right and even a responsibility of Hiram's citizens under "specified" mob circumstances. Southern abolitionists, wife beaters, harsh government agents, scandalously immoral persons, and a prophet were its victims.[2]

The instigators of this cruelty had once been followers of Joseph. These erstwhile followers had accepted Church membership, been blessed with fellowship, received callings from God, and witnessed miracles. Yet they rejected their blessings, denounced Joseph as a deceiver, and chose to destroy him. They themselves became the deceived, for they lost their heritage with the Saints of God; Joseph became the blessed, because he endured, with undiminished love and trust in God, the persecution of tar and feathers.

Let us analyze the setting, the people, and the events that led to the brutal attack on the young prophet.

Entree to Hiram

Events leading to Joseph Smith's brief yet highly significant experience in Hiram, Ohio, began in the nearby community of Kirtland. In 1831, the people of Kirtland experienced an unusual eruption of excitement over spiritual manifestations. (D&C 50:2.) This excitement was heightened by the arrival of Joseph Smith, who professed to be a prophet of God.

Many church-going citizens of Kirtland and the neighboring vicinity, most out of curiosity and a few out of a sincere desire to know if Joseph had a prophetic calling, visited him. Among those who came were fifty-three-year-old John Johnson[3] and his wife, Elsa, from Hiram, and Ezra Booth[4], a Methodist minister from nearby Mantua.

During their visit with Joseph, a miracle occurred. As they conversed on the godly gifts that had been conferred during Christ's ministry, one of the visitors exclaimed, "Here is Mrs. Johnson with a lame arm; has God given any power to man on earth to cure her?" Joseph, taking Elsa's hand, proclaimed, "Woman, in the name of the Lord Jesus Christ I command thee to be whole."[5] Immediately Elsa raised her arm, even though she had been afflicted by chronic rheumatism in her shoulder. By accounts of both believers and nonbelievers, she was thereafter able to do even heavy scrubbing without difficulty or pain.[6]

A later critic discounted the possibility of a divine miracle: "The company were awe-stricken at the infinite presumption of the man, and the calm assurance with which he spoke. The sudden mental and moral shock—I know not how better to explain the well attested fact—electrified the rheumatic arm."[7]

Despite this skeptical view of the event, the result was an impressive healing followed by the baptism of John Johnson and his wife and the Methodist minister in the spring of 1831. After baptism, John and Elsa returned to their farmhouse in Hiram. Ezra Booth accompanied them; he had been called to serve a mission there.

Ezra's brief mission included a visit to Hiram's Campbellite minister, Symonds Ryder.[8] At this visit, Booth requested an opportunity to speak to Ryder's congregation. This request was granted. Booth's remarks concerning Joseph so impressed Ryder that he sought audience with the Prophet in Kirtland.

Little is known of the particulars of Ryder's visit to Joseph in Kirtland, except that Ryder read a newspaper describing great destruction caused by an earthquake in Peking, China. When he read the account, he recalled having heard a young Mormon girl predicting the event. A skeptical account continues: "This appeal to the superstitious part of his nature was the final weight in the balance and he threw the whole power of his influence upon the side of Mormonism."[9]

He accepted baptism in early June 1831, was ordained an elder on 6 June by Joseph Smith, Sr., and on 8 June was called to the ministry. (See D&C 52:37.)[10] When he received communication of his ministerial call signed by the Prophet Joseph Smith and Sidney Rigdon, "both in the letter he received and in the official commission to preach, however, his name was spelled R-i-d-e-r, instead of R-y-d-e-r . . . he thought if the 'Spirit' through which he had been called to preach could err in the matter of spelling his name, it might have erred in calling him to the ministry as well; or, in other words, he was led to doubt if he were called at all by the Spirit of God, because of the error in spelling his name!"[11]

Another historian indicated that Ryder's later apostasy was influenced by more than the misspelling of his name. He concluded that the reason was that Joseph "advocated communism of goods."[12] Ryder confirmed this conclusion by writing of his misunderstanding of the law of consecration and stewardship:

"When they went to Missouri to lay the foundation of the splendid city of Zion, and also of the temple, they left their papers behind. This gave their new converts an opportunity to become acquainted with the internal arrangement of their church, which revealed to them the horrid fact that a plot was laid to take their property from them and place it under the control of Joseph Smith the prophet."[13]

Whatever his reasons, he not only left the Church but carried an intense determination to eradicate from all residents in Hiram what he saw as the seducing error of Mormonism. As Ryder shifted the whole power of his influence, first toward and then against the Mormons, his mentor, Booth, was following the same course.

At the June conference that yielded the orthographic turning point for Symonds Ryder, his gospel teacher, Ezra Booth, became a high priest. He immediately began serving as a missionary with Isaac Morley, traveling through Ohio, Indiana, and Illinois to Missouri. (See D&C 52:23.) His mission was a disappointment to him and became the impetus for his determination to immediately leave the Church and denounce Joseph. In a series of nine letters that appeared in the *Ohio Star*, he elaborated on his experienced deception and the "Mormon menace."[14]

This action led to his censure at a conference held on 6 September 1831. In the minutes of the conference, Oliver Cowdery recorded, "Upon testimony satisfactory to this conference, it was voted that Ezra Booth be silenced from preaching as an Elder in this Church."[15] Obviously this silencing did not deter him and in fact may have encouraged him to preach and write further against Joseph Smith and Mormonism.

In late summer of 1831, Booth united with Ryder in planting the seeds of hatred toward Joseph and Mormonism in Hiram. This action annulled their previous effective missionary influence, noted by a community historian, A. S. Hayden: "Perhaps in no other place, except Kirtland, did the 'Latter-day Saints' gain a more permanent footing than in Hiram."[16] The seeds of hatred found fertile soil, since most "Hiramites left the Mormonites faster than they had ever joined them."[17]

Even as Booth and Ryder were trying to rid Hiram of the "Mormon menace," John Johnson was extending a cordial invitation to Joseph and his family to be his guests there. John had been a resident of Hiram since 1818. By September 1831, he could be referred to as a prosperous resident, owning a new farmhouse located on his 304-acre estate.[18]

Joseph and Sidney Rigdon viewed Johnson's invitation as the answer to the Lord's directive to "seek them a home, as they are taught through prayer by the Spirit." (D&C 63:65.) Thus, Joseph accepted his hospitality. He wrote, "On the 12th of September, I removed with my family to the township of Hiram, and commenced living with John Johnson."[19] Joseph's family then consisted of his wife, Emma, and the six-month-old twins of John Murdock, whom Joseph and Emma were rearing as their own.[20]

When Joseph removed to Hiram, so did several faithful followers, including Sidney Rigdon. Sidney had been aware of the efforts of Booth and Ryder to ignite hatred in the community. He challenged Ryder in the *Ohio Star* to a debate on the authenticity of the Book of Mormon. Ryder published his refusal to meet Sidney in a public forum, citing as his excuse Rigdon's "irascible temper, loquacious extravagance, impaired state of mind, and want of due respect to his superiors."[21]

Sidney responded to this indictment by claiming that Ryder "presented himself before the public as an accuser; he has been called upon before the same public, to support his accusations; and does he come forward and do it? nay, but seeks to hide himself behind a battery of reproach, and abuse, and low insinuations."²²

This name-calling and haranguing furthered sparked the smoldering fuels of mobocracy, but in the interim it did not prevent Joseph's stay in the Johnson farmhouse from being productive. The seven months in the home proved vital to the spiritual growth and definition of the Church. Joseph received at the home sixteen of the most important revelations on the development of the Church.²³ Among these revelations was section 76 on the three degrees of glory. Other significant events included a decision to compile and publish the Book of Commandments, five Church conferences, and the translation of portions of the Bible.

These months of uninterrupted spiritual outpourings came to an abrupt end on the night of 24 March, when violence displaced peace and crushed the sense of haven for Joseph, Sidney, and their families. Although Mormon and anti-Mormon sources disagree on the details, all agree that the local citizens tarred and feathered Joseph and Sidney. The local history praises "the good people of Hiram and some others," saying that they "went to the house of Smith and Rigdon, took them out, stripped them to the buff, and treated them to a coat of tar and feathers and a rail ride, which induced them to leave."²⁴

The Night of 24 March 1832

On 24 March 1832, Joseph and Emma were taking turns caring for the eleven-month-old twins, who were seriously ill with measles. As the evening began, Emma nursed the children while Joseph rested. His rest was violently interrupted when a dozen men with blackened faces burst into the room. Emma's screams of "Murder!" were too late. The men grabbed Joseph with vengeance. An example of their fury was provided by Carnot Mason, who jerked a handful of hair, including a patch of scalp, from Joseph's head, during the ruckus in the room.

The men had their "hands . . . in my hair,²⁵ and some

had hold of my shirt, drawers and limbs."[26] Joseph struggled to free himself. In this attempt, he cleared one leg, "with which I made a pass at one [Warren Waste who] fell on the door steps."[27] The mob threatened him with death if he continued his resistance. They swore "by G—, they would kill me if I did not be still, which quieted me."[28] The threat was punctuated by further death threats by Waste, who returned to the fray with a bloody hand, which he thrust in Joseph's face, muttering with a hoarse laugh, "Ge, gee, G— d— ye, I'l fix ye."[29]

True to his threat, he seized Joseph by his throat and choked him until he lost consciousness. In this state, Joseph was carried by the mobbers some thirty yards from the farmhouse. As consciousness returned, he saw men "disguised with colored faces and stimulated by whiskey" coming from every direction. Symonds Ryder later described them more favorably as "a company formed of citizens from Shalersville, Garrettsville, and Hiram."[30] These men were known to be Campbellites, Methodists, and Baptists.

More ominous to Joseph than the growing mob was his recognition of the bloodied body of Sidney Rigdon lying on the frozen ground. Sidney had been attacked, tarred and feathered, and mercilessly dragged toward the farmhouse. His head was repeatedly lacerated as it struck icy protrusions. He became unconscious from loss of blood.

At the sight of Sidney, Joseph fully understood his own peril. He pled with his captors, "You will have mercy and spare my life, I hope," to which they replied with harsh profanities, "Call on yer God for help, we'll show ye no mercy."[31]

The mob proceeded thirty rods past Sidney Rigdon to the meadow. There they held council. Joseph assumed the topic in question was whether to kill him or not. Joseph reported their decision was "not to kill me, but to beat and scratch me well, tear off my shirt and drawers, and leave me naked."[32]

It appears this decision was not accepted by all. A

167

mobber named Dr. Dennison tried to force a vial of poisonous nitric acid into Joseph's mouth. He then proposed to emasculate Joseph. In this attempt Joseph's clothes were torn off. His naked body was then attacked by the fingernails of an unknown mobber, who "like a mad cat, [fell on Joseph] and muttered: G— d— ye, that's the way the Holy Ghost falls on folks!"[33] Dennison, however, seeing Joseph's body stretched on a plank, weakened in his resolve and refused to operate.

The refusal seemed to spur on the shouts and assaults by other mobbers, "Simonds, Simonds, where's the tar bucket? I don't know, answered one, where 'tis Eli's left it."[34] When the tar was fetched the mob tried to force the tar paddle into Joseph's mouth. Joseph twisted his head so they could not. An angry mobber cried, "G— d— ye, hold up yer head and let us giv ye some tar."[35] They forced tar into his mouth, which all but smothered him. They covered his scratched and beaten body with the loathsome substance. Joseph lost consciousness again. As the final touch to this barbarity, in mockery they feathered a prophet of God.

As quickly as they had entered the quietude of Joseph's world, the mob fled to the old brickyard of Hiram to wash themselves and bury their filthy clothes, hoping that their participation in the deed would be hidden. Joseph was left alone. When he regained consciousness, he struggled to rid the tar from his mouth in order to breathe more freely. He attempted to rise but failed, due to his weakened condition. In a second effort to rise, he saw two lights in the distance. "I made my way towards one of them, and found it was Father Johnson's."[36]

When Joseph neared the farmhouse, he called from the shadows to Emma. With her emotions highly stressed, Emma saw Joseph covered with what she assumed was blood, rather than tar. She concluded that he was "all crushed to pieces."[37] She fainted. It was not until further pleas by Joseph to neighbors now ministering to Emma that a blanket was extended to him. Wrapping it around himself, he staggered into the farmhouse.

Throughout the night his friends scraped, washed, and attempted to lubricate the tar from his wounded body.

The Aftereffects of the Mobbing

The local press publicly decried the vicious attack as "a base transaction, an unlawful act, a work of darkness, a diabolical trick."[38] Nevertheless, even the press hinted at the widespread sympathy by the condoning comment, "but bad as it is, it proves . . . that Satan hath more power than pretended prophets of Mormonism."[39]

It is obvious from the attitude of the local press and the local sympathy for "appropriate" mob rule that Joseph was not safe in Hiram. Still, he remained at the Johnson farm for about a week. His activities during that week tell much about his character.

On the following morning, 25 March, Joseph appeared in a public church service "all scarified and defaced." In this setting were some of Joseph's avowed enemies who had participated in the mob. His response to them illustrates his greatness. He wrote, "I preached to the congregation as usual."[40] In other words, despite the vicious attack of the previous night and the reality of continuing death threats, Joseph fulfilled his responsibilities as directed by the Lord. In the afternoon Joseph baptized three people.

On Monday morning, 26 March, Joseph went to the log cabin across the street from the farmhouse to comfort his friend and brother in the gospel, Sidney. He reported, "I found him crazy."[41] The abusive mobbing of Sidney had rendered him seriously ill. He was suffering from a concussion and delirium. Instead of an exchange of consoling words to each other, Joseph listened to Sidney's delirious harangue, punctuated by abusive language: he wanted a razor to use as a weapon to kill Joseph. Yet never once did Joseph reprimand his friend.

On Thursday of that week, 29 March, Joseph buried his eleven-month-old son, Joseph Murdock Smith. The mobocrats at the farmhouse had caused doors to gape open and the seriously ill babies to be exposed to the cold. Young baby Joseph, the first martyr of mobocracy in this dispensation, developed a severe cold, which, added to his measles, caused his death.

The sorrowing father left Hiram on 1 April, leaving Emma and the other baby, Julia, behind. His destination was Missouri. As he traveled toward Missouri, he was threatened by mobbers, who pursued him from Hiram to Cincinnati. Seeing that the mob was not yet satiated, he now feared for the immediate safety of Emma and his child. He instructed Emma by letter that she quickly move back to Kirtland to stay with Newel K. Whitney's family.

A prophet and his family were not safe in Hiram. But were the mobbers who had attacked him? Did they need to hide from the law or prosecution because of their villainous deed? Symonds Ryder, the apostate leader of the mob, was safe in Hiram. McClentic, who had his hands in Joseph's hair; Streeter, son of a Campbellite minister; Felatiah Allen, Esq., who supplied the mob a barrel of whiskey—all were safe in Hiram. Even Mason, Fullars, Cleveland, and Dr. Dennison found in Hiram a haven of peace. None of these known mobbers or the estimated fifty unknown mobbers experienced any repercussions from their attempt on Joseph's life. An example of the fellowship they enjoyed in Hiram was the eulogy preached by B. A. Hinsdale in the Hiram Church for Symonds Ryder: "God grant that we may do our work as well as he did his; then we may go to our graves in equal peace."[42]

After the event, if anyone inquired of the whereabouts of any of the mobbers of 24 March, an appropriate alibi was ready. These alibis were even passed to the next generation. For example, according to Ryder's son, Hartwell, Ryder was not involved in the tarring and feathering of Joseph Smith. Nor did he preach on the following Sunday in the south schoolhouse on Ryder Road and glory that he had been an instrument of the Lord in driving the Mormons out of Hiram. Instead, Hartwell wrote, Ryder was "ill in bed at the time."[43]

Conclusion

Hiram, Ohio, was Joseph's introductory experience to physical brutality. This brief introduction to fury was a prologue to what was to continue throughout his life. It culminated on 27 June 1844 in Carthage, Illinois. Despite his efforts to "preach to the congregation as usual," "appropriate" mob rule seemed to have triumphed momentarily. The martyr's crown was forged in Hiram on 24 March 1832, but thanks to the council's decision not to kill him and Dr. Dennison's quivering personal refusal, Joseph lived. For twelve years the forged crown waited to be worn, despite the plots of a host of false brethren, lies, reviling, and continual persecution. Joseph escaped death from 1832 to 1844 only because his work was not complete.

Hiram was a preparatory ground for Joseph. In this community he saw former friends plotting his destruction, faithful friends murmuring, and the effects of unleashed vengeance. Yet in Hiram, he learned of the glories of heaven that await those who endure the suffering and vicissitudes when one "could not deny, neither dared I do it; at least I knew that by so doing I would offend God, and come under condemnation." (Joseph Smith–History 1:25.)

Joseph knew of the truth he professed, that like Paul of old, "though they should persecute [me] unto death, yet [I] knew, and would know to [my] latest breath." (Joseph Smith–History 2:24.) His testimony was tested by severe physical suffering in Hiram. Joseph left the community that had turned on him. The reputedly upright citizens viewed Joseph as a deceiver. They embraced Symonds Ryder and Ezra Booth while mocking a prophet of God. They reviled the Lord's anointed, leaving him "scarified and defaced." Yet Joseph did not abandon his divine calling: "Behold, thou art Joseph, and thou wast chosen to do the work of the Lord. . . . and thou art still chosen." (D&C 3:9–10.)

Notes

1. Hiram was the third township settled in Portage County. It included the highest elevation in the Western Reserve, thirteen hundred feet above sea level. The town was once composed of the territory known as Mantua, Shalersville, Freedom, Windham, and Nelson.

The first settlers of Hiram moved from Pennsylvania in 1799. They had a reputation of being "poor but law abiding." They had been attracted to Hiram by land prices from seventy-two cents to three dollars an acre and rumors of fertile soil. Their success on this highest plateau in the Western Reserve attracted stable families, who expanded farm living to include publishing newspapers and building schools and churches. *Portage Heritage*, ed. James B. Holm (Portage, Ohio: The Portage County Historical Society, 1957), pp. 372–80; see also *History of Portage County, Ohio* (Chicago: Warner, Beers, and Co., 1885), pp. 466–75.

2. Pouring molten tar over the body and covering it with feathers was an official punishment in England as early as the twelfth century. This practice continued in the United States until the late nineteenth century, even though it was never legal. H. E. Barnes, "The Story of Punishment," *Dictionary of American History* (New York: Charles Scribner's Sons, 1976), 6:461–62.

3. John Johnson, the son of Israel Johnson and Abigail Higgins, was born 11 April 1778 in Chesterfield, Cheshire, New Hampshire. He married Elsa Jacobs on 22 June 1800 in Chesterfield, Cheshire, New Hampshire. Susan Easton Black, *Membership of The Church of Jesus Christ of Latter-day Saints, 1830–1848* (Salt Lake City, Utah: Corporation of the President, 1988), 25:580–83.

4. Ezra Booth was born in 1792 in Connecticut. He married Dorcas Taylor on 10 March 1819 in Nelsonville, Athens, Ohio. Ibid., 6:168–69.

5. Joseph Smith, *History of The Church of Jesus Christ of Latter-day Saints*, 7 vols., 2d ed. rev., ed. B. H. Roberts (Salt Lake City, Utah: The Church of Jesus Christ of Latter-day Saints, 1932–51), 1:215–16.

6. Ibid.

7. Ibid.; A. S. Hayden, "Life and Character of Symonds Ryder," *Early History of the Disciples in the Western Reserve, Ohio* (Cincinnati: Chase and Hall Publishers, 1876), pp. 250–51.

8. Symonds Ryder was born on 20 November 1792 in Hartford, Washington, Vermont. He married Mahitable Loomis in November 1818. Black, *Membership of the Church*, 38:70–71.

9. J. H. Kennedy, *Early Days of Mormonism* (Scribner's and Sons, 1888), as cited in Smith, *History of the Church*, 1:158.

10. In Doctrine and Covenants 52:37, Simonds is directed to receive that which Heman Bassett had lost. Heman was a participant in the abnormal spiritual activities in 1831 and was one of the earliest converts to withdraw in Ohio. *Painesville Telegraph*, vol. 2, no. 50 (24 May 1831), stated that he "declared it all a miserable hoax." Max H. Parkin, *Conflict at Kirtland: A Study of the Nature and Causes of External and Internal Conflict of the Mormons*

in Ohio between 1830 and 1838 (Salt Lake City, Utah: Max Parkin, 1966), p. 91.

11. Another historian claimed that when Joseph Smith "misspelled" Ryder's first name *Si-m-o-n* instead of *Symonds*, Ryder lost faith in him, feeling that if the Lord really did speak to Smith, he would spell his name "correctly." Holm, *Portage Heritage*, p. 171; see also Smith, *History of the Church*, 1:261.

12. This historian explains his conclusion by stating, "After a time something leaked out in regard to the Saints having an eye on their neighbor's property, that it was their design to get into their possession all the lands of those whom they converted." Holm, *Portage Heritage*, p. 171; see also *History of Portage County, Ohio*, p. 474.

13. Symonds Ryder to A. S. Hayden, 1 Feb. 1868, as cited in Parkin, *Conflict at Kirtland*, p. 254.

14. The letters have also been published in E. D. Howe, *Mormonism Unvailed* (Painesville, Ohio: E. D. Howe, 1834), pp. 175–221.

15. Smith, *History of the Church*, 1:217.

16. Hayden, *Early History of the Disciples*, p. 220; see also Parkin, *Conflict at Kirtland*, p. 248.

17. Symonds Ryder to A. S. Hayden, as cited in Parkin, *Conflict at Kirtland*, p. 254.

18. John Johnson first purchased 100 acres of land in Hiram, Ohio, on 19 March 1818, from Amos Spicer and A. Norton. On 4 April 1820, he purchased 60 acres from John Whipple. On 14 March 1823, he purchased 100 acres from Mary Hutchinson, et al. On 20 December 1827, he purchased 54 acres from Clarissa Eggleston. When Joseph Smith arrived in Hiram, John owned 304 acres. Salt Lake Genealogical Library, Film 899057, "Locality of Record, Recorders Office, Portage County Courthouse, State of Ohio, Index to Deeds, 1795–1917."

The Johnson farmhouse was purchased by the Church in 1956. It was dedicated by Elder James A. Cullimore, Assistant to the Quorum of the Twelve Apostles. *Church News*, 17 May 1969, p. 3.

19. Smith, *History of the Church*, 1:215.

20. Emma Smith had given birth to twins, Louisa and Thaddeus, on 30 April 1831. These twins lived for approximately three hours. On the same day, John Murdock's wife gave birth to twins, named Joseph Smith Murdock and Julia Murdock. John's wife died in childbirth. John gave his motherless twins to Joseph and Emma "in the fond hope that they would fill the void in [Emma's life] occasioned by the loss of her own." Smith, *History of the Church*, 1:260.

21. *Ohio Star*, vol. 2, no. 52 (29 Dec. 1831), n. p., as cited in Parkin, *Conflict at Kirtland*, p. 118.

22. *Ohio Star*, vol. 3, no. 2 (12 Jan. 1832), n. p., as cited in Parkin, *Conflict at Kirtland*, p. 119.

23. See Doctrine and Covenants 1; 65; 67; 68; 69; 71; 73; 74; 76; 77; 78; 79; 80; 81; 99; 133.

24. *History of Portage County, Ohio*, p. 474.

25. Carnot Mason is reported to be the man who dragged Joseph by the hair. Later, Joseph showed Levi Hancock a patch of his hair that had been pulled out by the roots, leaving his scalp bare. Levi Hancock, *Levi Hancock Journal*, p. 73; a copy is located at Brigham Young University, Provo, Utah; see also Luke Johnson, "History of Luke Johnson," *Millennial Star*, vol. 26, no. 53 (31 Dec. 1864): 834–35.

26. Smith, *History of the Church*, 1:261.

27. Waste reportedly regarded himself as the "strongest man in the Western Reserve, and had boasted that he could take the Prophet out of the house alone." Waste later observed, however, "the Prophet was the most powerful man he ever had hold of in his life." Luke Johnson, "History of Luke Johnson," p. 835.

28. Smith, *History of the Church*, 1:261.

29. Ibid., p. 262.

30. Symonds Ryder to A. S. Hayden, 1 Feb. 1868, as cited in Parkin, *Conflict at Kirtland*, p. 254.

31. Smith, *History of the Church*, 1:262.

32. Ibid.

33. Ibid., p. 263.

34. Ibid.

35. Ibid.

36. Ibid.

37. Ibid.

38. *Warren News-Letter and Trumbull County Republican*, vol. 4, no. 8 (10 Apr. 1832), n. p., as cited in Parkin, *Conflict at Kirtland*, p. 252.

39. Ibid.

40. Smith, *History of the Church*, 1:264.

41. Ibid., p. 265.

42. Doris Messenger Ryder, "A History of Symonds Ryder," *The Report* [Ohio Genealogical Society], vol. 9, no. 2 (Apr. 1969), pp. 1–2.

43. Ibid.

Chapter 10

The Prophet Translates
the Bible by
the Spirit of Revelation

Robert J. Matthews

Dean of Religious Education
Brigham Young University

Introduction

That the Prophet Joseph Smith made what he termed a "new translation" of the Bible is quite well known among members of The Church of Jesus Christ of Latter-day Saints. What is not so well known is *why* and *how* he did it, and even less appreciated is the effect it has had on the membership of the Church. Virtually every member of the Church in the 150 years since that day until the present, and everyone who will yet be a member, has been or will be affected by that translation. Even those who know nothing about the facts of the translation, nor of a single textual correction, are affected by it in their daily lives as Church members.

As one becomes familiar with the historical facts of the translation, and learns of the textual corrections, improvements, and additions, that person's understanding of the doctrinal restoration becomes more clear. A history of the Prophet's translation of the Bible parallels much of the history of the book of Doctrine and Covenants and the history of the Church from 1830 to 1833. These concepts, although possibly not known and understood generally in the Church, have been discussed at least partially in other publications[1] and hence will be touched upon only lightly in this essay. The main purpose of this essay is to put forth the Prophet Joseph Smith as a superior example of one who learned by the inspiration of the Spirit, lived by the Spirit, and taught by that same Spirit. This essay is intended to illustrate that as the Prophet Joseph Smith searched the scriptures, he obtained light and knowledge by the spirit of revelation. That acquisition enabled him to translate the text and give the meaning in plainer words than did the King James text. It also provided material that had been lost from the King James text. In observing this revelatory process, the Prophet's work with the Bible becomes an example, a signboard, and an invitation to every one of us to acquire like spiritual insight.

To develop the theme we will briefly consider *what* the Joseph Smith Translation of the Bible is, *why* he did it, *how* it was done, and the *results* that have come from it. As noted above, we will in this essay pay less detailed attention to the precise doctrinal contributions (although they are highly significant) and more to the underlying message that is generated by the translation activity itself. In so doing we must draw a distinction between the *process* of translation and the *product* of the translation, or the printed Bible. The process will capture our most direct attention.

What Is the Joseph Smith Translation of the Bible?

The Joseph Smith Translation of the Bible is a work done by the Prophet Joseph Smith and his scribes chiefly during the years from 1830 to 1833, with some additional revisions until his death in June 1844. It consists of a manuscript of 477 pages, each measuring approximately eight and one-half inches by fourteen inches.

The work has been known by various names. The Prophet Joseph consistently called it the New Translation. When first published in 1867 by the Reorganized Church (hereafter called RLDS) it was titled *Holy Scriptures*. Due to terminology that became increasingly common among the RLDS, the title was enlarged in a printing of 1937 to read *Holy Scriptures, Inspired Version*. It has also frequently been dubbed unofficially as the Inspired Revision. The work has now been titled the Joseph Smith Translation by official action of the First Presidency and the Quorum of the Twelve Apostles of The Church of Jesus Christ of Latter-day Saints. This action was taken in connection with the publication in 1979 of an edition of the King James Version of the Bible containing study and reference notes including excerpts from the Joseph Smith Translation.

The manuscript notes and other paraphernalia connected with the Prophet's translation of the Bible are now in the possession of the RLDS Church, Independence, Missouri. The RLDS have also published the work repeatedly in varying editions and formats since 1867.

The Joseph Smith Translation is inseparably connected with the revelations that are published in the Doctrine and Covenants and also with the daily activities of the Prophet Joseph Smith during the early years of the Church. This relationship is clearly delineated in seven separate section headings and in seventeen footnotes of the 1981 edition of the Doctrine and Covenants published by The Church of Jesus Christ of Latter-day Saints, Salt Lake City, Utah. See, for example, the headnotes to sections 35; 71; 74; 76; 77; 86; 91; see also the footnote references to Doctrine and Covenants 9:2; 35:20; 37:1; 41:7; 42:56; 45:12, 60; 49:21; 73:3; 76:17; 84:14, 24; 93:53; 94:10; 104:58; 107:2; 124:89. There is no substantive difference between the revelations in the Doctrine and Covenants and the revelations in the Joseph Smith Translation, even though the latter are labeled a "translation." They are a "translation" in the sense of being a clarification or restoration of a text, but not in the usual sense in which the word *translation* is used, meaning the rendering of a subject from one language to another.

The work was not finished nor published in its entirety by the Prophet Joseph. During his lifetime, excerpts appeared in *The Evening and the Morning Star,* the *Times and*

Seasons, and *Lectures on Faith.* There was also a broadside tract of Matthew 24 issued in Kirtland about 1835. Later, excerpts were published in the *Millennial Star* and the Pearl of Great Price.[2] It is clear, however, that the Prophet was planning a complete publication of the Joseph Smith Translation before the time of his death. His extensive efforts toward publication are a strong suggestion that even if it were not a finished product, enough was accomplished to merit its use among the Saints. The Prophet went through the entire Bible from Genesis through Revelation and made thousands of changes but did not make all of the corrections that might someday need to be made. The printed edition of the Joseph Smith Translation has at least thirty-four hundred verses that read differently from the King James text.

Why Was a Translation of the Bible Made by the Prophet Joseph Smith?

There are really two questions that should be considered here. First, why was the Bible translated yet again, and second, why was Joseph Smith the one to do it?

The simplest and most direct answer to the second question is that the Lord commanded him to do it. This is evident from Doctrine and Covenants 45:60–62 and 76:15, which clearly assign the Prophet to the work. He regarded his work with the Bible as "a branch of his calling" as a Prophet.[3]

The answer to the first question is just as simple and direct: the Bible needed it. We can see from Moroni's words to the Prophet in September 1823 that some passages as they stand in the King James Version needed to be rephrased for clarity. The Prophet noted in his history that several of the quotations by Moroni were given with a little variation from the way they read in our Bibles. (Joseph Smith–History 1:36–41.) Joseph Smith had also learned by experience that the various teachers of religion interpreted "the same passages . . . so differently as to destroy all confidence in settling [some questions] by an appeal to the Bible." (Joseph Smith–History 1:12.) He also saw that it caused great contention among the ministers. This certainly would give a signal to him that the Bible is not sufficiently clear in many instances. Nephi also informs us that many plain and precious parts containing important points of doctrine, and also many covenants of the Lord have been taken out of the Bible. (See 1 Nephi 13:21–42.)

Another reason for making the translation is that the Prophet in his early years (he was twenty-five when he began the translation) needed the experience as well as the information that the translation process would bring to him. Furthermore, the Church membership and the world needed, or would need, the doctrinal information and also the example of the spiritual benefits that come from searching the scriptures.

That the Christian world senses the need for a better translation than the King James Version is abundantly evident from the large number of translations that have been made since the King James Version first appeared. One who wishes to purchase a Bible today has a selection of more than two dozen English translations from which to choose,[4] all of which have come into being since the time of the Prophet Joseph Smith.

How Did the Prophet Joseph Proceed with the Translation?

We wish we had a detailed account by the Prophet Joseph's own hand as to how he made the translation of the Bible, but we do not. From various comments by himself and others, and from examining the handwritten manuscript, we are able to reconstruct the process and establish the time frame.

The Prophet and Oliver Cowdery began the translation in June 1830, using an edition of the King James Version printed in 1828 by H. and E. Phinney in Cooperstown, New York. This Bible they had purchased on 8 October 1829 for $3.75 from the E.B. Grandin Bookstore in Palmyra, New York. It appears that the Prophet would read from the King James text and dictate to the scribe, who would record the material. The first scribe in point of time was

Oliver Cowdery, the second John Whitmer. The third and major scribe was Sidney Rigdon. Other persons helped to a lesser degree.[5] The main translation activity was completed by 2 July 1833, after which there was considerable revision and editing to prepare the document for publication. This procedure resulted in the original draft's being supplemented or in some instances even replaced with a revised and edited copy.

The translation was a revelatory process, not based on a knowledge of the biblical languages nor the perusal of ancient manuscripts. The evidence of the handwritten documents and of the markings placed in the Phinney edition of the King James Version indicates that the basic text was the English language King James Version. The substantial variations from that text were due to the inspiration received by the Prophet Joseph while he was studying the text.

Translating by the Spirit of Revelation

Four items serve to illustrate the revelatory process of the translation. First, on page 3 of the Old Testament manuscript is found this caption, "A Revelation given to the elders of the Church of Christ on the First Book of Moses." This extends to material from Genesis 1:1 through Genesis 3. On page 8 of the manuscript there is another caption, "A Revelation concerning Adam after he had been driven out of the Garden of Eden."[6]

Second, on page 1 of the New Testament manuscript are these words, which indicate how the Brethren felt about what they were doing: "A Translation of the New Testament Translated by the Power of God."[7]

Third, is the wording of Doctrine and Covenants 76:15–18, given in connection with the vision of the degrees of glory. We read in this case that as the Prophet and Sidney were doing the work of translation, they came to the text of John 5:29, and it was revealed to them that it should read differently than it stands in the King James Version. Concerning this rewording the Prophet said: "Now this caused us to marvel, for it was given unto us of the Spirit."

(D&C 76:18.) The words "given to us of the Spirit" are a clue to the process of translation.

The fourth illustration is from Doctrine and Covenants 45:60–62 and is a confirmation of the other three, showing that the process was a learning activity. We particularly note these words: "It shall not be given unto you to know any further concerning this chapter until the New Testament be translated, and *in it* all these things *shall be* made known." (D&C 45:60; italics added.) This clearly attests to the fact that the translation was to be a learning experience to the Prophet, which would bring him to an understanding of things heretofore not known by him. He was not reading the Bible in order to find errors so that he could offer his premeditated corrections. Rather, he was by divine appointment searching the text for its intended meaning, and in the process the Lord gave him knowledge to clarify and purify the text and even to restore lost material where necessary.

A Lesson in Spirituality

The Prophet Joseph Smith lived by the spirit of revelation. He made decisions by it, he learned by it, and he taught by it. Because of this spirit, which is the gift of the Holy Ghost, the Prophet could unlock the closed doors of biblical knowledge and could obtain "the true meaning and intention" of even the most vague and "mysterious passages." (Joseph Smith–History 1:74.) He learned how to recognize the voice of the spirit and thus to get revelation when it was needed. Although such an ability is a *gift*, it is also an *attainment* and requires energy, experience, and practice, even for a prophet.

That the gift of revelation requires effort and experience is manifest in several instances. For example, we read in Doctrine and Covenants 9:6–10 that the Lord chided Oliver Cowdery for expecting that he could translate "when [he] took no thought save it was to ask me." He was counseled that he must "study it out in [his] mind" and then respond to the burning in his bosom, if it was right, or to the "stupor of thought," if it was wrong. In the infancy of this dispensation when the gospel was being unfolded day by day and when even the leaders were beginners, one can sense the Lord tenderly working with them (and with us) in showing how to commune with the Spirit. In Doctrine and Covenants 6:5, 10, 11, 12, 14, we find these instructions to Oliver Cowdery: "If you will ask of me you shall receive; if you will knock it shall be opened unto you, . . . behold thou hast a gift. . . . Remember it is sacred and cometh from above—and if thou wilt inquire, thou shalt know mysteries; therefore thou shalt *exercise* thy gift. . . . Trifle not with sacred things. . . . As often as thou hast inquired thou hast received instruction of my Spirit." (Italics added.)

A few days later the Lord again counseled Oliver about how to use the Spirit. This is found in the Doctrine and Covenants 8:2–4: "Yea, behold, I will tell you in your mind and in your heart, by the Holy Ghost, which shall come upon you and which shall dwell in your heart. Now, behold, *this is the spirit of revelation;* behold, this is the spirit by which Moses brought the children of Israel through the Red Sea on dry ground. Therefore this is thy gift; *apply unto it*." (Italics added.)

We can benefit from the instruction to exercise the gift and to "apply unto it." Still later, the Lord spoke to Hyrum Smith, saying: "I will impart unto you of my Spirit, which shall enlighten your mind, which shall fill your soul with joy . . . and . . . by this shall you know, all things whatsoever you desire of me. . . . appeal unto my Spirit." (D&C 11:13–14, 18.) These things show that even though the gift of revelation is bestowed, the recipient must still *apply himself* to the task and become familiar with the workings of the Spirit.

This same developmental process is demonstrated in the experience of the Prophet Joseph Smith. We are indebted to Elder Orson Pratt for an enlightening comment on this point, which is an excerpt from the minutes of the School of the Prophets in Salt Lake City, 14 January 1871, and has to do with the translation of the Book of Mormon and also the Bible:

"He [Elder Pratt] mentioned that as Joseph used the

Urim and Thummim in the translation of the Book of Mormon, he wondered why he did not use it in the translation of the New Testament. Joseph explained to him that the experience he had acquired while translating the Book of Mormon by the use of the Urim and Thummim had rendered him so well acquainted with the Spirit of Revelation and Prophecy, that in the translating of the New Testament he did not need the aid that was necessary in the 1st instance."[8]

Translating by the spirit of revelation as the Prophet searched the scriptures is both a lesson and an invitation to all of us. Although none of us is commissioned by the Lord to make another translation of the Bible, yet it is plain to see that light, inspiration, and revelation come to those who pursue it for the right reasons through searching the scriptures. We have before us in the history of the Church several examples showing this principle at work. It was reading James 1:5 that caused the Prophet to seek for additional information that led to the First Vision in 1820; it was reading the newly translated account from the Book of Mormon that led Joseph and Oliver to inquire about baptism, which resulted in John the Baptist conferring the Aaronic Priesthood upon them in 1829; and it was President Joseph F. Smith's pondering over the meaning, after having read 1 Peter 3 and 4, that parted the veil and gave him a view of how the gospel is preached in the world of departed spirits. (See D&C 138:1–11.) President Smith said, "As I pondered over these things which are written [1 Peter 3–4], the eyes of my understanding were opened, and the Spirit of the Lord rested upon me, and I saw the hosts of the dead, both small and great." (D&C 138:11.)

Such experiences are patterns that show us there is understanding and new knowledge to be gained when we search, pray, ponder, and meditate upon the holy scriptures and hear the voice of the Lord through his Spirit. In this way we come to know not only the doctrines of the gospel and the will of the Lord as revealed in ancient time but also the application to us individually in our own time.

Speaking of this spirit of revelation the Prophet Joseph

explained: "A person may profit by noticing the first intimation of the spirit of revelation; for instance, when you
feel pure intelligence flowing into you, it may give you
sudden strokes of ideas, so that by noticing it, you may
find it fulfilled the same day or soon; (i.e.) those things
that were presented unto your minds by the Spirit of God,
will come to pass; and thus by learning the Spirit of God
and understanding it, you may grow into the principle of
revelation, until you become perfect in Christ Jesus."[9]

As we consider the marvelous things in the Joseph
Smith Translation—the clarifications, additions, and corrections that far exceed the content of all other versions of
the Bible—it is a cause for rejoicing that these great truths
were made known to the Prophet, not through language
and ancient manuscripts, as only a few of the learned might
be privileged to learn them, but rather through the spirit
of revelation, which every faithful Saint may possess. It is
likewise an encouragement to strive to develop within us
that same spirit and enjoy its same fruits, for "God hath
not revealed anything to Joseph, but what He will make
known unto the Twelve, and even the least Saint may know
all things as fast as he is able to bear them."[10]

What Were the Results of the Prophet's Translation of the Bible?

First, as indicated, the translation process was to be a
learning experience for the Prophet. This is always the case
if the Holy Ghost is involved, for "no [one] can receive
the Holy Ghost without receiving revelations."[11] Information isn't revelation unless it comes from outside of the
individual and is new to his awareness. Such is the meaning also of *inspiration*. This word comes from the Latin
word meaning to "infuse" or "to enter" from without. It
is my conviction that the first and most important result
of the translation of the Bible was the spiritual education
of the Prophet himself.

Second, one revelation often calls for more revelation,
for by the very nature of things we learn line upon line,
precept upon precept, here a little and there a little, as we

are able to bear it. As noted, the major period of translation was from June 1830 through 2 July 1833. It is wonderfully significant that during this same period most of the doctrinal revelations now published in the Doctrine and Covenants were received. Even such major doctrinal statements as sections 107 and 132, which are now dated later than 1833, were based on revelation actually received in 1831, as is explained in the headnotes to these two sections.[12] This historical and topical parallel between the Joseph Smith Translation and the Doctrine and Covenants is not a coincidence; it is a consequence. While the Prophet labored intently with the text of the holy scriptures, the Lord through his Spirit gave him detailed knowledge and also understanding of the doctrines and the history of the gospel from the premortal world through the Millennium. This resulted in an improved biblical text as well as a collection of revelatory material for the Doctrine and Covenants.

Expressing a similar conviction, President George Q. Cannon wrote: "The labor was its own reward, bringing in the performance a special blessing of broadened comprehension to the Prophet and a general blessing of enlightenment to the people through his subsequent teachings."[13]

Some of the great revelations coming through the Prophet and preserved in the Joseph Smith Translation are the visions of Moses (also found in Moses 1) and an outpouring of knowledge about the Grand Council and about the Creation, Adam, Satan and Cain, and Enoch and Noah, as recorded in Genesis 1–7 of the Joseph Smith Translation (and also published as chapters 2–8 of the book of Moses in the Pearl of Great Price).

The revelation concerning Enoch given in December 1830 (JST, Genesis 6–7; Moses 6–7) laid the groundwork for the next twenty-five or so revelations in the Doctrine and Covenants about Zion and about the law of stewardship and consecration received from February through October 1831. (See D&C 42–65.) The age of accountability, set at eight years of age by the Lord, was revealed to the

Prophet in about April 1831 in connection with Joseph's translation of Genesis 17:11, dealing with Abraham. This was several months before it occurs in Doctrine and Covenants 68:25–28 in November 1831. Knowing the age at which children begin to become accountable determines the practice of the Church relative to baptism of children and has thus affected the lives of millions and will continue to do so. The relation of the Joseph Smith Translation to the vision of the degrees of glory has already been mentioned. To this list we would add the revelation on the plurality and eternity of marriage, now published as section 132 of the Doctrine and Covenants, which in its present form was written in July 1843, but which was initially revealed in 1831. Furthermore, the revelation on priesthood councils and quorums, now identified as Doctrine and Covenants 107, also has an early attachment to the work of the Bible translation, as we have already mentioned.

We therefore see that the age for baptism, the concept of building Zion, the degrees of glory in the afterlife, and the eternal marriage and family covenant were all closely allied with the process of the Bible translation. That is, these four fundamental doctrines, which are cornerstones in the gospel of Jesus Christ, are inseparably connected with the Prophet Joseph's translation activity. The connection is both historical and doctrinal, because it was in the process of the Bible translation that these doctrines were revealed to the Prophet. They were drawn forth and amplified to him as he examined the traces of these concepts that remain in the Bible. On the basis of these four fundamental cornerstones of faith and doctrine, one feels confident in repeating the earlier assertion that the Joseph Smith Translation has in some way affected the life of every member of the Church in the past 150 years and will yet affect the lives of all future members of the Church.

In addition to the revelations establishing the doctrine of the Church, the Prophet's work has also provided us with the most correct edition of the Bible currently available. Even though all of the translations available through the scholarly world have some variation among them, they are primarily the result of minor translation preferences and choices of words. Although we would not discount the value of the refinements made due to the academic process, these scholarly Bibles are still very much alike in content, whereas the Bible produced by the Prophet Joseph Smith is much different. The Joseph Smith Translation is less concerned with these small refinements and is more concerned with sweeping innovations introducing new material—or, rather, restoring lost material. Huge sections, sometimes containing hundreds of words, were added to Genesis 5, Genesis 14, Genesis 48, Genesis 50, Isaiah 29, Matthew 21:48–56, and Luke 3:4–10. Moreover, supplementary portions of varying shorter lengths are added to all of the sixty-six books of the Bible except fourteen (Ruth, Ezra, Esther, Ecclesiastes, Lamentations, Obadiah, Micah, Habakkuk, Zephaniah, Haggai, Malachi, 2 John, and 3 John; The Song of Solomon was deleted). The books of Genesis, Exodus, Isaiah, Matthew, Luke, Romans, and Revelation received the most corrections. The Joseph Smith Translation is a miraculous work embodying revelation and restoration by the Spirit. With the Joseph Smith Translation as with the Book of Mormon, the translation was by the "unlearned man" whose tools were faith and inspiration, rather than the "learned," who might trust in his knowledge of languages, worldly theology, and ancient manuscripts. (Compare 2 Nephi 27 and Isaiah 29.)

Evaluating the doctrinal correctness and usability of the Joseph Smith Translation, Elder Bruce R. McConkie left no doubt about his confidence in the work when he made the following public statement in 1984: "Use and rely on the Joseph Smith Translation, the so-called Inspired Version. [This] can scarcely be stated with too great an emphasis. The Joseph Smith Translation, or Inspired Version, is a thousand times over the best Bible now existing on earth. It contains all that the King James Version does, plus pages of additions and corrections and an occasional deletion. It was made by the spirit of revelation, and the changes and additions are the equivalent of the revealed word in the Book of Mormon and the Doctrine and Covenants."[14]

Two years earlier Elder McConkie had counseled the Regional Representatives and other leaders of the Church not to neglect the spiritual value of the Joseph Smith Translation: "Mark a new set of the standard works. Use the footnotes and teaching aids in our new editions. Pay particular attention to the inspired changes made by the Prophet Joseph Smith in the Bible."[15]

President Gordon B. Hinckley, writing on the history of the Church and the spiritual growth of the Prophet Joseph Smith, offers the following observation:

"One of the projects undertaken by Joseph Smith before his removal to Ohio was a revision of the English Bible. He did not discredit the King James translation, but he knew, as has since been more generally recognized, that certain errors and omissions in that record had led to numerous difficulties among the sects of Christendom. . . .

"Upon his arrival in Ohio, Joseph continued with this labor, working as time permitted. . . .

"We have seen how Joseph Smith and the Church developed as various questions and problems arose. He sought the Lord for guidance and testified to the world that he received it. Most of the revelations which have since regulated the Church were received during this Ohio-Missouri period."[16]

Thus the work of the Prophet Joseph Smith with the Bible was the means, first of all, of informing the Prophet; second, of providing a better Bible — even the best Bible — for the Saints and the world to profit thereby; and third, of major significance, is the example and lesson the work itself sets before us of seeing the fruits of a Prophet of God at work with the scriptures — searching the word of the Lord for inspiration and preparing himself for and receiving additional revelation. A translation that is conducted by the use of languages and based on a manuscript is limited to the knowledge of the translator and the content of the document to be translated, whereas, by comparison, a translation by a prophet, through the spirit of revelation, can expand to the extent that God chooses to reveal what he knows about the subject.

Summary

The translation of the Bible by the Prophet Joseph Smith is a storehouse of revealed doctrinal and historical knowledge, and every person interested in the gospel of Jesus Christ can benefit immensely from it, gaining intelligence and information not provided in any other source. And even beyond the factual benefit, we look to the process by which the Prophet was able to make the translation and realize that he has shown us the way that we too can gain knowledge unattainable by any other source or method. The unmistakable demonstration of this revelatory process has to be counted as extremely significant, along with the other contributions and advantages of the Prophet Joseph Smith's translation of the Bible.

It would make but little difference whether the Prophet were translating the Bible, the Book of Mormon, or the Abrahamic manuscripts, if the process is by the spirit of revelation, the *product* is a piece of divine truth, and because it comes from outside of the person (revelation), it goes beyond the fund of knowledge previously available.

Notes

1. See, for example, Robert J. Matthews, *A Plainer Translation: Joseph Smith's Translation of the Bible, A History and Commentary* (Provo, Utah: Brigham Young University Press, 1975). See also *The Joseph Smith Translation,* Robert L. Millet and Monte S. Nyman, eds. (Provo, Utah: Religious Studies Center Monograph Series, Brigham Young University, 1985).

2. The first publication of the entire text of the New Translation was in 1867, by the RLDS Church. Certain portions had been published by the LDS Church before that time, however. Most of these were published during the lifetime of the Prophet Joseph Smith, but some were later. A list of these extracts, arranged chronologically in the order of publication, follows. Biblical citations are as given in the printed Inspired Version, but, of course, these were not so identified in the original publications.

The Evening and the Morning Star (Independence, Missouri)

August 1832:	Genesis 7:1–78b
March 1833:	Genesis 6:45–71; Genesis 7:20–25

April 1833: Genesis 4:1–5:4b; Genesis 6:61–64; Genesis 7:5–13;
          Genesis 8:1–18; Genesis 9:17–23

Lectures on Theology (Kirtland, Ohio), first published in the Doctrine and Covenants in 1835 as "Lectures on Faith"
Lecture First: Hebrews 11:1
Lecture Second: Genesis 1:27–31; Genesis 2:18–25, 27; Genesis
          3:13–25; Genesis 4:1–9; Genesis 5:6b–9b; Genesis
          5:17–25
Lecture Third: Romans 10:14

Broadside Tract, "Extract from the New Translation of the Bible," published probably in Ohio, sometime between 1832 and 1837
          Matthew 24

Times and Seasons (Nauvoo, Illinois), January 1843, pp. 71–73.
          "A Revelation to Joseph Smith, jun., given in
          June 1830" (Visions of Moses)

The Millennial Star (Liverpool, England), 15 March 1851, pp. 90–93.
          Genesis 1:1–3:12b

Pearl of Great Price (Liverpool, England), July 1851, pp. 1–17, 30–32.
          All of the foregoing portions of Genesis
          (except Genesis 9:17–23)
          Matthew 24

3. The Prophet's journal contains several references to his divine appointment to translate the Bible. On one occasion he labels it a "branch of my calling." Smith, *History of the Church,* 1:238 (1 Dec. 1831).

4. For example, the Revised Version (RV) published in England in 1871 and the American Standard Version (ASV) in the United States in 1881; the Revised Standard Version (RSV) 1946–52; The New English Bible (NEB) 1961; the New World Translation (Watchtower Society) 1950; and the New American Bible (English Roman Catholic edition) 1970. See *The New Testament from Twenty-six Translations* (Grand Rapids, Mich.: Zondervan Publishing House, 1967) as a sourcebook on the many translations available. In addition to these Christian publications, there are various recent Jewish translations of the Old Testament now available.

5. For a more complete discussion of the scribes and their work, see Matthews, *A Plainer Translation,* chapters 2 and 3.

6. Old Testament Manuscript 2, pp. 1–8. This manuscript is in the possession of the RLDS Church, Independence, Missouri. Permission was given the writer to peruse the manuscript and make a typescript.

7. New Testament Manuscript 1, p. 1, in possession of the RLDS Church, Independence, Missouri. A photocopy is published in Matthews, *A Plainer Translation,* p. 267.

8. Manuscript in the Historical Library, The Church of Jesus Christ of Latter-day Saints, Salt Lake City, Utah.

9. Joseph Smith, *Teachings of the Prophet Joseph Smith,* sel. Joseph Fielding Smith (Salt Lake City, Utah: Deseret Book Co., 1938), p. 151.

10. Smith, *Teachings of the Prophet Joseph Smith,* p. 149.

11. Smith, *Teachings of the Prophet Joseph Smith,* p. 328.

12. Further discussion on the early dating of these sections is found in Robert J. Woodford, "The Historical Development of the Doctrine and Covenants" (Ph.D. dissertation, Brigham Young University, 1974); see also Doctrine and Covenants 84; 107; 132.

13. George Q. Cannon, *Life of Joseph Smith the Prophet* (Salt Lake City, Utah: Deseret Book Co., 1958), pp. 147–48.

14. Bruce R. McConkie, "The Bible, a Sealed Book," in the supplement to *A Symposium on the New Testament* (Salt Lake City, Utah: The Church of Jesus Christ of Latter-day Saints, 1984), p. 5.

15. Regional Representatives' Seminar, 2 Apr. 1982, Salt Lake City, Utah.

16. *Truth Restored,* 5th ed. (Salt Lake City, Utah: The Church of Jesus Christ of Latter-day Saints, 1954), pp. 99–100.

Chapter 11

Zion's Camp: A Refiner's Fire

Bruce A. Van Orden
Assistant Professor of Church History and Doctrine
Brigham Young University

"Brethren, when we learn [of] your sufferings, it awakens every sympathy of our hearts," wrote the Prophet Joseph Smith to the exiled Saints in Missouri when he first discovered the particulars of their being driven from their homes in Jackson County. "[W]e cannot refrain from tears, yet, we are not able to realize, only in part, your sufferings: and I often hear the brethren saying, they wish they were with you, that they might bear a part of your sufferings."[1]

Joseph's heart was indeed broken when he learned that Zion had been desecrated by enemies of the Church. In nothing had the Prophet placed greater hopes for the future than in establishing the resplendent New Jerusalem, robed in righteousness. The Lord had revealed to him the precise location of the city of Zion (see D&C 57:1–3) but had also warned, "Ye cannot behold with your natural eyes, for the present time, the design of your God concerning those things which shall come hereafter, and the glory which shall follow after much tribulation." (D&C 58:3.) So in this same letter to the Missouri exiles, Joseph reflected: "I cannot learn from any communication by the Spirit to me, that Zion has forfeited her claim to a celestial crown, notwithstanding the Lord has caused her to be thus afflicted. . . . I have always expected that Zion would suffer some affliction, from what I could learn from the commandments which have been given . . . [but] I know that Zion, in the due time of the Lord, will be redeemed; but how many will be the days of her purification, tribulation, and affliction, the Lord has kept hid from my eyes; and when I inquire concerning this subject, the voice of the Lord is: Be still, and know that I am God! all those who suffer for my name shall reign with me, and he that layeth down his life for my sake shall find it again."[2]

With this reassuring letter, Joseph Smith promised his brothers and sisters in Missouri that somehow the Lord would come to their aid in redeeming Zion. Joseph himself desired desperately to help in any way he could. For the next several weeks, the Prophet wrestled with ideas about how to redeem Zion. Finally the Lord through revelation confirmed the idea of some of the Saints that they should gather a paramilitary force of loyal Saints in the East to go to Missouri and assist their compatriots in Zion. Thus began the chapter in Joseph Smith's life known as Zion's Camp. This bold venture did not succeed as hoped in returning the exiled Saints to their sacred properties in Jackson County, but it provided yet another refiner's fire in the growth of the Prophet and developed leaders who could help shoulder the burdens of the emerging kingdom of God on the earth.

Joseph Smith had first visited Missouri in July 1831, identifying Independence as the City of Zion and establishing Jackson County as a gathering spot for Latter-day Saints. In 1832 he had visited the area again and conducted further business in the cause of Zion. These were the Prophet's only two visits to Missouri before the march of Zion's Camp.

As hundreds of Saints arrived in Jackson County in 1831 and 1832, the original settlers became increasingly nervous about the Mormons' presence. To these generally rough, proslavery southerners, Mormonism was a strange and threatening religion. Some feared that Mormons were abolitionists and that they would establish an alliance with the Indians. The presence of ever-increasing numbers of Mormons threatened the old settlers economically, politically, religiously, and socially. In the summer of 1833 these frontier settlers, deciding to take action into their own hands, demanded the removal of all Mormons from their county. By November they had violently driven the Saints across the Missouri River.

Letters of the Saints' plight reached Joseph Smith in late November and December. In one pathetic epistle, William W. Phelps wrote of the patience, humility, and bewilderment of the Saints who had remained faithful under their great trials. He said, "I know that it was right that we should be driven out of the land of Zion, that the rebellious might be sent away. But, brethren, if the Lord will, I should like to know what the honest in heart shall do? Our clothes are worn out; we want the necessaries of life, and shall we lease, buy, or otherwise obtain land where we are, to till, that we may raise enough to eat?"[3]

Upon receiving this letter, the Prophet sought the will of God and received a lengthy revelation, which he immediately sent to his beloved brothers and sisters in Missouri. The revelation mingled chastisement, comfort, and assurance that Zion would stand: "I, the Lord, have suffered the affliction to come upon them, wherewith they have been afflicted, in consequence of their transgressions. . . . Therefore, they must needs be chastened and tried, even as Abraham, who was commanded to offer up his only son." (D&C 101:2, 4.)

"Behold, I say unto you, there were jarrings, and contentions, and envyings, and strifes, and lustful and covetous desires among them; therefore by these things they polluted their inheritances." (D&C 101:6.)

"And they that have been scattered shall be gathered. And all they who have mourned shall be comforted. And all they who have given their lives for my name shall be crowned. . . . Zion shall not be moved out of her place, notwithstanding her children are scattered." (D&C 101:13–15, 17.)

Meanwhile the exiled Saints in Clay County, Missouri,

petitioned Governor Daniel Dunklin for assistance. He immediately ordered a court of inquiry to study the matter, but made no mention of military assistance in recovering the Mormons' lost land. In late November, however, the state's attorney general, Robert W. Wells, wrote the Saints, probably on his own authority, stating that "if they [the Mormons] desire to be replaced on their property, that is, their houses in Jackson County, an adequate force will be sent forthwith to effect that object."[4] Although Wells was acting without the formal authority of the governor, his letter served as both motivation and justification for the formation of Zion's Camp.

The Saints in Clay County conducted a conference on New Year's Day 1834. It was decided that two elders should be sent to Ohio to consult with the Prophet and other leaders of the Church as well as to discuss the attitude of the Missourians. Owing to poverty and inclement weather, no one readily volunteered, but two determined brethren, Parley P. Pratt and Lyman Wight, at length agreed to go. On 22 February 1834 these emissaries of the beleaguered Missouri Saints arrived on foot in Kirtland, Ohio, and presented to both the Prophet and the Saints in Kirtland their moving requests for aid.

Conditions of the Saints in Ohio were hardly conducive to providing quick and sufficient assistance. New converts, most of them lacking material goods, were thronging to Kirtland. The Church's meager resources were being tested to provide housing, work, and food for the newcomers. The Lord had assigned the Kirtland Saints to dedicate themselves to building a temple, so that project took what time, energy, and money were available to the Church. Another troublesome problem at this time was the anti-Mormon activity of apostate Philastus Hurlbut, who had been hired by a Kirtland committee to expose Mormonism. Hurlbut brought a lawsuit against Church property. Subsequent lawyer and court costs worsened an already pinched financial situation. Sidney Rigdon undertook a vigorous campaign against Hurlbut, which enraged the latter, who then made a public threat on the life of Joseph

Smith. In turn Joseph brought out a public complaint against Hurlbut.

Yet in spite of these challenges, Joseph Smith was most anxious to come to the aid of his Missouri compatriots. On 24 February he convened a meeting of the high council in Kirtland to hear the report of Elders Pratt and Wight. These emissaries convinced the brethren that military support from the Saints in the East would demonstrate to the Missouri government that the Mormons would have sufficient protection in returning to their Jackson County properties. At the conclusion of the meeting, Joseph Smith announced that he was going to Zion to help redeem it. He asked for a vote of the council to sanction his decision. It carried unanimously. When the Prophet asked for volunteers to go with him, thirty to forty of those present volunteered. Joseph was selected to be the "commander-in-chief of the armies of Israel."[5]

That same day Joseph had received a revelation (D&C 103) calling for the formation of a small paramilitary force. Eight men, including the Prophet and the Missouri elders, Parley P. Pratt and Lyman Wight, were called to gather young and middle-aged members and also to raise money to help the oppressed members in Missouri. They were to raise a company of five hundred men, if possible, but not fewer than one hundred, to march to Missouri for "the restoration and redemption of Zion." (D&C 103:29.) The revelation also stated, "Let no man be afraid to lay down his life for my sake; for whoso layeth down his life for my sake shall find it again. And whoso is not willing to lay down his life for my sake is not my disciple." (D&C 103:27–28.)

Recruiting volunteers for Zion's Camp, as the Lord's army in this instance came to be called, proved to be a difficult task. The Prophet and his associates fastened great hopes on obtaining volunteers and substantial financial contributions from members of the Church in various eastern states, but the tiny response was disheartening. In a letter to one of the recruiters, Orson Hyde, Joseph Smith lamented, "The fact is, unless we can obtain help, I myself cannot go to Zion, and if I do not go, it will be impossible to get my brethren in Kirtland, any of them, to go, . . . for unless [we] do the will of God, God will not help [us]; and if God does not help [us], all is vain." The Prophet also added a prophecy: "Now, Brother Orson, if this Church, which is essaying to be the Church of Christ will not help us, when they can do it without sacrifice, with those blessings which God has bestowed upon them, I prophesy—I speak the truth, I lie not—God shall take away their talent, and give it to those who have no talent, and shall prevent them from ever obtaining a place of refuge, or an inheritance upon the land of Zion."[6]

One of the few who responded from the East was twenty-seven-year-old convert Wilford Woodruff of Connecticut. Wilford, impressed with the impassioned appeal of Parley P. Pratt for volunteers, nevertheless was hesitant to go because of his business affairs. "He [Parley] told me it was my duty to try to prepare myself and go up to Zion," Wilford recorded in his journal. "And accordingly, I used every exertion to settle my accounts, arrange my affairs, and prepare myself to join my brethren to go to Missouri."[7]

Were it not for the approximately one hundred men who volunteered for the army from Kirtland and other parts of Ohio, Joseph Smith would not have felt justified in going up to Zion. Numerous able-bodied young men who had recently returned to Kirtland from missionary labors that had strengthened their faith joined the ranks. One of these was Brigham Young, who one day was trying to convince his older brother Joseph to go too. When Joseph Smith witnessed this conversation, he exclaimed, "Brother Brigham and brother Joseph, if you will go with me in the camp to Missouri and keep my counsel, I promise you, in the name of the Almighty, that I will lead you there and back again, and not a hair of your heads shall be harmed." Hearing this, Joseph Young agreed to participate, and the three men clasped hands in confirmation of this covenant.[8]

Leaving wives and children at home in Kirtland proved to be one of the challenges of Zion's Camp. To prevent undue hardships, many kind members of the Church planted gardens that spring so the women and children could harvest corn and other crops during the army's absence. A few elders, with Oliver Cowdery and Sidney Rigdon designated as the leaders, were left behind to supervise the continuing construction of the temple and direct the affairs of the Church in Kirtland.

Lack of sufficient supplies, money, and training also plagued the organization of Zion's Camp. Most of the one hundred plus volunteers who prepared to leave Kirtland in May 1834 would have to travel on foot. Some were armed with whatever they could find—muskets, pistols, and swords. Most were poorly clothed, some even wore makeshift outfits. George A. Smith, first cousin of the Prophet, was selected to go on the expedition though he was not yet seventeen. His father provided him with a Queen's Arm musket, and his mother made him a pair of pantaloons from bed ticking. His new boots did not fit him well, he had very little extra clothing, and he had only one blanket for bedding.[9] Even with the considerable soliciting over the previous two months, Zion's Camp left Kirtland with only five hundred dollars and twenty wagons of clothing and provisions for the relief of the Saints in Missouri. Hardly anyone in the army had previous military training. Some who did, such as dynamic missionary Heber C. Kimball, were given leadership roles as captains over groups of twelve men.

Physical hardships en route over the nearly nine-hundred-mile trek proved at once to be one of the greatest challenges of Zion's Camp. It was not unusual for the company to march thirty-five miles a day amid the discomfort from blistered feet, oppressive heat, heavy rains, high humidity, hunger, and thirst. Feeding the camp was one of the most persistent problems. The men were often required to eat limited portions of coarse bread, rancid butter, cornmeal mush, strong honey, raw pork, rotten ham, and maggot-infested bacon and cheese. On occasion the men strained swamp water to remove "wigglers" (mosquito larvae) before drinking it. Milk and butter were often obtained from local farmers under unsanitary conditions, and this raised fears of "milk sickness," "puking fever," or even death. But Joseph Smith advised them to "use all they could get from friend or enemy," unless the milk was obviously contaminated, and promised them it would do them good and "none [would] be sick in consequence of it." "Although we passed through neighborhoods where many of the people and cattle were infected with the sickness, yet my words were fulfilled," he later affirmed.[10]

In spite of the hardships and the military conditions, Zion's Camp placed great emphasis upon spirituality. In addition to company prayers, the men were admonished to pray privately morning and evening. On Sundays the camp rested, held meetings, and partook of the sacrament. One of the most prized privileges was to hear the Prophet teach the doctrines of the kingdom. "It was a great school for us to be led by a Prophet of God a thousand miles through cities, towns, villages, and through the wilderness," remembered Wilford Woodruff.[11] The brethren maintained an implicit faith that the Lord was accompanying them. "God was with us, and His angels went before us," recalled Joseph Smith, "and the faith of our little band was unwavering. We know that angels were our companions, for we saw them."[12]

The Lord also blessed the brethren to travel safely through sometimes threatening circumstances. Members of the camp generally tried to conceal their identity and objectives as they marched. Occasionally the army appeared to be numerically larger than it actually was to those who tried to determine its strength. Near Dayton, Ohio, a dozen men who entered the camp concluded there were six hundred soldiers. Faced with opposition at Indianapolis, Joseph Smith assured his brethren that they would pass through the city without anyone being aware of their doing so. He divided them into small groups, which dispersed and, taking different routes through the community, passed through undetected. When they crossed the Illinois River, the ferryman thought there were five hundred in the company.

Quarreling and contention within Zion's Camp became

its most vexing problem. Several men feared possible dangers ahead, some complained about changes in their lifestyle, and a few questioned the decisions of the leaders. For forty-five days they marched together, and inevitably personality clashes arose, exacerbated by the harsh conditions of their travel. Grumblers often complained to Joseph Smith and blamed him for their discomfort. Sylvester Smith, a sharp-tongued group captain apparently not related to the Prophet, was frequently in the forefront of the dissension. He complained about poor food, about the lack of preparation for the journey, and about how Joseph's watchdog kept him awake at night.

Throughout most of the march, Joseph Smith was remarkable in his humility and forbearance. He took his full share of the fatigues of the journey, suffering blisters and bloody feet with the rest. Even with Sylvester Smith he remained patient. But on 3 June, as the camp neared the Mississippi River and after Sylvester had threatened to kill Joseph's watchdog, the Prophet stood on a wagon wheel and scolded Sylvester Smith and other contentious brethren for their lack of humility, their murmuring and faultfinding, and their "fractious and unruly spirits." Because of these trangressions, he said some of them would "die like sheep with the rot." He also prophesied, "As the Lord lives, the members of this camp will suffer for giving way to their unruly temper."[13] This prophecy, sadly, was fulfilled within a few weeks.

After crossing the Mississippi River into Missouri, the army was joined by additional men from Michigan, recruited by Hyrum Smith and Lyman Wight. Through Ohio, Indiana, and Illinois, others had also been recruited. The total number in Zion's Camp now reached about 207 men, eleven women, eleven children, and twenty-five baggage wagons.

Meanwhile, the anti-Mormons in Jackson County had learned of the advancing army when the postmaster in Chagrin, Ohio, wrote to his counterpart in Independence that "the Mormons in this region are organizing an army to restore Zion, that is take it by force of arms."[14] Believing that a Mormon invasion was imminent, Jackson County troops began to drill, and sentries were posted at all ferries along the Missouri River, the entrance to Jackson County. In a vindictive spirit and perhaps to discourage the return of the Saints, mobbers had earlier burned 150 homes belonging to Mormons in the county.

At the same time Church leaders now residing in Clay County continued to petition Governor Daniel Dunklin for assurance that he would support the Saints in returning to their homes, in obtaining their property, and in living in peace in Jackson County. The governor acknowledged that the Mormons had been wronged by being driven from their homes, and he sought to have the arms that were taken from them the previous November returned to them. Furthermore, he recognized that an armed force sent by the state would be necessary to successfully reinstate the Mormons on their lands and protect them while the courts decided the legal issues involved.

Once Zion's Camp was in Missouri, Joseph Smith sent Elders Orson Hyde and Parley P. Pratt to Jefferson City, the state capital, to ascertain if Governor Dunklin was still willing to honor his supposed promise to reinstate the Saints in Jackson County with the assistance of the state militia. The interview was a bitter disappointment. Dunklin conceded that if he called out the militia, Missouri would be plunged into an open civil war. He advised the Mormon emissaries to avoid bloodshed by relinquishing their rights, selling their lands, and settling elsewhere. He also advised them to continue to appeal to the court, probably realizing that many officers of the court in Jackson County were among the enemies of the Mormons. "That poor coward ought, in duty, to resign," remarked Orson and Parley to each other as they left the governor's office.[15]

Meanwhile, in an effort to resolve the dispute, Judge John F. Ryland of Clay County arranged a meeting for 16 June at the courthouse in Liberty between a committee of citizens from Jackson County and representatives of the Saints in Clay County. A large, unruly, and belligerent crowd gathered at the meeting. The non-Mormons proposed to purchase within thirty days all property owned by the Saints in Jackson County or have the Mormons buy all their property. This proposal was unrealistic, since the Saints did not have sufficient funds to purchase even a fraction of the non-Mormon land, nor were they willing to sell their land in Zion, which they had been commanded of the Lord to purchase and retain. These facts, of course, were known by the anti-Mormons. Tempers flared as Jackson County representative and Protestant minister Samuel Owens swore that the Missourians would fight for every inch of ground rather than let the Saints return. A Baptist minister added that the Mormons had lived long enough in Clay County and should be cleared out of there too. Judge Joel Turnham, moderator of the meeting, pled for restraint. "Let us be republicans; let us honor our country, and not disgrace it like Jackson county. For God's sake don't disfranchise or drive away the Mormons. They are better citizens than many of the old inhabitants."[16] Any further negotiations between the Saints and their oppressors proved futile. Many Jackson County residents armed themselves in preparation for battle with the Mormons.

All the while, Zion's Camp marched nearer to join their fellow Church members in Clay County. On 18 June the army arrived within a mile of Richmond, the seat of Ray County, about fifteen miles from Liberty, where most of the Mormons were residing. As the men encamped, Joseph Smith, having a premonition of danger, went into the woods and petitioned God for safety. The Prophet was assured that the Lord would protect them. The men were roused in the early morning hours and left without prayers or breakfast. As they marched through Richmond, a black slave woman agitatedly told Luke Johnson, "There is a company of men lying in wait here, who are calculating to kill you this morning as you pass through."[17] Fortunately the men met no resistance, but were able to make only nine miles, being slowed down by broken wagon wheels.

Instead of reaching their intended destination of Liberty, they pitched camp just inside Clay County between two branches of the Fishing River, a location vulnerable to an ambush. Joseph Smith knelt and prayed again for divine protection when he learned that mobs were preparing to attack. These fears were confirmed when five armed Missourians rode into camp, cursing, and swore that the Mormons would "see hell before morning." They boasted of nearly four hundred men who would join forces in Jackson County from Ray, Lafayette, and Clay counties as well as Jackson County, then prepare to cross the Missouri River. Their plan was to utterly destroy the Mormons. Sounds of gunfire were heard, and some of the men wanted to fight, but the Prophet promised that the Lord would protect them. "Stand still and see the salvation of God," he declared.[18]

A few minutes after the Missourians' departure, a small black cloud appeared in the clear western sky. It moved eastward, unrolling like a scroll, filling the heavens with darkness. As the first ferryload of mobbers crossed the Missouri River to the south, a sudden squall made it nearly impossible for the boat to return to pick up another load of men. The storm was so intense that the men of Zion's Camp abandoned their tents and found shelter in an old Baptist log meetinghouse nearby. Wilford Woodruff noted that when Joseph Smith came in, he exclaimed, "Boys, there is some meaning to this. God is in this storm."[19] It was impossible for anyone to sleep, so the group sang hymns while the lightning and rain storm raged outside.

Elsewhere the mobbers sought refuge wherever they could. The fury of the storm broke branches from trees and destroyed crops. It soaked and rendered useless their ammunition, frightened and scattered their horses, and raised the level of Fishing River, preventing them from attacking Zion's Camp. "[I]t seemed as if the mandate of vengeance had gone forth from the God of battles, to protect His servants from the destruction of their enemies," the Prophet recalled.[20]

Following the storm, members of Zion's Camp met with local Church leaders in Clay County. After some discussion about what to do next, the brethren realized that even though the Lord had protected them, there was little chance of either peacefully marching into Jackson County or negotiating a mutually agreeable solution with Jackson County residents. The Prophet sought the Lord's will and received another revelation. In it the Lord first expressed his dissatisfaction with some members of the Church for their disobedience and selfishness. They "do not impart of their substance, as becometh saints, to the poor and afflicted among them; and are not united according to the union required by the law of the celestial kingdom." The Saints must learn their duty and gain more experience, the Lord explained, before Zion could be redeemed. But the Lord also promised the obedient that they would receive an endowment from on high if they continued faithful. Regarding those of Zion's Camp who had sacrificed so much for this march, the revelation stated, "I have heard their prayers, and will accept their offering; and it is expedient in me that they should be brought thus far for a trial of their faith." (D&C 105:3–4, 19.)

To a small minority of the army, the Lord's command not to do battle was the final trial of their faith. Disappointed and angry, a few apostatized. As a result of the insurrection of some, Joseph Smith again warned the camp that as a consequence of the unrighteous complaints, the Lord would send a devastating scourge upon them. The day before the revelation, two men contracted cholera, a dreaded disease that had come to America only two years earlier and had afflicted thousands, particularly along the waterways. The epidemic spread among the men, causing severe diarrhea, vomiting, and cramps. Before it ended, about seventy people, including the Prophet, were stricken; thirteen camp members died. On 2 July Joseph Smith told the camp that "if they would humble themselves before the Lord and covenant to keep His commandments," the plague would be "stayed from that hour," and there would "not be another case of the cholera among them." The brethren, with uplifted arms, covenanted to keep the commandments, after which, the Prophet certified, "the plague was stayed."[21]

On 25 June 1834, during the height of the cholera attack,

Joseph divided Zion's Camp into several small groups to demonstrate the Saints' peaceful intent to the Missourians. Ten days later formal written discharges were prepared for each faithful member. Some younger and single members were urged to stay in Missouri to help the Saints. Others were allowed to prepare to return to Ohio. Lyman Wight reported that Joseph Smith "was fully satisfied that he had done the will of God, and that the Lord accepted our sacrifice and offering, even as he had Abraham's when he offered his son Isaac; and in his benediction asked the heavenly Father to bless us with eternal life and salvation."[22]

To the relief of the Saints in Kirtland who were worried about reports that the Prophet had been killed in Missouri, he and a few other leaders of Zion's Camp arrived back in Kirtland in early August. Later in the month a high council court heard complaints of Sylvester Smith and others who were still bitter over Zion's Camp. Ten men who had participated on the march disputed the charges of Smith and testified that Joseph was not guilty of improper conduct. After reviewing the evidence, Sylvester admitted he was in error and had behaved improperly. He also added, "I have received testimony from the heavens, that the work of the Lord, brought forth by means of the book of Mormon, in our day, through the instrumentality of bro. Joseph Smith Jr. is eternal truth, and must stand, though the heavens and the earth pass away."[23]

To many contemporaries of Joseph Smith and to some twentieth century historians, the Zion's Camp episode was a debacle. True, the camp failed to help the Missouri Saints regain their lands and was marred by disease, death, dissension, apostasy, and unfavorable publicity. Nevertheless, a number of positive and ultimately decisive results derived from the journey. By volunteering, the members demonstrated their faith in the Lord and his prophet as well as their own earnest desire to comply with latter-day revelation. Their concern for the exiled Missouri Saints was manifest in a willingness to lay down their lives if necessary to bring assistance. Money and supplies brought with the camp aided their stricken brothers and sisters. The march itself provided important field training for several men who would lead the great exoduses of the Church which lay ahead, first out of Missouri and later to the Rocky Mountains.

This rugged journey also served as a test to determine those who were worthy to serve in positions of ecclesiastical leadership and to receive the partial endowment in the Kirtland Temple. Joseph Smith later explained: "God did not want you to fight. He could not organize His kingdom with twelve men to open the Gospel door to the nations of the earth, and with seventy men under their direction to follow in their tracks, unless He took them from a body of men who had offered their lives, and who had made as great a sacrifice as did Abraham."[24] In February 1835 the Quorum of the Twelve Apostles and the First Quorum of the Seventy were organized. Nine of the original apostles, all seven presidents of the Seventy's quorum, and all sixty-three other members of that quorum had served in the army of Israel that marched to western Missouri in 1834.

Zion's Camp also chastened, polished, and refined many of the Lord's servants, the Prophet Joseph Smith among them. The observant and dedicated received invaluable practical training and spiritual experience that served them well in future struggles for the Church. Joseph was able to add numerous trustworthy souls to the body of official Church leadership that would assist him through the challenges that lay ahead. Many leaders trained in Zion's Camp would eventually succeed Joseph Smith after the Prophet's martyrdom. The most vital of these, Brigham Young, would tell a skeptic what he had gained from Zion's Camp: "I would not exchange the knowledge I have received this season for the whole of Geauga County."[25]

Notes

1. Joseph Smith, *History of The Church of Jesus Christ of Latter-day Saints*, 7 vols., 2d ed. rev., ed. B. H. Roberts (Salt Lake City, Utah: Deseret Book

Co., 1932–51), 1:454; see also Dean C. Jessee, ed., *The Personal Writings of Joseph Smith* (Salt Lake City, Utah: Deseret Book Co., 1984), p. 309.

2. Smith, *History of the Church*, 1:453–54; see also Jessee, *Personal Writings of Joseph Smith*, p. 308.

3. Smith, *History of the Church*, 1:457.

4. Robert W. Wells to Amos Reese and others, 21 Nov. 1833, in "History," *Times and Seasons* 6 (1 June 1845): 912.

5. Smith, *History of the Church*, 2:39–40. See Peter Crawley and Richard L. Anderson, "The Political and Social Realities of Zion's Camp," *Brigham Young University Studies* 14 (Summer 1974): 406–20 for a thorough discussion of the Mormons' assumption that the march of Zion's Camp would result in aid from the Missouri government.

6. Smith, *History of the Church*, 2:48.

7. *Wilford Woodruff's Journal*, ed. Scott G. Kenney, 9 vols. (Midvale, Utah: Signature Books, 1983–85), 1:7; spelling and punctuation standardized.

8. *Manuscript History of Brigham Young, 1801–1844*, ed. Elden Jay Watson (Salt Lake City, Utah: Smith Secretarial Service, 1968), p. 8.

9. Merlo J. Pusey, *Builders of the Kingdom: George A. Smith, John Henry Smith, George Albert Smith* (Provo, Utah: Brigham Young University Press, 1981), p. 10.

10. Smith, *History of the Church*, 2:66–67.

11. Matthias F. Cowley, *Wilford Woodruff: History of His Life and Labors* (Salt Lake City, Utah: Bookcraft, 1964), p. 40.

12. Smith, *History of the Church*, 2:73.

13. Smith, *History of the Church*, 2:80.

14. "Henderson to Independence Postmaster," in the Columbia, Missouri, *Intelligencer and Boon's Lick Advertiser* (7 June 1834), as quoted in Pearl Wilcox, *The Latter-day Saints on the Missouri Frontier* (Independence, Mo.: n. p., 1972), p. 121.

15. *The Autobiography of Parley P. Pratt*, edited by his son Parley P. Pratt, 6th ed. (Salt Lake City, Utah: Deseret Book Co., 1964), p. 115.

16. Smith, *History of the Church*, 2:97–98.

17. Smith, *History of the Church*, 2:102.

18. Journal of Joseph Holbrook, Archives of The Church of Jesus Christ of Latter-day Saints, Salt Lake City, Utah, p. 19.

19. Smith, *History of the Church*, 2:104.

20. Smith, *History of the Church*, 2:105.

21. Smith, *History of the Church*, 2:120.

22. *History of the Reorganized Church of Jesus Christ of Latter Day Saints* (Independence, Mo.: Herald Publishing House, 1967), 1:515–16.

23. *Messenger and Advocate* 1 (Oct. 1834): 11.

24. Smith, *History of the Church*, 2:182.

25. *Journal of Discourses*, 26 vols. (Liverpool: Latter-day Saints' Book Depot, 1855–86), 2:10.

Chapter 12

Establish a House of Prayer, a House of God: The Kirtland Temple

Milton V. Backman, Jr.
Professor of Church History and Doctrine
Brigham Young University

On a broad plateau near the crest of a steep hill stands one of the important historic landmarks in Ohio, the Kirtland Temple. Although its surroundings near the present metropolis of Cleveland differ markedly from its original environment, this temple still appears as both an esthetic and a spiritual monument to the faith and zeal of early Latter-day Saints. Acknowledged for many years as a unique architectural and historic site, this building is included in the current edition of the National Register of Historic Places.[1]

Buildings are always more than mere physical constructions: their history is interwoven with the struggles and motivations of their builders. The planning and construction of the Kirtland Temple were characterized by incidents of unusual faith, and the uncommon sacrifices were preludes to a powerful pentecostal season. During an era in which the heavens resounded, some of the greatest visions in the history of the world occurred within the walls of this sacred edifice.

There are many less well known but important characteristics of the Kirtland Temple. This building was the first temple and the first major meetinghouse constructed by Latter-day Saints. It was also built in harmony with a commandment of the Lord and in accordance with visions and revelations received by Joseph Smith and other Church leaders. On 27 December 1832, the Lord told the Saints, "Organize yourselves . . : and establish a house, even a house of prayer, a house of fasting, a house of faith, a house of learning, a house of glory, a house of order, a house of God." (D&C 88:119.) When the Saints delayed construction of this temple, the Lord chastised them and emphasized again certain features of this building. The Saints were told on 1 June 1833 that they would receive in this temple an endowment of power from on high and that it would be built according to plans unfolded by the Lord. The interior was to be fifty-five feet wide and sixty-five feet long. The lower part of the inner court was to be dedicated as a place of worship; the second floor was to serve as a school of the apostles. (See D&C 95:1, 8, 13–17.)

When the Saints received the initial instructions to build this temple, the Kirtland branch numbered only about one hundred members. Many converts, including most who joined the Church in Kirtland township, had migrated to western Missouri, the main gathering place for the Saints. Subsequently, in 1833 Latter-day Saints were not only few in number but they also owned fewer than two hundred acres and lacked money for such a project as building a temple. In 1833 only ten members of the Church were assessed a land or personal property tax (the latter tax being an assessment on horses, cattle, or merchandise).[2] Moreover, not one member in that community had practical architectural knowledge of the kind needed for planning a major building. They did not lack faith, however; they believed the revelation that they would receive guidance from the Lord.

The Lord possibly played a greater direct role in the planning of this temple than in the planning of any other building constructed in the latter days. According to Orson

Pratt (who used Kirtland during the 1830s as a base for his missionary labors), Latter-day Saints built this house of the Lord according to a heavenly pattern unfolded by visions.[3] Truman O. Angell, who became one of the supervisors in the construction of the temple, explained that after the First Presidency (Joseph Smith, Sidney Rigdon, and Frederick G. Williams) knelt in prayer, the building appeared before them in vision. He also reported that while standing in the foyer of the temple, Frederick G. Williams told him that the hall coincided precisely with that which he beheld in vision. Further, Joseph Smith told him that the seats were located where he had seen them in vision.[4] And Truman Coe, Presbyterian minister of Kirtland, verified an understanding in that community that the temple was built "according to the pattern shown to Joseph in vision."[5]

The building of the Kirtland Temple was a massive communal enterprise, successful only because of great sacrifice, dedication, and cooperation of all the Mormon community. Latter-day Saints worked together with an inspiration and spirit that distinguished them from many other people.[6] Many laborers worked at least one day a week without compensation, cutting and hauling stone for masons to fashion. "Come, brethren," Joseph Smith would say, "let us go into the stone-quarry and work for the Lord."[7] Some men worked full time on the temple, receiving only food and clothing in payment. Women labored as diligently on this project as the men. They made clothes and provided meals for the workers, drove the wagons that hauled stone from the quarry, assisted the masons, and made carpets, draperies, and veils for the temple. Along with the men, women made great financial sacrifices throughout the building of this house for the Lord. Although china and glassware were mixed with the stucco, giving a sparkle to the exterior, no surviving contemporary records inform us of the extent of the women's contribution of this glass.[8]

For three years, from the summer of 1833 to March 1836, most Kirtland Saints sacrificed their time, talents, and material goods for the building of this house for the

Lord. Most materials used for the construction of the temple were secured locally. For example, oak timber that was cut into massive beams was obtained from nearby forests, and most of the stone was chiseled from a quarry located about one mile south of the building. There were a few major expenses for such materials as glass and special tools and for payment to a contractor for plastering the building. Since only a few workers were paid, and much of the building material was secured at little or no cost, contemporary estimates that the building cost $40,000 to $60,000 are rough approximations.[9]

Recognizing the need for help and sensing a missionary responsibility, elders of Kirtland, throughout the building of the temple, devoted part of their time to missionary work. They not only preached and baptized but they also solicited contributions for that building and encouraged converts to gather in Kirtland. Their labors and the service of other self-supporting missionaries proved fruitful. During the mid-1830s there was an accelerated growth of Latter-day Saints in that community. Primarily as a result of the gathering of converts to Kirtland, Church membership increased from about one hundred in early 1833 to thirteen hundred in 1836. By 1838 there were more than two thousand members in the Kirtland branch.[10]

From an architectural perspective, the Kirtland Temple is an unusual structure. The exterior of the building resembles many New England and Western Reserve meetinghouses (with its rectangular design and bell tower focus), but the sides resemble a massive gothic structure. More than any other architectural characteristic, however, the interior designs and pulpits distinguish it from all other buildings. This temple is an uncommon and harmonious "blend of diverse architectural elements exhibiting Venetian, Georgian, Gothic, Egyptian, and Grecian structural motifs and decorations." Three unusual tiers of pulpits are located on the east and west sides of the large halls on the first and second floors. The corners of the building are strongly articulated by contrasting stone cornerstones, and stone trim of essentially the same color frames the doors and windows. Another uncommon aspect of this temple was that the exterior stone was originally covered by stucco glaze and lined slightly to give it the appearance of a brick building.[11]

Nevertheless, the most distinguishing characteristic of the Kirtland Temple was the unusual events that occurred inside this house of the Lord. Recalling incidents that transpired in that building in 1836, Orson Pratt testified, "God was there, his angels were there, the Holy Ghost was in the midst of the people, the visions of the Almighty were opened to the minds of the servants of the living God; the veil was taken off from the minds of man; they saw the heavens opened; they beheld the angels of God; they heard the voice of the Lord, and they were filled from the crown of their heads to the soles of their feet with the power and inspiration of the Holy Ghost. . . . In that Temple, set apart by the servants of God, and dedicated by a prayer that was written by inspiration, the people were blessed as they never had been blessed for generations and generations."[12]

During a thirteen-week period, extending from 21 January to 1 May 1836, more Latter-day Saints beheld visions and witnessed other unusual spiritual manifestations than during any other era in the history of the restored Church. During at least ten meetings or different sessions of meetings, Latter-day Saints saw heavenly beings. During eight of these sessions, many saw angels; and on five different occasions, Latter-day Saints testified that they saw the Savior, Jesus Christ. While the Saints were communing with heavenly hosts and singing with heavenly choirs, many prophesied, others spoke in tongues, and some received the gift of interpretation of tongues.[13]

While describing one of the meetings he attended in the temple early in 1836, Harrison Burgess recalled that the Spirit of the Lord rested upon him. It seemed, he said, as though the interior of the temple had been illuminated by a power from God. The Prophet, his brother Hyrum, and Roger Orton, he added, seemed to be engulfed in this light. Then Joseph Smith exclaimed aloud that he beheld the Savior, Hyrum Smith said that he saw the angels of heaven, and Roger Orton testified that he saw the chariots of Israel. Concluding his description of this solemn assembly, Elder Burgess affirmed that the power of God was manifest, and many prophesied.[14]

Latter-day Saints enjoyed another spiritual feast on 27 March 1836, the day of the temple's dedication. This service began at 9:00 A.M. Following a scriptural reading, an invocation, and the singing of hymns, Sidney Rigdon spoke for two and half hours, drawing tears from many eyes. After praising the Saints for building the temple amid sacrifices, privations, and persecution, he described one of its unusual characteristics. This building, he testified, was different from all other houses of worship. It was the only building on earth, he asserted, "that was built by divine revelation." He also reminded the Saints of the sacrifices of the Savior. If the Redeemer appeared in that day of "science" and "intelligence," President Rigdon concluded, he would likely say that which he uttered when he walked the earth: "The foxes have holes, and the birds of the air have nests; but the Son of Man hath not where to lay His head."[15]

During the afternoon service, Joseph Smith offered the dedicatory prayer, which had been written by revelation. This temple, he declared, had been built by commandment as a place for the Savior to visit and manifest himself to his people. He prayed that the Saints would go forth in power to gather the righteous to Zion, that they would be protected from the wickedness and calamities of the last days, and that they would be crowned with glory and honor and gain eternal life. He also prayed for others, including leaders of nations, the children of Judah, and all of Israel. (See D&C 109.)[16]

Some who attended this solemn assembly testified that the Savior was present. Others declared that the apostle Peter had come to accept the dedication. David Whitmer testified that he saw angels during the service; and the official minutes kept by Oliver Cowdery stated that during the dedicatory service, Frederick G. Williams testified that a holy angel of God appeared and sat between him and Joseph Smith, Sr.[17]

Following closing remarks by Hyrum Smith and Sidney Rigdon and a prayer by President Rigdon, the congregation sealed the proceedings with the Hosanna Shout, shouting, "Hosanna! Hosanna! Hosanna to God and the Lamb" three times and sealing each series of hosannas with three amens.[18]

Following the Hosanna Shout, Brigham Young arose and spoke in an unknown tongue, which was interpreted by David Patten, another apostle, after which Elder Patten delivered a short exhortation in tongues. About 4:00 P.M., after the Prophet blessed the congregation, the seven-hour dedicatory service concluded.[19]

It was difficult for those who participated in this solemn assembly to reiterate that which had transpired. "No mortal language" could "describe the heavenly manifestations of that memorable day," Eliza R. Snow recalled. The congregation, she added, felt the "sweet spirit of love and union," "a sense of divine presence," and "each heart was filled with joy inexpressible and full of glory." Benjamin Brown, another participant, declared that the Spirit of God was poured out profusely, as on the day of Pentecost. "We had a most glorious and never to be forgotten time."[20]

Unusual spiritual experiences were not restricted to those who gathered in that building. Many persons described uncommon manifestations that transpired outside the house of the Lord during its dedication. Several reported seeing an unusual light hover over the temple. Others testified of hearing heavenly singing coming from the roof of the building.[21] Some said they saw angels or heavenly beings on top of the temple; and during a priesthood meeting held in that building on the night of its dedication, some not only saw angels but heard a vibrant sound, like a mighty rushing wind, penetrate this house of worship.[22]

According to contemporaries, the power of God was also manifest during this pentecostal season in the homes of the Kirtland Saints. While some Saints enjoyed "sweet heavenly communion with the Holy Ghost," others were blessed physically. Lorenzo Snow declared that in many instances "the sick were healed — the deaf made to hear — the blind to see and the lame to walk."[23]

An unusual outpouring of the Spirit continued for months following the dedication of the temple. Many enjoyed spiritual feasts during the fast and testimony meetings held in the temple on the first Thursday of each month. During one of these days of fasting, Prescindia Huntington, who had moved to Kirtland in May 1836 and was baptized the following June, said that one afternoon an excited, bewildered young girl rushed to her home and said that a meeting was being held on top of the temple. "I went to the door," Prescindia explained, "and there I saw on the temple angels clothed in white covering the roof from end to end. They seemed to be walking to and fro; they appeared and disappeared. The third time they appeared and disappeared before I realized that they were not mortal men." She testified that a number of children in Kirtland saw this assembly of angels and that when members of the congregation returned to their homes, they reported that the power of God had been manifest both inside and outside the temple. While interpreting an unknown language during the meeting, one Latter-day Saint declared that angels were "resting" upon the house of the Lord.[24]

While angels were ministering to Latter-day Saints, the testimonies of the Saints were strengthened, increased knowledge was revealed from heaven, and special keys of the priesthood were restored. In one of the greatest visions that occurred in the Lord's house, Joseph Smith learned the principle of salvation for the dead. During a gathering of the priesthood on 21 January 1836 in the west room of the upper loft, the heavens were opened. During this meeting in which many saw angels and the face of the Savior, Joseph Smith beheld in vision the celestial kingdom. He saw "the blazing throne of God, whereon was seated the Father and the Son." He "saw the beautiful streets of that kingdom, which had the appearance of being paved with gold." He beheld "Fathers Adam and Abraham" and the modern apostles (those who had been called and ordained in 1835). He also saw his father (who was in the room with him at the time), his mother, and his brother Alvin, who had died before the restoration of the priesthood and organization of the Church. Joseph marveled how Alvin obtained an inheritance in that kingdom without being baptized for the remission of sins. While Joseph pondered, the voice of the Lord spoke to him, saying, "All who have died without a knowledge of this gospel, who would have received it if they had been permitted to tarry, shall be heirs of the celestial kingdom of God; also all that shall die henceforth without a knowledge of it, who would have received it with all their hearts, shall be heirs of that Kingdom, for I, the Lord will judge all men according to their works, according to the desire of their hearts." (D&C 137:1–9.)[25]

In another significant vision that occurred in the Lord's house, Joseph Smith and Oliver Cowdery received special keys of the priesthood. On Easter Sunday, 3 April 1836, following a meeting in which the sacrament was administered by Church leaders to members who crowded into the temple, Joseph and Oliver retired by one of the pulpits. They knelt in prayer behind drapes that had been lowered, creating an atmosphere of privacy. "The veil was taken from our minds, and the eyes of our understanding were opened," the Prophet recorded in his diary, "and we saw the Lord standing upon the breastwork of the pulpit. . . . Under his feet was a paved work of pure gold in color like amber." The Prophet testified that during this vision the Redeemer forgave them of their sins and accepted that house of worship, adding that its fame would spread to foreign lands. The Lord also said that the people who had built that house had received their endowment and should rejoice. (See D&C 110:1–10.)[26]

When the Lord instructed early converts to gather in Ohio he promised them that they would receive there "an endowment from on high." (D&C 38:32.) This endowment, which bearers of the priesthood received in the Kirtland

Temple, was different from that which Latter-day Saints later obtained in Nauvoo. The Kirtland endowment was a gift of knowledge and power that prepared members to be more effective ambassadors of the Lord. In summarizing this gift, members said that they participated in a washing and anointing ceremony in Kirtland.

This Kirtland endowment consisted in part of four preparatory ordinances—washing of the body, anointing, sealing the anointing, and washing of the feet. All except one of these rites was performed in the temple. The washing ceremony was performed in the homes of the Saints or in the building (that served as a school for the elders, as a printing office, and as an office for Church leaders) constructed adjacent to the temple. This initial ordinance was not merely a washing of the body but was a spiritual experience in which members attempted to cleanse themselves inwardly by promising to keep the commandments of the Lord. The last ordinance, washing of the feet, had earlier been introduced to members of the School of the Prophets but had been discontinued temporarily. It was instituted in the temple shortly before the Savior told Joseph that members had received an endowment.[27]

Following the visitation of the Savior, three personages appeared in separate visions and bestowed upon Joseph Smith and Oliver Cowdery special keys of the priesthood. Moses conferred upon these leaders "the keys of the gathering of Israel from the four parts of the earth" and the keys of "the leading of the ten tribes from the land of the north." (D&C 110:11.) Elias conferred upon them keys of "the dispensation of the gospel of Abraham, saying that in us and our seed all generations after us should be blessed." (D&C 110:12.) Elijah committed to them the keys of ordinances, powers, and endowments of the fulness of the Melchizedek Priesthood in fulfillment of the prophecy of Malachi that "before the great and dreadful day of the Lord," Elijah would come "to turn the hearts of the fathers to the children and children to the fathers, lest the whole earth be smitten with a curse." (D&C 110:13–16.)[28]

Elijah's appearance not only fulfilled a prophecy that

had been uttered more than twenty-two centuries earlier but it also occurred during the Jewish Passover. In compliance with an ancient tradition, Jewish people set a special place with a cup of wine for Elijah and during this meal opened the door for him to enter. Instead of appearing to the Jewish people during this feast, held on Friday, 1 April, however, Elijah appeared in the Kirtland Temple on Easter Sunday, the second day of Passover, "the day of the presentation of the first fruits of the harvest."[29]

There is striking similarity between the vision of 3 April in the Kirtland Temple and a vision on the Mount of Transfiguration. About six months before the death of Jesus, the Savior, Moses, and Elias (Elijah) gave the keys of the priesthood to Peter, James, and John, who later conferred these same keys upon the apostles.[30] These same heavenly beings conferred similar priesthood keys upon Joseph Smith and Oliver Cowdery who in turn bestowed them upon members of the Quorum of Twelve Apostles.

While explaining the significance of this series of visions and other visitations in which priesthood keys were restored, a modern apostle, Elder Bruce R. McConkie, reminded us that we live in the dispensation of the fulness of times, or the fulness of dispensations. "Every key, power, and priesthood ever held by a mortal on earth," he added, was restored to the Prophet Joseph Smith. "These keys are now vested in the First Presidency and the Twelve. They lie dormant, in a sense, in all but the senior Apostle of God on earth."[31]

According to Elder McConkie, included among the keys restored by Elias in the Kirtland Temple was the "marriage discipline of Abraham. . . . It is a system that enables a family unit to continue in eternity; it is the system out of which eternal life grows." It is a holy order, and a new and everlasting covenant of marriage.[32]

That the promises made to Abraham, Isaac, and Jacob might bless the lives of those living in the latter days, Elijah restored the sealing powers of the priesthood. Elijah's authority included more than the work of salvation for the dead: "By virtue of this sealing power all ordinances, both for the living and dead, may be binding on earth and in heaven."[33]

Although the authority to perform temple ordinances was restored in the Kirtland Temple, the Kirtland endowment was not the same as that which was performed in the Nauvoo temple or in Latter-day Saint temples of today. Joseph Smith's keen mind was gradually "awakened and expanded," a modern apostle, Elder Neal Maxwell, reflected, "as the tutoring words of the Lord and of past prophets flowed through his quickened consciousness."[34] He in turn had a responsibility to unfold gospel principles and practices to others, line upon line and precept upon precept.

The pentecostal season did not continue indefinitely in Kirtland. According to Daniel Tyler, after bearers of the priesthood had received their endowment, Joseph Smith cautioned them, "Brethren, for some time Satan has not had power to tempt you. Some have thought that there would be no more temptation. But the opposite will come, and unless you draw near to the Lord you will be overcome and apostatize."[35] Nancy Tracy, another Latter-day Saint who reflected on the unusual spiritual experience that took place in Kirtland, suggested that these blessings prepared Latter-day Saints for the trials that awaited them. "We have opposing elements to contend with," she noted, and then added, the Saints "shall be made perfect through suffering."[36]

Two and a half years following the dedication of the Kirtland Temple, most Saints who sacrificed to build a house for the Lord abandoned this building, left their homes, and headed westward. The exodus from Kirtland of more than sixteen hundred settlers in less than six months was another demonstration of the faith of these converts, for the Latter-day Saints abandoned Kirtland amid intensified persecution, including apostate mobocracy. As aptly described in a letter written by one contemporary, Hepzibah Richards, "They are driven out of this place as truly as the Saints were driven out of Jackson County four years ago, though in a different manner. There they were driven out by force of arms, here by persecution, chiefly from the dissenters."[37] While describing conditions in Kirtland, early Church historians wrote that the year 1837 ended amid "apostasy, persecution, confusion, and mobocracy."[38] Early in January 1838, Joseph Smith and Sidney Rigdon fled from that community.[39] Many contemporaries sincerely believed that if they had not left they would have been killed by their enemies. Persecution continued after the exodus of these leaders; and amid increased threats on lives and property, other Saints headed west. By the end of July 1838 fewer than one hundred Latter-day Saints lived in the shadow of the majestic temple.[40]

Although Joseph Smith and a few other leaders had lived in fear of persecution during most of their residence in Kirtland, the enemy outside the Church was not sufficiently strong to force Latter-day Saints to leave Kirtland before 1838. In the spring and summer of that year, however, oppressors, aided by Mormon dissidents, forced nearly all Latter-day Saints to abandon that community. An apostasy of one-third of the General Authorities and about eleven percent of the membership of the Kirtland branch was a prelude to the major exodus of the Saints.[41]

Latter-day Saints who lived in Kirtland during this crisis concluded that apostates lost the spirit of the Lord through pride, selfishness, greed, immorality, and criticism of the Prophet. Eliza R. Snow aptly observed that after members of the Church had been recipients of marvelous blessings, many were lifted up in the pride of their hearts. Most Kirtland Saints, she explained, were poor, but after the completion of the temple, they sought economic improvement and witnessed the dawn of prosperity. A spirit of speculation gripped many members, including bearers of the priesthood, and some became "haughty." "As the Saints drank in the love and spirit of the world, the Spirit of the Lord withdrew from their hearts, and they were filled with pride and hatred toward those who maintained their integrity."[42]

Some twentieth-century historians have tended to concentrate on economic forces, especially the demise of the Kirtland Safety Society, as the paramount factor triggering dissension within the Church. The failure of this joint-stock company and an economic collapse created by the Panic of 1837 created irritations. Joseph Smith became the scapegoat. People blamed him for their economic plight and claimed he was a fallen prophet. Although some reasoned that the bank had been born of revelation and its failure was evidence that Joseph Smith was no longer an inspired prophet, Joseph defended himself. He insisted that he had never predicted that the bank could not fall. A study of the records of this institution indicates that some of the criticism leveled at Joseph was more a justification than a real cause of the economic irritation. A high percentage of stockholders in the Kirtland Safety Society remained faithful, and not one of the major stockholders was disfellowshipped or excommunicated. In fact, only 8 percent of the investors left the Church, and almost half (45 percent) of this group returned to the Church.[43]

The last major group of Saints to migrate from Geauga County (now Lake) in 1838 was the Kirtland Camp. Organized by the seventies quorum, more than 515 pioneers gathered and formed a long train of wagons that began rolling from that community on 6 July. Elias Smith, the quorum clerk and historian of this group, expressed in his journal the impressions of many who abandoned their homes and temple. "The feelings of the brethren on leaving Kirtland were somewhat peculiar," he wrote, "notwithstanding the scenes they had passed through in Kirtland; but the consciousness of doing the will of their heavenly Father, and obeying His commandments in journeying to Zion, over balanced every other consideration that could possibly be presented to their minds, and buoyed up their spirits."[44]

Although one of the most difficult periods in the life of Joseph Smith was the Kirtland era (many of his closest friends and associates rejected his leadership, and enemies from within and without forced him to flee westward to escape death), the Prophet remained steadfast in his determination to build the kingdom of God. Sustained by new knowledge, strengthened by the reception of new keys, and bolstered by gifts of increased faith and power received in the Kirtland Temple, the Prophet Joseph Smith continued his mission of restoration. George Q. Cannon aptly summarized the Prophet's perseverance amid the trials of life when he asserted:

"Think of what he passed through! Think of his afflictions, and think of his dauntless character! Did any one ever see him falter! Did any one ever see him flinch! Did any one ever see any lack in him of the power necessary to enable him to stand with dignity in the midst of his enemies, or lacking in dignity in the performance of his duties as a servant of the living God? God gave him peculiar power in this respect. He was filled with integrity to God, with such integrity as was not known among men. He was like an angel of God among them. Notwithstanding all that he had to endure, and the peculiar circumstances in which he was so often placed, and the great responsibility that weighed constantly upon him, he never faltered; the feeling of fear or trembling never crossed him—at least he never exhibited it in his feelings or actions. God sustained him to the very last."[45]

Notes

1. *The National Register of Historic Places* (Washington, D.C.: U.S. Government Printing Office, 1972), pp. 368–69.

2. Geauga County Tax Records, Kirtland Township, 1833, microfilm copy located in Family Records Library, The Church of Jesus Christ of Latter-day Saints, Salt Lake City, Utah.

3. Orson Pratt, in *Journal of Discourses*, 26 vols. (Liverpool: Latter-day Saints' Book Depot, 1855–86), 14:273.

4. Autobiography of Truman O. Angell, microfilm of holograph, Archives of The Church of Jesus Christ of Latter-day Saints, Salt Lake City, Utah, p. 4. For additional references to the temple being built in harmony with visions and revelations received by the First Presidency, see "Extract from Journal of Heber C. Kimball," *Times and Seasons* 6 (15 Jan. 1845): 771, and Autobiography of George W. Johnson, typescript, Brigham Young University, Provo, Utah, p. 2.

5. *The Ohio Observer* [Hudson, Ohio], 11 Aug. 1836.

6. Thomas E. O'Donnell, "The First Mormon Temple, at Kirtland, Ohio," *Architecture* 50 (1924): 266.

7. Heber C. Kimball, in *Journal of Discourses*, 10:165; Joseph Smith, *History of The Church of Jesus Christ of Latter-day Saints*, 7 vols., 2d ed. rev., ed. B. H. Roberts (Salt Lake City, Utah: The Church of Jesus Christ of Latter-day Saints, 1932–51), 2:161.

8. Linda King Newell and Valeen Tippetts Avery, "Sweet Counsel and Seas of Tribulation: The Religious Life of the Women in Kirtland," *BYU Studies* 20 (Winter 1980): 155–56.

9. Milton V. Backman, Jr., *The Heavens Resound: A History of the Latter-day Saints in Ohio, 1830–1838* (Salt Lake City, Utah: Deseret Book Co., 1983), p. 161.

10. Ibid., p. 140. According to the census of 1830 there were 1,018 people living in Kirtland township. The non-Mormon growth in Kirtland continued until 1833, when this growth stopped at about 1200. Consequently in 1836 the Mormon population exceeded that of the non-Mormon, and by 1838 there were almost double the number of Saints in Kirtland than non-Mormons. Ibid.

11. *The National Register of Historic Places*, p. 368.

12. Orson Pratt, in *Journal of Discourses*, 18:132.

13. The most complete account of the visions that took place in the Kirtland Temple was recorded in Joseph Smith's 1836 diary and later published in his *History of the Church*. After Joseph's history was published, many contempories verified in their sermons and writings the reliability of that history. See Backman, *Heavens Resound*, pp. 283–304.

14. Backman, *Heavens Resound*, p. 292; Autobiography of Harrison Burgess, photocopy of holograph, Archives of The Church of Jesus Christ of Latter-day Saints, Salt Lake City, Utah, pp. 3–4; Diary of Stephen Post, holograph, Jan. 1836, Archives of The Church of Jesus Christ of Latter-day Saints, Salt Lake City, Utah; Smith, *History of the Church*, 2:386–87.

15. Smith, *History of the Church*, 2:413–15. An account of the dedicatory service written by Oliver Cowdery was published in the March 1836 edition of the *Messenger and Advocate*; Oliver Cowdery, Sketch Book, 27 Mar. 1836, Archives of The Church of Jesus Christ of Latter-day Saints, Salt Lake City, Utah; *Messenger and Advocate* 2 (Mar. 1836): 274–81.

16. Smith, *History of the Church*, 2:420–26; Orson Pratt, in *Journal of Discourses*, 18:132.

17. Autobiography of Truman O. Angell, p. 5; Heber C. Kimball, in *Journal of Discourses*, 9:376; Autobiography of Heber C. Kimball, Archives of The Church of Jesus Christ of Latter-day Saints, Salt Lake City, Utah, p. 66; George A. Smith, in *Journal of Discourses*, 2:215; Journal of Edward Partridge, 27 Mar. 1836, Archives of The Church of Jesus Christ of Latter-day Saints, Salt Lake City, Utah; *Messenger and Advocate* 2 (Mar. 1836): 281.

18. Smith, *History of the Church*, 2:427–28.

19. Smith, *History of the Church*, 2:428. For additional information on events that transpired during the dedicatory service, see Smith, *History of the Church*, 2:410–28, and Backman, *Heavens Resound*, pp. 294–300.

20. Eliza R. Snow, *Eliza R. Snow, an Immortal: Selected Writings of Eliza R. Snow*, comp. Nicholas G. Morgan (Salt Lake City, Utah: Nicholas G. Morgan Foundation, 1957), pp. 58, 62; Benjamin Brown, *Testimonies for the Truth* (Liverpool, 1853), pp. 10–11.

21. Orson Hyde Elliott, *Reminiscences, in the Life of Orson Hyde Elliott* (San Francisco, 1899), p. 44; George A. Smith, in *Journal of Discourses*, 2:215; Autobiography of Aroet L. Hale, holograph, p. 4, Archives of The Church of Jesus Christ of Latter-day Saints, Salt Lake City, Utah.

22. Brown, *Testimonies for the Truth*; Autobiography of Aroet L. Hale; Oliver Cowdery, Sketch Book, 27 Mar. 1836.

23. Eliza R. Snow Smith, *Biography and Family Record of Lorenzo Snow* (Salt Lake City, Utah: Deseret News Co., 1884), p. 11.

24. Edward W. Tullidge, *The Women of Mormondom* (New York, 1877), p. 207.

25. Smith, *History of the Church*, 2:380–82.

26. Smith, *History of the Church*, 2:434–35; Diary of Joseph Smith, 3 Apr. 1836, Archives of The Church of Jesus Christ of Latter-day Saints, Salt Lake City, Utah.

27. Backman, *Heavens Resound*, pp. 265–66, 285–94, 300–302.

28. Smith, *History of the Church*, 6:251; Andrew F. Ehat and Lyndon W. Cook, eds., *The Words of Joseph Smith* (Provo: Religious Studies Center, Brigham Young University, 1980), p. 329.

29. John P. Pratt, "The Restoration of Priesthood Keys on Easter 1836," *Ensign* 15 (July 1985): 55, 59.

30. Smith, *History of the Church*, 3:387.

31. Bruce R. McConkie, "This Final Glorious Gospel Dispensation," *Ensign* 10 (Apr. 1980): 21–23.

32. Ibid., p. 23.

33. Ibid.

34. Neal A. Maxwell, in Conference Report, Oct. 1983, p. 76.

35. Daniel Tyler, "Incidents of Experience," *Scraps of Biography* (Salt Lake City, Utah: Juvenile Instructor, 1883), pp. 32–33.

36. Autobiography of Nancy Alexander Tracy, typescript, Archives of The Church of Jesus Christ of Latter-day Saints, Salt Lake City, Utah, p. 9.

37. Hepzibah Richards to friends, 19 Feb. 1838, in Manuscript History of the Great Lakes Mission—Ohio, 19 Feb. 1838, Archives of The Church of Jesus Christ of Latter-day Saints, Salt Lake City, Utah.

38. Smith, *History of the Church*, 2:529.

39. Smith, *History of the Church*, 3:1.

40. Backman, *Heavens Resound*, pp. 342–47, 368.

41. Ibid., pp. 327–29, 361.

42. Eliza R. Snow, *Biography and Family Record of Lorenzo Snow*, pp. 20–24.

43. For a discussion of the effect of the Kirtland Safety Society on

Church history, see Backman, *Heavens Resound,* pp. 314–21. See also Marvin S. Hill, C. Keith Rooker, and Larry T. Wimmer, *The Kirtland Economy Revisited* (Provo, Utah: Brigham Young University Press, 1977). This latter work suggests that the Panic of 1837 did not lead to the demise of the Kirtland Safety Society but actually prolonged its life. The bank was legally destroyed because it lacked a charter. The Panic of 1837, however, intensified the problems of Joseph Smith and others because it caused a decline in land prices and made it more difficult for Joseph Smith to pay his debts (including securing delays in payment of debts). Most of Joseph's debts were Church debts that had occurred primarily as a result of buying land in Kirtland that was sold to Saints for less than that charged by others. For a more detailed discussion of forces that led to an apostasy and Mormon persecution in Kirtland, see Backman, *Heavens Resound,* chap. 17, and Max H. Parkin, "The Nature and Cause of Internal and External Conflict of the Mormons in Ohio Between 1830 and 1838," Master's thesis, Brigham Young University, 1966.

44. Backman, *Heavens Resound,* p. 357; Smith, *History of the Church,* 3:100.

45. George Q. Cannon, in *Journal of Discourses,* 23:362.

Chapter 13

Let Far West Be Holy and Consecrated

Clark V. Johnson
Associate Professor of Church History and Doctrine
Brigham Young University

The Latter-day Saint migration into Missouri began in the early 1830s. About eight months after the Church was organized the Prophet Joseph Smith received a commandment to move to the Ohio. Once established in Ohio, about February 1831, Joseph began receiving revelations about future doctrines and movements of the church. The Kirtland-Missouri period was one of the eminent revelatory periods in Church history.[1]

The priesthood councils, the Presiding Bishopric (see D&C 41), the High Council (see D&C 102), the First Presidency, the Quorum of the Twelve Apostles, the First Council of Seventy (see D&C 107)—the governing bodies of the Church—were organized. During this period God revealed and elaborated on the ideal of Zion to his prophet. The Lord defined Zion as the pure in heart and declared that Zion was a place in Missouri, where the pure in heart dwell. (See D&C 97; 52; 57.) Outgrowths from the concept of Zion included the reemphasis of the Ten Commandments (see D&C 59), the Sermon on the Mount (see 3 Nephi), the doctrines of premortal life (see Moses), the law of consecration (see D&C 51), the united order (see D&C 104), tithing (see D&C 119), spiritual gifts (see D&C 46), the degrees of glory (see D&C 76), the priesthood (see D&C 84; 107), temples in which the Saints of God received the mysteries of godliness (sacred ordinances that had long been withheld from man, but which increased their knowledge of God; see D&C 57; 84), the Word of Wisdom (see D&C 89), the principles of light and truth upon which all creation operates (see D&C 88; 93), and the doctrine of eternal life (see D&C 76; 137). Or, as it was summed up later by a new convert during this period, "As man is, God once was: As God is, man may be."[2]

These revelations stretched their minds beyond anything they had ever imagined. These principles challenged them to raise their aims not only to achieve success in mortality but also to place in perspective earth-life as a continuance in immortality.

The unfolding history of this period is one in which Church members struggled to incorporate in their lives the principles set forth in the revelations. Church leaders sought to implement the revelations regarding priesthood councils and to give direction to the Church. Following revelatory directions, the Prophet Joseph Smith first traveled to Missouri in 1831. There he held a conference, and Sidney Rigdon consecrated the land for the "gathering of the saints." (D&C 57:1; see also 52:1.)[3]

Life in Kirtland was on the edge of the frontier, but life in Missouri proved to be the "raw" frontier. The principle of "survival of the fittest" dominated life in Missouri. The principles of Jacksonian democracy that governed American life during the 1830s were nowhere more forcibly expressed than on the frontier. Freedom of speech and action characterized life on the frontier. "Backwoodsmen . . . sold their rude clearings or even abandoned them at the first approach of civilization." The frontier farmer, "a restless man" who lived in a world of "cheap land . . . often moved as he felt attracted by the thought of better soils."[4] The comforts of life mattered little. All who came to the frontier faced the same "rigorous hardships, the same deprivations and the same grueling labors."[5] The strong survived; the weak did not.

When Joseph entered Missouri in 1831, he became acutely concerned about the lawless element that dominated life there.[6] He worried about the members of The Church of Jesus Christ of Latter-day Saints who migrated into this environment. These Saints brought a commitment to establish the kingdom of God on the earth. They attempted to implant this ideal in the heart of the frontier.

The 1830s saw constant collisions of Church members with the frontier society as the Saints sought to live the ideals of their new faith and perhaps share these standards with their neighbors through missionary work. Parley P. Pratt wrote that by the summer of 1833 there were nearly twelve hundred Church members in Jackson County. The Missourians considered the Mormons intruders. Soon mobs arose, and during the winter of 1833–34 they drove the Saints from Jackson County.[7]

Church members fled primarily into Clay and Ray counties, where they remained for two years.[8] When the Mormons fled from Jackson into Clay and Ray counties, Ray County included what today is Caldwell, Daviess, and Harrison counties, thus stretching to the Iowa border.[9] Carroll County, where Dewitt is located, had been a part of Ray County until 1833, the same year the Mormons left Jackson county. With both Caldwell and Daviess counties being created in 1836 from Ray County, some of the Latter-day Saints did not actually move but became citizens of a different county when the Missouri legislature organized the counties.[10]

The Location of Far West

On 11 March 1836, the Prophet Joseph Smith charged Edward Partridge, Isaac Morley, John Corrill, and William W. Phelps to purchase lands in Missouri where the Saints could settle.[11] Following an exploration of the areas north of Liberty, Missouri, Presidents William W. Phelps and John Whitmer, members of the Church Presidency in Missouri, purchased the town plot of Far West on 8 August

1836. They laid out the city one mile square.[12] On 15 November 1836 Jacob Whitmer, Elisha H. Groves, and George M. Hinkle were appointed to assist the Presidency in building a temple.[13] Problems soon arose among Church leaders over the acquisition of property and the location of the city of Far West. Some felt that Phelps and Whitmer had exceeded their trust.[14] Especially was this true regarding the temple site, which had also been selected by these men. The consensus seemed to be that Whitmer and Phelps had surpassed their authority by purchasing lands without council approval and that cities of Zion ought to be located by prophetic decree, not by arbitrary selection by those of lesser authority.[15] Although it is not mentioned in the records, Whitmer and Phelps likely justified themselves by their position in the Presidency of the Church in Missouri, and their commission had come directly from the Prophet Joseph Smith.

The location and perimeters of Far West were a frequent topic of disagreement as the Presidency, High Council, and Presiding Bishopric met in 1837. In April this body transferred "the Town Plot with 4 eighties, which are on the Commons, into the hands of the Bishop of Zion, & that the avails arising from the sale of said lands should be appropriated to the benefit & upbuilding of 'Poor Bleeding Zion'."[16] Even with the transfer of property to the Presiding Bishopric, disputations on the subject of Far West did not die. In November 1837 the Corporation of Far West wanted to decrease the width of the streets so that each block would contain "four acres of ground and each block be divided into four lots."[17] Apparently this action was taken, as Albert P. Rockwood noted that the four main streets would be eight rods wide and the public square would contain ten acres. The other streets were to be six rods wide, and the blocks were to contain four acres each. Thus each block would contain four buildings.[18] Several days later, on 10 November 1837, the council voted to enlarge Far West to two square miles.[19] This subject was still being debated in early 1838 as the council authorized Thomas B. Marsh and John Corrill to draft a petition so that the boundary extension could be acted on in the next session of court.[20] Apparently the action to double the size of Far West was never taken; subsequent land studies show that the city plot remained one mile square.[21]

In spite of these difficulties, Far West soon emerged as the center of Mormon influence, smaller settlements, such as Haun's Mill, Bear Creek, Adam-ondi-Ahman, and De-witt being settled during the same period.

Disagreement and Confusion

The dispute among Church leaders over the settlement of Far West carried over into other issues as the various councils struggled for their place in Church government. Unfortunately, these disagreements over authority and jurisdiction became more serious. As the leading quorums — the Church Presidency in Missouri, the High Council, and the Quorum of Twelve Apostles — came into conflict, untimely decisions were made that rocked the Church. Letters suggest that Oliver Cowdery, John Whitmer, and David Whitmer, members of the Presidency of the Church in Missouri, did not feel that the Traveling High Council (Quorum of the Twelve Apostles) and the High Council at Far West had jurisdiction over them. Also, Oliver judged some of the men who presided over the Church to be "hotheaded."[22]

About 1 November 1837 Joseph arrived at Far West to settle the difficulties among Church leaders. During the ten days he was at Far West, the Prophet met in council with local authorities; they solved most of the problems regarding the city plot and the width of streets. He agreed with the earlier decisions made by the council; however, his suggestion that the location of the temple be deferred until the Lord had revealed his will nullified the High Council's earlier decision. The council acceded to the Prophet's proposals, which were also sanctioned in a conference with the local membership.[23] Except for some problems between Oliver Cowdery, Thomas B. Marsh, and Joseph the trip was a success.[24] On 10 November Joseph returned to Kirtland.[25]

Harmony among Church leaders was only temporary. In a council meeting held near the end of January 1838, charges were brought against W. W. Phelps, David Whitmer, John Whitmer, and Oliver Cowdery, the Presidency of the Church in Missouri,[26] who were accused of violating the Word of Wisdom and selling their lands in Jackson County. The accused admitted to certain violations.[27] The council then resolved that these brethren not be received as Presidents and that this action be presented to the Church. Between 5 and 9 February 1838, the charges were presented at various branches of the Church throughout the area. Even though some spoke in favor of retaining the Presidency temporarily until Joseph Smith arrived, the majority rejected them as the Presidency of the Church in Missouri.[28]

On 10 March 1838 at a High Council meeting, charges were brought against W. W. Phelps and John Whitmer. These charges ranged from unchristian conduct to the most serious accusation, fraudulent use of Church funds.[29] At this trial Oliver Cowdery tried to intervene in the defendants' behalf by sending a letter to Thomas B. Marsh, who presided over the council at the Church trial. Oliver maintained that his purpose was to pacify the council and to reason with the men who were meeting. The letter noted that it was "contrary to the principles of the revelations of Jesus Christ and His gospel . . . to try a person . . . by an illegal tribunal or by men prejudiced against him or by authority that has given an opinion or decision beforehand or in his absence."[30] Unfortunately, the letter had the opposite effect on the members of the council. Rather than calming them, it convinced the council members that Phelps and Whitmer were in rebellion; the council excommunicated them from the church.[31]

These events show that the Quorum of the Twelve and the High Council at Far West did not feel themselves subservient to the Presidency at Far West whom they had previously released. Nor did the Presidency at Far West acknowledge that the Far West High Council or the Quorum of the Twelve had the power to release them. Therefore, the excommunicants did not feel they were subject to the council's decisions.

As Thomas B. Marsh called into question the conduct of these leaders, conflict among Church leadership boiled as each began to take sides—the Cowderys and the Whitmers against the Marshes. In a letter dated 24 February 1838, Oliver wrote his brothers in Kirtland of "a great stir here, and so far as I am able to learn, the names of all who refuse to confess those disorganizing doctrines [organization of quorums] lately introduced into the Church, to be correct, are denounced as wicked, devilish . . . and not friendly to Joseph." Continuing, Oliver observed that he considered such notions as "perfect foolery"; he felt "that those desperate and hot-headed power-seeking ignorant men . . . will drive the intelligent and independents to declare their unbelief to an astonished world."[32] The tone of Oliver's letter indicates the frustration as well as the concern he personally felt about the direction the Church was heading in Missouri. It is apparent that he felt that the priesthood councils lacked direction, refused to admit any discussions to procedures within meetings, and moved too rapidly in making decisions. Oliver also maintained that he had "long been pointed out for a victim" of such priesthood councils.[33] During the next month, on 12 April 1838, he was excommunicated from the Church.[34]

The Arrival of Joseph Smith and Sidney Rigdon at Far West

In the middle of this turmoil, on 12 January 1838, the Prophet Joseph Smith and Sidney Rigdon left Kirtland, Ohio. Joseph arrived at Far West 14 March 1838, but Sidney Rigdon did not arrive until 4 April 1838.[35]

Whitmer's and Phelps's memberships had already been withdrawn before Joseph's arrival, and Oliver Cowdery's excommunication followed a few days later. Shortly after the Prophet's arrival, Oliver sought to counsel with him, but the interview never took place, much to Cowdery's disappointment.[36]

Even though Joseph took part in the council meetings

and presided during this time, he never contravened the council's decisions. Why he chose not to intervene in behalf of the Whitmers and Cowderys and other issues decided by the council is not stated; however, it needs be noted that Church government, which is government by council, began to develop at this date.[37] In a letter to Brigham Young in 1843, Oliver Cowdery took a different view of the matter. He felt that designing men were envious of the "harmony existing between [himself] and the first elders of the Church."[38] Oliver accused them of character assassination that drove a wedge between himself and the Prophet.[39]

Joseph's presence in Far West calmed Church members for a few weeks. On 17 April he received a revelation directing him to call others to positions vacated by those who had left the Church. (See D&C 114.) In a revelation near the end of April the Lord accepted Far West and commanded that it be built up and that a temple be built. (See D&C 114:2; 115:7–12.)

During the weeks preceding these revelations, Joseph and others explored the region selecting possible sites for future cities. In May, by revelation, he named Adam-ondi-Ahman, where Lyman Wight and others had already settled. (See D&C 116.) On 1 June Joseph returned to Far West from an exploring and surveying expedition to be with Emma while she gave birth to a son, Alexander Hale Smith, the following day.[40]

During the first days of July, several families left Far West for Carroll County. They settled at Dewitt[41] and joined other Latter-day Saints already living there.[42] In spite of previous difficulties, these were special times in which the Saints were edified by their association with the Prophet.

The Fall of Far West

In the early summer of 1838, things looked bright for the Church. New locations had been selected for cities, and the eastern migration was on its way. At a church meeting in June 1838, Sidney Rigdon preached his famous "Salt Sermon," wherein he said to the Church members assembled, "Ye are the salt of the earth; but if the salt have lost his savor, wherewith shall it be salted?" Referring to those who had left the Church, he continued, "It is thenceforth good for nothing, but to be cast out, and to be trodden under foot of men."[43] Fearing for their personal safety, David and John Whitmer, W. W. Phelps, and Oliver Cowdery fled from Far West within a few days.

Rigdon's second discourse came as part of the Independence Day celebration at Far West. This celebration included a parade composed of Church leaders, militia, and cavalry, "which marched to music." It culminated at the Far West temple lot, where the Prophet Joseph Smith directed the laying of the temple cornerstones.[44] Sidney Rigdon was the orator of the day. In his speech, known as "The Mormon Declaration of Independence," Rigdon declared that it was "better, far better to sleep with the dead, than to be oppressed among the living."[45] This speech notified everyone that the Mormons insisted upon their constitutional rights.

Problems until this time had been pretty much confined within the Church as the members struggled to establish Zion; however, events from within the Church influenced non-Mormons. For at least four reasons, the Missourians felt threatened by Rigdon's 4 July speech. First, they knew what had happened to the Phelpses, the Cowderys, and the Whitmers. Second, they feared increased Mormon influence because of the influx of Latter-day Saint migration into Missouri. Third, they did not understand and they were afraid of the Mormon belief in a living prophet and the Mormons' determination to follow him. And fourth, county political leaders in Daviess, Clinton, Lafayette, Livingston, and Carroll counties realized that a large migration would give the followers of Joseph Smith control of the counties just as the Saints controlled Caldwell County. Soon the social pressures from outside the Church began to increase, until only a spark was needed to ignite the flame.

This catalyst occurred a few weeks later at Gallatin on election day, 6 August. Citizens denied Mormons the right to vote; when the Mormons insisted on voting, a riot broke out.[46] An account by John L. Butler, a participant, gave the victory to the Mormons; Joseph H. McGee wrote that he "had witnessed many knock downs . . . but none on so grand a scale," and he concluded that the Missourians "had carried the day."[47] The true outcome of the Gallatin election-day riot differs from account to account. The following day, Joseph Smith received an erroneous notice that three Mormons had been killed. Shortly after obtaining this news, the Prophet, Sidney Rigdon, Hyrum Smith, and fifteen or twenty others, under the command of George W. Robinson, rode toward Gallatin to investigate the report. They were joined by additional brethren as they traveled. Fortunately, the Prophet and his party took a circuitous route rather than riding directly into Gallatin, stopping at Lyman Wight's house in Adam-ondi-Ahman. They learned from several men who had been at Gallatin that "none of the brethren were killed, although several were badly wounded."[48] Recognizing the volatile nature of the state of affairs, the Prophet spent the next few days visiting old settlers in the area, promoting peace.[49] Among those he visited was Adam Black, a justice of the peace for Daviess County. The Saints asked Black to sign an agreement that "he would not associate himself with any mob against the Mormons." Black, after refusing to sign the already prepared statement, wrote one of his own that he did sign in which he promised to support the state and United States constitutions. By the middle of August 1838, however, Adam Black and William Peniston brought charges against Joseph Smith and Lyman Wight, accusing them of insurrection.[50] Expecting to be acquitted of these charges, the Prophet, Wight, and others met at a Mr. Raglin's, where a hearing was finally held before Judge King in Daviess County. To the surprise of those present, the judge ordered the Prophet and Wight to stand trial before the circuit court. They were released "on $500 bond while awaiting the proceedings."[51]

During the days and weeks that followed, raids began on rural Mormon homes and small communities, terrorizing the inhabitants. A mob army laid siege to Dewitt, and two mobs were operating near Haun's Mill. The small villages of Gallatin and Millport were burned, each side blaming the other.[52] Both sides took prisoners and organized themselves.[53] In late August and September, armed Missourians attacked isolated Mormon farms. To protect outlying settlers, the Mormons incorporated into the militia a small, highly mobile unit named the Danites. They were organized first as a defensive force, to show local mobs that the Mormons were determined to defend themselves and to help isolated Mormon families who were beleaguered by lawless citizens. Soon, however, this unit, under Sampson Avard, exceeded its original charge and became an unofficial avenging force, which matched Missourian brutality blow for blow.[54]

Excitement in western Missouri escalated. A mob-army lay siege to Dewitt near the end of September, preventing the inhabitants from leaving to gather food. They also shot up the town and stampeded the settlers' animals. Starved and repeatedly shot at day and night, the people of Dewitt surrendered on 11 October 1838, then moved to Far West.[55] The mobbers harassed them along the way, and as a result one woman died and was buried, wrapped only in a blanket.[56] The riots, false accusations, and anarchy soon led to a face-to-face confrontation between Mormons and mobs.

The Mormons learned that a mob army was threatening outlying farms on Crooked River in Caldwell County. Acting under the advisement of government officials and Missouri state law, the Saints had previously organized a militia unit within Caldwell County.[57] George M. Hinkle served as commander of the militia headquartered at Far West, with Lyman Wight, David W. Patten, and John Killian serving as officers over the various units within the command. When word reached Far West that a mob-army was collecting on Crooked River and that the mob was holding three of the brethren captive in their camp, Captain David W. Patten left Far West with about sixty men. He encountered Samuel Bogart's company at Crooked River. When the fighting ceased, Gideon Carter lay dead, Patten and Patrick O'Banion were mortally wounded, and Samuel Hendricks and several others were wounded.[58] One member of Bogart's command was killed, Moses Rolland; and a number were wounded—Thomas H. Lloyd, Edwin Odell, James Lochard, Martin Dunnaway, Samuel Tarwater, and Wyatt Crawen.[59]

The day following the battle at Crooked River, Jacob Haun visited the Prophet at Far West at the request of the settlers near the mill located on Shoal Creek. The thirty-five families had been unsuccessful in negotiating peace treaties with the mobs, so community leaders sent Haun to Far West to seek the Prophet's advice. Joseph Smith advised Haun to abandon the mill and move into Far West. Haun explained that he felt the people to be strong enough to defend the mill.[60] The Prophet cautioned him to "move in, by all means, if you wish to save your lives. . . . You had much better lose your property than your lives, one can be replaced, the other cannot be restored; but there is no need of your losing either if you will only do as you are commanded."[61] Haun returned and told those at the mill that "if we thought we could maintain the mill it was Joseph's council for us to do so if we thought not to come to Farewest."[62] The following day, 30 October 1838, a Missouri militia unit under the command of Colonel William O. Jennings and Nehemiah Comstock attacked the Mormon settlement at Haun's Mill. It is estimated that this army of from 240 to 300 well-armed men fired seventeen hundred rounds at the thirty-five defenders. Eighteen men and boys died, and another twelve were wounded during the attack.[63]

Throughout this time, both sides continually appealed to the heads of government for protection. On 27 October 1838, just three days before the incident at Haun's Mill, Governor Lilburn W. Boggs had issued an order demanding that all Mormons leave the state or be exterminated.[64] The governor enforced his order by sending General John B. Clark to command the state militia already approaching Far West.

On the evening the Haun's Mill massacre occurred, the

Missouri Militia of twenty-five hundred to three thousand soldiers approached Far West. At first the citizens of Far West felt relief, but relief turned to apprehension as the army bivouacked within sight of the city and informed the Saints that the army had been ordered by the governor to stop the Mormon rebellion. The people of the city spent the night bolstering fortifications and standing guard. The following day, under a flag of truce, Colonel George M. Hinkle, commander of the forces at Far West, entered the army encampment. General Samuel D. Lucas demanded the surrender of certain Mormon leaders—Joseph Smith, Sidney Rigdon, Parley P. Pratt, Lyman Wight, and George W. Robinson.[65] Returning to the city, Hinkle reported to Church leaders that General Lucas wished to talk over the current condition with them. Consequently, later that day Colonel Hinkle and the men Lucas had requested left Far West for the army camp. As they neared the camp, the army officers started toward them with what at first appeared to be an honor guard, but as the Mormons drew nearer, the guard rushed forward surrounding them. They were conducted back to the militia camp as prisoners. There a court-martial was held. The Prophet and others were tried in absentia and sentenced to be shot the next morning. The execution of the prisoners was thwarted by the actions of General Alexander W. Doniphan, who, risking disgrace, refused to carry out the execution order that had been given to him by General Lucas.[66] The following day, Hyrum Smith and Amasa Lyman were arrested and put with the other prisoners.

Once the leaders had been arrested, the militia entered Far West and demanded that the citizens surrender their arms. After giving up their arms, the men were ordered into the town square, where they were forced to sign away their property to defray the cost of the war. Meanwhile, the army looted the houses. They "tore up floors, upset haystacks, plundered . . . wantonly wasted and destroyed a great amount of property . . . [and violated] the chastity of women."[67] On 3 November the prisoners were taken into Far West and permitted under strict guard to take leave of their families. The Prophet noted: "I found my wife and children in tears. . . . When I entered my house, they clung to my garments, their eyes streaming with tears, while mingled emotions of joy and sorrow were manifested in their countenances [they feared he had been killed]. I requested to have a private interview with them, . . . but this privilege was denied me by the guard. I was then obliged to take my departure."[68] Joseph and those arrested with him were first marched to Independence and later to Richmond to stand trial.[69]

On 5 November 1838, about eighty men were arrested by General John W. Clark at Far West, and fifty-three were escorted to Richmond to await trial before Judge Austin A. King's court of inquiry that began 12 November 1838. Following this preliminary investigation, the prisoners were bound over for trial by the circuit court.[70] Joseph and five others were sentenced by Judge King to Liberty Jail to await trial.

While Church leaders spent the winter of 1838–39 in Missouri jails, they prayed for their people. Meanwhile the Latter-day Saints made their escape from Missouri. Under the direction of Brigham Young, Heber C. Kimball, and others, almost twelve thousand people—men, women, and children—headed eastward across Missouri into Iowa and Illinois. They settled in some ten counties in Illinois and two counties in Iowa, where they remained until the return of their leaders in the spring of 1839.[71]

By the late spring of 1839, the Mormons had abandoned Far West. When the Mormons left Missouri, "the deserted farms and houses offered inducement to emigration that was not despised, and new settlers rapidly filled the places of the departed hosts."[72]

Conclusions

Certainly the Kirtland-Missouri period was the greatest revelatory period in the history of the Church. During this time the Prophet Joseph Smith received revelations, explained the doctrines, and organized the councils that govern the Church. After 1835, when the presiding priesthood quorums were organized, Joseph's function became somewhat different. While still the center and clearly the most popular figure of the Church, he permitted the various quorums to function; and at Far West it seems he took a "back seat," allowing the members of those quorums to define the boundaries of their authority.

Thus, the Prophet displayed at Far West a contrast in his leadership, compared to leadership patterns of earlier Church history. During the formative years, the settlement at Far West was not directed by the Prophet, because the location had been chosen by others; and even after his arrival he did not assume the responsibility to govern the community. Even though Church and community government were nearly the same, Joseph left the actual functioning to others, such as Thomas B. Marsh, David W. Patten, Brigham Young, and Elias Higbee. He also chose to take a supporting position in political and military decisions. Documents during this time describe him as a comforter, counselor, and teacher. While he did preside during meetings of the Far West High Council and the Traveling High Council, he also approved of their decisions.

After its initial settlement, Far West was accepted by the Lord, and the Saints were commanded to gather there and build a temple. Soon Far West emerged as the most populous city in Caldwell County and the center of Mormon activity. Weakened by the confusion among its own leadership, the Church fell prey to non-Mormon agitators, who feared the loss of position, wealth, and power. Within a few weeks, anarchy escalated to such a pitch that the state militia, including some of the mobbers, intervened; and with the Governor's proclamation in hand, the militia drove the Mormons from the state.

After the Mormon expulsion, the city fell into decay, and the one-time county seat of Caldwell County degenerated into scattered farms, the land tilled by other hands. In time virtually the only remaining evidence of its promised splendor was the foundation stones for the temple, laid 4 July 1838.[73]

Notes

1. The Prophet Joseph Smith received eighty-eight revelations that were published in the Doctrine and Covenants during the Kirtland-Missouri period. See Doctrine and Covenants, 1981 ed., "Chronological Order of Contents."

2. Eliza R. Snow Smith, *Biography and Family Record of Lorenzo Snow* (Salt Lake City, Utah: Deseret News Co., 1884), p. 46.

3. Joseph Smith, *History of The Church of Jesus Christ of Latter-day Saints*, 7 vols., 2d ed. rev., ed. B. H. Roberts (Salt Lake City, Utah: The Church of Jesus Christ of Latter-day Saints, 1932–51), 1:196. See Smith, *History of the Church*, 1:188–96, for Joseph Smith's travels and work in Missouri during his first visit.

4. George Dangerfield, *The Era of Good Feelings* (New York: Harcourt, Brace, and Co., 1952), pp. 111–12.

5. Leland Homer Gentry,"A History of the Latter-day Saints in Northern Missouri from 1836 to 1839" (Ph.D. dissertation, Brigham Young University, 1965), p. 16.

6. Smith, *History of the Church*, 1:189.

7. P. P. Pratt, *History of the Late Persecution Inflicted by the State of Missouri upon the Mormons* (Detroit: Dawson & Bates, 1839), pp. 18–23. See also Parley P. Pratt, *Autobiography of Parley Parker Pratt*, edited by his son Parley P. Pratt, 6th ed. (Salt Lake City, Utah: Deseret Book Co., 1966), p. 105.

8. Clark V. Johnson, "The Missouri Redress Petitions: A Reappraisal of Mormon Persecutions in Missouri," *BYU Studies* 26 (Spring 1986): 31–32. See also Pratt, *History of the Late Persecution*, pp. 22–24, and Pratt, *Autobiography*, p. 107.

9. George B. Everton, Sr., *The Handy Book for Genealogists* (Logan, Utah: Everton Publishers, 1971), pp. 127–33.

10. Jacob Haun purchased land in Caldwell County as early as 1835, where he built his mill on Shoal Creek. See Caldwell County land records.

11. W. W. Phelps wrote a letter from Liberty, Missouri, to President Oliver Cowdery at Kirtland, Ohio, detailing a recent exploration of the "Far West" (meaning uninhabited land north and west of Liberty, Missouri). They visited Plattsburg, the Clinton County seat. Without a compass they were lost much of one day, but in the afternoon they found a house on Shoal Creek when they reentered Ray County. He described the land around Shoal Creek as having "some tolerable mill sites; but the prairies, . . . peering one over another, as far as the eye can glance, flatten all common calculation as to timber for boards, rails or future wants, for a thick population according to the natural reasoning of men." See Journal of Edward Partridge, Book of John Whitmer, and Journal of John Murdock, Archives of The Church of Jesus Christ of Latter-day Saints, Salt Lake City, Utah; Smith, *History of the Church*, 2:444–45; Donald Q. Cannon and Lyndon W. Cook, eds., *Far West Record* (Salt Lake City, Utah: Deseret Book Co., 1983), pp. 105–6.

12. Cannon and Cook, *Far West Record*, pp. 103–4, 110. They also purchased "four adjacent eighties." The city was laid out in accordance with a plan for cities of Zion given by Joseph in 1833. Far West is located in the northern part of the Mirable Township, encompassing the NE qr., sec. 15; NW qr., sec 14; SE qr., sec 10; SW qr., sec 11. *An Illustrated Historical Atlas of Caldwell County, Missouri* (Philadelphia: Edwards Brothers, of Missouri, 1876), pp. 8, 48.

13. Cannon and Cook, *Far West Record*, p. 102.

14. Smith, *History of the Church*, 2:433–34. See also Council Minutes for 3, 5, 6, and 7 Apr. 1837; Cannon and Cook, *Far West Record*, pp. 107–10.

15. One must remember that until 1836, Joseph Smith had almost single-handedly directed the Church. If any questions arose, he was consulted and most often gave the answer. By 1836 the priesthood organization of the Church with all its quorums and appendages had been organized, which included the First Presidency, the High Council (both at Kirtland and Missouri), the Assistant President, the Quorum of Twelve Apostles, the First Quorum of Seventy, and the Aaronic Priesthood quorums.

16. Cannon and Cook, *Far West Record*, p. 110. John Whitmer and W. W. Phelps silently agreed to the proposition. The council also voted to relieve them from their obligation to pay the $1000 each they had subscribed to build the temple. "Poor bleeding Zion" refers to those who had been driven from Jackson County and who were still in a desperate situation.

17. Ibid., p. 119.

18. See letter of Albert P. Rockwood to his sister, 6 Oct. 1838, Historical Department, The Church of Jesus Christ of Latter-day Saints, Salt Lake City, Utah. See also Cannon and Cook, *Far West Record*, p. 120.

19. Cannon and Cook, *Far West Record*, p. 125. Edward Partridge and his counselors were appointed as a committee to investigate the cost of the surrounding lands to see if the cost of such action was feasible.

20. See Council Minutes, 20 Jan. 1838; Cannon and Cook, *Far West Record*, p. 135.

21. *Historical Atlas, Caldwell County, Missouri*, p. 8.

22. Letter of Oliver Cowdery to his brothers Lyman and Warren F. Cowdery, who were residing at Kirtland. The letter written at Far West, Missouri, is undated, but was probably written 10 February 1838. RLDS Church Historian's Office, The Auditorium, Independence, Missouri.

23. Smith, *History of the Church*, 2:521–24.

24. Ibid. See also Cannon and Cook, *Far West Record*, p. 120.

25. Smith, *History of the Church*, 2:524.

26. Two apostles, Thomas B. Marsh, president of the Quorum of the Twelve Apostles, and David W. Patten, were present at the meetings.

27. W. W. Phelps said he kept the Word of Wisdom. Oliver Cowdery admitted that he had drunk tea because of ill health during the winter. David and John Whitmer stated that they did not consider their use of tea and coffee as violation, since they did not feel they were hot drinks. All of them admitted selling their lands in Jackson County, stating that they felt

it their right to do so. Finally, they "declared they would not be controlled by an ecclesiastical power or revelation whatever in their temporal concerns." Cannon and Cook, *Far West Record,* 26 Jan. 1838, pp. 135–36.

28. Meetings were held at Far West, S. Carter's settlement, Edmund Durfee's and Nahum Curtis's homes, and Haun's Mill; Cannon and Cook, *Far West Record,* pp. 137–40.

29. See minutes of High Council meeting held 10 March 1838; Cannon and Cook, *Far West Record,* pp. 145–49.

30. See undated letter of Oliver Cowdery to his brothers Lyman and Warren F. Cowdery.

31. Cannon and Cook, *Far West Record,* p. 149.

32. Undated letter of Oliver Cowdery to his brothers Lyman and Warren F. Cowdery.

33. Ibid.

34. Cannon and Cook, *Far West Record,* p. 169. This is also evident in a letter, dated 12 April 1838, he wrote to the High Council on the same day that he was excommunicated: "I could have wished that those charges might have been deferred until after my interview with President Smith; but as they are not, I must waive the anticipated pleasure with which I had flattered myself of an understanding on those points which are grounds of different opinions on some Church regulations, and others which personally interest myself." Smith, *History of the Church,* 3:16–18.

35. Smith, *History of the Church,* 3:8, 13. Rigdon was delayed by the illness of his wife.

36. Smith, *History of the Church,* 3:16–18.

37. Even though the councils had been authorized by revelation in 1835, it is during this period that the Traveling High Council (Quorum of Twelve Apostles) began to function and assumed control of Church leadership at Far West. See Doctrine and Covenants 107:22–30, 33, 35–36.

38. Letter from Oliver Cowdery to Brigham Young, 25 Dec. 1843, Huntington Library, San Marino, California. See also Cannon and Cook, *Far West Record,* p. 170 n. 6.

39. Ibid. This is most interesting in light of the fact that during his church trial Oliver was accused of slandering Joseph Smith. See Cannon and Cook, *Far West Record,* p. 163.

40. Smith, *History of the Church,* 3:37.

41. Dewitt is also spelled DeWitt. See Andrew Jenson, *Historical Record,* 8:697–98, and *National Geographic Atlas of the World,* 4th ed.

42. Henry Root and a few other Mormon families had settled at Dewitt early in 1838. By October, seventy families had settled at Dewitt. Smith, *History of the Church,* 3:450–51.

43. John Corrill, *Brief History of the Church of Latter Day Saints* (St. Louis: Printed for the Author, 1839), p. 30. B. H. Roberts, *A Comprehensive History of The Church of Jesus Christ of Latter-day Saints,* 6 vols. (Provo, Utah: Brigham Young University Press, 1965), 1:438–40. Following his address, Rigdon prepared a document addressed to leading apostates Oliver Cowdery, David

Whitmer, John Whitmer, William W. Phelps, and Lyman E. Johnson commanding them to leave the county under penalty of a "more fatal calamity." Ibid., p. 438. This document was signed by eighty-four men. See *Documents, Correspondence, Orders, etc., Relating to the Disturbances with the Mormons* (Jefferson City, Mo.: Missouri General Assembly, 1841), pp. 103–6.

44. Smith, *History of the Church,* 3:41–42.

45. Roberts, *Comprehensive History,* 1:440.

46. Smith, *History of the Church,* 3:56–59. See Journal of John L. Butler, 6 Aug. 1838.

47. John L. Butler, see Smith, *History of the Church,* 3:57–58; Joseph H. McGee, see Leland Gentry, "A History of the Latter-day Saints in Northern Missouri," pp. 256–57.

48. Smith, *History of the Church,* 3:58–59.

49. A committee of Mormons (Lyman Wight, Vinson Knight, John Smith, Reynolds Cahoon, and others) met with several citizens of Millport (Joseph Morin, John Williams, James B. Turner, and others) to negotiate peace. Smith, *History of the Church,* 3:60.

50. Smith, *History of the Church,* 3:59–62. Black issued his statement on 8 August; Peniston swore his statement two days later, on 10 August. Judge Austin A. King issued a warrant for the arrest of Joseph Smith and Lyman Wight.

51. Smith, *History of the Church,* 3:73; see also 3:69–74.

52. Reportedly the citizens of Millport abandoned and burned their own property and blamed the Mormons for it. Roberts, *Comprehensive History,* 1:463, 478.

53. Nathan Pinkham, Addison Green, Moses Kelly, William Seeley, and John Smith were among those taken prisoner by various mob-militia forces. See Clark V. Johnson, Redress Petitions: The Missouri Conflict, 1833–1838 (unpublished manuscript, n.d.). John B. Comer, William L. McHoney, and Allen Miller were taken prisoners by the Mormons. Smith, *History of the Church,* 3:75.

54. Leland H. Gentry, "The Danite Band of 1838," *BYU Studies* 14 (Summer 1974): 421–50.

55. The Mormons were warned by mobbers that they should leave Dewitt on 22 August 1838. The mobbers began their siege of Dewitt 2 September by firing upon the town's inhabitants. Smith, *History of the Church,* 3:64, 77, 85, 159.

56. A woman by the name of Jensen, who had recently given birth to a child, died. Smith, *History of the Church,* 3:159–60.

57. In the 1830s the county governments within Missouri acted as independently as the various states in the union in matters of issuing writs of habeas corpus, traveling through a county by a group from another county, and calling to arms their own militia. A county judge could call the local militia unit into active duty upon reception of a complaint by a local citizen. If the county militia was not sufficient to handle a situation, then the local judge could call upon the judicial district of the circuit judge; and

if the forces were still insufficient, then the judges could appeal to the governor of the state for help. Thus when General Alexander Doniphan visited Far West, he advised and authorized them to protect themselves and call out the militia. An affidavit was made to one of the county judges, who issued orders to the county sheriff, who ordered the commanding officer of the militia at Far West, Colonel George M. Hinkle, to activate those forces necessary to stop the marauding mobs. Smith, *History of the Church,* 3:162, 455–56.

58. Smith, *History of the Church,* 3:170–71.

59. Jenson, *Historical Record,* 8:702.

60. See Journal of David Lewis, Special Collections of the Merrill Library, Utah State University, Logan, Utah, p. 11; see also *Juvenile Instructor* 27:95.

61. Gentry, "A History of the Latter-day Saints in Northern Missouri," pp. 432–33.

62. Journal of David Lewis, pp. 11–12.

63. See Isaac Leany and Joseph Young's account of the Haun's Mill Massacre. Clark V. Johnson, "The Petition of Isaac Leany," *BYU Studies* 23 (Winter 1983): 94–103, and Redress Petitions: The Missouri Conflict (unpublished manuscript), pp. 799–805; Smith, *History of the Church,* 3:182–87.

64. Smith, *History of the Church,* 3:175.

65. Smith, *History of the Church,* 3:187–88. Lucas also demanded that the citizens of Far West sign over their property to pay for the war, and he ordered all Mormons to leave the state. Smith, *History of the Church,* 3:188.

66. Ibid., pp. 188–89. Pratt, *History of the Late Persecution,* pp. 40–41.

67. Smith, *History of the Church,* 3:192. See also Pratt, *History of the Late Persecution,* p. 43.

68. Smith, *History of the Church,* 3:193.

69. Pratt, *Autobiography,* pp. 228–30.

70. Stephen C. LeSueur, *The 1838 Mormon War in Missouri* (Columbia: University of Missouri Press, 1987), pp. 197, 204–5. Joseph Smith, Lyman Wight, Caleb Baldwin, Hyrum Smith, Alexander McRae, and Sidney Rigdon were accused of treason, and Parley P. Pratt, Morris Phelps, Lyman Gibbs, Norman Shearer, and Darwin Chase were to await trial for murder. Others were indicted with lesser crimes.

71. Roberts, *Comprehensive History,* 1:509–10. Smith, *History of the Church,* 3:249–54. See Johnson, "The Missouri Redress Petitions: A Reappraisal," pp. 31–32.

72. Not all the Mormons left. David and John Whitmer, the Bozarths, George Walters, Abner Scoville, Avery Smith, and others remained. See *An Illustrated Historical Atlas of Caldwell County,* p. 8.

73. Crosby Johnson noted that had the Mormons remained, perhaps at Far West, "instead of being a farm with scarcely sufficient ruins to mar the spot where it once stood, there would have been a right and populous city." Ibid.

Chapter 14

The Founding of Nauvoo

Donald Q. Cannon
Associate Dean of Religious Education
Brigham Young University

The decision of the Latter-day Saints to settle in Illinois in 1839 resulted directly from their experience in Missouri. They had been driven from one county to another and finally were expelled from the state.

The first and foremost concern of the Latter-day Saints in 1839 was to leave Missouri. Since Illinois was convenient, they fled there. The state of Illinois, however, had not been designated as Zion or as a special gathering place in the same sense that Missouri had. Indeed, as late as 25 March 1839 Joseph Smith had no definite place in mind for the future settlement of the Saints.

In February 1839 a large number of Mormon refugees arrived at the community of Quincy, Illinois, whose people received the refugees with compassion and understanding. As Joseph Smith later said, "We found a hospitable people and a friendly home."[1] Quincy, the largest town in the area, was located about 150 miles from Far West, Missouri.

While at Quincy the Saints had to decide whether to gather in one place or to disperse themselves among non-Mormons. Ultimately, they decided to settle in one place. The decision about where to locate was the result of careful exploration and consultation. As early as the fall of 1838 some Mormons had fled from Missouri and located near the mouth of the Des Moines River in the Iowa territory. These Mormon settlers considered the possibility of settling in the so-called Half-Breed Tract in eastern Iowa. They also learned that Dr. Isaac Galland held title to most of that land.

Upon learning of the desperate condition of the Mormons, Galland offered to sell them twenty thousand acres of land in Lee County, Iowa, for two dollars an acre. Eventually, the Saints bought land from Galland on both sides of the river. Traditionally, Latter-day Saints and Latter-day Saint historians have considered Galland a swindler, who took advantage of the Church. Recently, however, some historians have viewed Galland in a more favorable light. Lyndon W. Cook, for example, writes that "Dr. Isaac Galland was clearly a Mormon benefactor."[2]

While the Mormons settled in Illinois, Joseph Smith languished in Liberty Jail. On 6 April 1839 Judge Austin King ordered the prisoners removed from Liberty Jail and taken to Daviess County for trial. Following two days of hearings, the prisoners procured a change of venue to Boone County. During their travels to Boone County, the sheriff and guards, perhaps acting under instruction, allowed the prisoners to escape. It is a distinct possibility that the lawyer-friend of the Mormons, Alexander W. Doniphan, engineered this escape. In any case, Joseph and his companions fled to safety in Illinois. A Mormon by the name of Dimick Huntington wrote a descriptive account of the Prophet's arrival at Quincy on 22 April 1839:

"I Dimick Huntington saw Joseph land from the Quincy ferry boat about 8 o'clock in the morning. He was dressed in an old pair of boots, blue cloak with collar turned up, wide-brim hat, rim sloped down, not been shaved for some time, looked pale and haggard."[3]

On 1 May 1839, the Latter-day Saints made their first land purchase in Commerce, Illinois. It is instructive to note that the Saints did not make any land purchase until after Joseph Smith arrived. They bought a 135-acre farm from Hugh White for five thousand dollars, and forty-seven acres of unimproved land from Isaac Galland. Later, additional hundreds of acres were purchased from Daniel H. Wells, Hiram Kimball, Davidson Hibbard, and the firm of Horace R. Hotchkiss, et al. Within a few days of the initial land purchases in Commerce, Joseph Smith and his family moved to Commerce. On 19 May 1839 the Prophet, Emma, and their four small children moved into a small log cabin on the White property, on the bank of the Mississippi River, about a mile south of Commerce City.

During the month of June the Saints made additional land purchases on both sides of the river. The most extensive purchases were from Galland on the Iowa side. In fact, Galland sold the whole town of Nashville, part of Keokuk, and the settlement known as Montrose. Their purchases at Montrose included Fort Des Moines, with its barracks, which had been built during the Black Hawk War. The terms Isaac Galland offered were advantageous to the Saints. Galland offered the land at a reasonable rate and on long-term credit and also agreed to exchange lands in Illinois and Iowa for lands owned by the Mormons in Missouri.[4]

In July 1839 the Saints began to feel the effects of their suffering in Missouri. Their weakened condition, coupled with the mosquito-infested swampland along the shore of the Mississippi, caused many to fall seriously ill with malaria, which they called fever or ague. Outbreaks of malaria and cholera were frequent in the Mississippi River Valley in the nineteenth century. The summer season was the time when most sickness occurred.[5]

The Saints sought relief from these illnesses with the standard remedies of the day, especially Sapinton's Pills, a compound of quinine. Mormons on both sides of the river were affected by this onslaught of disease and suffering.

Although sick himself, Joseph Smith rose from his bed and called upon the Lord in fervent prayer. Clothed in the power of the priesthood and being assured that God was with him, he healed everyone in his house and also those camped near his home. Following these miraculous events,

Joseph and some of the Twelve went about Commerce and visited the sick, healing almost everyone they administered to.

One of the most remarkable examples of faith-healing in Latter-day Saint history occurred at this time, when Joseph visited Elijah Fordham, who was considered a dying man. When Joseph asked if he had faith to be healed, Brother Fordham replied that it was too late. The Prophet Joseph then commanded him in the name of Jesus Christ to be made well. Elijah got up from his bed, ate a bowl of bread and milk, and then accompanied Joseph Smith into the street, where they healed others.[6]

In the midst of poverty, sickness, and the colossal task of building a new city, the Twelve Apostles began departing for a mission to England. Their departure demonstrated both their faith and also their zeal for preaching the gospel. In all of this missionary effort, Joseph Smith led the way and directed the work of the Twelve, although he did not go to England himself. John Taylor and Wilford Woodruff left for England before the others. Both men had been very sick, and Wilford Woodruff reportedly said, "I feel and look more like a subject for the dissecting room than a missionary."[7]

Their valiant efforts, in the midst of poverty and sickness, paid rich dividends. The mission of the Twelve to the British Isles resulted in a bountiful harvest of souls. Many of these new converts, convinced of the truthfulness of the Restoration and influenced by the doctrine of gathering, emigrated to Nauvoo.

During August, while some of the Apostles were leaving for England, Joseph Smith purchased additional land in and around Commerce. Much of the land purchased in this period was bought from the firm of Horace R. Hotchkiss, et al.

During this busy time, Joseph Smith named the new settlement Nauvoo. The Prophet declared that *Nauvoo* was a Hebrew word meaning beautiful place or beautiful situation. Joseph Smith's knowledge of Hebrew as well as the accuracy of his definition of *Nauvoo* have been attested to by Hebrew scholar Louis Zucker.[8] The first formal use of the new name, Nauvoo, was in a caption on the published plat of the City of Nauvoo, 30 August 1839. It should be noted, however, that the name of the post office was not officially changed from Commerce to Nauvoo until 21 April 1840.

In October the Nauvoo Stake was organized, the first stake established in the area; and the organization of the stake occurred in conjunction with the first general conference of the Church held in Nauvoo. The new Nauvoo Stake consisted of three wards. By 1842 the Nauvoo Stake had ten wards, with a bishop presiding over each ward. William Marks was set apart as the first stake president. The Saints also voted for the creation of a stake in Iowa, which they called the Zarahemla Stake.

By the end of 1839, the Mormons had established a growing community at the head of the rapids on the Illinois side of the Mississippi. The site of Nauvoo was directly across the Mississippi River from Montrose, Iowa, 12 miles north of Keokuk, Iowa, 15 miles from Warsaw, Illinois, 53 miles from Quincy, Illinois, and 191 miles from St. Louis, Missouri. During that year they had successfully fled from Missouri, identified a location for gathering in Illinois, purchased land, organized the Church in the area, and constructed several homes and buildings. The foundation of Nauvoo had been firmly laid. All these things had been accomplished under the inspired leadership of Joseph Smith.

While Nauvoo was the focal point of Mormon settlement in Illinois, it was certainly not the only community founded by the Mormons in the Prairie State. Joseph Smith's vision of Latter-day Saint settlement was not limited to Nauvoo. In March 1843 he said, "There is a wheel; Nauvoo is the hub: we will drive the first spoke in Ramus, second in La Harpe, third Shokoquon, fourth in Lima: that is half the wheel. The other half is over the river."[9]

Joseph Smith and his followers planned seventeen communities in Hancock County besides Nauvoo. Of these, Ramus (Webster and Macedonia) and Lima are what

I would call major colonies. Other settlements, such as Plymouth, Green Plains, Golden's Point, Yelrome (Tioga), and Camp Creek I have designated minor colonies. There were also missionary towns, places where the Saints constituted a minority and hoped to convert others to the faith. Such towns included Carthage, Bear Creek, La Harpe, and Fountain Green. Other small settlements surrounded Nauvoo like suburbs—Stringtown, Mormon Springs, Rocky Run, Sonora, and Davis Mound.[10]

Nauvoo and the settlements in Hancock County offer a glimpse of Joseph Smith as colonizer. The Illinois settlements, when coupled with the Iowa settlements, constitute an extensive network of Mormon communities. Looking at these settlements, we could consider Joseph Smith as a forerunner of Brigham Young, the great colonizer of the Utah period.

There were other settlements, but Nauvoo was by far the largest town created by the Saints. The City of Nauvoo covered the entire flatland along the Mississippi River, as well as a portion of the land above the bluffs, where the business section of Nauvoo is located today. The map engraved by Gustavus Hills during the 1840s and reproduced by Nauvoo Restoration, Inc., in 1971 depicts a city much larger than the one the Saints actually built. This map represents an idealized Nauvoo, the city which Joseph Smith dreamed about. Although all of the area depicted on the map was called the incorporated city limits, it was not all platted and divided into blocks with streets on each side. During the time of Joseph Smith, Nauvoo measured 3733.11 acres. In contrast, the Nauvoo of today measures 1842.67 acres, or about 49 percent of the original town. Today only the west-central portion of the original city remains.[11]

Joseph Smith envisioned a city on a grand scale and also one that was ordered and well planned. The city of Nauvoo was platted in June 1839 according to the Prophet's design with a square grid system. There were 150 squares, or blocks, of four square acres each, divided into four equal lots. The streets ran north-south and east-west both on the flats near the river as well as on the bluffs. With the exception of Main and Water Streets, the streets measured forty-nine and one-half feet. Main Street was eighty-seven feet wide; Water Street measured sixty feet in width.[12]

Such a city was designed for individual family homes with spacious lots for trees and gardens. The earliest Mormon homes were log cabins. Within a short time some frame homes were erected. Eventually brickyards sprang into operation, and fine brick homes were built. In order to provide opportunities for all, Joseph Smith gave lots to the poor who could not afford to buy them. His desire was to make sure that everyone had a suitable home. For him Nauvoo was a city of Zion in the best sense of the phrase.[13]

As the city grew, demand for public buildings increased, and several significant structures were built by the Saints. Some of the most important public buildings include the temple, the Red Brick Store, the Seventies Hall, the Masonic Hall (Cultural Hall), and the Times and Seasons Complex.

In January 1841, Joseph Smith received a revelation commanding the Saints to build a temple in Nauvoo. The revelation, later published as section 124 of the Doctrine and Covenants, underscored the importance of the temple and furnished details of construction, including building materials to be used. In this heavenly communication the members of the Church also received significant information pertaining to the purposes of the temple. Emphasizing the need for the temple the revelation proclaimed: "For there is not a place found on earth that he may come to and restore again that which was lost unto you, or which he hath taken away, even the fulness of the priesthood." (D&C 124:28.)

The Saints hired William Weeks as architect, and work began as soon as weather would allow. On 6 April 1841, they laid the cornerstones in an elaborate ceremony. From the outset the construction of the temple became a high priority for the Saints. The erection of this religious edifice occupied the time and talents of most of Nauvoo's craftsmen for five years. Some men even lost their lives while working on the temple. Moses Horn died in a blasting accident that occurred at the quarry where workers obtained limestone for the massive walls of the temple. Elijah Cunningham drowned while working in the Wisconsin Pineries, where they had gone to obtain pine lumber for the temple.[14]

This magnificent building was created by a people who had very little capital for such a venture. In place of money, the building was constructed by voluntary labor and through the exercise of faith. In order to provide a labor force, Church leaders initiated a tithing-in-time system. Each man and boy gave every tenth day in labor on the building. In addition to this voluntary system, many members worked full-time on the temple.[15]

Sacrifice was the order of the day. Donations of time and means came from almost every one of the Saints. Expressing the total dedication to the completion of the temple, Eliza R. Snow wrote: "Every talent and exertion are peculiarly needed for the erection of the temple."[16] Sarah Burbank, who had come as a young girl with her family from Canada to Nauvoo, recalled: "I used to go past the temple and watch the men work on it. Men worked on the temple with nothing to eat but cornbread and bacon."[17]

The Saints were willing to sacrifice their time and energy because they recognized the vital importance of the temple. This was not just another building; it was the house of the Lord. Heber C. Kimball, one of the Twelve, put it this way: "God is favoring us day by day; and leading our enemies as a horse is led by the reins. For what purpose? In order that he may carry on his work, and erect that building. I do not go out of doors, and look at that house, but the prayer of my heart is 'O, Lord save this people, and help them to build thy house.' "[18]

By the fall of 1841, the Saints had completed the basement, including the baptismal font. On 8 November 1841 this area was dedicated and immediately put to use. Baptisms for the dead, which had previously been performed in the Mississippi River, were now performed in the large baptismal font of the temple. The first font was built of pine timber from Wisconsin, but this temporary structure was replaced in 1845 with a stone font.[19]

As other portions of the temple were completed they were dedicated and put to use. Thus when the endowment rooms were completed in November 1845, they were immediately dedicated and pressed into service for the endowment ceremony.

The temple was not officially dedicated until 1 May 1846, after most of the Saints had left Nauvoo. Orson Hyde and Wilford Woodruff officiated. Wilford Woodruff noted in his diary that a one dollar admission fee was charged. Orson Hyde and Wilford Woodruff spoke, and Orson Hyde offered the dedicatory prayer.[20]

By the time of its completion in 1846, the Nauvoo Temple was the largest structure in the United States north of St. Louis and west of Cincinnati. It was also one of the most widely known buildings in the entire country. Within a few months, the Saints had left Nauvoo, and the temple fell into other hands.[21]

By 1849 the Nauvoo Temple had come into the possession of Etienne Cabet, leader of a socialist group called the Icarian Community. The sacred edifice also became the victim of fire and the ravages of nature. In October 1848, it was burned by a suspected arsonist; and in May 1850, a tornado toppled some of the walls.[22]

Construction of the Seventies Hall commenced in the fall of 1843; dedicatory services were held on 1 December 1844. This building provided a meeting place and a training facility for the Seventies. On the first floor was a large lecture-preaching room. Equipped with pulpit and pews, this room was ideal for missionaries. The second floor housed a library and office. In 1845 the library held 675 volumes.[23]

The Masonic Hall, also called the Cultural Hall, was a tall building, a building that dominated the landscape for miles around. In the 1840s and in its restored condition it was and is an impressive building. Its beauty derives in no small measure from the impressive facade, which has the appearance of marble and stands in sharp contrast with the red brick walls on either side. This building served many purposes. A careful examination of early Mormon diaries indicates that the hall had at least twenty-six different uses. The residents of early Nauvoo attended theatrical productions, concerts, Church meetings, Masonic ceremonies, military meetings, police meetings, political gatherings, art exhibits, business meetings, funerals, dinners and court sessions, all at this location.[24]

In 1842, James Ivins, a convert from New Jersey, purchased a lot at the corner of Kimball and Main Streets. Eventually three red-brick buildings were erected on this site. In 1845 Ivins sold the buildings to the Church, and the printing offices were moved to this complex. In these buildings the Saints printed the *Times and Seasons* and the *Nauvoo Neighbor*. The complex also housed the Nauvoo post office for a time.[25]

What was life like for the citizens of Nauvoo? Basically, they experienced the same kinds of things that most nineteenth-century Americans did. Space in this essay will not permit an extensive examination of life in Nauvoo; instead, the economic activities of old Nauvoo will be discussed as an example of the people's life-style.

Agriculture played a major role in the economic life of Nauvoo, as it did in many nineteenth-century American cities of similar size. Essentially there were three major components of Mormon agriculture in Illinois. First, most families in Nauvoo did maintain a garden with fruit trees, grapevines, and vegetables. These gardens were ideal on the large lots, which were typically one square acre. Second, the community farm, also called the Big Field, provided farming and gardening opportunities for those on the lower end of the economic scale who did not have their own land. To provide regulation of crops planted, acreage cultivated, and so forth, an organization called the Big Field Association was created. Third, on the outskirts of Nauvoo and in outlying areas of Hancock County, other individual owners operated their farms. These farmers raised wheat, oats, rye, and potatoes and also had livestock, including cattle, sheep, and hogs.[26]

Even Wilford Woodruff, one of the Twelve, was heavily involved in agricultural pursuits. During much of October 1841 Elder Woodruff engaged in cutting and hauling hay. In September 1842 he was harvesting corn. In June 1843 rain delayed his corn planting. On New Year's Day 1844 he got off to an early start by working in his orchard. "I planted 4 Apricotts, 13 Plums, 11 Shugar Cherry and 30 choice peachstones," he wrote.[27]

It was not until the 1860s that Americans settled into only one occupation. Thus people in Nauvoo were found engaged in a variety of things to give them sustenance. Over two hundred professions have been identified that cover a wide variety of skills. More than one-third of the male inhabitants considered themselves farmers, while another third were stonemasons, bricklayers, blacksmiths, and shoemakers. Others made part of their living by gathering rags, painting portraits, selling palm leaf hats, mining coal, or trapping and exterminating bedbugs. A few of the Latter-day Saints in Nauvoo were lawyers, doctors, or dentists, and more than eighty people taught school.[28]

One of the major businesses in Nauvoo involved buying, selling, and exchanging land. Indeed, Nauvoo's economy revolved around the exchange of property. Land transactions for the Church were conducted by or under the direction of Joseph Smith, especially in the early years. Private landholders and real estate investors also sold land to new settlers. The Church gave special consideration to the poor, who obtained land either without cost or at a low rate.[29]

Other businesses in Nauvoo of the 1840s included stores, brickyards, sawmills, lime kilns, flour mills, bakeries, tailorshops, printing offices, blacksmith shops, a tin shop, and shoe shops. As in other nineteenth-century American cities, these businesses were not located in a single district. They sprang up everywhere in the city, in shops and sometimes in homes. No zoning laws were in operation.[30]

The most important general store in Nauvoo belonged to Joseph Smith. His Red Brick Store provided a wide variety of merchandise, including food, clothing, dry goods, and books. The Red Brick Store served as a community center as well as a store. The Prophet conducted Church business in his office and in the large hall on the second floor. Here, for example, the Relief Society was organized on 17 March 1842. Because of the large amount of community and church business conducted in Joseph Smith's store, it became one of the most important buildings in Nauvoo. While general stores were important in most early American communities, the Red Brick Store was a focal point of Nauvoo social, economic, political, cultural, and religious life. The significance of the Red Brick Store far exceeded the commercial role played by other general stores.[31]

Joseph Smith was not a successful businessman, and eventually he leased the store to Ebenezer Robinson. One factor that contributed to Joseph Smith's lack of success in this business venture was his open-handed generosity. He constantly extended credit to those unable to pay for their goods, just as he had done in Kirtland. Joseph Leech recalled how the Prophet provided employment for him and his brother-in-law, Henry Nightingale. After they had dug a ditch for the Prophet, he paid them very generously with some of the best pieces of meat in his inventory, as well as a sack of flour for each of the workers. Realizing his generosity, they expressed: "We thanked him kindly, and went on our way home rejoicing in the kind-heartedness of the Prophet of our God." Joseph Smith's attitude about his business in the Red Brick Store was aptly summarized in the statement he made as he opened the store: "I love to wait upon the Saints and be a servant to all."[32]

Manufacturing in Nauvoo centered in homes and shops. Products created by Nauvoo craftsmen included leather goods, matches, gloves, bonnets, pottery, and jewelry. Major industries, such as textile mills, were contemplated but were never realized. They failed to develop because capital was unavailable.[33]

One major business enterprise grew out of the desire for pine lumber. The Saints needed lumber for the temple, for the Nauvoo House, a hotel built by the Saints to accommodate visitors, and for homes and shops. Since pine was scarce on the Illinois prairie, they turned their attention to the Wisconsin pineries, some five hundred miles to the north. A sizable contingent of Latter-day Saints, led by Bishop George Miller, a member of the Council of Fifty, Nauvoo City Council, and trustee-in-trust for the Church, settled in the Black River Falls area and established lumber camps and sawmills. Millions of board feet of lumber were floated down the Black and the Mississippi rivers to Nauvoo.[34]

Much of the exchange in Nauvoo commercial transactions consisted of barter—exchange of land and goods. Paper and specie, or hard money, was also used, however. The Saints minted their own coin money, printed currency, and also used money from other towns in the Mississippi Valley. The unstable banking system and lack of controls in issuing money led to counterfeiting. Use of illegal money was common in frontier regions, because each town could mint its own money. Merchants had to be on guard to detect bogus money. Although some Latter-day Saints were involved in counterfeiting, Church leaders neither condoned nor engaged in that rather common frontier practice.[35]

The economy that developed in Nauvoo was successful in limited areas, but it was never strong enough to properly support the population. Possibly the economy might have achieved maturity if the Latter-day Saints had been allowed to stay. But that was not Nauvoo's destiny.[36]

From the preceding discussion of economic activities in Nauvoo it is apparent that the Mormons under the direction of Joseph Smith succeeded in founding a relatively successful city. They were proud of their city and what it represented.

How did Joseph Smith feel about Nauvoo? Believing it was a beautiful place, he consequently gave it the Hebrew name *Nauvoo*. Despite reports of the unhealthy climate and the presence of disease in the area, he persisted in the belief that Nauvoo was a healthy place to live. In a letter to the Saints in the *Times and Seasons,* he wrote that "Nauvoo is rising in glory and greatness."[37] As he was leaving for Carthage, with the feeling that he would never return, he exclaimed, "This is the loveliest place and the best people under the heavens."[38] Later, as he spent the night in Carthage Jail, his affection for the people and his beloved city became apparent as he told Dan Jones, "I would to God that I could preach to the Saints in Nauvoo once more."[39]

Notes

1. Joseph Smith, *History of The Church of Jesus Christ of Latter-day Saints,* 7 vols., 2d ed. rev., ed. B. H. Roberts (Salt Lake City, Utah: The Church of Jesus Christ of Latter-day Saints, 1932–51), 4:540.

2. Lyndon W. Cook, "Isaac Galland—Mormon Benefactor," *BYU Studies* 19 (Spring 1979): 284.

3. Journal of Dimick Huntington, Archives of The Church of Jesus Christ of Latter-day Saints, Salt Lake City, Utah.

4. Cook, "Galland," pp. 271–84.

5. M. Guy Bishop, Vincent Lacey, and Richard Wixom, "Death at Mormon Nauvoo, 1843–1845," *Western Illinois Regional Studies* 19 (Fall 1986): 71–77.

6. Smith, *History of the Church,* 4:4.

7. Matthias F. Cowley, *Wilford Woodruff: History of His Life and Labors* (Salt Lake City, Utah: Deseret News, 1909), p. 109.

8. Louis C. Zucker, "Joseph Smith As a Student of Hebrew," *Dialogue* 3 (Summer 1968): 49–55.

9. Smith, *History of the Church,* 5:296. For information on settlements across the Mississippi River, see Stanley B. Kimball, "Nauvoo West: The Mormons of the Iowa Shore," *BYU Studies* 18 (Winter 1978): 132–42.

10. Donald Q. Cannon, "Spokes on the Wheel: Early Latter-day Saint Settlements in Hancock County, Illinois," *Ensign* 16 (Feb. 1986): 62–64.

11. Interview with James L. Kimball, Jr., Archives of The Church of Jesus Christ of Latter-day Saints, Salt Lake City, Utah, 1 May 1987. James Kimball has done extensive research on Nauvoo, both in his Ph.D. program and in his work for Nauvoo Restoration, Inc.

12. Robert Bruce Flanders, *Nauvoo: Kingdom on the Mississippi* (Urbana: University of Illinois Press, 1965), pp. 42–43.

13. David E. Miller and Della S. Miller, *Nauvoo: The City of Joseph* (Salt

Lake City, Utah: Peregrine Smith, 1974), p. 77; hereafter referred to as *City of Joseph*; Flanders, *Kingdom*, p. 126.

14. Miller and Miller, *City of Joseph*, pp. 108–9.

15. Ibid.

16. Maureen Ursenbach, "Eliza R. Snow's Nauvoo Journal," *BYU Studies* 15 (Summer 1975): 405–6.

17. Leonard J. Arrington, et al., eds., *Voices of the Past: Diaries, Journals and Autobiographies* (Provo, Utah: Campus Education Week, 1980), p. 27.

18. Stanley B. Kimball, "Heber C. Kimball and Family, the Nauvoo Years," *BYU Studies* 15 (Summer 1978): 475.

19. Miller and Miller, *City of Joseph*, pp. 116–17.

20. *Wilford Woodruff's Journal, 1833–1898*, ed. Scott G. Kenney, 9 vols. (Midvale, Utah: Signature Books, 1983–84), 3:42.

21. *The Nauvoo Temple, 1841–1865* (Nauvoo, Ill.: Nauvoo Restoration, 1971), p. 21.

22. Miller and Miller, *City of Joseph*, pp. 117–19. For information on the Red Brick Store, see discussion of economic activities in Nauvoo.

23. Miller and Miller, *City of Joseph*, pp. 126–28.

24. Nauvoo Restoration, Inc., Study of Masonic Hall conducted by Donald Q. Cannon (1979–1980).

25. "Printing Office Complex" (Nauvoo, Ill.: Nauvoo Restoration, 1972).

26. Miller and Miller, *City of Joseph*, p. 79.

27. *Wilford Woodruff's Journal*, 2:133, 188, 243, 337.

28. Flanders, *Kingdom*, pp. 144–54.

29. Ibid., pp. 115–43.

30. Ibid., p. 154; Miller and Miller, *City of Joseph*, pp. 81–82.

31. Miller and Miller, *City of Joseph*, pp. 84–86.

32. *Juvenile Instructor* 27 (Mar. 1892): 152–53.

33. Flanders, *Kingdom*, pp. 149–55.

34. Dennis Rowley, "The Mormon Experience in the Wisconsin Pineries, 1841–1845," paper delivered at the Mormon History Association Meetings in Omaha, Nebraska, 1983.

35. Donald Q. Cannon, "Counterfeiting in Nauvoo," unpublished paper in possession of author.

36. Flanders, *Kingdom*, pp. 177–78.

37. *Times and Seasons*, 29 July 1843.

38. Smith, *History of the Church*, 6:554.

39. Joseph Smith, *Teachings of the Prophet Joseph Smith*, sel. Joseph Fielding Smith (Salt Lake City, Utah: Deseret Book Co., 1976), pp. 383–84.

Chapter 15

As a Prophet Thinketh in His Heart, So Is He: The Mind of Joseph Smith

Chauncey C. Riddle
Professor of Philosophy
Brigham Young University

One important question a thinking Latter-day Saint might ask concerning Joseph Smith is, What are the basic beliefs of his thinking? In other words, what are the fundamental ideas which are part of all that he felt, thought, and did?

This question is important because the mind of Joseph Smith was shaped by God himself; the thinking as represented in the scriptures which came through him is a prime clue to the nature of the mind of God. And since it is the opportunity of each Latter-day Saint to come to have one mind with God and with all of the holy prophets since the beginning, this question also comes down to what each of us should believe.

I will attempt to isolate the most important features of the thinking of the Prophet Joseph Smith. This is not a work of scholarship, for no scholarly methodology enables one to make the value judgments necessary to this task. This writing is more a personal testimony, an editorial on the life and thought of the Prophet. Admittedly it represents my personal opinions, based on a lifetime of study of the scriptures and pondering of the doctrines of the restored gospel. A similar effort on the part of everyone is an important labor in establishing Zion as we strive to attain one mind, the Savior's mind.

This paper lists and elaborates the ideas which I believe are central to the thought of Joseph Smith and to the thought of all others who pursue the revelations of the true and living God in the hope of being saved from ignorance and impurity. My method is to give the reader a trisection by which to contemplate these ideas. One aspect will be quotations from the nonscriptural writings of the Prophet, another will be scriptural references, and still another will be my comments.

1. *The heart of man is the key, the most important factor of man's being.* "Thus you see, my dear brother, the willingness of our heavenly Father to forgive sins, and restore to favor all those who are willing to humble themselves before Him, and confess their sins, and forsake them, and return to Him with full purpose of heart, acting no hypocrisy, to serve Him to the end."[1]

The four parts of man are the heart, which is the function of desiring and choosing; the mind, which is the function of understanding, knowing, and planning; the strength, which is the physical body of man, having the functions of sensing, acting, and procreating; and the might, which is the influence of a person (of the heart, mind, and strength) as that person acts in the world. Thus the four important things to understand about any person in a given situation are the person's motive (heart), intention (mind), action (strength), and resulting influence (might) — the most important of these being heart, for it is the independent variable. (2 Nephi 31:13: "Follow the Son, with full purpose of heart.")

2. *Man's life consists of using one's heart and mind to choose and act.* "A man may be saved, after the judgment, in the terrestrial kingdom, or in the telestial kingdom, but he can never see the celestial kingdom of God, without being born of water and the Spirit. He may receive a glory like unto

the moon [i. e. of which the light of the moon is typical], or a star, [i. e. of which the light of the stars is typical], but can never come unto Mount Zion, and unto the city of the living God, the heavenly Jerusalem, and to an innumerable company of angels; to the general assembly and Church of the Firstborn, which are written in heaven, and to God the judge of all, and to the spirits of just men made perfect, and to Jesus the Mediator of the new covenant, unless he becomes as a little child, and is taught by the Spirit of God."[2]

To live is to act. To act is to sense a problem, perceive the situation, choose and plan a solution, and act to create a change in the world in the hope of solving the problem. The world is one's environment. A person acts to change that environment so that the desires of the person will be fulfilled. Actions do not always result in the fulfillment of desire, but persons always act to fulfill desire. (Proverbs 23:7: "As he thinketh in his heart, so is he.")

To every action there is an equal and opposite reaction, in people as well as in particles, so whenever a person acts to change his environment, that action also changes himself. (2 Nephi 2:11: "Opposition in all things.") The specific change of self involved in a given action is that every choosing creates a propensity to make a similar choice at a later time. That propensity, if reinforced with similar choices, will eventually create a habit in the person, and habits create a character. (Alma 62:41: "Hardened, . . . softened.")

To live a human life is to attempt to reshape one's environment; this attempt may or may not succeed, but the attempt always creates a set of habits, a character, in the person. A person always succeeds in shaping the self into the image of that person's own desires. (D&C 123:11–17: "Cheerfully do all things that lie in our power.")

To live spiritually is to act under the direction of the Holy Spirit, which leads to eternal life, which is the fulness of acting spiritually. (Moses 6:59: "Enjoy the words of eternal life in this world, and eternal life in the world to come, even immortal glory.")

3. *In every action man must choose between what he believes to be the better and the worse, between darkness and light.* "We again make remark here—for we find that the very principle upon which the disciples were accounted blessed, was because they were permitted to see with their eyes and hear with their ears—that the condemnation which rested upon the multitude that received not His saying, was because they were not willing to see with their eyes, and hear with their ears; not because they could not, and were not privileged to see and hear, but because their hearts were full of iniquity and abominations; 'as your fathers did, so do ye.' The prophet, forseeing that they would thus harden their hearts, plainly declared it; and herein is the condemnation of the world; that light hath come into the world, and men choose darkness rather than light, because their deeds are evil. This is so plainly taught by the Savior, that a wayfaring man need not mistake it."[3]

What a person thinks is better, the person calls good; and what a person thinks is worse may be called evil. This is to say that every human has agency. The agency consists in being subject to a person's own desires, thus enabling that person to call some things good because they are desired by the person, and to call some things evil, or bad, or undesirable, because they are not desired by the person. (Alma 42:7: "Subjects to follow after their own will.") Every person has some desires that he or she may act upon and others which he or she is powerless to attain. But in either case, the desiring and planning when one is powerless to act and the desiring and planning and acting when one is able to act both result in habit and character formation. (Mosiah 4:24–25: "you who deny the [poor] . . . say in your hearts.")

4. *In every action one is influenced toward the good by God and toward evil by Satan.* "We admit that God is the great source and fountain from whence proceeds all good; that He is perfect intelligence, and that His wisdom is alone sufficient to govern and regulate the mighty creations and worlds which shine and blaze with such magnificence and splendor over our heads, as though touched with His fin-

ger and moved by His Almighty word. And if so, it is done and regulated by law; for without law all must certainly fall into chaos. If, then, we admit that God is the source of all wisdom and understanding, we must admit that by His direct inspiration He has taught man that law is necessary in order to govern and regulate His own immediate interest and welfare; for this reason, that law is beneficial to promote peace and happiness among men. And as before remarked, God is the source from whence proceeds all good; and if man is benefitted by law, then certainly, law is good; and if law is good, then law, or the principle of it emanated from God; for God is the source of all good; consequently, then, he was the first Author of law, or the principle of it, to mankind."[4]

God and Satan may influence man directly or indirectly. Direct influence comes in the form of personal revelation from either, God acting upon the spirit (heart and mind) and body of man, and Satan working upon the body. Or the influence may be indirect, through other human beings, through illness or calamity, or through natural events. The person receiving these influences might not recognize either God or Satan as existing or having any effect in a given situation. But it is fundamental to scripture-based thinking to recognize that all good that is really good comes from God and that everything that is evil is sent forth by the power of Satan. (Moroni 7:11–12: "All things which are good cometh from God; and that which is evil cometh of the devil.")

Every person who attains accountability in this world knows both good and evil. But they do not come labeled. Thus there may be a difference between what a given person says is good and what God commends as good. The things individuals call good are relative goods, the desires of the person, and may differ from person to person. (See Moroni 7:14.) The good of God is righteousness and is absolute. Righteousness is so absolute that no human being can find it on his own. Thus it is that the true and living God of righteousness, which is Jesus Christ, is also "the fountain of all righteousness" to mortals on this earth. (Ether 12:28.)

Evil is inherently relative, never absolute, because it is always simply anything other than the righteousness which God commends at any given moment. Evil admits of degrees; some things are more evil than others. But righteousness admits of no degrees: one is either righteous or not, which is to say that one is either yielding to the influence of God to do what is right at a given moment, or one is not. (James 2:10: "Offend in one *point,* he is guilty of all"; italics added.)

5. *The righteousness of God is wise sharing in love; the evil of Satan is selfishness.* "Let the Saints remember that great things depend on their individual exertion, and that they are called to be co-workers with us and the Holy Spirit in accomplishing the great work of the last days; and in consideration of the extent, the blessings and glories of the same, let every selfish feeling be not only buried, but annihilated; and let love to God and man predominate, and reign triumphant in every mind, that their hearts may become like unto Enoch's of old, and comprehend all things, present, past and future, and come behind in no gift, waiting for the coming of the Lord Jesus Christ."[5]

Righteousness is of God. It is acting under the direction of God to share the good things one has and can do with others in such a way that the eternal happiness of any beings affected by that action is maximized. (2 Nephi 26:24: "He doeth not anything save it be for the benefit of the world.") Selfishness is to shorten the God-ordained blessings of some being in order to try to fulfill one's own personal desires. (3 Nephi 1:29: "They became for themselves.") One work of God among men is to direct them as to where and how to be generous with those who are less fortunate than they are. Satan essentially says to each human that one should look out for himself first, that one should feather his own nest. (Moses 5:29–31: "Murder and get gain.")

As a person yields to the influence of God, that person grows in generosity and care for the welfare of others until his love is full, pure, and universal. Thus, over time, that person acquires the character of God. As unselfishness becomes the essence of the person, God is able to share with that person his own purity of heart and fullness of mind and strength. Thus the person grows to be as God, which process eventuates in becoming a god. (D&C 50:24: "Until the perfect day.")

As a person who was once cleansed by the blood of Jesus Christ yields to the influence of Satan, he becomes selfish and possessive in character. If he does not repent of that selfishness before temporal death, then Satan seals that one to himself. (Alma 34:35: "He doth seal you his.") But if one turns away from selfishness before one's character is finally fixed and partakes to some degree of righteousness through Jesus Christ, that one may become righteous in character to that same degree and able to endure a kingdom of glory in eternity. (D&C 76:50–106: "Just men made perfect.")

It follows also that no action of any human being is temporal only. Every action has moral ramifications and eternal consequences. Every action is either a yielding to the influence of God to do the work of righteousness, or it is yielding to the influence of Satan to sin. In every act, humans fill the God-given opportunity to make the world a place of happiness, wisdom, and truth; or, they fulfill the Satan-inspired opportunity to be self-indulgent, uncaring for others, promoting darkness and lies. (D&C 29:34–35: "Not at any time have I given unto you a law which was temporal.")

One measure of the degree of evil a person is perpetrating when he acts is the limits of the circle within which that person is willing to be good to others. Thus an absolute devil has concern only for himself; everything and anything else, including all human beings, God, and Satan are simply tools to be used by that person to get what he wants. A less evil being is "good" to perhaps one other person but acts selfishly toward anyone else. A being yet less evil may include in the circle of persons with whom he desires to share all of his immediate or extended family.

A being still less evil may extend the boundaries of his positive concern to his village, state, or nation. But a being cannot become righteous until he is willing to share with everyone — with his enemies, with all other human beings regardless of their nationality, religion, class orientation, education, health, or gender, and also with God, Satan, rocks, trees, animals, stars, etc., ready to share with all in the manner commended to him by God. (2 Nephi 26:24: "Benefit of the world.")

Human tragedy is made when a person attempts to do good for those whom he loves, tries to do evil to those whom he does not love, and finds that the evil he tries to do to the unloved ones destroys those whom he desires to love. The tragedy is occasioned, of course, by the fact that his love for those whom he desires to love is not pure love, because it does not first focus on love of God. Thus the person finds that his relative, personal love is another form of evil, of which he must repent if he wishes to come to God and be reconciled to true righteousness. (See Matthew 5:43–48.)

6. *Acuteness of heart and mind in man consists in learning to discern the influence of God and to distinguish it from the influence of Satan.* "The Spirit of Revelation is in connection with these blessings. A person may profit by noticing the first intimation of the spirit of revelation; for instance, when you feel pure intelligence flowing into you, it may give you sudden strokes of ideas, so that by noticing it, you may find it fulfilled the same day or soon; (i.e.) those things what were presented unto your minds by the Spirit of God, will come to pass; and thus by learning the Spirit of God and understanding it, you may grow into the principle of revelation, until you become perfect in Christ Jesus."[6]

Life is an intelligence test. Of all the things a person may attempt in this life, the most important and for some the most difficult task is that of sorting out his or her own heart and mind. Three things must be carefully and accurately identified: the influence of God, the desires and ideas of the self, and the influences of Satan. (D&C 46:7: "Not be seduced by evil spirits.") This is not strictly a mind problem, as many would make it. It is a heart *and* a mind problem.

God is to be identified by the fact that he is the source of good and of truth. The self is to be identified as a source of desires and ideas which do not always square with good and truth. Satan is to be identified by his insistence that our own desires and ideas are really very good when we ourselves in our "heart of hearts" know that they are not. (Moroni 7:16–17: "The way to judge.")

The person who has not made such identifications lives life in a fog where everything is relative and nothing is holy except perhaps himself. This person is driven to and fro with every wind of doctrine, having no anchor and no rudder. He or she will likely be an imperfect copy of some stronger nearby human being. (James 1:5–7: "He that wavereth.")

One begins to live as an individual only when one makes these discriminations and begins to use them. One then knows that God exists and is good, that Satan exists and is evil, and that one's self is not either God or Satan but that one may choose between them. This can be an auspicious beginning of good things in the person's life.

7. *Wisdom for man is to learn to act only under the influence of God.* "There is one thing under the sun which I have learned and that is that the righteousness of man is sin because it exacteth over much; nevertheless, the righteousness of God is just, because it exacteth nothing at all, but sendeth rain on the just and the unjust, seed time and harvest, for all of which man is ungrateful."[7]

"Every word that proceedeth from the mouth of Jehovah has such an influence over the human mind the logical mind that it is convincing without other testimony. Faith cometh by hearing.

"If 10000 men testify to a truth you know would it add to your faith? No, or will 1000 testimonies destroy your knowledge of a fact? No."[8]

Man is free to serve God or to serve himself. Satan's only leverage is to encourage an individual to disobey God in following his own desires. (James 1:13–14: "Own lust.")

But by paying careful attention, a person may learn to serve God only, never to indulge the desires of self. (Helaman 3:35: "Purifying . . . sanctification.")

The self is motivated to make this dedication only after it has learned to identify and distinguish carefully between the influence of God and the influence of Satan. Having attained that enlightenment, the self will then quickly discern that when one follows the influence of God, things go well: one's beliefs then are regularly discovered to be true, and one's actions are seen to lead to kindness, love, sharing, and an increase of the happiness of others whom one affects. Having observed such results, the self then sees that the only intelligent thing to do is to yield to the influence of God in all things. (Alma 32:26–43: "Ye must needs know that the seed is good.")

There will be momentary doubts for most. To satisfy those doubts one needs but to relapse into selfishness for a season and bask in its misery to be reassured that the way of God is real and correct. God is kind and permits such experiments, but not forever. Before mortal death, each person who has heard the gospel of Jesus Christ must declare himself or herself. (D&C 88:83: "Seeketh me early.")

8. The only way wisdom can be attained is to learn to love with God's love. "The names of the faithful are what I wish to record in this place. These I have met in prosperity, and they were my friends; and I now meet them in adversity, and they are still my warmer friends. These love the God that I serve; they love the truths that I promulgate; they love those virtuous, and those holy doctrines that I cherish in my bosom with the warmest feelings of my heart, and with that zeal which cannot be denied. I love friendship and truth; I love virtue and law; I love the God of Abraham, of Isaac, and of Jacob; and they are my brethren, and I shall live; and because I live they shall live also."[9]

"Until we have perfect love we are liable to fall and when we have a testimony that our names are sealed in the Lamb's book of life we have perfect love and then it is impossible for false Christs to deceive us."[10]

This is to say that one must not just play at learning to yield to the influence of God in all things. One must throw one's whole heart and soul into the fray. Until one fastens all the affections of his heart on God and his righteousness, so much so that serving God and establishing his righteousness on earth become an all-consuming passion, one will not be able to yield to the influence of God unerringly. (Alma 37:37: "Counsel with the Lord.") The pressures to care for self are so great and so pervasive that mind alone can never deliver a soul to God. (Matthew 13:22–23: "Care of the world . . . choke the word.") Nevertheless, heart and mind combined and dedicated can make this all-important delivery. But heart must lead the way, for heart is stronger and more important than mind. Mind facilitates, and that in a most ingenious and admirable manner, but heart points the mind and controls the occupation of the mind almost entirely. (D&C 59:5: "Thou shalt love.")

9. *The only way one can love God with all of one's heart, might, mind, and strength is through the law and the ordinances of the new and everlasting covenant.* "It is a duty which every Saint ought to render to his brethren freely — to always love them, and ever succor them. To be justified before God we must love one another: we must overcome evil; we must visit the fatherless and the widow in their affliction, and we must keep ourselves unspotted from the world: for such virtues flow from the great fountain of pure religion. Strengthening our faith by adding every good quality that adorns the children of the blessed Jesus, we can pray in the season of prayer; we can love our neighbor as ourselves, and be faithful in tribulation, knowing that the reward of such is greater in the kingdom of heaven. What a consolation! What a joy! Let me live the life of the righteous, and let my reward be like this!"[11]

To be able to deliver oneself — heart, might, mind, and strength — to Jesus Christ is a matter of power. No human being has that power naturally, though many go a remarkable distance toward that goal outside the covenant. The power that makes that delivery possible is the gift of

271

the Holy Ghost, which is the pearl of great price. Through the Holy Ghost a person's heart may be purified, cleansed of all selfishness; then the soul can reflect back to God that pure love and also extend it to a neighbor. By that power the mind can eliminate all errors of belief, which are the chains of hell inflicted by Satan on the world, and also gain that precious knowledge of the truth which one must have to be saved. Through the power of the Holy Spirit, one may keep his body clean and pure and have it renewed in rebirth unto sufficiency to accomplish every mission to which the person is appointed by God. And through that power one receives priesthood might, enough might to show that one will use it obediently and fully in the service of God. (Moroni 7:25–48: "Lay hold upon every good thing.")

Thus through the new and everlasting covenant one can fulfill all that is possible for man: to become as God is. (D&C 132:19–20: "Then shall they be gods.") This new creation will not be accomplished completely in this mortality, but enough will be accomplished here that the individual may become a great power in extending the influence of God in the earth. (Mosiah 8:15–18: "Becometh a great benefit.")

The law of the celestial kingdom is that one must act only in faith in the Lord Jesus Christ. (D&C 132:12: "No man shall come unto the Father but by me or by my word, which is my law.") All righteous acts are acts of faith in him, and whatsoever is not that faith is sin. To say that we should love the Lord, our God, with all of our heart, might, mind, and strength is linguistically equivalent to saying that we should exercise full faith in Jesus Christ through the new and everlasting covenant.

10. *The key to knowledge (truth) is to learn first of the whole, which is God, then of the parts, which are nature and man.*

"2. Let us here observe, that three things are necessary in order that any rational and intelligent being may exercise faith in God unto life and salvation.

"3. First, the idea that he actually exists.

"4. Secondly, a correct idea of his character, perfections and attributes.

"5. Thirdly, an actual knowledge that the course of life which he is pursuing is according to his will. For without an acquaintance with these three important facts, the faith of every rational being must be imperfect and unproductive, but with this understanding it can become perfect and fruitful, abounding in righteousness, unto the praise and glory of God the Father, and the Lord Jesus Christ."[12]

The world would have one study the parts and through them discern the whole. But this is not really possible. No one can intelligently study a part of something without having at least a working hypothesis of the nature of the whole of that something. If the hypothesis about the whole is faulty, the part will be analyzed in a faulty way. This is the real lesson of systems thinking, thinking popularized in the present century but employed by responsible thinkers from time immemorial.

The whole is God. The universe is personal, not natural, because the hand of God is in every thing. (D&C 59:21: "Confess . . . his hand in all things.") Until one understands the nature and being of God, one cannot understand correctly the rest of the universe. Nature is the handiwork of God, and when one sees any natural occurrence in the universe, one is beholding "God moving in his majesty and power." (D&C 88:46–47.) Men are the children of God, and when one sees a human being, one sees the literal offspring of gods, a potential heir of Jesus Christ. Whatsoever one does to any of those heirs, Jesus Christ counts it as done unto himself. (Matthew 25:40: "Ye have done it unto me.") Each of these heirs may inherit all He is and has if that heir will only deny selfishness and grow in spiritual stature unto the measure of the fulness of his stature through faith in Him and through the power brought by the covenants. (Ephesians 4:13: "Fullness of Christ.")

11. *Jesus Christ is the Truth. The gospel of Jesus Christ is the truth which points the way to find the Truth.* "And now what remains to be done, under circumstances like these?

I will proceed to tell you what the Lord requires of all people, high and low, rich and poor, male and female, ministers and people, professors of religion and non-professors, in order that they may enjoy the Holy Spirit of God to a fullness and escape the judgments of God, which are almost ready to burst upon the nations of the earth. Repent of all your sins, and be baptized in water for the remission of them, in the name of the Father, and of the Son, and of the Holy Ghost, and receive the ordinance of the laying on of the hands of him who is ordained and sealed unto this power, that ye may receive the Holy Spirit of God; and this is according to the Holy Scriptures, and the Book of Mormon; and the only way that man can enter into the celestial kingdom. These are the requirements of the new covenant, or first principles of the Gospel of Christ: then 'Add to your faith, virtue; and to virtue, knowledge; and to knowledge, temperance; and to temperance, patience; and to patience, godliness; and to godliness, brotherly kindness; and to brotherly kindness, charity [or love]; for if these things be in you, and abound, they make you that ye shall neither be barren nor unfruitful, in the knowledge of our Lord Jesus Christ.'[13]

"Again, if others' blessings are not your blessings, others' curses are not your curses; you stand then in these last days, as all have stood before you, agents unto yourselves, to be judged according to your works."[14]

Man is saved no faster than he gains knowledge of the Truth. This truth one must know is not just any truth, such as one would encounter in a phone book or on a topographic map. The truth which saves is Jesus Christ. Only he can and will save from sinning, from hell, from death. Only as one comes to know him personally can one be saved. (John 8:31–36: "Ye shall know the truth.")

Everyone on earth is invited to come to know the Truth through the teaching of the gospel of Jesus Christ. If a person accepts that gospel and lives it completely, the path entered upon will lead such a one to know the Savior personally. The scriptures speak of the gospel as the truth because it is that portion of truth in the world which everyone must come to know to fulfill their mortal probation in accepting or rejecting Jesus Christ. (D&C 123:11–12: "Know not where to find [the truth].")

The responsibility for seeing that every child of God encounters the gospel of Jesus Christ rests on the shoulders of the Savior himself. He enlists others to assist him, that they too might become as he is through faithful service. But he also respects the agency of men. He allows men to teach their children the truth or lies, as they will. Some teach the lies of Satan or part truths in ignorance, but some do not. (D&C 123:7–8: "Chains . . . of hell.") It suffices to know that God is just, and thus every soul will hear the truth taught to him in his own tongue, in all humility, by a servant of Jesus Christ. This will happen before he or she becomes fully accountable for his or her sins and therefore liable for the final judgment which will come to all human beings. Partial accountability comes to each person through the light of Christ. But the light of Christ witnesses of truth and good. It does not tell one how to repent of sinning nor how to be able to make amends for all the evil one has done. That is the message of the gospel of Jesus Christ. (Moses 6:55–62: another law: all men must repent through Christ.)

As defined by the Lord himself in scripture (see 3 Nephi 27:13–21), there are but a few simple, powerful ideas which constitute the truth, the gospel of Jesus Christ. These are as follows:

1. Jesus Christ was sent into this world to do the will of God, his Father.

2. His Father's will was that he be lifted up upon the cross and atone for the sins of all men.

3. After Jesus had been lifted up, he was to draw all men to himself, that each might receive a final judgment as to whether each one's works were good or evil.

4. Whosoever would desire to be found guiltless at the day of judgment must:

   a. Exercise full faith in Jesus Christ, unto

   b. Repenting of sinning, and

   c. Being baptized in his name, of water; then to

d. Receive the Holy Ghost unto the remission of sins; then to

e. Endure to the end.

5. Whosoever receives the Holy Ghost and endures not unto the end will be hewn down and cast into the fire.

12. Family is the important social relationship. "Except a man and his wife enter into an everlasting covenant and be married for eternity, while in this probation, by the power and authority of the Holy Priesthood, they will cease to increase when they die; that is, they will not have any children after the resurrection. But those who are married by the power and authority of the priesthood in this life, and continue without committing the sin against the Holy Ghost, will continue to increase and have children in the celestial glory. The unpardonable sin is to shed innocent blood, or be accessory thereto. All other sins will be visited with judgment in the flesh, and the spirit being delivered to the buffetings of Satan unto the day of the Lord Jesus.

"Salvation means a man's being placed beyond the power of all his enemies.

"The more sure word of prophecy means a man's knowing that he is sealed up unto eternal life by revelation and the spirit of prophecy, through the power of the holy priesthood. It is impossible for a man to be saved in ignorance."[15]

All human beings have one literal Heavenly Father and thus are brothers and sisters in the spirit. All human beings have one physical set of parents, Adam and Eve, and thus are brothers and sisters in the flesh. One purpose of the gospel of Jesus Christ is to allow men to know and affirm this family relationship, that all might learn again to serve their Father, the true and living God. (Acts 17:22–31: "God that made the world.")

The marriage covenant is of God, and marriage and the begetting of children unto God are to be holy undertakings, functions of the holy priesthood of God. The most important personal bond between any two persons is the bond between any human being and the Savior, as one learns to love the Savior, his new father, with all of his heart, might, mind, and strength. (Ether 12:4; Mosiah 5:7: "Children of Christ.") The next most important bond for any human being is the bond of love which the new and everlasting covenant makes possible between husband and wife. This second bond can be successful only if the first one is in place, the bond of love between each individual and the Savior. When a husband and wife bond in the pure love of Christ, they create an eternal unit and they can then be exalted. It is that nuclear, bonded family consisting of three persons, the Savior as father, and the faithful husband and the faithful wife, which is and can be exalted, not the individuals separately. (D&C 132:8–25: singly saved.)

13. *The greatest power on earth is the Holy Priesthood.* "It has been the design of Jehovah, from the commencement of the world, and is His purpose now, to regulate the affairs of the world in His own time, to stand as a head of the universe, and take the reins of government in His own hand. When that is done, judgment will be administered in righteousness; anarchy and confusion will be destroyed, and 'nations will learn war no more.' "[16]

"Other attempts to promote universal peace and happiness in the human family have proved abortive; every effort has failed; every plan and design has fallen to the ground; it needs the wisdom of God, the intelligence of God, and the power of God to accomplish this. The world has had a fair trial for six thousand years; the Lord will try the seventh thousand Himself; 'He whose right it is, will possess the kingdom, and reign until He has put all things under His feet;' iniquity will hide its hoary head, Satan will be bound, and the works of darkness destroyed; righteousness will be put to the line, and judgment to the plummet, and 'he that fears the Lord will alone be exalted in that day.' "[17]

The holy priesthood is the power of God. By it the worlds are created, governed, and destroyed; and by it the work of God in all the universe is accomplished. (D&C 38:1–3: "All things came by me.")

Man is given the opportunity, through faith in Jesus

Christ, to receive and use this priesthood if he will use it only as God instructs him. As God commands men, they do the most important work they do on earth through the priesthood power. That work is to establish eternal family relationships between God and men through the teaching of the gospel of Jesus Christ and through the administration of the new and everlasting covenant. (D&C 128:17–18: "Turn the heart of the fathers.")

Because of the fall of Adam, men must do the work to earn their bread by the sweat of their brows. This is part of the individual salvation each must work out as each seeks to be obedient to God. But the time will come for the faithful, perhaps in the next world, where all work will be done by priesthood power. As one is true and faithful to his priesthood covenants here, one prepares to wield the greatest power in all of eternity, the holy priesthood of God. (D&C 84:33–38: "These two priesthoods.")

All associations or alliances made on earth which are not made through the new and everlasting covenant "have an end when men are dead." (D&C 132:6–7.) The only associations which may be made eternal through that covenant are family relationships.

The power of the holy priesthood is also the only power by which righteous and lasting government can be established on the earth. The civil governments of men are better than nothing, usually, but none can solve all problems or achieve either equity or righteousness. The nations of the earth must suffer until they are willing to accept the Savior as their lawgiver; then he will reign through love and the power of priesthood.

The thinking of the Prophet Joseph Smith is as wide and as deep as eternity. It compasses all of God and all of space, time, and matter. Truth and righteousness are his themes, but righteousness reigns as head. For him it is the God of Righteousness who rules the universe, who is the source of truth, who is the "Spirit of Truth" to all who hunger and thirst after righteousness.

Notes

1. Joseph Smith, *History of The Church of Jesus Christ of Latter-day Saints,* 7 vols., 2d ed. rev., ed. B. H. Roberts (Salt Lake City, Utah: The Church of Jesus Christ of Latter-day Saints, 1932–51), 2:315.

2. Joseph Smith, *Teachings of the Prophet Joseph Smith,* sel. Joseph Fielding Smith (Salt Lake City, Utah: Deseret Book Co., 1938), p. 12.

3. Ibid., pp. 95–96.

4. Ibid., pp. 55–56.

5. Ibid., pp. 178–79.

6. Ibid., p. 151.

7. Ibid., p. 317.

8. Andrew F. Ehat and Lyndon W. Cook, eds., *The Words of Joseph Smith* (Provo, Utah: Brigham Young University Religious Studies Center, 1980), p. 237.

9. Smith, *History of the Church,* 5:108–9.

10. Smith, *Teachings of the Prophet Joseph Smith,* p. 9.

11. Smith, *History of the Church,* 2:229.

12. *Lectures on Faith* (Salt Lake City, Utah: Deseret Book Co., 1985), no. 3, p. 38.

13. Smith, *Teachings of the Prophet Joseph Smith,* p. 16.

14. Ibid., p. 12.

15. Ibid., pp. 300–301.

16. Ibid., pp. 250–51.

17. Ibid., p. 252.

Chapter 16

Joseph Smith's Mission and Timetable: "God Will Protect Me until My Work Is Done"

Ronald K. Esplin

Director of Joseph Fielding Smith Institute for Church History
Brigham Young University

For those interested in Joseph Smith's life and mission, Nauvoo is key. As one historian observed, Nauvoo was "the first full-scale model" of the kingdom of God as envisioned by Joseph Smith. Perhaps more importantly, as noted another, Joseph Smith's Nauvoo program and teachings stand as "a deliberate last will and testament of his work."[1] From the first, the "shadow of Carthage" added urgency to the Prophet's Nauvoo actions and decisions. Propelled, as we shall see, by premonitions of death, Joseph Smith toiled in Nauvoo to complete, whatever the cost, the essential elements of his life's work.

Joseph Smith's Nauvoo was complex. Dissenters and critics could find much to criticize. There was also much to admire and, inescapably, much to ponder. All could see the Prophet's highly visible involvement in business and political affairs. One might deal with him as store keeper, land salesman, or mayor. In a theocracy where religious belief informed every aspect of life, he was political adviser and chief economic booster as well as prophet-leader and spiritual mentor. But important as the civic and temporal may have been to Joseph Smith and the Nauvoo Saints, these did not define "the core" or get to the heart of what Nauvoo meant for them. Other things, less visible, held that honor — especially the temple and associated priesthood keys, ordinances, and teachings.

With little understanding of his sense of mission and purpose, critics then and now often measured Joseph Smith's Nauvoo performance by a set of expectations very different from his own. One modern observer, for example, after focusing on what might be called the Prophet's "secular" program, concluded that in Nauvoo, Joseph Smith "was losing control of many affairs, and perhaps of himself." He could not otherwise understand why the Prophet pushed certain things when reason alone should have indicated caution and suggested the probable disastrous results.[2] From this perspective, Joseph Smith in Nauvoo was a flawed hero in a Greek tragedy moving inexorably to a fate which his own blind actions and imperfect character helped determine.

This assessment fails to take into account the religious goals and understandings that influenced, almost compelled, so many Nauvoo decisions. It ignores the religiously based personal timetable and sense of urgency, one that had little to do with city development or politics, that prodded the Prophet in Nauvoo. Assessing his Nauvoo accomplishments on the basis of visible civic involvements alone overlooks aspects of his Nauvoo program most important to his own sense of mission and ignores the perspective from which his closest associates evaluated the Nauvoo experience.

Coreligionists who understood the religious meaning of Nauvoo measured Joseph Smith by a different standard than outsiders and, after measuring, proclaimed success. Joseph Fielding represents those who found pattern and purpose in Nauvoo events, even in the problematic ones. "My consolation," he wrote while still mourning the death of Joseph and Hyrum, is that they "had done all that they could have done and the Foundation of the great Work of the last Days was laid so that it could be finished by the 12 Appostles who had been instructed in all things." For Fielding, these reflections "in a great measure took off the Edge of the Grief that I might else have felt, for I thought that [Joseph] had . . . fulfilled his own Purposes, and I felt willing to say amen to it." Though an eyewitness of some of the difficulties critics pointed to in dismissing Joseph Smith, for Joseph Fielding, the explanation was simple: "It seems as though the Lord had pushed things forward rather prematurely on account of the shortness of Joseph's Time."[3]

Was Joseph Smith's Nauvoo a success or a failure? Was his death the result of misjudgment and events out of control, or the result of fearlessly pursuing the essential regardless of the cost? Examining the Prophet's own gradually developed understanding of mission, mortality, and personal timetable permits us to better understand his Nauvoo "program" and to see his death, as did his closest associates, as foreshadowed and timely.

"I understand my mishion & business," Joseph Smith declared from the pulpit in Nauvoo. "God Almighty is my shield & what Can man do if God is my friend? I shall not be sacrafised untill my time comes. Then I shall be offered freely."[4] No casual remark, this declaration bespoke a hard-won confidence that finally he comprehended fully what God expected of him. It had not always been so. Between the Sacred Grove and Carthage stretched a difficult road as he strived to learn his duty and then to do it. Only gradually did he gain an understanding of his mission and unwavering confidence that God would stand by him until it was completed.

That Joseph Smith came to understand his mission "line upon line, precept upon precept," should not surprise us. Like other mortals—even Christ grew "in wisdom . . . and in favour with God and man"—Joseph Smith only gradually comprehended what God required of him, and more gradually still, found means to do it.[5] If Joseph

Smith in Nauvoo was confident, strong, and fully aware of his responsibilities, he started out none of these. Instead he was, as acknowledged in scripture, among the "weak things of the world, those who are unlearned and despised" but who, if faithful, might be "made strong" in the Lord.[6]

In Joseph Smith's earliest account of his youthful experience in the Sacred Grove, he stressed that he had sought the Lord after mourning "for my own sins and for the sins of the world." Neighborhood preachers awakened in him a deep awareness of human frailty but failed, in his mind, to offer either consolation or salvation. Young Joseph emerged from the grove immersed in God's acceptance. He also learned, to his surprise, that all the Christianity of his day was incomplete and defective. He left the grove instructed to join no church, "until further directed."[7] Though Joseph must have understood, however vaguely, that God intended to remedy the shortcomings in the Christian world, he left no hint that he yet perceived how, or that he would be an instrument.

From his own perspective, the years immediately following this "First Vision" were marked by "foolish errors," "the weakness of youth," and "the foibles of human nature" which often left him feeling condemned for his "weakness and imperfections." It was such a feeling that led him in September 1823 to again seek "forgiveness of all my sins and follies, and also for a manifestation . . . that I might know of my state and standing" before God. In response a messenger, Moroni, appeared to instruct him in his responsibilities and to inform him of things to come. The messenger quoted scriptures promising future priesthood powers and foreshadowing important events of the Restoration. These likely provided young Joseph with a broad framework, the "big picture" into which he might later fit details as he came to comprehend them. He undoubtedly learned something about the gathering and restoration of Israel, a grand work requiring much preparation, and that in all this "God had a work for me to do."[8] But there is little evidence that he yet understood the full meaning of this work or foresaw clearly his own role in it. Moroni then provided specific details of only his first assignment: to obtain "a book . . . written upon gold plates," which contained the fulness of the gospel.[9]

Though Joseph Smith's daily life for the next several years resembled that of other young men of his community, he could no longer be unaware of unusual responsibility. In addition to clearing land, taking odd jobs, and otherwise helping support a large family in a region not far removed from the frontier, he now also had to prepare himself to obtain the plates. It is possible that he did not yet realize that he would be responsible not only to obtain the record but to translate it. Annual visits with the messenger at the hill where the plates were buried no doubt clarified his responsibilities and helped prepare him for what was to come.

In September 1827, four years after their first encounter, Moroni finally permitted Joseph Smith to remove the plates. After emphasizing to Joseph that he was now responsible for them, Moroni added a solemn warning with a promise, the first of several Joseph would receive in the process of learning, step by step, what God required of him: "If I should let them go carelessly or through any neglect of mine," he was warned, he could be "cut off"; but if he was diligent, "they should be protected."[10]

Joseph soon clearly understood that he had both the responsibility and the gift to translate the record. He also learned that anything else — by implication there would be other gifts and other assignments — must be future. He was to "pretend to no other gift" nor would God grant other gifts, "until my purpose is fulfilled in this; for I will grant unto you no other gift until it is finished."[11] This was not simply a matter of timing and priority but also of process: translating prepared Joseph Smith for further responsibility. Here he gained experience, learned principles and doctrine vital to his mission, received authority, and in general readied himself for what was to come. He also learned what God next expected of him: that by virtue of restored priesthood authority, he and his fellow laborer Oliver Cowdery were to baptize and then to organize those baptized into a church infused with the authority they had received.

As Joseph Smith grew in understanding of his mission, revelation continually stressed something he had first learned from Moroni: all was conditional and depended upon his faithfulness. Repeatedly chastisements and solemn warnings accompanied revealed instruction and promise, identifying these early years as ones where young Joseph struggled, learned from mistakes, and occasionally took his eye off the mark.

A person might have revelations and "power to do many mighty works," read a revelation of July 1828, but if he "sets at naught" the counsels of God he will fall. "How oft you have transgressed," it continued, in part by fearing men more than God. "Behold, thou art Joseph, and thou wast chosen to do the work of the Lord, but because of transgression, if thou art not aware, thou wilt fall" and "have no more gift." Delivering sacred things to Martin Harris occasioned this chastisement, but there was more: "thou hast suffered the counsels of thy director to be trampled upon from the beginning."[12] A similar warning several months later concludes with a promise, one that foreshadowed, even in 1829, what was to come in Nauvoo: if Joseph was faithful, "behold I grant unto you eternal life, even if you should be slain."[13]

In 1830 experience and revelation further clarified for Joseph Smith the scope of his mission. The April organization of the church brought to Joseph and Oliver the responsibility to preside and oversee. A revelation given the day of organization described Joseph Smith as "a seer, a translator, a prophet, an apostle of Jesus Christ" and an elder of the newly organized church. He had been inspired, it said, "to lay the foundation thereof, and to build it up." "His word ye shall receive, as if from mine own mouth," the revelation counseled the church, for "him have I inspired to move the cause of Zion in mighty power for good, and his diligence I know."[14] Several weeks later another revelation confirmed that although he had formerly been "called and chosen" specifically to produce the

Book of Mormon, since the organization of the Church his mission had expanded. "Thou shalt devote all thy service in Zion," he was told, "and in this thou shalt have strength." Specifically he was to teach, confirm, and organize. The revelation also warned that "in temporal labors" he would not have strength, "for this is not thy calling."[15]

Each step forward provided Joseph Smith an expanded view of what would be expected of him. With the Book of Mormon, priesthood restoration, the organization of the Church, and beyond, the process was the same: performance of duty today was a prerequisite for more complete understanding tomorrow. Later, in Nauvoo, Joseph Smith looked back and described his growth and education during this early period. It came, he declared, through "the voice of God" and other messengers "at sundry times and in diverse places," each "giving line upon line, precept upon precept; here a little, and there a little; giving us consolation by holding forth that which is to come, confirming our hopes."[16] This process would continue until at least 1836, when experiences associated with the Kirtland Temple prepared the Prophet more fully to understand and complete what remained of his life's work.

Following the organization of the Church in April 1830, several developments occurred of significance for Joseph's understanding of his mission. Perhaps nothing was more important to the young prophet in this connection than his work translating the Bible. Beginning in June 1830, he periodically applied himself intensely to the prayerful study, contemplation, and inspired "translation" of large portions of the Old and New Testament. While Joseph Smith never recorded for us the details of the process, it clearly provided him with what we might call his doctrinal (and perhaps spiritual) graduate education. The translating process produced important expansion and commentary on many biblical passages, served as the catalyst for significant revelations now part of the Doctrine and Covenants, and brought forth both a book of Moses and a book of Enoch.[17]

The books of Moses and Enoch were of special significance to Joseph Smith in understanding his responsibilities. Recognizing the "delicate situation" of the church in June 1830, says the Prophet's history, the Lord granted them "line upon line of knowledge — here a little and there a little," specifically, the "Visions of Moses."[18] Work later that year and in the early part of 1831 produced the rest of the book of Moses, including what is today known as Moses 6–7 but is in reality a book of Enoch.

These revelations provided Joseph Smith concrete examples of prophets of ancient dispensations as models for his own. Enoch created a "Zion society" on earth, one of peace and prosperity based on love, equality, and righteousness. The City of Enoch became for Joseph the archetypal Zion community, the model of what modern Israel was to bring to pass in the latter days. When prudence later dictated that names be disguised before certain revelations circulated, it was not accidental that Joseph Smith selected *Enoch* for his own pseudonym.[19]

Moses also served him as model. The life of Moses, leader of ancient Israel, provided instructive parallels to Joseph, the Moses of modern Israel. A revelation of September 1830, the same month as part of the book of Moses, suggests Oliver Cowdery would be a spokesman to Joseph as Aaron was to Moses. Revelations in 1834 and 1835 specifically identify Joseph Smith as the one who shall lead in this dispensation "as Moses led the children of Israel."[20] In connection with the Kirtland Temple, Joseph Smith first received "the blessings, of Moses, to lead Israel in the latter days, even as moses led him in days of old," and then, from the ancient patriarch himself in the temple, "the keys of the gathering of Israel."[21] Identifying with his ancient predecessors clearly taught Joseph Smith much about his responsibilities.[22]

More than once during these early years revealed instruction suggested that additional insight, knowledge, or authority depended on first fulfilling certain requirements. Counsel came in July 1830, for example, that Joseph should continue translating the scriptures and laboring with the Colesville Saints until the next conference, "and then it shall be made known what you shall do."²³ Similarly, in December Joseph Smith received a commandment to cease translating until the Saints could "assemble together at the Ohio." Though he was not yet in a position to comprehend fully its significance, a January expansion of that instruction indicated that the move to Ohio was essential so that a righteous people might "be gathered unto me," for "there will I give unto you my law; and there you shall be endowed with power from on high."²⁴

Within days of his arrival in Kirtland, Ohio, Joseph Smith received, as promised, "the law of the Church," now section 42 of the Doctrine and Covenants. The blessings associated with the gathering and the temple, also foreshadowed in the New York revelation, would take much longer. While both became important to the Prophet's understanding of mission in Kirtland and were partially realized there (the "power from on high" in connection with the 1836 dedication of the Kirtland Temple), learning and then implementing all essential aspects of his temple-related responsibilities became for Joseph Smith a central concern the entire last decade of his life. Not until Nauvoo, just before his death, did he implement the full promise suggested here. A New York revelation described Joseph Smith as one "inspired to move the cause of Zion in mighty power." In Kirtland he came to see the gathering and the temple as cornerstones of the "program" for Zion.

Joseph and others moved from New York to Ohio in response to revelation requiring that the church "assemble" and "gather," in Ohio. But even as he settled in at Kirtland, he knew that it was not to be the only gathering place. Almost immediately he began preparations for Missouri. Ohio had a special commission as the place for "an endowment from on high." Missouri, soon known as Zion, would be designated the "center place."

In the fall of 1830, Oliver Cowdery, Parley Pratt, and others traveled to the Missouri on a special mission to the Indians. By the spring of 1831, news from the travelers combined with the Prophet's growing expectations for Missouri to make the Indian mission and "the gathering of the Saints to that place" a major topic of discussion.[25] Who would go to Missouri? when? to what specific part? what about Kirtland? In connection with a Kirtland conference in early June, the Prophet received a word of the Lord directing that the next conference be held in Missouri "upon a land which I will consecrate unto my people." In Missouri, the revelation promised, "the land of our inheritance" would be designated. And, if Joseph Smith and Sidney Rigdon were faithful, it would then be made known to them "what they shall do."[26]

Two weeks later Joseph Smith left Ohio for Missouri to learn, as the revelation promised, what more the Lord required of him. In July, on the banks of the Missouri River he contemplated the rough frontier town of Independence and the great western wilderness and its native inhabitants beyond the nearby border. Moved, he sought to know of the Lord: "When will the wilderness blossom as the rose? When will Zion be built up in her glory, and where shall Thy temple stand?" "The place which is now called Independence is the center place," came the response, "and the spot for the temple is lying westward . . . not far from the court-house."[27] That revelation, and another soon to follow, directed that the land be consecrated, the temple site dedicated, and land purchases and settlement (the gathering) begun, even though it would be "many years" before most of the elders could receive their inheritance in Zion.[28]

In early August Sidney Rigdon dedicated the land of Zion for the gathering of the Saints and Joseph Smith dedicated the temple site.[29] A conference followed. Then Joseph Smith, Oliver Cowdery, and Sidney Rigdon left for Ohio, as required by revelation, "to accomplish the residue of the work which I have appointed unto them in their own land."[30] Convinced, however, that "the land of Zion was now the most important temporal object in view," once in Kirtland, Joseph Smith sought from the Lord additional information about the land and the gathering.[31]

Important as was Zion in Missouri to Joseph Smith and his mission, the vital "residue of the work . . . appointed," was in Kirtland. That residue probably included continuing his work as revelator and translator as well as expanding church organization to meet the needs of a growing church. Without question it included the temple. In September, as some Kirtland residents prepared to move, by assignment, to Missouri, the word of the Lord declared that Kirtland was to remain an important "strong hold" for five years. Only after that time would all be free to leave for Missouri.[32] Why five years? Five years would see the temple dedicated and initial ordinances and revelatory experiences complete.

What did Joseph Smith understand Zion to be, and what was its relationship to the gathering and the temple? According to the New York revelations on Enoch, the Lord called his *people* Zion "because they were of one heart and one mind, and dwelt in righteousness" with no poor among them. A *place* could also be called Zion, a place where people lived together in unity, equality and righteousness before the Lord, even as Enoch's city which was "called the City of Holiness, even Zion."[33] This was the goal. But Zion also was *process,* and the "program of Zion" comprised the means by which the Saints could become a Zion's people. The gathering and the temple were essential parts of the process of creating a Zionic community bound together by God's law and enjoying his power.

In Nauvoo the Prophet taught publicly concepts related to Zion that he clearly understood in Kirtland.[34] Obviously a "gathering" was needed in order to bring together those who would become part of a new society. But the main object of gathering the people of God in any age, Joseph Smith declared, "was to build unto the Lord an house whereby he could reveal unto his people the ordinances."[35] A fulness of priesthood power, of the saving ordinances, and of instruction was impossible without a temple; a temple was impossible without gathering. Gathering and temple provided the foundation for Zion.

In Joseph Smith's world view, nothing could be more important. The "building up of Zion is a cause that has interested the people of God in every age," he taught, "a work that is destined to bring about the destruction of the powers of darkness, the renovation of the earth, the glory of God, and the salvation of the human family." In this connection his mission was "to lay a foundation that will revolutionize the whole world," not by sword or gun but by the power of priesthood, of truth and of changed hearts.[36] The gathering and a temple were prerequisites.

If Joseph Smith did not understand this before, it was made perfectly clear in 1833. In May Kirtland focused on the necessity of constructing several buildings essential to a Zion community—a building for the presidency, one for education, another for printing—each "wholly dedicated to the Lord from the foundation thereof."[37] A building committee commenced work. Then a June revelation chastened the leaders for not pressing forward with "the building of mine house" as a priority above all others. Though important, the other buildings could not compare with the commandment to build a house in which "I design to endow those whom I have chosen with power from on high." The June revelation that renewed the commandment promised, "If you keep my commandments you shall have power to build it." Within a week, work on the temple began.[38]

Once Joseph Smith understood this program, his challenge was to teach it to the Latter-day Saints and, together, develop the means to implement it. Brigham Young later spoke of his introduction to these concepts during a visit to Kirtland in July 1833, one month after the temple revelation. The promised blessings, he learned, depended on fulfilling duties both temporal and spiritual: God required not only that they preach and pray but that they build. To the assembled elders, the Prophet delivered the word of the Lord: "it was simply this: Never do another day's work to build up a Gentile city; never lay out another dollar while you live, to advance the world in its present state." Instead, it was their duty to "sustain the Kingdom of God to your uttermost" and in every way.[39]

Brigham Young here learned the purpose for the gathering and the necessity of the temple. He here first

291

understood that even labors often called "temporal" were essential and had sacred meaning in the kingdom of God. And here he made the decision to move himself and his family to Kirtland to assist in building that kingdom both temporally and spiritually. Years later he characterized "the nature and beauty of Joseph's mission" as an inspired bringing together of heaven and earth.[40]

The Prophet's commitment to temple and Zion were not the only aspects of his mission evident to the Saints in early Kirtland. His work as translator continued to be important, both to him and to the Church, even as additional revelations clarified his roles as revelator and presiding officer.[41] These revelations underscored Joseph Smith's uniqueness in both calling and authority even among those who shared with him the keys of priesthood leadership. Only he had been appointed "to receive commandments and revelations" for the Church.[42] Because he was both translator and revelator, holding the "keys of the mysteries of the kingdom," additional revelation would come through him; the Church must either sustain him or not receive "the glories of the kingdom."[43] These responsibilities were his and his alone, "if he abide in me." The continuation of these gifts depended upon faithfulness. Should he fail—requiring that someone else complete his mission—"he shall not have power except to appoint another in his stead,"[44] thus preserving order in the Church.

As presiding officer—designated first elder, then first apostle, and finally president of the high priesthood[45]— Joseph Smith also oversaw the organizational development of the Church. By the mid-1830s, an elaborate organization replaced the small, loosely organized congregations of the New York period. By 1833 church organization included Aaronic and Melchizedek priesthood offices and special presiding officers such as bishops and a general, or "first," presidency. In 1834 Joseph Smith organized stakes, one in Kirtland and one in Missouri, each with a high council and stake presidency. The Quorum of Twelve Apostles and the first Seventies came in 1835.[46] This essentially marked the end of administrative innovation until, in connection with the Nauvoo Temple near the end of his life, the Prophet added several finishing touches.

Although by 1834 Joseph Smith understood priorities, hard lessons about "timetable" were still ahead: nothing would come as quickly or as easily as he might have hoped. Zion, he would learn, would be redeemed on the Lord's timetable, not man's, and even an understanding of order and priority did not reveal the timetable.

In 1833 enemies drove the Missouri Saints from Jackson County, their center place. Joseph Smith in 1834 led an armed band from Ohio in the hopes of reinstating the Saints on their Jackson County lands. After considerable hardship, Zion's Camp, as it was called, disbanded before entering Jackson County. Without the governor's promised assistance, they managed only to resupply the Saints in their temporary homes, not reinstate them in their former ones.[47]

On 22 June, before disbanding Zion's Camp, Joseph Smith delivered, on the banks of the Fishing River, a pointed and enlightening revelation. A later revelation suggested that even when the Saints do all in their power to fulfill God's commands, the timetable might be altered by the opposition of men.[48] In this case, however, the word of the Lord was that the Saints had not done enough. Were it not for the collective transgressions of the Missouri Saints, declared the revelation, they might even now enjoy their lands.[49] The revelation emphasized that Zion can only be built upon celestial principles; the Saints' lack of unity and lack of obedience violated cardinal rules for Zion. Therefore, because of transgressions, "it is expedient in me that mine elders should wait for a little season for the redemption of Zion."[50]

With chastisement came counsel and promise. Before Zion could be redeemed, the Saints must be "taught more perfectly, and have experience, and know more perfectly their duty." None of this could occur "until mine elders are endowed with power from on high" — the priority again of the temple. Since the temple must come first, it was essential that the redemption of Zion "wait for a little season." The promise, though, remained: if obedient, the Saints "shall have power after many days to accomplish all things pertaining to Zion."[51]

No doubt this warning and promise moved Joseph Smith and his associates to contemplate both their duty and the future endowment. It might also have suggested that establishing the new society in Missouri would be a slow and lengthy process.[52] Two months later, writing to church leaders in Missouri, Joseph Smith was more optimistic. After reemphasizing that the elders must "receive their endowment in Kirtland before the redemption of Zion," he made it clear that he believed that if the church were united and made every possible effort — "we have a great work to do, and but little time to do it in" — Zion might be redeemed in two years.[53] For the next eighteen months, the Prophet directed all possible resources to complete the temple with the firm idea of following that up with the "redemption" of Zion. But, as he would learn in the temple in May 1836, the Lord apparently had in mind a different timetable.[54]

It is instructive to see Joseph Smith growing through all of this — and, based on experience, expanding his knowledge of duty and mission. After expending a great deal of energy on church organization before leaving Ohio with Zion's Camp in 1834, he apparently saw his work largely in organizational terms and judged his mission complete. He returned with a different understanding.

"I supposed I had established this Church on a permanent foundation when I went to Missouri," he told the Quorum of the Twelve in 1835, "and indeed I did so, for if I had been taken away it would have been enough, but I yet live, and therefore God requires more at my hands." The additional requirements were related to the temple. "There is one great deficiency or obstruction . . . that deprives us of greater blessings," he told the apostles on this occasion. They must "attend to certain duties that we have not as yet attended to" in the temple. He fully understood by 1835 that his work could not be finished nor "the foundation of this church complete and permanent" without temple-related powers, ordinances, and teachings.[55]

Apparently this understanding came home to him with full power only at Fishing River. When he left for Missouri, he told the Twelve, he thought his mission complete. Two days after the Fishing River revelation he did not. Cholera struck the camp 24 June. Seventy men fell violently ill, among them Joseph, and fourteen died, hastily buried without coffins. "If my work were done," he told his brethren then, "you would have to put me in the ground without a coffin, too."[56] That his work was not finished implied a promise that he would have time to see it through.

The year 1836 was both the year of the temple and the year planned for the redemption of Zion. On 17 January, Church leaders held an emotional and lengthy meeting which resolved difficulties and brought harmony. Apostle Heber Kimball later characterized this meeting as opening "a joyful season . . . truly the beginning of good days."[57] The following week the Prophet presided over the first ordinance work associated with the still-unfinished temple. (It is here that Father Smith anointed Joseph and sealed on him "the blessings of Moses, to lead Israel in the latter days.") Joseph Smith's record of the day reports visions and manifestations as the "heavens were opened upon us."[58] Similar sessions followed.

As the temple dedication neared, thoughts also turned to Zion. Since the previous fall Joseph had contemplated leading an enlarged Zion's Camp to help the Missouri Saints recover their Jackson County lands. In October he had instructed the Twelve to prepare to move their families to Missouri in the spring. Now, on 13 March, a council of leaders concluded to emigrate 15 May "if kind providence smiles upon us and openes the way before us."[59] It was not to be.

On 27 March Joseph Smith dedicated the temple. Before beginning the ordinances two days later, the Prophet and several associates knelt "in the most holy place in the Lords house" to be taught by revelation "concerning our going to Zion, and other important matters." With the appointed day fast approaching, he wanted confirmation of the plan. The voice of the Spirit was that if they would humble themselves, fasting and praying in the temple through the night, they would learn His will. Although the diary preserves no answer, the Prophet's instructions to the Twelve the next day, and his own actions thereafter, indicate that the answer removed his personal feeling of urgency about Zion.[60]

March 30, the day appointed for the solemn assembly, was a day of blessings, ordinances, spiritual confirmation, and instruction. It had been necessary to remain in Kirtland until the endowment was received, affirmed Joseph, but the time was at hand when they could go forth empowered. Modifying the former instruction that the Twelve move to Missouri, he told them they were now "at liberty to go wheresoever they will," to Zion if they pleased, or elsewhere. Though the urgency was gone, the goal remained. "Let the redemption of Zion be our object," he advised, preaching and gathering "the strength of the Lords house where ever we find them."[61]

On this occasion Joseph Smith also declared that he "had now completed the organization of the church." He indicated they had received all the necessary ordinances and instruction and "were now at liberty . . . to go forth and build up the kingdom of God." Had Kirtland temple experiences ended here, the Prophet might have concluded that his work was done.[62]

There occurred on the Sunday following one of the most significant events associated with the Kirtland Temple. After preliminaries, Joseph Smith and Oliver Cowdery retreated behind lowered veils for "solemn and silent prayer." "The eyes of their understandings were opened," Joseph reported in his diary, and they saw Christ, acknowledging acceptance of the temple, and then in turn Moses, with the keys of the gathering of Israel; Elias, with the keys of Abraham; and Elijah with vital keys of redemption and sealing.[63] Joseph received the first essential priesthood keys in 1829; here, in 1836, he received the last.

These temple events of 1836 marked an important shift in Joseph Smith's understanding of mission, priorities, and even daily activities. The Prophet's Kirtland diary ends, for example, with the entry recording the manifestations of 3 April. After the spring of 1836, he devoted his principal energies not to temple or to Zion but to strengthening Kirtland as a gathering place for the Saints.[64]

This is not to suggest that he no longer felt responsibility for temple or Missouri; within two years he lived in Missouri, and the temple soon became even more important to him and his mission, not less. The appearance of Elijah in April with additional temple-related keys opened the way for—indeed, required—expanded temple ordinances. Implementing the ordinances suggested here and passing on the keys would become Joseph Smith's highest priority.

Although Joseph Smith probably understood in the spring of 1836 his additional temple-related responsibilities, he could not immediately carry them out because the Saints were not yet prepared. "All these things were to be done in their time, place, and season," George A. Smith later explained. In the Kirtland temple the Lord proceeded "with such great caution that, at all hazards, a few . . . might be able to understand and obey." Even so, some apostatized because there was too much, some because there was not enough, and "if the Lord had on that occasion revealed one single sentiment more . . . I believe He would have upset the whole of us."[65] Before the Saints were ready for more, Joseph and others were forced to flee Kirtland, leaving the temple behind.

Though the Prophet, too, learned "line upon line, precept upon precept," at this point he clearly was well in advance of the Saints. The evidence suggests that from this point on he understood, at least broadly, the full scope of his responsibility. His challenge now was not to learn his duty but to do it—to prepare the people to receive the fulness and find the proper time and pace to proceed.

Joseph Smith arrived in Far West, Missouri, in March 1838. Though most of the Saints remained loyal to the

Prophet and his vision of a new Zion on earth, some leaders had not. Dissenters, vexatious lawsuits, and threats finally had made it unwise to remain in Kirtland.[66] Far West, located in Caldwell County, a new county north of Jackson County and populated mainly by the Saints, became the new headquarters. Though there seemed no realistic possibility of returning to the designated "center place" immediately, Far West offered an appropriate place to continue preparing a Zion's people.

Given the nature of Joseph Smith's mission, it is not surprising that one month after his arrival in Missouri revelation designated Far West a gathering place and directed construction of a temple. The revelation, moreover, commanded that the temple be commenced without delay and that Far West be "built up speedily by the gathering of my Saints."[67] Under the circumstances, however, no effort could build the temple or the city rapidly enough. Violence first erupted in late summer. Fall saw the imprisonment of Joseph Smith and the Presidency, hostages essentially for their people, and during the winter of 1838–39 the Saints were driven from Missouri. Once again obstacles prevented Joseph Smith from completing the indispensable temple-related aspects of his mission.

Joseph Smith's Missouri imprisonment, from November 1838 into April 1839, had a profound effect on his sense of urgency about completing his life's work. He had long been aware of his own mortality and no doubt considered it many times as he contemplated his unfolding calling. "Even if you should be slain," read the 1829 passage; "I yet live, and there is more," he noted in 1835. But this was different. He had narrowly avoided death when first taken and now "to all human appearance, could not be delivered" alive from his enemies, to borrow Brigham Young's phrase. In July he had declared: "all the world is threatening my life, but I regard it not, for I am willing to die any time when God calls for me."[68] And now it appeared He would.

In spite of the prospects, Joseph Smith and close associates shared in 1838 an assurance that God would protect him. Too much remained unfinished. Joseph Smith wrote from Liberty Jail that, though their enemies seemed to have triumphed, "we most assuredly know, that their triumph will be but short, and that God will deliver us out of their hands."[69] Brigham Young, Heber Kimball, and Willard Richards, among others, claimed similar reassurance.[70] But Joseph Smith did not emerge from Liberty Jail feeling invulnerable. To the contrary, just as firmly as he believed he would be delivered, he apparently believed that he would not live to see forty.[71] While he had often contemplated the possibility of death, it is possible that in Liberty Jail, for the first time, he realized that his allotted time was both fixed and short.

Imprisonment brought Joseph Smith long days and weeks to contemplate these things and to review his labors. If he felt satisfaction in the progress from the publication of the Book of Mormon through the dedication of the Kirtland Temple, he could only have felt frustration to note how little more of the essential had been accomplished in the nearly three years since. As he wrote from Liberty Jail in March, "I never have had opportunity to give [the Saints] the plan that God has revealed to me."[72] Pondering past problems, and perhaps his own performance, he concluded that "many things were introduced among the Saints, before God had signified the time, . . . notwithstanding the principles and the plans may have been good." Timing was important. The Saints must be prepared and God must approve before pressing forward again, but Joseph felt certain the time was near "when God will signify many things."[73] Freed from prison in April 1839, Joseph Smith arrived among the Saints with an internal agenda, a sense of personal urgency, and a conviction that the city that became Nauvoo represented his last opportunity.

Whatever Joseph Smith's hopes in 1839, reality dictated that resources be used to regroup and to survive. The Missouri experience had been devastating, destroying morale and health as well as goods. So discouraged were the Saints that many wondered if they should "gather" again.

Rallied by Brigham Young, the Saints voted in March to try once more, a decision Joseph ratified as soon as he was free. The gathering, of course, was essential. But the first need was for refuge, then for a temple city. Unlike in Kirtland and Far West, so enormous were the challenges that in spite of the Prophet's sense of urgency, the Saints had been in Nauvoo more than eighteen months before revelation authorized the construction of a temple.[74]

During 1839 and 1840, Joseph Smith applied his energies to many projects important to him and to the Saints. "I cried Lord what will you have me to do," he said later, "& the answer was build up a city & call my saints to this place!"[75] He laid the foundations of a major city for a new gathering place; and he helped the Twelve prepare for their mission to Britain, a tremendously successful enterprise that infused Nauvoo and the whole church with new energy and resources. He taught the Twelve many new principles, promising that "God hath not revealed any thing to Joseph, but what he will make known unto the Twelve." Furthermore, he added, alluding as he often did to the temple, "even the least Saint may know all things as fast as he is able to bear them."[76]

The lack of progress on essential temple-related responsibilities remained a concern. In July 1840 the Prophet spoke of his commitment to build "as great a temple as ever Solomon did," adding emotionally that if it should be the will of God "that I might live to behold that temple completed . . . I will say, 'Oh Lord it is enough let thy servant depart in peace.' "[77]

Joseph's reaction to a September 1840 blessing by his father also reveals the internal tension he felt. During the deathbed blessing of his children, Father Smith promised Joseph, "You shall even live to finish your work." According to his mother, Joseph, upon hearing this, "cried out, weeping, 'Oh! my father, shall I.' 'Yes,' said his father, 'you shall live to lay out the plan of all the work which God has given you to do. This is my dying blessing upon your head in the name of Jesus. . . . for it shall be fulfilled.' "[78] While no doubt reassured by this promise, the sense of urgency remained; he could not shake the conviction that he must press ahead.

In January 1841, Joseph received an important revelation. "I am well pleased with your offering and acknowledgements," it began, "for unto this end have I raised you up, that I might show forth my wisdom through the weak things of the earth." This suggests that his frailties and earlier stumblings were part of the plan so that all might know his strength was not of himself but in the Lord. In Nauvoo, indeed since the Kirtland Temple, revelations often acknowledged that Joseph "hath sincerely striven to do thy will,"[79] instead of the earlier chastisements and warnings, as if he were finally tested and true. The Prophet's own statements in Nauvoo also reflect a growing confidence that he had done his duty acceptably before God.

"Your prayers are acceptable before me," the January 1841 revelation continued, "and in answer to them, I say unto you" proclaim the restored gospel to the world, establish Nauvoo as a cornerstone of Zion, gather the Saints, "and build a house to my name."[80] A temple was urgent, "For there is not a place found on earth that he may come to restore again that which was lost . . . even the fulness of the priesthood." Further, the revelation defined this power, and the ordinances, revelation, and teachings "of my holy house, which my people are always commanded to build" as the essential "foundation of Zion." Joseph will be shown "all things pertaining to this house, and the priesthood thereof," the passage continued; construction should now begin "on the place where you have contemplated building it."[81]

The ceremonial laying of the cornerstones for the Nauvoo Temple was the centerpiece of the April 1841 general conference.[82] But substantial work did not begin immediately, partly because of limited resources and competing priorities and perhaps because the Twelve, who would become the temple's strongest supporters, were still in England. Upon their return, Joseph Smith called in August 1841 an "extraordinary conference" at which he essentially realigned the Twelve as church leaders. The time had come, he announced, for the Twelve "to stand in their place next to the First Presidency," and to assist, for the first time, in managing all the affairs of the Church.[83] The "business of the church given to the 12" — Willard Richards's phrase[84] — soon included gathering and directing resources for the temple.

During the 1830s, especially before the dedication of the Kirtland Temple, Joseph Smith frequently received and circulated to the Saints in writing the "word of the Lord." In the early days of Nauvoo he did not. After the revelation (on the temple, among other things) of January 1841, Nauvoo "word of the Lord" revelations, which today are part of scripture, consist only of two short passages of very specific counsel and the important revelation on celestial marriage, written down in 1843 but apparently received earlier.[85] In Nauvoo the Prophet often enlarged the understanding of the Saints through both written and oral teaching. Much of this was considered inspired and some was later canonized, including two important letters relating to the temple written in September 1842.[86] But "thus saith the Lord" formal revelations were few indeed.

The difference, in part, may have been the need, in the beginning, to firmly establish the principle that God can and does speak today as in times past. Beyond that pattern, however, was the need to lay a revealed foundation for the Restoration. At first, revelation time after time opened totally new understandings. We have also seen that the Prophet had to learn his mission "line upon line." Since by 1836 these needs had been largely filled, it is reasonable to expect a decrease in the number of occasions calling for a formal, written "word of the Lord." Brigham Young later noted that the Kirtland Temple required more revelation than later ones, concluding, "it is only where experience fails, that revelation is needed."[87]

Joseph Smith pointed out still another reason. "Some say Joseph is a fallen Prophet because he does not bring forth more of the word of the Lord," he acknowledged in a December 1841 meeting with the Twelve. "Why does he not?" he then asked. "Are we able to receive it? No (says he) not one in this room."[88] It was the Prophet's responsibility to share what he now knew, yet many did not accept new teachings easily and some not at all; not even close associates were prepared to receive all that had been revealed.[89] Of necessity there would be less new revelation until the Saints were prepared to better understand, accept, and act on what had already been received.

The Prophet often returned to this theme in Nauvoo. Clearly he felt tension between the sense of urgency to complete his work and the relative lack of preparation for the Saints to receive it. "Many seal up the door of heaven," he complained, "by saying so far God may reveal and I will believe" but no further.[90] He also compared the difficulty of getting "anything into the heads of this generation. . . . [e]ven the Saints were slow to understand," with trying to split a hemlock knot "with a Corn do[d]ger for a wedge and a pumpkin for a beetle." It could not be done. In this statement, made not long before his death, he continued: "I have tried for a number of years to get the minds of the Saints prepared to recieve the things of God, but we frequently see some of them after suffering all they have for the work of God will fly to peaces like glass as soon as anything Comes that is Contrary to their traditions. They cannot stand the fire at all."[91]

In Nauvoo the Prophet carefully labored to prepare the Saints for innovations, and he succeeded in introducing many. But in some cases he concluded to move ahead privately among those he felt would embrace new teachings, preserve them, and eventually deliver them to the Church. In all of this, he was committed to doing what God required of him — his duty as he understood it — whatever the cost. "The object with me is to obey and teach others to obey God in just what he tells us to do," he taught several months before his death. "It mattereth not whether the principle is popular or unpopular. I will always maintain a true principl even if I Stand alone in it."[92] Understanding that such religiously based imperatives drove him, we can see purpose in Nauvoo decisions and actions that may otherwise seem premature and unwise. This applies, for example, to the introduction during the early 1840s of plural marriage.

Inevitably plural marriage brought complications into the Prophet's life and into the church, as he knew it would. No explanation for its introduction works as well as the simple one: he believed God required it of him and of the Saints. Even so, he would not have introduced it *then*, given other priorities and the unavoidable certainty of accompanying difficulties, except that he believed God required it then. Several witnesses claim that he began only after an angel declared he must act or his calling would be given to another.[93] When he did implement in Nauvoo a principle that he had understood for several years, he did so aware of the probable costs. Brigham Young remembered his stating more than once that he was determined to press ahead though it would cost him his life, for "it is the work of God, and He has revealed this principle, and it is not my business to controle or dictate it."[94]

Though perhaps less dangerous, moving ahead with his temple responsibilities presented a no less difficult challenge. Progress on the structure itself was slow. Writing from the British Mission in December 1841, Parley Pratt expressed his joy that the temple was underway and his "great desire to push it forward," adding, "I hope it will be enclosed by next fall."[95] In Nauvoo that same December, Brigham Young likewise stressed the importance of obeying the word of the Lord through Joseph, "& as the Lord had commanded us to build a Temple we should do it spedily."[96] Though as committed to the temple as Elder Pratt, Joseph Smith and those with him in Nauvoo knew that the building was not as far along nor would it move as rapidly as Parley expected — or as the Prophet needed.

That winter, pondering the progress on the temple and his renewed forebodings about his death, Joseph Smith made a momentous decision: he would complete, outside the temple, the responsibilities central to his mission. Fearing that construction might require more time than he had, he concluded that a set-apart upper room would have to substitute.[97]

Of necessity, without a temple only a select few could, at first, receive the additional teachings and ordinances. This approach did offer the advantage that the Prophet could now proceed with the whole program even though not all the Saints were prepared to receive it. Those selected, he made clear, would be a vanguard not an elite, receiving only "what will be made known to all the Saints . . . so soon as they are prepared to receive, and a proper place [the temple] is prepared to communicate them."[98] The challenge remained, then, of continuing to teach publicly as much as possible to prepare all the Saints — a task actually made more difficult by the inevitable rumors associated with private teachings.[99] But there was little choice. In spite of problems, the work would finally be advancing. Progress, and the arrangement making it possible, provided Joseph Smith a satisfying freedom. Heber Kimball, one of the select group, understood: "Brother Joseph feels as well as I Ever see him," he wrote to Parley Pratt. "One reason is he has got a Small company, that he feels safe in thare ha[n]ds. And that is not all, he can open his bosom to[o] and feel him Self safe."[100]

Throughout the winter and spring of 1842, the Prophet prepared for temple ordinances. Perhaps it was no coincidence that in March he published the book of Abraham, decided to permit the establishment of the Nauvoo Masonic Lodge (he did not request it), and helped organize the Nauvoo Female Relief Society. He may have seen these, along with important public discourses, as playing a role in preparing the Saints. It is clear that these preparations were directed toward preparing the people, not the program or himself. Since 1836 he had understood what more was required. The many years of preparation, and the fact that what he introduced in Nauvoo meshed tightly with the Kirtland Temple experiences, tends to confirm that these preliminaries were for teaching the ordinances, not for completing them.

During this period, the Prophet Joseph spoke his mind

freely to the newly organized Nauvoo Female Relief Society. Their minutes of his remarks provide a window from which to view him during this season of such importance to his mission. Especially revealing was the meeting of 28 April 1842. It was "nonsense of the human heart," he told the sisters on this occasion, for a person to aspire to office or to always find fault with the management of things; "big elders" had proved troublesome from the beginning. "If God has appointed him, and chosen him as an instrument to lead the Church, why not let him lead it through? Who knows the mind of God? Does he not reveal things differently from what we expect?" In spite of all opposition, with God's help, Joseph thought he "always came out right in the end." Now he intended to "organize the Church in proper order." That could not be done, he hinted, unless the sisters, too, were properly organized under priesthood, something possible only in connection with the temple.[101]

On this occasion he also shared his premonitions. He would make use of this opportunity with them, he insisted, for "he did not know as he should have many opportunities of teaching them . . . they would not long have him to instruct them — that the church would not have his instruction long, and the world would not be troubled with him a great while . . . he spoke of delivering the keys to this Society — and to the Church — that according to his prayers God had appointed him elsewhere."[102] Sisters who had heard him three weeks earlier could not have missed his meaning. At the funeral of a young boy, he spoke solemnly of the pain he felt at the passing of his own brothers. Such losses are hard to bear, he said, and sometimes "I should have been more reconciled to have been called myself if it could have been the will of God." And well it might be in the future "with me as well as you. Some has supposed that Br. Joseph could not die but this is a mistake. It is true their has been times when I have had the promise of my life to accomplish such & such things, but having accomplished those things I have not at present any lease of my life & am as liable to die as other men."[103]

As he spoke he was preparing for the moment, now

less than a month away, when he would at last introduce
the ordinances necessary to complete his mission and calling. In early May 1842, Joseph Smith instructed nine close
associates, among them Brigham Young and Heber Kimball of the Twelve, "in the principles and order of the
Priesthood." This was the occasion of the first full temple
ritual, or endowment.[104] There were only men; women,
too, must yet receive the ordinances. Also, there must be
enough Saints so endowed and instructed to ensure, whatever happened to him, that the ordinances would be preserved and given to the church in the Nauvoo Temple.
But finally he was completing what he knew was required
of him.

What was now lacking he might have finished in a
relatively short time—and apparently expected to—until
realities beyond his control once again intervened. Though
we cannot here detail the obstacles that forced changes in
the timetable,[105] we can note that he did not return to
complete what was begun here until the fall of 1843. In
the meantime, as he readjusted his agenda to external
realities, one thing remained constant. Knowing that he
still had not completed his mission, he felt, again, a promise of protection until he could.

"I have the whole plan of the kingdom before me, and
no other person has," he declared in August.[106] Two days
later he explained that his feelings "at the present time are
that inasmuch as the Lord Almighty has preserved me until
today, [He] will continue to preserve me by the united
faith and prayers of the Saints, until I fully accomplished
my mission in this life and so fully established the dispensation of the fulness of the Priesthood . . . that all the
powers of Earth and Hell can never prevail against it."[107]
In January 1843 he announced that he understood his mission and with God as his shield "I shall not be sacrafised
untill my time comes. Then I shall be offered freely."[108] "I
defy all the world, and I prophecy they never will over-
throw me till I get ready," he declared later that year.[109]
"I cannot lie down until my work is finished," he affirmed

307

---

in the spring of 1844, followed the next month by "God will always protect me until my mission is fulfilled."[110]

Another constant throughout this period was work on the temple. Though it was not finished sufficiently for ordinance work during the Prophet's lifetime, he continually reminded the Saints of its importance, and of the promised blessings available to all within. "Let the work of my temple . . . be continued on and not cease," read one reminder, "let your diligence, and your perseverance, and patience, and your works be redoubled, and you shall in nowise lose your reward."[111]

In September 1843, Joseph Smith returned to the ordinance work begun in the spring of 1842. By December and January, a number of men and women had received temple ordinances at the hands of the Prophet. These met together frequently to assist in the ordinance work for others and to receive instruction. Before the Prophet's death, approximately seventy men and women received these ordinances under his direction. By January 1844, nine members of the Quorum of the Twelve, along with some others, had also received the "fulness of the Priesthood" ordinances, essentially completing the Prophet's temple-related agenda.[112] At last the stage was set for Joseph Smith's final essential duty.

In the last months of his life, the Prophet continued meeting privately with the Twelve and with others who had received temple ordinances, teaching them more fully their temple-related powers, responsibilities, and related doctrine. He also emphasized to the Twelve the importance of finishing the temple and commissioned them to "investigate the locations of Callifornia & oregon & find a good location where we can move after the Temple is completed."[113] In March, the Prophet introduced his final institutional model, the Council of Fifty—a priesthood-directed organization within which members and non-members could work cooperatively in carrying out economic and political enterprises.[114]

The climax came in an extraordinary council in late March involving the Quorum of the Twelve and others.

Though dozens of reminiscent accounts comment on the council, soon after the Prophet's death the Twelve prepared the most detailed account. According to that account, "depressed in Spirit," Joseph Smith had opened his heart "concerning his presentiments of the future":

"Brethren, the Lord bids me hasten the work in which we are engaged. . . . Some important Scene is near to take place. It may be that my enemies will kill me, and in case they should, and the Keys and power which rest on me not be imparted to you, they will be lost from the Earth; but if I can only succeed in placing them upon your heads, then let me fall a victim to murderous hands if God will suffer it, and I can go with all pleasure and satisfaction, knowing that my work is done, and the foundation laid on which the kingdom of God is to be reared."

The Twelve could not be all killed at once, the Prophet continued, "and should any of you be killed, you can lay your hands upon others and fill up your quorum. Thus can this power and these keys be perpetuated in the Earth." He then rolled the burden of the kingdom onto their shoulders, "for the Lord is going to let me rest a while." That done, he declared: "I feel that I am free. I thank my God for this deliverance."[115]

As part of this "final charge" to the Twelve, as the apostles later called this council, Joseph Smith conferred "the keys of the sealing power," received from Elijah in 1836, upon Brigham Young, President of the Twelve. This, taught the Prophet, was the "last key," the "most sacred of all," and it pertained "exclusively to the first presidency."[116] The Prophet could now declare "that he had conferred upon [them] every key and every power that he ever held himself before God."[117] His life's work was complete.

In April conference, the Prophet testified to the Saints that he was far from being, as some charged, "a fallen prophet," for he had never been "in any nearer relationship to God than at the present time."[118] A few weeks later, on the eve of his departure for Carthage, George Laub heard him speak for the last time. "The enemy is seeking my life and are laying planns to kill me, but if they kill me they kill an Inocent man. This I will call on God, angels & men to witness. . . . But I have laid the foundation of the work of what the Lord hass gave me to doo, therefore have noe longer leas of my life. I have acco[m]plished my work that was given me & others can build on the same."[119]

In August 1842 Joseph Smith saw himself as the only man with "the whole plan of the kingdom before me." By the spring of 1844 that was no longer true. The summer the Prophet was killed, Orson Hyde put into perspective for the Nauvoo Saints what had occurred. His comments, reported in a letter, summarize admirably the Prophet's Nauvoo completion of his mission:

"Orson Hyde told last Sunday what it was for, that they [the Twelve] were in Council with Joseph so much last spring. He said that Joseph was preparing them for the work that they have now got to do which is to hold the keys and build up this kingdom in all the world. Joseph commited unto them all the keys of the Priesthood otherwise the *fulness* would not have been upon the Earth now he is taken away. He also took them through all the ordinances which is necessary for the Salvation of Man, that they haveing experienced them all, by passing through them, might be prepared to lead the People . . . when he had finished his work ordained and anointed the twelve to lead this people and build upon the foundation which he had laid he was *filled with joy* & sayes he it is now but little matter what becomest of me. . . . from many things which he said and did it is evident that he [k]new an eventful period had arrived, that his exit was at hand, for he said, 'I will die for this people' and he has gone."[120]

"Though the enemy had the power to kill our Prophet," Brigham Young asked rhetorically, "did he not accomplish all that was in his heart to accomplish in his day? He did, to my certain knowledge . . . he prepared the way."[121]

Notes

1. Robert B. Flanders, "Dream and Nightmare: Nauvoo Revisited," *The Restoration Movement: Essays in Mormon History,* F. Mark Mckiernan, et al., eds. (Lawrence, Kans.: Coronado Press, 1973), p. 156; hereafter cited as "Nauvoo Revisited"; Richard L. Anderson, Joseph Smith's Martyrdom: Prophecies and Submission, unpublished paper, 1988, p. 1.

2. Flanders, "Nauvoo Revisited," p. 152.

3. Andrew F. Ehat, ed., " 'They Might have Known That He Was Not a Fallen Prophet' — The Nauvoo Journal of Joseph Fielding," *BYU Studies* 19 (Winter 1979): 153–54.

4. *Wilford Woodruff's Journal, 1833–1898,* ed. Scott G. Kenney (Midvale, Utah: Signature Books, 1983), 22 Jan. 1843, 2:217.

5. Luke 2:56 (see also Luke 2:40); Doctrine and Covenants 128:21.

6. Doctrine and Covenants 35:13–14, 17; 50:16. Later, in Nauvoo, an 1841 revelation, now Doctrine and Covenants 124:1, said that the Lord raised up Joseph Smith "that I might show forth my wisdom through the weak things of the earth."

7. Dean C. Jessee, ed., *The Personal Writings of Joseph Smith* (Salt Lake City, Utah: Deseret Book Co., 1984), pp. 5–6 (1832 account) and pp. 201–2 (1838 account).

8. Jessee, *Personal Writings of Joseph Smith,* pp. 202–3. In recording this event, Joseph Smith mentioned a number of passages quoted by the messenger and then observed: "He quoted many other passages of scripture and offered many explanations which cannot be mentioned here." Ibid., p. 204.

Writing in 1835, Oliver Cowdery indicated that the messenger provided important information to prepare Joseph Smith for his later work, including an understanding that Joseph was to be "an instrument" in the Lord's hand to help prepare the way for the restoration of Israel. Cowdery added his opinion that on this occasion "our brother [Joseph] was permitted to see and understand much more full and perfect than I am able to communicate in writing." *Messenger and Advocate* 1 (Feb. 1835): 79–80; 1 (Apr. 1835): 109.

Because of this lengthy instruction (and perhaps other experiences not recorded), the possibility remains that Joseph Smith understood more about his mission than records reveal. Surviving records, however, do indicate that he did not know "the end from the beginning" and that he clearly learned details about specific responsibilities only as events unfolded. Indeed, as we shall see, several times he was told that he could learn more only by actively accomplishing something else. It is likely that many of Moroni's explanations, and other instruction that foreshadowed important future events, took on full meaning to Joseph Smith only as his mission unfolded.

9. Jessee, *Personal Writings of Joseph Smith,* pp. 202–3. In the "Wentworth Letter," March 1842, Joseph Smith reported that Moroni said he "was chosen to be an instrument . . . to bring about some of His purposes in this glorious dispensation," but again provided no details not relating to his responsibility with the plates. Joseph Smith, *History of The Church of Jesus*

Christ of Latter-day Saints, 7 vols., 2d ed. rev., ed. B. H. Roberts (Salt Lake City, Utah: The Church of Jesus Christ of Latter-day Saints, 1932–51), 4:537.

10. Jessee, *Personal Writings of Joseph Smith,* p. 208.

11. Doctrine and Covenants 5:4.

12. Doctrine and Covenants 3:1–15. See also Doctrine and Covenants 6:18–20; 20:5–8.

13. Doctrine and Covenants 5:21–22; see also vv. 31–35. "Even if he should be slain," was the original, third person, wording of Book of Commandments 4:7. This phrasing was changed in 1835. One month later (see D&C 6:29–30) the Lord told Joseph and Oliver that enemies "can do no more unto you than unto me," that is, take their lives, and even if they did, "you shall dwell with me in glory." Such foreshadowings, coupled with later threats against his life, caused the Prophet to think through the risks and accept them long before Carthage.

14. Doctrine and Covenants 21:1–8.

15. Doctrine and Covenants 24:1, 3–7, 9.

16. Doctrine and Covenants 128:20–21; taken from a letter dated 6 September 1842.

17. This work occupied Joseph Smith periodically for three years, from mid-1830 until mid-1833. For a detailed look at its importance to Joseph Smith and to the Church, see Robert J. Matthews, *"A Plainer Translation," Joseph Smith's Translation of the Bible: A History and Commentary* (Provo, Utah: Brigham Young University Press, 1975). See especially chapter 2, "The Making of the New Translation," pp. 21–54, where Matthews reviews chronologically the periods of intense activity.

18. Smith, *History of the Church,* 1:98.

19. For examples, see Smith, *History of the Church,* 1:333 (D&C 92); 1:352 (D&C 96); 2:54 (D&C 104).

See also Davis Bitton, "Joseph Smith, Like Unto . . . Competing Categories of Understanding," paper presented at the Annual Meeting of the Mormon History Association, Logan, Utah, May 1988. Bitton discusses Enoch, Joseph of Egypt, Moses, and Paul as prophetic models with whom Joseph Smith identified.

20. Doctrine and Covenants 28:2–3; 103:15–17, 21; 107:91–92. See also 2 Nephi 3:9, 15, which indicates that a prophet named Joseph after his father would be "great like unto Moses."

21. Diary of Joseph Smith, 21 Jan. 1836, Joseph Smith Papers, Archives of The Church of Jesus Christ of Latter-day Saints, Salt Lake City, Utah; Doctrine and Covenants 110:11.

Brigham Young has also been referred to as the Moses of this dispensation. In his own mind, he was Joshua to Joseph's Moses — the surrogate Moses who led the children of Israel to the promised land that Moses had prepared for but was not permitted to enter. More than once, he referred to Joseph as "our Moses that the Lord has given us." See, for example, Brigham Young to Mary Ann Angel, 16 Oct. 1840, Blair Collection, Archives of The Church of Jesus Christ of Latter-day Saints, Salt Lake City, Utah.

22. Several passages describe the responsibilities of such prophet-

leaders. Doctrine and Covenants 103:35 says such leaders must "preside in the midst of my people, and organize my kingdom upon the consecrated land, and establish the children of Zion upon the laws and commandments which have been and which shall be given." Doctrine and Covenants 107:91–92 say that the "President" of the "High Priesthood is to preside over the whole church, and to be like unto Moses," that is to be "a seer, a revelator, a translator, and a prophet, having all the gifts of God which he bestows upon the head of the church."

23. Doctrine and Covenants 26:1. "Go to the west" in this revelation apparently did not mean Ohio, the location designated in revelations later that year, but west to Fayette, New York, where conference convened September 26–27, 1830.

24. Doctrine and Covenants 37:1, 3 (Dec. 1830); 38:31–32 (Jan. 1831). See also Doctrine and Covenants 39:14–15 (Jan. 1831).

25. Smith, *History of the Church*, 1:181–82.

26. Doctrine and Covenants 52:2–6. This passage also included the warning that if they were not faithful, they would be cut off. See also verse 42, which describes Missouri as "the land of your inheritance."

27. Doctrine and Covenants 57:3. For the context, see Smith, *History of the Church*, 1:189.

28. Doctrine and Covenants 58:44. Verses 1–5 may also be significant for the "timetable" of Zion. The passage reminds us that mortals cannot know "the design of your God concerning those things which shall come hereafter, and the glory which shall follow after much tribulation. For after much tribulation come the blessings."

29. See Smith, *History of the Church*, 1:196, 199.

30. Doctrine and Covenants 58:58.

31. Smith, *History of the Church*, 1:207.

32. Doctrine and Covenants 64:21–22. For the context, see Smith, *History of the Church*, 1:211.

33. Moses 7:18–19. This was Joseph's conception when he told Brigham Young in 1834 that if he lived to see Zion redeemed, he would see "the day of god's power and every person will be of one heart and of one mind." Minutes, Reunion of Zion's Camp Veterans, 10 Oct. 1864, Brigham Young Papers, Archives of The Church of Jesus Christ of Latter-day Saints, Salt Lake City, Utah.

34. In Kirtland the Prophet began to teach and implement the principles associated with Zion, including the unity of temporal and spiritual under prophetic leadership. Organizing temporally under priesthood meant a role for ecclesiastical leaders quite different from the traditional role in Protestant America. Strong feelings about the advisability of this unity of temporal and spiritual contributed to the difficulties of later Kirtland. For a detailed examination of the principles involved and reactions to them, see Ronald K. Esplin, "The Emergence of Brigham Young and the Twelve to Mormon Leadership, 1830–1841" (Ph.D. dissertation, Brigham Young University, 1981), chapter 5: "The Kirtland Experience: Diverse Perceptions of the Sacral Kingdom, 1836–1837."

35. Joseph Smith Sermon, 11 June 1843, in *Wilford Woodruff's Journal*, 2:240. For other accounts of this important sermon, see Andrew F. Ehat and Lyndon W. Cook, eds., *The Words of Joseph Smith: The Contemporary Accounts of the Nauvoo Discourses of the Prophet Joseph* (Provo, Utah: Religious Studies Center, Brigham Young University, 1980), pp. 209–16.

36. Editorial from *Times and Seasons*, 2 May 1842, in Smith, *History of the Church*, 4:609–10; Joseph Smith Sermon, 12 May 1844, in Ehat and Cook, *Words of Joseph Smith*, p. 267.

37. Doctrine and Covenants 94:3–12; see also Smith, *History of the Church*, 1:342, 349. Note that the language of the building committee circular emphasizing the importance of constructing "a house" would seem to apply to and suggest a temple but in fact refers to the other dedicated buildings then under contemplation.

38. Doctrine and Covenants 95:1–11; Smith, *History of the Church*, 1:353.

39. Brigham Young discourses, 3 Feb. 1867, in *Journal of Discourses*, 26 vols. (Liverpool: Latter-day Saints' Book Depot, 1855–86), 11:294–95, and 16 June 1867, 12:59. This occurred at the 13 July 1833 gathering described in Smith, *History of the Church*, 1:388–89.

40. Brigham Young discourse, 7 Oct. 1857, in *Journal of Discourses*, 5:332.

41. For examples of the importance of the work of translation, see Smith, *History of the Church*, 1:215, and Doctrine and Covenants 41:7.

42. Doctrine and Covenants 28:2; 43:3.

43. Doctrine and Covenants 24:5–6; 28:6–7; 35:17–18; 43:12–14; 64:5; 100:9–11.

44. Doctrine and Covenants 43:3–7. On the conditional nature of Joseph Smith's call, see also Doctrine and Covenants 35:17–18; 64:5. On the requirement that ordinations be open, known to the Church, and follow prescribed order, see also Doctrine and Covenants 42:11.

45. Doctrine and Covenants 20:2; 107:65–66.

46. For a brief overview, see James B. Allen and Glen M. Leonard, *The Story of the Latter-day Saints* (Salt Lake City, Utah: Deseret Book Co., 1976), pp. 77–81.

47. See Richard L. Anderson and Peter Crawley, "The Political and Social Realities of Zion's Camp," *BYU Studies* 14 (Summer 1974): 406–20.

48. Doctrine and Covenants 124:49–51. The wording suggests that this applied to the prolonged effort of the Saints in Missouri from 1831 to 1839. But for the years up to 1833, apparently the fault lay more with the Saints. See Doctrine and Covenants 101:1–10.

49. Doctrine and Covenants 105:2 says "might have been redeemed even now." In many cases, including this one, usage suggests that the "redemption of Zion" does not mean the coming of Zion in glory, or that the Saints would suddenly be prepared to fully live as Zion's people; rather, "redeeming Zion" in the short term means simply returning the Saints to their lands to resume the process.

50. Doctrine and Covenants 105:2–6, 9.

51. Doctrine and Covenants 105:10–13, 37. References to the promised

"endowment of power from on high" are scattered throughout the section; see vv. 11, 12, 18, 33.

52. Especially is this so if the suggestions here are paired with Doctrine and Covenants 58:44, which says "the time has not yet come, for many years" for most to receive their inheritance there.

53. Joseph Smith to Lyman Wight, Edward Partridge, et al., 16 Aug. 1834; Jessee, *Personal Writings of Joseph Smith,* pp. 329–31.

54. In 1831, as the Saints first learned of Missouri as the "center place," the Lord made clear that "Ye cannot behold with your natural eyes, for the present time, the design of your God concerning those things which shall come hereafter," adding that it would only be "after much tribulation." Doctrine and Covenants 58:3.

The gathering, the temple, and the teachings composing the essential foundation for Zion were clearly part of Joseph Smith's work and calling. Perhaps "redeeming Zion" in Missouri was not. (It was not a central concern, for example, in Nauvoo, as he wrapped up his work, nor in the same way after the Kirtland Temple as it was before.)

55. Diary of Joseph Smith, 12 Nov. 1835.

56. Smith, *History of the Church,* 2:114. So strongly did Joseph Smith feel about the priority of the temple after Doctrine and Covenants 105 was received in June 1834 that he severely reproved the apostles a year later when reports suggested they had inappropriately emphasized redeeming Zion more than temple during their summer mission in the East. See Smith, *History of the Church,* 2:239–40; Esplin, "Emergence of Brigham Young," pp. 166–67, 213.

57. "History of Heber Chase Kimball," ms., Heber C. Kimball Papers, Archives of The Church of Jesus Christ of Latter-day Saints, Salt Lake City, Utah; Diary of Joseph Smith, 17 Jan. 1836.

58. Diary of Joseph Smith, 21 Jan. 1836.

59. Diary of Joseph Smith, 13 Mar. 1836; see also 24 Sept. 1835; 5, 29 Oct. 1835.

60. Diary of Joseph Smith, 29 Mar. 1836; Jessee, *Personal Writings of Joseph Smith,* p. 181.

61. Diary of Joseph Smith, 30 Mar. 1836; Jessee, *Personal Writings of Joseph Smith,* pp. 182–83.

Nothing here indicates a change in the goal described when the Saints were first driven from Jackson County in 1833: "let your hearts be comforted concerning Zion; for all flesh is in mine hands; be still and know that I am God. Zion shall not be moved out of her place, notwithstanding her children are scattered. . . . there is none other place appointed." Doctrine and Covenants 101:16–17, 20.

The promise of Zion was firm; what had changed was their understanding of urgency or timetable.

62. Diary of Joseph Smith, 30 Mar. 1836; Jessee, *Personal Writings of Joseph Smith,* pp. 183–84.

63. Diary of Joseph Smith, 3 Apr. 1836; Jessee, *Personal Writings of Joseph Smith,* pp. 186–87; this is the original for what is now Doctrine and Covenants 110.

Ronald K. Esplin

Historian of religion Jan Shipps has suggested that the visitation of ancient prophets reported here was one of the five most pivotal events in Mormon history. She feels that this claimed contact with Old Testament prophets influenced the way Joseph Smith and his associates thereafter viewed the Old Testament and themselves as modern Israel, similar to Christ's transfiguration (with Moses and Elijah) tying his time directly to the prophetic era. Notes on file from conversation of 13 February 1980.

64. Esplin, "Emergence of Brigham Young," pp. 224–28 ff.

65. George A. Smith discourse, 18 Mar. 1855, in *Journal of Discourses,* 2:214–15; see also Brigham Young discourse, 6 Apr. 1853, in *Journal of Discourses,* 2:32. Compare this with Doctrine and Covenants 50:40, "ye are little children and ye cannot bear all things now; ye must grow in grace and in the knowledge of the truth." See also vv. 23–25.

66. For detailed discussion of the Kirtland difficulties from the perspective followed here, see Esplin, "Emergence of Brigham Young," pp. 273–307.

67. Doctrine and Covenants 115:5–12, 17. This also reaffirms the Prophet Joseph's essential role both in the construction of the temple "according to the pattern which I shall show," and as the one holding "the keys of this kingdom and ministry." See vv. 14–16, 19. Later that summer a second temple site was designated at Adam-ondi-Ahman.

68. Brigham Young discourse, 1 Aug. 1854, in *Journal of Discourses,* 1:364; William Swartzell, *Mormonism Exposed, Being a Journal of a Residence in Missouri* (Pekin, Ohio: By Author, 1840), p. 40, as quoted by Anderson, "Joseph Smith Martyrdom," p. 3. The quotation continued: "I am of age and care not how long I live. Not my will be done, but thine, O Lord!"

69. Joseph Smith to the Church, 16 Dec. 1838, later printed in *Times and Seasons* 1 (Apr. 1840): 83; see also his account written after deliverance, in *Times and Seasons* 1 (Nov. 1839): 7–8.

70. See Esplin, "Emergence of Brigham Young," p. 359 n. 73.

71. Upon learning of the Prophet's death in 1844, Lyman Wight, cellmate with Joseph Smith in Missouri, informed Wilford Woodruff "that Joseph told him while they were in Joal that he should not live to see forty years but told him not to reveal it untill he was dead." *Wilford Woodruff's Journal,* 28 July 1844, 2:432. Such a presentiment helps account for numerous statements by Joseph Smith in Nauvoo about impending death.

72. Joseph Smith to Mrs. Norman Bull, 15 Mar. 1839; Smith, *History of the Church,* 3:286.

73. Joseph Smith, et al., to Bishop Partridge and the Church, 25 Mar. 1839; *Times and Seasons* 1 (July 1840): 132–33.

74. Doctrine and Covenants 124 (19 Jan. 1841).

75. Diary of Joseph Smith, 13 Apr. 1843.

76. Comments of Joseph Smith, 27 June 1839, in Ehat and Cook, *Words of Joseph Smith,* p. 4.

77. Joseph Smith Sermon, 19 July 1840, recorded by Martha Jane Knowlton [Coray], in Dean C. Jessee, ed., "Joseph Smith's 19 July 1840

316

Discourse," *BYU Studies* 19 (Spring 1979): 394. See also Ehat and Cook, *Words of Joseph Smith*, p. 418.

78. Lucy Smith, *Biographical Sketches of Joseph Smith, the Prophet . . .* (Liverpool & London: 1853), p. 267.

79. Doctrine and Covenants 109:68. See also 132:53, 57.

80. Doctrine and Covenants 124:1–3, 25–27.

81. Doctrine and Covenants 124:28, 34, 39–44. For any concerned that the temple should instead be built in Jackson County, vv. 49–51 explains why, given the circumstances, the Lord will "require that work no more" at the present.

82. See Smith, *History of the Church*, 4:327–31.

83. "History of Brigham Young," Brigham Young Papers, p. 2. For a full discussion of this meeting, and the sources for it, see Esplin, "Emergence of Brigham Young," 501–4.

The Twelve returned from their successful mission to England experienced and prepared to serve at the very time Joseph Smith urgently needed their services in managing Nauvoo and the expanding Church. It could be that practical needs alone account for this change. But it is possible, given Joseph Smith's awareness of mortality, that he also saw this as a preparation for succession, which in retrospect it clearly turned out to be.

84. Diary of Willard Richards, 16 Aug. 1841, Willard Richards Papers, Archives of The Church of Jesus Christ of Latter-day Saints, Salt Lake City, Utah.

85. See Doctrine and Covenants 125–26; 132. See also Danel W. Bachman, "New Light on an Old Hypothesis: The Ohio Origins of the Revelation on Eternal Marriage," *Journal of Mormon History* 5 (1978): 19–32.

86. Doctrine and Covenants 127–28; see also 129–31.

87. Brigham Young discourse, 6 Apr. 1853, in *Journal of Discourses*, 2:32.

88. *Wilford Woodruff's Journal*, 19 Dec. 1841, 2:142.

89. By Nauvoo the Prophet had understood many of these things for several years. Brigham Young reported that in Kirtland Joseph had said to him: "if I was to reveal to this people what the Lord has revealed to me, there is not a man or woman who would stay with me." Brigham Young discourse, 25 May 1862, in *Journal of Discourses*, 9:294. This included not only such challenging practices as plural marriage but even doctrinal explanations. Speaking of the vision of degrees of glory, written in 1832 and now Doctrine and Covenants 76, the Prophet proclaimed that he "could explain a hundred fold more than I ever have of the glories of the kingdoms manifested to me in the vision, were I permitted, and were the people prepared to receive them." Smith, *History of the Church*, 5:402.

90. Joseph Smith Diary, 11 June 1843. Compare this with his letter from Liberty Jail to Isaac Galland, 22 March 1839, *Times and Seasons* 1 (Feb. 1840): "where is the man who is authorized to put his finger on the spot and say, thus far thou shalt go and no farther: there is no man. Therefore let us receive the whole, or none."

91. *Wilford Woodruff's Journal*, 21 Jan. 1844, 2:342–43.

92. *Wilford Woodruff's Journal,* 21 Feb. 1844, 2:351.

93. Danel W. Bachman, "A Study of the Mormon Practice of Plural Marriage Before the Death of Joseph Smith," Master's thesis, Purdue University, 1975), pp. 74–75.

94. Brigham Young discourse, 8 Oct. 1866, Brigham Young Papers.

95. Parley Pratt to Brigham Young, 4 Dec. 1841, Brigham Young Papers.

96. *Wilford Woodruff's Journal,* 19 Dec. 1842, 2:143.

97. The year before, he began temple-related baptisms for the dead without a temple. Doctrine and Covenants 124:28–35 discusses the performance of baptisms for the dead ("which belongeth to my house") outside the temple under certain circumstances. Though not his preference, he now extended this model to include other ordinances. Before the completion of the St. George Temple in 1877, this was also done in early Utah, first in dedicated rooms, then in a building erected for the purpose.

98. Smith, *History of the Church,* 5:2. The quotation continues: "therefore, let the Saints be diligent in building the Temple." Compare this with the Prophet's public teaching of some temple-related principles, 16 July 1843, followed by the declaration "that he could not reveal the fulness of these things untill the Temple is completed." Ehat and Cook, *Writings of Joseph Smith,* p. 233.

99. For a brief discussion of how private teachings complicated Nauvoo society, see Ronald K. Esplin, "Joseph, Brigham and the Twelve: A Succession of Continuity," *BYU Studies* 21 (Summer 1981): 302–6.

100. Heber C. Kimball to Parley P. Pratt, 17 June 1842, Parley Pratt Papers, Archives of The Church of Jesus Christ of Latter-day Saints, Salt Lake City, Utah.

101. Minutes of the Nauvoo Relief Society, 28 Apr. 1842, Archives of The Church of Jesus Christ of Latter-day Saints, Salt Lake City, Utah.

102. Ibid.

103. *Wilford Woodruff's Journal,* 9 Apr. 1842, 2:167–68.

104. Smith, *History of the Church,* 5:2.

105. Difficulties with John C. Bennett erupted less than ten days after the first endowments. His excommunication for moral failings prompted a public "exposé" of, among other things, supposed temple-related ritual, making it difficult to continue and, for a season, diverting attention and resources. In addition to the always heavy demands upon him as father, city-father (replacing John C. Bennett as mayor of Nauvoo), and spiritual head of his people, there were also unusual demands such as time spent in hiding to avoid capture by Missouri enemies and, on one occasion, capture and escape. That some of those closest to the Prophet were not ready in 1842 to receive the ordinances also influenced the timetable.

106. Smith, *History of the Church,* 5:139. (Original diary entry differs only in punctuation.)

107. Joseph Smith to the Relief Society, 31 Aug. 1842, Minutes of the Nauvoo Relief Society.

108. *Wilford Woodruff's Journal,* 22 Jan. 1843, 2:217.

109. Diary of Joseph Smith kept by Willard Richards, 15 Oct. 1843, Joseph Smith Papers. Richards jotted down brief phrases to stand for complex thoughts. These later were fleshed out. Compare with Smith, *History of the Church,* 6:58, which reads: "I defy all the world to destroy the work of God; and I prophesy they never will have power to kill me till my work is accomplished, and I am ready to die."

110. Minutes of April Conference, *Times and Seasons* 5 (15 Aug. 1844): 617; Thomas Bullock Minutes, 12 May 1844, Archives of The Church of Jesus Christ of Latter-day Saints, Salt Lake City, Utah.

111. Doctrine and Covenants 127:4 (extract from Joseph Smith letter, 2 Sept. 1842).

112. See "A Summary of Data on the Individuals Who Received the Endowment Before Ordinance Work Began in the Nauvoo Temple," in Andrew F. Ehat, "Joseph Smith's Introduction of Temple Ordinances and the 1844 Mormon Succession Question " (Master's thesis, Brigham Young University, 1982), pp. 102–3. For a brief overview of ordinance work for the Twelve, see Esplin, "A Succession of Continuity," pp. 314–16.

113. Diary of Joseph Smith, 20 Feb. 1844. For a full treatment of Joseph Smith's role in the later move to a western refuge, a Zion in the West, and that enterprise's relationship to his calling, see Ronald K. Esplin, " 'A Place Prepared': Joseph, Brigham and the Quest for Promised Refuge in the West," *Journal of Mormon History* 9 (1982): 85–111.

114. See D. Michael Quinn, "The Council of Fifty and Its Members, 1844–1945," *BYU Studies* 20 (Fall 1979): 163–97; Andrew F. Ehat, " 'It Seems Like Heaven Began on Earth': Joseph Smith and the Constitution of the Kingdom of God," *BYU Studies* 20 (Spring 1980): 253–79.

115. Undated Certificate of the Twelve, fall or winter, 1844–1845, Brigham Young Papers. For another version, see Orson Hyde, "Rigdon Trial Minutes," *Times and Seasons* 5 (15 Sept. 1844): 651.

116. Proclamation of Parley P. Pratt, 1 Jan. 1845, *Millennial Star* 5 (Mar. 1845): 151. Compare Doctrine and Covenants 132:7–8.

117. Undated Certificate of the Twelve, Brigham Young Papers.

118. *Wilford Woodruff's Journal,* 6 Apr. 1844, 2:374.

119. George Laub's account of June sermon as published in Eugene England, "George Laub's Nauvoo Journal," *BYU Studies* 18 (Winter 1978): 160.

120. Samuel W. Richards to Franklin D. Richards, 23 Aug. 1844, Franklin D. Richards Collection, Archives of The Church of Jesus Christ of Latter-day Saints, Salt Lake City, Utah.

121. Brigham Young discourse, 6 Apr. 1853, in *Journal of Discourses,* 1:132.

Chapter 17

Joseph Smith's Final Self-Appraisal

Richard Lloyd Anderson
Professor of Ancient Scripture
Brigham Young University

Joseph Smith stood on the platform near the temple to address the Latter-day Saints. It was Sunday morning, 16 June 1844, eleven days before his assassination. Watching the rain clouds that threatened the meeting that wet spring, he made them a positive symbol with typical humor: "I have contemplated the saying of Jesus—as it was in the days of Noah, so shall it be at his second coming—and if it rains, I'll preach: the plurality of Gods."[1] A casual reading of this Joseph Smith discourse would not show its context as a hard-hitting answer to his enemies, nor would short scanning give an understanding of life's thunder clouds which the Prophet knew were darkening around him. Such realities made this 16 June speech a solemn valedictory on the significance of his God-given mission and its revolutionary theology.

Though the Prophet did not fully realize it then, this sermon would be noted in a journal as "Joseph Smith's last public discourse on doctrine."[2] The following Tuesday he spoke in full uniform as the commander of the Nauvoo Legion, but the subject of that last public speech was different—the safety of Nauvoo and the civil rights of the Saints. These events are dramatic, but Joseph Smith's motivation in courageously facing them is all important. No biographer can weigh his prophetic mission without knowing his inner thoughts in calm and crisis. Yet subjective probing is the very thing that history, the slavish recorder of externals, is least able to do. The realistic solution is to let Joseph Smith explain himself, for his private and public comments are richly recorded and regularly contain autobiographical insights. The speeches of his closing months consistently highlight a handful of themes on his calling and message. Thus Joseph Smith is the best commentator on the meaning of his "last public discourse on doctrine." Yet the thrusts of that talk can be understood only by recreating the questions and problems that Joseph Smith then addressed.

The Setting of the 16 June Speech

"Oh, apostates, did ye never think of this before?"[3] With such Pauline public dialogue Joseph Smith punctuated his Nauvoo answer to his detractors. He regretted opposition but was beyond the point of apologizing that it existed: "I have reason to think that the Church is being purged."[4] Indeed, Joseph Smith's dynamic teachings constantly conflicted with the doctrines of factions that clung to the beliefs of nineteenth-century Christian orthodoxy. Such tension alienated apostles before the Ohio and Missouri exodus, and the process was repeating in Nauvoo. Opponents of polygamy and other doctrines then clustered about William Law, counselor in the First Presidency from 1841 through 1843. The cleavage culminated on 18 April 1844, when a special council of leaders cut off "Robert D. Foster, Wilson Law, William Law, and Jane Law, of Nauvoo . . . for unchristianlike conduct."[5] Other key figures in this group were excommunicated 18 May, including James Blakesley, Francis M. Higbee, and Austin Cowles.[6]

Law's group organized a counter church and opposed definite doctrines of Joseph Smith. Researcher Lyndon Cook recently uncovered a transcript of the 1844 William

Law journal, which outlines his agony at isolation from and anger at the Prophet. He wrote of estrangement in early January 1844, when Joseph Smith notified him that he had been dropped from the First Presidency. After an April conference dominated by Joseph Smith's sweeping doctrines on the nature of God, Law gathered his own "conference" on Sunday, 21 April, and "held public meetings every Sabbath day" thereafter until early June.[7] Word came to Joseph Smith a week after organization that "the new church . . . decided that Joseph was a fallen prophet, etc., and William Law was appointed in his place."[8] Sympathizer Sarah Scott wrote about the "conference" that "reorganized the Church," calling it "The Reformed Church."[9] President Smith finally commented publicly on 26 May with irony: "Inasmuch as there is a new church, this must be the old; and of course we ought to be set down as orthodox."[10]

William Law was a talented opponent: he financed a press to bring down the Prophet and attacked through legal actions. The first and only issue of the *Nauvoo Expositor* was distributed 7 June, containing specifics on plural marriage, a devastating attack, because the practice violated Illinois statutes. Such publicity was particularly dangerous in inflaming public opinion, since so many sought a pretext to rid the state of Mormons by legitimate violence. The *Expositor* attacked two main doctrines of the Prophet: "a plurality of Gods above the God of this universe" and also "the plurality of wives, for time and eternity."[11] For the second doctrine, the Prophet chose calculated silence, but nine days after the *Expositor*'s charges, he devoted his entire 16 June discourse to the doctrine of multiple gods and to his authority as a latter-day prophet.[12]

After extended debate in the city council, Mayor Joseph Smith declared the *Expositor* a nuisance and authorized destruction of the press, which was done at sundown on Monday, 10 June. The following Sunday the Prophet gave his defense of the doctrine of plurality of gods but in an atmosphere of critical danger to himself and his city. He had long avoided court hearings outside of Nauvoo, because he feared, not the law, but lynch law. One of the dissidents, Francis M. Higbee, had sued Joseph Smith for slander, only to have Joseph Smith resist going to Carthage, telling the Nauvoo court that this was a "malicious prosecution" with the motive "to throw your petitioner into the hands of his enemies" — to "carry out a conspiracy which has for some time been brewing against the life of your petitioner."[13] This statement illustrates Joseph Smith's later unwillingness to answer charges at Carthage on the destruction of the *Expositor* press until Governor Ford arrived and made it an executive issue.

Joseph Smith's last doctrinal discourse was given in the midst of maneuvers to get him to Carthage for trial, a cause which was attracting hundreds of volunteers to the county seat to force Mormon conformity. Here were ballots by bullet that had so plagued Mormon settlements in three other states. When Joseph Smith had faced a similar situation in Missouri eight years before, he gave himself up as a hostage for the safety of his people, a possibility that he well recognized as he spoke publicly at the end of May in the face of mounting regional opposition: "When I shrink not from your defense, will you throw me away for a new man who slanders you?"[14]

Before the destruction of the *Expositor* and its aftermath, Law's faction had already filed several cases designed to bring Joseph Smith to the hostile county seat of Carthage. Thus the destruction of the press, the filing of riot charges against Joseph Smith, and the public demand that he go to Carthage to answer were but one avenue to manipulate the Prophet into range of the courts or the guns of his enemies. When criminal charges were filed for the destruction of the press, the Prophet exercised his option of a Nauvoo hearing. Then flames raged out of the control of governor and courts as public opinion accepted the cry that the Mormons claimed to be above the law. Aggressive protest meetings in Carthage and Warsaw demanded retribution against Joseph Smith and Nauvoo. Once again, "volunteers" arose — ostensibly to defend the law, yet only to make mockery of it.[15]

So when Joseph Smith stood to speak on 16 June he was well aware that his doctrinal defense might be his last before flight, imprisonment, or even murder. That he retained the composure to give a careful scriptural analysis shows how deeply he valued these teachings. That day, as mayor of Nauvoo, he also composed—or approved for publication—a warning to the surrounding countryside:

"We have no disturbance or excitement among us, save what is made by the thousand and one idle rumors afloat in the country. . . . Of the correctness of our conduct in this affair, we appeal to every high court in the state, and to its ordeal we are willing to appear at any time that his Excellency, Governor Ford, shall please to call us before it. I therefore, in behalf of the Municipal Court of Nauvoo, warn the lawless, not to be precipitate in any interference in our affairs, for as sure as there is a God in Israel, we shall ride triumphant over all oppression."[16]

Joseph gave his final sermon on that tense Sunday morning; in the afternoon he addressed the men of the city in an appeal to send correct information throughout the county, but to be ready: "to keep cool, prepare their arms for defence of the city, as it was reported a mob was collecting at Carthage."[17] The same afternoon, Joseph Smith sent an urgent appeal to Governor Ford, showing the seriousness of events on the day of his last doctrinal discourse. Newspapers had carried responsible reports "that an energetic attempt is being made by some of the citizens of this and the surrounding counties to drive and exterminate 'the Saints' by force of arms." The immediate intervention of the governor would probably be "the only means of stopping an effusion of blood."[18] Thus the Prophet spoke that morning, with awareness of critical danger for himself and his people. He preached under threat of death, answering his critics and clarifying his prophetic position to all who would learn of him.

Themes of the 16 June Speech

The accuracy of the Prophet's last doctrinal discourse is clear, because Thomas Bullock's copy survives with his own notation: "Sermon of Joseph Smith, written by T. Bullock at the time."[19] And these minutes are in Bullock's looser penmanship, with many abbreviations, which suggest rapid notes under dictation. In Utah, Bullock and others who had heard the Nauvoo discourses helped to round out sentences from memory for the final Church history. Both raw and polished versions have historical validity, though the dictation at the time has textual priority and will be followed here.[20] The Laub and McIntire journals also have verifying summaries of the 16 June discourse, but Bullock's detailed record includes their essence and has far more. This is consistent with the high quality of Bullock's recording of discourses, such as Joseph Smith's King Follett sermon at the 1844 April conference. The Bullock notes there are more detailed than even those of Woodruff and Clayton.[21]

On 16 June Joseph Smith's stated goal was to explain the "plurality of Gods"; he had already done this in some detail in the King Follett sermon, which the Nauvoo *Expositor* had so roundly criticized. On 16 June the Prophet more carefully spelled out scriptural hints, precedents, and parallels that indicated the truth of that doctrine, but these technical arguments are not relevant to the larger issue here—how the Prophet viewed his own mission at the end. For in the process of teaching the doctrine of man's divine potential, Joseph Smith assessed his own role and the source of his calling and knowledge.

The Prophet's biblical proofs probed ultimate theology; Joseph Smith admitted that "there is but one God pertaining to us," or more properly but one triple presidency of Father, Son, and Holy Ghost. He said he had taught the separateness of these persons, and thus "the plurality of Gods," during a ministry of "15 years," which reached back to 1829, the year of the first baptisms and preliminary meetings of the Church.[22] In brief summary, Joseph Smith stressed Christ's statement that he was doing what he had seen his Father do, reasoning that the Father therefore had a mortal mission of his own at one time, and concluding that this was a process of development for other divine beings, a process also available to mortals of this earth.[23] The Prophet added a half dozen other biblical scriptures, most of which he had used in other discourses to extend Latter-day Saint horizons on the nature of divinity. But Joseph Smith featured a text at the outset and worked with it to the climax of the speech: John's Revelation depicted a future when Christ will have "made us kings and priests unto God and his Father." (Revelation 1:6.) Joseph reasoned that the essential role of the Father and Son was kingship. If their disciples also became kings, then those disciples became gods under gods.[24]

But another message is prominent in the 16 June sermon. If the plurality of gods was the subject, Joseph Smith's overarching purpose was to refute his opponents, who were using that doctrine as proof that he was a fallen prophet. So the larger topic was the nature of Joseph Smith's calling and his faithfulness to it. This issue was woven into the fabric of the sermon and concluded it. William Law's faction publicly acknowledged that Joseph Smith had once been a prophet, and Joseph Smith moved against the inconsistency of that position. They were converts to a faith that they could now only partially accept. The *Expositor* spoke for the genuineness of their earlier conversions:

"We all verily believe, and many of us know of a surety, that the religion of the Latter Day Saints, as originally taught by Joseph Smith, which is contained in the Old and New Testaments, Book of Covenants, and Book of Mormon, is verily true; and that the pure principles set forth in those books are the immutable and eternal principles of Heaven, and speaks a language which, when spoken in truth and virtue, sinks deep into the heart of every honest man."[25]

Joseph Smith quickly showed the fallacy of using modern revelation against the plurality of gods, quoting his vision of the three glories as authoritative: "Go and read the vision. There is glory and glory — sun, moon, and stars — and so do they differ in glory. And every man who reigns is a god. And the text of the Doctrine and Covenants damns themselves."[26] The reasoning is clear, even in these artificially chopped sentences of the recorder. The Prophet and Sidney Rigdon had beheld the celestial glory in early 1832, and by the end of that year their revelation had been in *The Evening and the Morning Star* and republished in the 1835 Doctrine and Covenants as binding truth. There the faithful were promised — as in the Prophet's sermon text of Revelation 1:6 — that they would be "priests and kings" and receive "of his fulness, and of his glory. . . . Wherefore, as it is written, they are gods, even the sons of God." (D&C 76:56, 58.)[27]

Quoting his earlier vision was far more than a tactic here, for underlying his many biblical texts is the theme of new information. Joseph made clear that he was a prophet speaking in his own right when he next used a verse from Moses' call and suggested his own youthful call: "Moses was a stuttering sort of a boy like me."[28] Joseph fully explained that he was not satisfied with the Bible alone on any issue, but typically sought the controlling principle behind each verse: "And when you take a view of the subject, it sets one free to see all the beauty, holiness, and perfection of the Gods. All I want is to get the simple truth — naked and the whole truth."[29] Joseph soon returned to this theme:

"When things that are great are passed over without even a thought, I want to see all in all its bearings and hug it to my bosom. I believe all that God ever revealed, and I never hear of a man being damned for believing too much, but they are damned for unbelief."[30]

So the Prophet saw the vulnerability of the seceders in their going part way with true principles and then stopping. By holding rigidly to human preconceptions about God, they closed off the perspective of his existence and power:

"And no man can limit the bounds, or the eternal existence of eternal time. Hath he beheld the eternal world, and is he authorized to say that there is only God? He makes himself a fool, and there is an end of his career in knowledge. He cannot obtain all knowledge, for he has sealed up the gate to [it.]"[31]

Such a teaching is given in the context of resisting divine direction; it does not promote philosophical speculation. In private conversation the year before, Joseph Smith had contrasted traditional Christians, who were "circumscribed by some peculiar creed," with the Latter-day Saints, who "have no creed, but are ready to believe *all true principles* existing, as they are made manifest to us from time to time."[32] But on this and other occasions the Prophet's opposites were not creed versus free thinking, but the difference between being religiously limited or religiously expansive. In the above 1843 statement, "true principles . . . are made manifest to us from time to time" — clearly synonymous language for direct revelation. Latter-day Saints would not be hobbled by earthly creeds but would be led to larger heavenly principles through their prophet. The result for Joseph Smith is indeed a structured religion, but one formed from eternal principles through heavenly communication. Again in 1843 the Prophet gave this message in similar vocabulary as he acknowledged that traditional creeds had "some truth." Yet his dissent from them then shows how accurately the last doctrinal discourse reports his basic views: "But I want to come up into the presence of God and learn all things, but the creeds set up stakes and say, hitherto shalt thou come and no further — which I cannot subscribe to."[33]

Many a nineteenth-century liberal theologian dissented from older creeds, for example, Emerson; but none left such a defined, confident theology to replace the creeds or established an effective organization to spread revitalized doctrine. This is precisely Joseph Smith's concluding point in his 16 June valedictory. He returned to another fundamental which he had explained well by the close of his ministry: "God always sent a new dispensation into the world."[34] Experienced Saints in Nauvoo knew that Joseph Smith's earlier revelations and preaching equated a new dispensation with angelic messengers who returned authority to reestablish God's work.[35] Thus Joseph Smith focused not only on truth but also on delegated power from God to teach it. So Law's "Reformed Church" was derivative and hence unable to have more strength than the restored Church from which it seceded. Joseph Smith called this a "principle of logic," but his dispensational context shows that he was talking of divine commission: "Here jumps off a branch and says, I am the true tree and you are corrupt. If the whole tree is corrupt, how can any true thing come out of it?"[36]

Thus in the closing sentences of 16 June, Joseph Smith restated the claim of delegated power from divine messengers, as well as further knowledge through God's direct communication. In brief, Joseph Smith insisted that he was called not as a reformer, but with full powers of a restorer:

"God always sent a new dispensation into the world, when men come out and build upon other men's foundation. Did I build on another man's foundation but my own? I have got all the truth and an independent revelation in the bargain. And God will bear me off triumphant."[37]

This note of victory has an eternal perspective in all the Prophet's expressions in his last months. Indeed, the close of several of the last discourses is remarkably similar, illustrating how Joseph Smith material interprets Joseph Smith. Two days later he closed his last speech to the Nauvoo Legion by asking Nauvoo men to act "invariable in the defensive, and if we die — die like men of God and secure a glorious resurrection."[38] Even when opposition had intensified a month before, Joseph spiritedly refuted his detractors by suggesting that his success would be in teaching truth, not in continuing his career: "I want to triumph in Israel before I depart hence and am no more seen."[39]

The close of that 12 May discourse gives the same self-appraisal as the above climax of the last doctrinal discourse. His detractors were already holding their meetings of complaint, but they did not really answer Joseph Smith's teachings: "When did I ever teach anything wrong from this stand? When was I ever confounded?" Then the Prophet moved to the double point of the strength of his

mission—divine direction and authority: "I never told you
I was perfect, but there is no error in the revelations which
I have taught. . . . I testify that no man has power to reveal
it but myself: things in heaven, in earth, and hell."[40]

Notes

1. Andrew F. Ehat and Lyndon W. Cook, eds., *The Words of Joseph
Smith* (Provo, Utah: Brigham Young University Religious Studies Center,
1980), p. 378. This text of Ehat and Cook is quite accurate in transcribing
the Nauvoo notes of scribe Thomas Bullock, manuscript at Historical Department, The Church of Jesus Christ of Latter-day Saints, Salt Lake City,
Utah. Quotations used here have been checked against the Bullock original,
though abbreviations are spelled out. In these and other historical quotations
of this article, minor modifications may appear, to clarify spelling and punctuation. Compare note 20, below.

2. William Patterson McIntire, "Minute Book," 26 June 1840, manuscript at Historical Department, The Church of Jesus Christ of Latter-day
Saints, Salt Lake City, Utah; see also Ehat and Cook, *Words of Joseph Smith*,
p. 383.

3. Ibid., p. 381.

4. Ibid., p. 380.

5. *Times and Seasons* 5 (15 Apr. 1844): 511; see also Joseph Smith, *History
of The Church of Jesus Christ of Latter-day Saints*, 7 vols., 2d ed. rev., ed. B.
H. Roberts (Salt Lake City, Utah: The Church of Jesus Christ of Latter-day
Saints, 1932–51), 6:341.

6. *Times and Seasons* 5 (15 May 1844): 543; see also Smith, *History of
the Church*, 6:398.

7. Diary of William Law, 8 Jan. and 1 June 1844; transcript in private
possession. Compare some Law diary entries and background material in
Lyndon Cook, "William Law, Nauvoo Dissenter," *BYU Studies* 22 (Winter
1982): 66–70.

8. Willard Richards, Journal of Joseph Smith, Sunday, 28 Apr. 1844,
Archives of The Church of Jesus Christ of Latter-day Saints, Salt Lake City,
Utah; adapted in Smith, *History of the Church*, 6:347.

9. Sarah Scott to Father and Mother, 16 June 1844, Nauvoo; see also
George R. Partridge, "The Death of a Mormon Dictator," *New England
Quarterly* 9 (Dec. 1936): 595–96; William Mulder and A. Russell Mortensen,
Among the Mormons (New York: Alfred A. Knopf, 1958), p. 145.

10. Joseph Smith, 26 May 1844 discourse, manuscript at Historical
Department, The Church of Jesus Christ of Latter-day Saints, Salt Lake
City, Utah; handwriting identified by Dean S. Jessee as Leo Hawkins with
corrections by Thomas Bullock; see also, with slight text change, in Smith,
History of the Church, 6:410, and Ehat and Cook, *Words of Joseph Smith*, p.
375.

11. *Nauvoo Expositor,* 7 June 1844, p. 2, bottom of col. 3.

12. In the 26 May 1844 discourse, Joseph Smith denied specific rumors but did not deny that he had had a revelation on plural marriage and had begun that practice. Afterward the *Expositor* published details of the revelation, but again the Prophet said nothing publicly to refute it.

13. Nauvoo Municipal Court hearing, 8 May 1844, *Times and Seasons* 5 (15 May 1844): 538, 536; partially quoted in Smith, *History of the Church,* 6:358.

14. Ms. cited at note 10, above; see also Smith, *History of the Church,* 6:412; Ehat and Cook, *Words of Joseph Smith,* p. 377.

15. See, for instance, Smith, *History of the Church,* 6:462–66, for the reprint from the *Warsaw Signal* of the report of the 13 June mass meeting at Warsaw, calling for "a war of extermination" against Mormon leaders and Nauvoo itself if the leaders were not immediately surrendered.

16. "Proclamation, Mayor's Office, Nauvoo, June 16, 1844," *Nauvoo Neighbor,* 19 June 1844; see also Smith, *History of the Church,* 6:485.

17. Richards, Journal of Joseph Smith, 16 June 1844; adapted in Smith, *History of the Church,* 6:479.

18. Joseph Smith to Thomas Ford, 16 June 1844, Nauvoo, in Dean C. Jessee, *The Personal Writings of Joseph Smith* (Salt Lake City, Utah: Deseret Book Co., 1984), p. 589; see also Smith, *History of the Church,* 6:480.

19. Notation in Bullock's hand in the margin of the sermon minutes, 16 June 1844, manuscript at Historical Department, The Church of Jesus Christ of Latter-day Saints, Salt Lake City, Utah.

20. Smith, *History of the Church,* 6:473–79, contains the version of the 16 June discourse rounded out by memory of the Utah historians; it contains useful clarifications. Compare note 1, above.

21. See Donald Q. Cannon and Larry E. Dahl, *The Prophet Joseph Smith's King Follett Discourse* (Provo, Utah: Brigham Young University Religious Studies Center, 1983), p. 3: Bullock's "minutes were by far the most nearly complete made on the King Follett Discourse."

22. Ehat and Cook, *Words of Joseph Smith,* p. 378; compare Smith, *History of the Church,* 6:474.

23. Ehat and Cook, *Words of Joseph Smith,* p. 380; compare Smith, *History of the Church,* 6:476–77. The biblical basis of this reasoning, also used in the King Follett sermon, was John 5:19. Compare George Laub's similar summary of this section of the 16 June sermon in Ehat and Cook, *Words of Joseph Smith,* p. 382.

24. Ehat and Cook, *Words of Joseph Smith,* p. 381; compare Smith, *History of the Church,* 6:478.

25. *Nauvoo Expositor,* p. 1, top of col. 6.

26. Ehat and Cook, *Words of Joseph Smith,* p. 381; compare Smith, *History of the Church,* 6:477.

27. Doctrine and Covenants 91:5 (1835 ed.).

28. Ehat and Cook, *Words of Joseph Smith,* p. 381; see also Smith, *History*

Richard Lloyd Anderson

of the Church, 6:478, with softening modification, though the Bullock manuscript clearly has the double t.

29. Ehat and Cook, *Words of Joseph Smith,* pp. 379–80; compare Smith, *History of the Church,* 6:476, where *Gods* is interpreted as plural, as required by the context and syntax. In the Bullock manuscript the writing itself is so cramped that the plural is unclear.

30. Ehat and Cook, *Words of Joseph Smith,* p. 381; compare Smith, *History of the Church,* 6:477.

31. Ehat and Cook, *Words of Joseph Smith,* p. 379; compare Smith, *History of the Church,* 6:474–75.

32. Journal of William Clayton, 1 Jan. 1843, underlining in original. Compare Smith, *History of the Church,* 5:215, where the simplification of the thought loses the strong statement of revealed knowledge "to us."

33. Richards, Journal of Joseph Smith, 15 Oct. 1843; see also Ehat and Cook, *Words of Joseph Smith,* p. 256; Smith, *History of the Church,* 6:57.

34. Ehat and Cook, *Words of Joseph Smith,* p. 382; compare Smith, *History of the Church,* 6:478–79.

35. Joseph Smith was extremely consistent in using "dispensation" in the sense of God's giving priesthood authority through the appearance of angels: Doctrine and Covenants 27:13; 110:12, 16; 112:30–32; 128:20–21. See also the early Nauvoo discourses on priesthood succession: Ehat and Cook, *Words of Joseph Smith,* pp. 8–10, 37–40.

36. Ehat and Cook, *Words of Joseph Smith,* p. 382; compare Smith, *History of the Church,* 6:478.

37. Ehat and Cook, *Words of Joseph Smith,* p. 382; compare Smith, *History of the Church,* 6:479.

38. Journal of William Clayton, 18 June 1844; see also Ehat and Cook, *Words of Joseph Smith,* p. 384.

39. Bullock ms. notes, 12 May 1844, Historical Department, The Church of Jesus Christ of Latter-day Saints, Salt Lake City, Utah; see also Ehat and Cook, *Words of Joseph Smith,* p. 369; Smith, *History of the Church,* 6:366. From 1842, Joseph Smith's statements on coming martyrdom are remarkably clear, as for instance in Wilford Woodruff's journal report of the discourse of 22 January 1843: "I shall not be sacrificed until my time comes—then I shall be offered freely." Compare Richard Lloyd Anderson, "Joseph Smith's Prophecies of Martyrdom," *Sidney B. Sperry Symposium* (Provo, Utah: Religious Instruction, 1980), pp. 1–14.

40. Bullock ms., 12 May 1844; Ehat and Cook, *Words of Joseph Smith,* p. 369. Compare Smith, *History of the Church,* 6:366–67. *Hell* is probably used in the sense of the spirit world, since this discourse has a specific reference to the gospel's being accepted there.

332

Chapter 18

A Tribute to Joseph Smith, Jr.

Daniel H. Ludlow

Director of Correlation Review
The Church of Jesus Christ of Latter-day Saints

It may seem strange to begin a tribute to Joseph Smith, Jr., by emphasizing what he is *not,* but many of the biographies and articles that have been written about him have tended toward one extreme or the other. Those who have spoken of the "good" of Joseph Smith have appeared in the eyes of some critics to have virtually deified him. On the other hand, other critics feel that those who have spoken of the "bad" of Joseph Smith have depicted him as a tool of the devil or even worse.

When the angel Moroni appeared to Joseph Smith on 21 September 1823, he told the seventeen-year-old youth that his "name should be had for good and evil among all nations, kindreds, and tongues, or that it should be both good and evil spoken of among all people." (Joseph Smith–History 1:33.) This statement has been fulfilled as is quickly evident when the various publications about Joseph Smith are examined closely.

Thus at the beginning of this tribute it might be well to point out that Joseph Smith is *not* Deity; the opposite extreme, that Joseph Smith was a tool of the devil, is not even a viable possibility so far as this author is concerned.

Joseph Smith Is Not Jesus Christ

Latter-day Saints have never claimed that Joseph Smith is a member of the Godhead. He is not Jesus Christ. He is not the Firstborn Son of God in the spirit. (See D&C 93:21.) He is not the Only Begotten Son of God in the flesh. These sacred titles belong uniquely and forever to Jesus Christ, the divine Son of God.[1]

Thus, Latter-day Saints do not worship Joseph Smith, as is indicated in this statement by President Gordon B. Hinckley:

"We do not worship the Prophet. We worship God our Eternal Father, and the risen Lord Jesus Christ. But we acknowledge him [Joseph Smith], we proclaim him, we respect him, we reverence him as an instrument in the hands of the Almighty in restoring to the earth the ancient truths of the divine gospel, together with the priesthood through which the authority of God is exercised in the affairs of his church and for the blessing of his people."[2]

Elder Neal A. Maxwell suggested that the word *venerate* might be appropriate for Joseph Smith:

"The Prophet Joseph Smith, of course, was not a perfect man. There has been only one such—Jesus Christ. But Joseph Smith was a special witness for Jesus Christ. . . .

"We do not, as some occasionally charge, worship Joseph Smith, nor place him on a par with Jesus. But we do venerate him, remembering, hopefully that *the highest and best form of veneration is emulation.*"[3]

Dr. Richard L. Bushman wrote that Joseph Smith never indicated anything other than that he was a servant of Jesus Christ:

"We never have to apologize for the place of Jesus Christ in Latter-day Saint theology. He heads the Church. He reveals His will to the Prophet. We depend upon Jesus Christ as the very rock and foundation of our lives and personal salvation, and look to Him as a model in every possible way. We worship no man; it is God we worship, and we worship Him through the Savior. Who would be more disappointed than Joseph Smith if ever these convictions faded in the hearts of the Latter-day Saints?

"At the same time, we honor Joseph Smith, and with good cause."[4]

As powerful and as great as Joseph Smith was and is in the eyes of members of the Church, it is well to remember that his greatness was and is derived from his devoted discipleship of the Lord and Savior of us all, Jesus Christ. Joseph Smith is great precisely because he was one chosen of God and of Jesus Christ to serve under them for the blessing of mankind. Perhaps the greatest tribute that could be given to Joseph Smith is that he had such great faith and he lived such a worthy life that he was able during his lifetime to call upon the powers of heaven and receive answers; he was able to commune directly with Jesus Christ and with angels and representatives sent from the presence of God. Thus Joseph Smith's greatness is derived directly from his faithful discipleship to the members of the Godhead.

The following circumstances, attributes, and characteristics explain the greatness of Joseph Smith:

1. He was foreordained in the premortal existence to head the dispensation of the fulness of times.

2. He set an example of obedience to God and of love for his fellowman.

3. He was entrusted with the priesthood power and authority necessary to reestablish and build up the kingdom of God on the earth.

4. He became a great prophet, seer, and revelator of the Lord.

5. He survived the tests of ridicule and persecution.

6. He has been assured of eternal life through his great faith and his worthy life.

Each of these will be considered in this chapter, with brief tributes from those who knew Joseph Smith personally or who have become acquainted with him through a careful study of his life.

Joseph Smith Was Foreordained to Head the Dispensation of the Fulness of Times

Praise to the man who communed
with Jehovah! . . .
Blessed to open the last dispensation, . . .
Ever and ever the keys he will hold.[5]

Because of his great faith and because he lived a worthy life that enabled him to commune with Jehovah, Joseph Smith was able to fulfill his foreordained calling. Concerning the foreordination of Joseph Smith, President Ezra Taft Benson stated: "Joseph was truly foreordained to his great mission.

"To get a vision of the magnitude of the prophet's earthly mission we must view it in the light of eternity. He was among 'the noble and great ones' whom Abraham described as follows:

" 'Now the Lord had shown unto me, Abraham, the intelligences that were organized before the world was; and among all these there were many of the noble and great ones;

" 'And God saw these souls that they were good, and he stood in the midst of them, and he said: These I will make my rulers; for he stood among those that were spirits, and he saw that they were good; and he said unto me: Abraham, thou art one of them; thou wast chosen before thou wast born' (Abraham 3:22–23).

"So it was with Joseph Smith. He too was there. He too sat in council with the noble and great ones. Occupying a prominent place of honor and distinction, he unquestionably helped in the planning and execution of the great work of the Lord to 'bring to pass the immortality and eternal life of man,' the salvation of all our Father's children (Moses 1:39). His mission had had and was to have, impact on all who had come to earth; all who then dwelt on earth and the millions yet unborn.

"The Prophet Joseph Smith made this eternal fact clear in the words: 'Every man who has a calling to minister to the inhabitants of the world was ordained to that very purpose in the Grand Council of heaven before this world was. I suppose that I was ordained to this very office in that Grand Council. It is the testimony that I want that I am God's servant, and this people His people.' "[6]

Brigham Young also testified concerning the foreordination of the Prophet Joseph Smith: "It was decreed in the counsels of eternity, long before the foundations of the earth were laid, that he [Joseph Smith] should be the man, in the last dispensation of this world, to bring forth the word of God to the people, and receive the fulness of the keys and power of the Priesthood of the Son of God. . . . He was foreordained in eternity to preside over this last dispensation."[7]

Elder Neal A. Maxwell wrote of this special calling of Joseph Smith: "Indeed, on the scale of impact, what has been written in the scriptures is unfoldingly true:

" 'Joseph Smith, the Prophet and Seer of the Lord, has done more, save Jesus only, for the salvation of men in this world, than any other man that ever lived in it' (D&C 135:3).

"It should not surprise us that it should be so, since he began the dispensation in which most of the people who ever lived will live, a dispensation in which there would be an explosion of knowledge and truth, as well as of people."[8]

Joseph Smith Is an Example of Obedience to God and Love of Fellowman

Because of his great faith and because he lived a worthy life that enabled him to commune with Jehovah, Joseph Smith learned early in life to be obedient to the commandments of God, and he demonstrated love for his fellowmen. Dr. Richard L. Bushman wrote of the obedience of Joseph Smith: "Joseph commented that 'as my life consisted of activity and unyielding exertions, I made this one rule: When the Lord commands do it.' "[9]

Brother Jerry Roundy also noted this attribute of Joseph Smith: "It is hard to study the life of the Prophet Joseph

Smith without remembering that he learned to serve the Lord fully, at all times, and at all costs."[10]

Two statements by Joseph Smith allude to his feelings of concern and love for his fellowman:

"Sectarian priests cry out concerning me, and ask, 'Why is it this babbler gains so many followers, and retains them?' I answer, It is because I possess the principle of love."[11]

"Love is one of the chief characteristics of Deity, and ought to be manifested by those who aspire to be the sons of God. A man filled with the love of God, is not content with blessing his family alone, but 'ranges through the whole world, anxious to bless the whole human race.' "[12]

Joseph Smith Had Priesthood Power and Authority Restored to Him to Build Up the Kingdom of God on the Earth

Great is his glory and endless his priesthood.
Ever and ever the keys he will hold.
Faithful and true, he will enter his kingdom,
Crowned in the midst of the prophets of old.[13]

Because of his great faith and because he lived a worthy life that enabled him to commune with Jehovah, Joseph Smith had priesthood power and authority bestowed upon him that enabled him to reestablish the kingdom of God upon the earth.

Elder Gordon B. Hinckley noted this important mission of Joseph Smith and quoted the words of William W. Phelps concerning these powers: "One is led to marvel at the energies of the man. The breadth of his vision, the intensity of his activity are explained only by his great sense of mission and the inspiration of heaven which quickened his understanding. He was a man possessed by a sense of destiny — and that destiny was nothing less than the building of the Kingdom of God in the earth."[14]

Brother Robert J. Matthews mentioned some of the

heavenly messengers who restored priesthood keys and authority to Joseph Smith:

"The story of the restoration of the gospel is truly one of the most stimulating of all time. Many personalities from beyond the veil visited Joseph Smith as the gospel's restoration unfolded — among them were persons whose mortal lives are discussed in the Old Testament, including, said President John Taylor, 'Abraham, Isaac, Jacob, Noah, Adam, Seth, Enoch, and Jesus and the Father, and the apostles that lived on this continent as well as those who lived on the Asiatic continent. He seemed to be as familiar with these people as we are with one another.' The Doctrine and Covenants has references to visits also by Moses, Elias, Elijah, and of 'divers angels, from Michael or Adam down to the present time.' "[15]

Joseph Smith Is a Prophet, Seer, and Revelator

Praise to the man who communed with Jehovah!
Jesus anointed that Prophet and Seer.[16]

Because of his great faith and because he lived a worthy life that enabled him to commune with Jehovah, Joseph Smith was called of God to be His prophet, seer, and revelator. Although in the minds of some, the terms *prophet, seer,* and *revelator* might seem to be synonymous, Ammon makes a distinction between the terms in his discussion with King Limhi:

"And Ammon said that a seer is a revelator and a prophet also; and a gift which is greater can no man have, except he should possess the power of God, which no man can; yet a man may have great power given him from God.

"But a seer can know of things which are past, and also of things which are to come, and by them shall all things be revealed, or, rather, shall secret things be made manifest, and hidden things shall come to light, and things which are not known shall be made known by them, and also things shall be made known by them which otherwise could not be known." (Mosiah 8:16–17.)

President Howard W. Hunter explained the calling of a prophet and begins by quoting Elder Widtsoe:

"Dr. John A. Widtsoe defines a prophet as a teacher — one who expounds truth. 'He teaches the body of truth, the gospel, revealed by the Lord to man; and under inspiration explains it to the understanding of the people.' The word 'prophet' is often used to designate one who receives revelation and direction from the Lord. Many have thought that a prophet is essentially a foreteller of future events and happenings, but this is only one of the many functions of a prophet. He is a spokesman for the Lord."[17]

President Harold B. Lee quoted the Prophet Joseph Smith concerning the calling of a prophet: "The Prophet Joseph Smith explained something about the refining process through which he went. He said, 'A Prophet is not always a Prophet. He is a Prophet only when he's acting as such.' This is an illuminating statement and doubtless holds good in the cases of most ancient men of God. Very likely the ancient Prophet received his polishing in much the same way that Joseph Smith said he was polished."[18]

Hyrum Smith left this testimony of his brother's calling as a prophet: "There were prophets before, but Joseph has the spirit and power of all the prophets."[19]

Joseph Smith's calling as a seer was foretold by his ancestor Joseph who was sold into Egypt:

"Wherefore, Joseph [who was sold into Egypt] truly saw our day. And he obtained a promise of the Lord, that out of the fruit of his loins the Lord God would raise up a righteous branch unto the house of Israel. . . .

"For Joseph truly testified, saying: A seer shall the Lord my God raise up, who shall be a choice seer unto the fruit of my loins.

"Yea, Joseph truly said: Thus saith the Lord unto me: A choice seer will I raise up out of the fruit of thy loins; and he shall be esteemed highly among the fruit of thy loins. And unto him will I give commandment that he shall do a work for the fruit of thy loins, his brethren, which shall be of great worth unto them, even to the bringing of them to the knowledge of the covenants which I have made with thy fathers.

"And I will give unto him a commandment that he shall do none other work, save the work which I shall command him. And I will make him great in mine eyes; for he shall do my work.

"And he shall be great like unto Moses." (2 Nephi 3:5–9.)

President Marion G. Romney testified that Joseph Smith was that "choice seer": "Joseph Smith was this great seer. Next to the Savior Himself there has, in my judgment, never been a greater seer on the earth."[20]

President Gordon B. Hinckley indicated that the seer-ship of Joseph Smith enabled him to prepare himself and the kingdom of God for the future: "Joseph Smith, the prophet of God . . . was indeed a mighty seer, who saw this day and greater days yet to come as the work of the Lord moves over the earth."[21]

Joseph Smith, the prophet and seer, was also a revelator of God's truths. The Lord promised Joseph Smith: "God shall give unto you knowledge by his Holy Spirit, yea, by the unspeakable gift of the Holy Ghost, that has not been revealed since the world was until now." (D&C 121:26.)

President Howard W. Hunter explained the role of a revelator: "A revelator makes known something presently unknown or which has been known previously by man and taken from his memory. Always the revelation deals with truth, and always it comes with the divine stamp of approval. Revelation is received in various ways, but it always presupposes that the revelator has so lived and conducted himself as to be in tune or harmony with the divine spirit of revelation, the spirit of truth, and therefore capable of receiving divine messages."[22]

Joseph Smith Has Survived the Tests of Ridicule and Persecution

Because of his great faith and because he lived a worthy life that enabled him to commune with Jehovah, Joseph

Smith was able to endure and overcome the tests of ridicule and persecution. Jesus Christ, the Savior of all mankind, suffered persecution above all others, which led to His eventual crucifixion. Few others who have lived upon the earth have even approached the ridicule and persecution heaped upon the Master, but Joseph Smith was one whose persecution also led to martyrdom.

President Hugh B. Brown reflected on the possible reasons for the persecution of Joseph Smith: "I've often wondered why those early American Christians persecuted Joseph Smith as they did. Many of the mobs that came against him were led by professed ministers of the gospel of Jesus Christ. Now why did they persecute him? Did he come to them and say, 'There is no Christ'? Did he say to them, 'I am the Christ'? He said none of these things. He said, 'Jesus of Nazareth is the Christ, the Son of God and His is the only Name under heaven whereby men must be saved.' That was his declaration. . . .

"I again ask why they persecute a man when he comes to them, professed Christians, and tells them that the one whom they claim to believe in is, in fact, the Christ? What they couldn't tolerate was his—to them—blasphemous statement, 'I have seen Him and I have heard Him.' Why should it be thought a thing incredible to any one who believes the Holy Bible that a man could see and hear and talk with God? Did not all the prophets make that claim?"[23]

Historian Dean Jessee also wrote about the scorn and antagonism heaped upon Joseph Smith: "Even though Joseph Smith was warned by a heavenly messenger at an early age that his name would be known for both good and evil among all nations, he was not quite prepared for the intensity of the scorn that was heaped upon him. It was a source of 'serious reflection' to him that one so obscure as he was, whose circumstances made him of 'no consequence in the world,' should attract such bitter opposition.

"But so it was. Few historical figures have confronted more antagonism during their lives than did Joseph Smith.

Practically everything written about him in the public print of his time was colored by a spirit of malice. Yet much of this writing was contradictory in detail, though it may have agreed in tone. On the other hand, those contemporaries who knew him best wrote sympathetic and praiseworthy accounts of his life. Such widespread disagreement makes the Prophet an intriguing subject for historians' scrutiny. But the careful examination of original sources has to a great extent resolved the puzzles, shedding helpful light on the Prophet and his critics."[24]

Summary Tributes to Joseph Smith

Praise to the man who communed
with Jehovah! . . .
Kings shall extol him, and nations revere.[25]

Perhaps the most widely quoted tribute to Joseph Smith is the one prepared by John Taylor, who subsequently served as the third president of the Church in this dispensation: "Joseph Smith, the Prophet and Seer of the Lord, has done more, save Jesus only, for the salvation of men in this world, than any other man that ever lived in it. . . . He lived great, and he died great in the eyes of God and his people; and like most of the Lord's anointed in ancient times, has sealed his mission and his works with his own blood." (D&C 135:3.)

John Taylor also testified: "I was with him living and with him when he died. . . . I have seen him under these various circumstances, and I testify before God, angels and men that he was a good, honorable, virtuous man, and that his doctrines were good, scriptural, and wholesome; that his precepts were such as become a man of God; that his private and public character was unimpeachable; that he lived and died as a man of God and a gentleman."[26]

Joseph Smith has been referred to as possibly the greatest American who has lived to date.[27] What kind of a definition should be applied to the question "Who is the greatest American?" Eventually, perhaps, the definition that will be applied to the greatest American of all time will be "the person who has had the greatest effect or influence on the largest number of people over the longest period of time." There have been some other Americans who have had tremendous effect on large numbers of people for a relatively short period of time, but when those persons have died, their influence has largely died with them. There have been some Americans who had great influence on small numbers of people over a long period of time. But if the significance and the importance of a person and his works are viewed from the perspective of eternity, perhaps there has been no American to date, and I doubt there ever will be an American citizen, who will have a greater influence on a larger number of people over a longer period of time than did the Prophet Joseph Smith.

We have rejoiced in the words of Joseph Smith, and of Sidney Rigdon, concerning Christ: "After the many testimonies which have been given of him, this is the testimony, last of all, which we give of him: That he lives!

"For we saw him, even on the right hand of God; and we heard the voice bearing record that he is the Only Begotten of the Father." (D&C 76:22–23.)

Now, if I may be permitted a paraphrasing of that scripture, and apply it to the Prophet Joseph Smith, I would say: "This is the testimony last of all that I give of him: he is indeed the Prophet of God, chosen to lead the dispensation of the fulness of times; he was indeed foreordained to be the choice seer of the latter days and, he—Joseph Smith the Prophet—has been faithful to his foreordained calling."

Notes

1. Hundreds of other terms and titles that apply to Jesus Christ would not be used by thoughtful Latter-day Saints to refer to Joseph Smith, including the following titles: Beloved Son of God (Matthew 3:17); Great I Am (Exodus 3:14; D&C 29:1); Alpha and Omega, the Beginning and the Ending, the First and the Last (Revelation 1:8, 11); Jehovah (Exodus 6:3; Psalm 83:18); Redeemer (Job 19:25) and Savior (Matthew 1:21); Lamb of God (John 1:29); Messiah (Daniel 9:25–26); King of Zion; Rock of Heaven (Moses 7:53); God, Lord God, God of Abraham, Isaac, and Jacob (Exodus 3:15); Good and Great

and True Shepherd (John 10:11–14; Hebrews 13:20; Helaman 15:13); Captain of Man's Salvation (Hebrews 2:10); Founder and Prince of Peace (Mosiah 15:18; Isaiah 9:6); Head and Chief Corner Stone (Psalm 118:22; Ephesians 2:20); Resurrection and the Life (John 11:25); First Born and First Begotten of the Dead (Colossians 1:18; Revelation 1:5); the First Fruits of them that slept (1 Corinthians 15:20; 2 Nephi 2:8–9); Father of Heaven (1 Nephi 22:9) and of Earth (Helaman 14:12); King of kings, and Lord of lords (1 Timothy 6:15; Revelation 17:14).

2. Gordon B. Hinckley, "Joseph the Seer," *Ensign,* May 1977, p. 65.

3. Neal A. Maxwell, "The Prophet—Joseph Smith: Spiritual Statesman," Annual Joseph Smith Memorial Sermons, Logan, Utah, 19 Jan. 1975, p. 12.

4. Richard L. Bushman, "The Teaching of Joseph Smith," Annual Joseph Smith Memorial Sermons, Logan, Utah, 18 Jan. 1976, p. 1.

5. *Hymns of The Church of Jesus Christ of Latter-day Saints* (Salt Lake City, Utah: The Church of Jesus Christ of Latter-day Saints, 1985), no. 27.

6. Ezra Taft Benson, "Joseph Smith—Man of Destiny," Annual Joseph Smith Memorial Sermons, Logan, Utah, 3 Dec. 1967, p. 3.

See Joseph Smith, *History of The Church of Jesus Christ of Latter-day Saints,* 7 vols., 2d ed. rev., ed. B. H. Roberts (Salt Lake City, Utah: The Church of Jesus Christ of Latter-day Saints, 1932–51), 6:364.

7. Brigham Young, in *Journal of Discourses,* 26 vols. (Liverpool: Latter-day Saints' Book Depot, 1855–86), 7:289–90.

8. Neal A. Maxwell, "The Prophet–Joseph Smith: Spiritual Statesman," Annual Joseph Smith Memorial Sermons, Logan, Utah, 19 Jan. 1975, p. 13.

9. Richard L. Bushman, "The Teaching of Joseph Smith," Annual Joseph Smith Memorial Sermons, Logan, Utah, 18 Jan. 1976, p. 10.

10. Jerry C. Roundy, "The Greatness of Joseph Smith and His Remarkable Visions," *New Era,* Dec. 1973, p. 12.

11. Joseph Fielding Smith, *Teachings of the Prophet Joseph Smith* (Salt Lake City, Utah: Deseret Book Co., 1938), p. 313.

12. Ibid., p. 174.

13. *Hymns,* 1985, no. 27.

14. Gordon B. Hinckley, "Joseph Smith from the Perspective of 150 Years," Annual Joseph Smith Memorial Sermons, Logan, Utah, 3 Feb. 1980, p. 8.

15. Brigham Young, in *Journal of Discourses,* 21:94; D&C 128:21; Robert J. Matthews, "Modern Revelation, Window to the Old Testament," *Ensign,* Oct. 1973, p. 23.

16. *Hymns,* 1985, no. 27.

17. John A. Widtsoe, *Evidences and Reconciliations,* p. 204; Howard W. Hunter, "Joseph—the Seer," Annual Joseph Smith Memorial Sermons, Logan, Utah, 15 Dec. 1960, p. 7.

18. Harold B. Lee, "Joseph Smith—His Mission Divine," Annual Joseph Smith Memorial Sermons, Logan, Utah, 4 Dec. 1955, p. 132.

19. Smith, *History of the Church,* 6:346.

20. Marion G. Romney, "Joseph Smith the Seer, and Truth," Annual Joseph Smith Memorial Sermons, Logan, Utah, 15 Jan. 1978, p. 3.

21. Gordon B. Hinckley, "Joseph the Seer," *Ensign,* May 1977, p. 65.

22. Howard W. Hunter, "Joseph—the Seer," Annual Joseph Smith Memorial Sermons, Logan, Utah, 15 Dec. 1960, pp. 8–9.

23. Hugh B. Brown, "Joseph among the Prophets," Annual Joseph Smith Memorial Sermons, Logan, Utah, 7 Dec. 1958, pp. 175–76.

24. Smith, *History of the Church,* 1:7, 11; Dean C. Jessee, "Joseph Smith's Reputation," *Ensign,* Sept. 1979, p. 57.

25. *Hymns,* 1985, no. 27.

26. Thomas S. Monson, "The Prophet Joseph Smith—Teacher by Example," Annual Joseph Smith Memorial Sermons, Logan, Utah, 11 Dec. 1963, p. 6.

27. William E. Berrett, "Joseph Smith and the Verdict of Time," Annual Joseph Smith Memorial Sermons, Logan, Utah, 6 Dec. 1953, p. 110.

Bibliography

In 1944 the Latter-day Saint institute of religion at what was then the Utah State Agricultural College (now Utah State University) started to sponsor an annual memorial sermon in honor of Joseph Smith. Forty-five of these sermons had been given by January 1988, and most of them are available in printed form at both the Logan Institute and the reference library of the Church Educational System at the Church Office Building in Salt Lake City, Utah. The complete list of sermons by number is provided below, even though some of the sermons have not been published.

1. "Joseph Smith, a Prophet," by Joseph F. Smith, 6 Feb. 1944.

2. "The Prophet Joseph Smith on Doctrine and Organization," by David O. McKay, 10 Dec. 1944.

3. "The Prophet Joseph Smith," by Howard S. McDonald, 9 Dec. 1945.

4. "Joseph Smith: The Significance of the First Vision," by John A. Widtsoe, 8 Dec. 1946.

5. "An Evaluation of Joseph Smith and His Work," by Sidney B. Sperry, 17 Dec. 1947.

6. "Joseph Smith: His Creative Role in Religion," by Lowell L. Bennion, 5 Dec. 1948.

7. "The Prophet Joseph, Equally Burdened with Moses," by J. Reuben Clark, 4 Dec. 1949.

8. "Joseph Smith and the Political World," by G. Homer Durham, 3 Dec. 1950.

9. "Joseph Smith, Prophet of the Restoration," by Joseph Fielding Smith, 2 Dec. 1951.

10. "Joseph Smith, Prophet-Martyr," by Stephen L Richards, 7 Dec. 1952.

11. "Joseph Smith and the Verdict of Time," by William E. Berrett, 6 Dec. 1953.

12. "Joseph Smith: The Wentworth Letter and Religious America of 1842," by T. Edgar Lyon, 5 Dec. 1954.

13. "Joseph Smith: His Mission Divine," by Harold B. Lee, 4 Dec. 1955.

14. "A New Dimension in Religious Thought and Action," by Wesley P. Lloyd, 2 Dec. 1956.

15. "Religion in a Changing World," by Henry B. Eyring, 15 Dec. 1957.

16. "Joseph among the Prophets," by Hugh B. Brown, 7 Dec. 1958.

17. "Joseph Smith, Prophet Teacher," by Boyd K. Packer, 6 Dec. 1959.

18. "Joseph the Seer," by Howard W. Hunter, 15 Dec. 1960.

19. "The Leadership of Joseph Smith," by Sterling W. Sill, 5 Dec. 1961.

20. "The Prophet Joseph's Work," by Henry D. Moyle, 2 Dec. 1962.

21. "The Prophet Joseph Smith, Teacher by Example," by Thomas S. Monson, 11 Dec. 1963.

22. "Joseph Smith Memorial Sermon," by Robert K. Thomas, 6 Dec. 1964.

23. "Joseph Smith and the Sources of Love," by Truman G. Madsen, 5 Dec. 1965.

24. "Joseph Smith, the Prophet," by N. Eldon Tanner, 4 Dec. 1966.

25. "Joseph Smith, Man of Destiny," by Ezra Taft Benson, 3 Dec. 1967.

26. "The Foundation in the Center Place of Zion," by Alvin R. Dyer, 8 Dec. 1968.

27. "The True Knowledge of God," by Mark E. Petersen, 14 Dec. 1969.

28. "The First Vision," by Spencer W. Kimball, 13 Dec. 1970.

29. "The Prophet Joseph Smith, a Beacon in Our Lives," by Victor L. Brown, 12 Dec. 1971.

30. "Joseph Smith Memorial Sermon," Hartman Rector, Jr., 10 Dec. 1972.

31. "A Walk through the Bible with the Prophet Joseph Smith," by Robert J. Matthews, 9 Dec. 1973.

32. "The Prophet Joseph Smith: Spiritual Statesman," by Neal A. Maxwell, 19 Jan. 1975.

33. "The Teaching of Joseph Smith," by Richard L. Bushman, 18 Jan. 1976.

34. "Joseph Smith's Contribution to an Understanding of Israel," by Daniel H. Ludlow, 16 Jan. 1977.

35. "Joseph Smith the Seer, and Truth," by Marion G. Romney, 15 Jan. 1978.

36. "Joseph Smith, a Life of Love," by Barbara B. Smith, 28 Jan. 1979.

37. "Joseph Smith from the Perspective of 150 Years," by Gordon B. Hinckley, 3 Feb. 1980.

38. (Copy unavailable), by James E. Faust, 1981.

39. "Joseph Smith—Not a Mystic" (unpublished), by Truman G. Madsen, 1982.

40. "Joseph Smith Memorial Sermon," by David B. Haight, 30 Jan. 1983.

41. (Copy unavailable), by Elaine Cannon, 1984.

42. "At the Heart of the Church," by Russell M. Nelson, 3 Feb. 1985.

43. (Copy unavailable), "Greatness of Joseph Smith," by Jeffrey R. Holland, 1986.

44. "How the Joseph Smith Translation Has Been a Blessing to the Church," by Robert J. Matthews, 25 Jan. 1987.

45. "Free Agency and Freedom," by Dallin H. Oaks, 17 Jan. 1988.

Most of the following references were obtained from the *Index to Periodicals of The Church of Jesus Christ of Latter-day Saints,* a very valuable resource.

Roy W. Doxey, "Lesson 100—Joseph Smith Evaluated," *Relief Society Magazine,* Oct. 1969, pp. 777–82.

Gordon B. Hinckley, "Joseph the Seer," *Ensign,* May 1977, p. 65.

Dean C. Jessee, "Joseph Smith's Reputation," *Ensign,* Sept. 1979, pp. 56–63.

Robert J. Matthews, "Modern Revelation Window to the Old Testament," *Ensign,* Oct. 1973, pp. 21–23.

Jerry C. Roundy, "The Greatness of Joseph Smith and His Remarkable Visions," *New Era,* Dec. 1973, pp. 7–12.

Index

introduces family to Book of Mormon, 7, 78; financial trials of, 7–10; dreams of, regarding religion, 11; religious leanings of, 12–13; baptism of, 16; patriarchal authority of, 37–38; ordination of, as priest, 59; becomes Church Patriarch, 63; bless Joseph, Jr., to finish work, 300

Smith, Joseph, III, 110

Smith, Lucy, 42

Smith, Lucy Mack, 1–3, 11–12, 25

Smith, Samuel (grandfather of Joseph, Sr.), 3–4

Smith, Samuel H. (brother of Joseph, Jr.), 41, 59, 75–76

Smith, Sophronia, 42

Smith, Sylvester, 141, 200, 205

Smith, William, 37–38, 41, 111, 141, 154

Snow, Eliza R., 214, 220, 253

Snow, Erastus, 149

Stewardships, 116–17, 123

Storekeeping, Joseph Smith's problems with, 126, 133, 257

Stowell, Josiah, 10, 13, 83

Tarring and feathering, 101–2, 161–62, 166–69, 172 n. 2

Taylor, John, 249, 343

Temple: priesthood authority restored in, 65–68; full endowment of, 66; record keeping in, 150; connection of, with gathering, 290–91; building, priority of, 291. *See also* Endowment, temple; Kirtland Temple; Nauvoo Temple

Temporal concerns: effect of, on spiritual well-being, 115–16, 267; Joseph Smith not to have strength in, 286; in building kingdom of God, 292

Tenant farming, 8

Thompson, Robert B., 149, 155

Tithing: law of, 128, 131; "in time," 253

Tongues, speaking in, 214

Tracy, Nancy, 219

Translation: of Bible, process of, 179–80; as Joseph's "only gift," 284

Treasure-seeking, 13–14

Truth, 274–75

Tucker, Pomeroy, 83, 85

Turnham, Judge Joel, 202

Twelve Apostles: calling of, 63; mission of, to England, 249; Joseph Smith instructs, 300, 308–9; to stand next to First Presidency, 301–2; conferral of all keys upon, 309

Twelve Nephite disciples, 52

Tyler, Daniel, 111, 219

United Order, 116–17, 119–20

Universalism, 5, 25

Universe, understanding, 273

Unselfishness, 266–68

Urim and Thummim, 183

Visions: Joseph Smith's first, 25–27, 31–32; of three degrees of glory, 99–100; of God and Christ, 110–11; in Kirtland Temple, 111–12, 212–14; of construction of Kirtland Temple, 210

Voting, Saints prohibited from, 234–35

Washing and anointing, 217

Waste, Warren, 167, 174 n. 27

Weeks, William, 252

Wells, Daniel, 24

Wells, Robert W., 195

Whitmer, Christian, 59

Whitmer, David, 57; receives translated lines from Oliver Cowdery, 75; provides refuge for translation work, 76; on proselyting efforts, 79; sees angels in Kirtland Temple, 213; disputes with, over authority, 230; charges brought against, 231

359